DROPPING OUT

DROPPING OUT

Why Students Drop Out of High School
and What Can Be Done About It

RUSSELL W. RUMBERGER

HARVARD UNIVERSITY PRESS
Cambridge, Massachusetts, and London, England

KH

First Harvard University Press paperback edition, 2012

Library of Congress Cataloging-in-Publication Data

Rumberger, Russell W.
  Dropping out : why students drop out of high school and what can be done about it / Russell W. Rumberger.
    p. cm.
  Includes bibliographical references and index.
  ISBN 978-0-674-06220-7 (cloth : alk. paper)
  ISBN 978-0-674-06656-4 (pbk.)
  1. High school dropouts—United States.   2. High school dropouts—United States—Prevention.   I. Title.
  LC146.6.R86   2011
  373.12'913—dc22   2011016123

11/26/12

For Sharon, Anne, Emily, and Jenna

CONTENTS

Acknowledgments   xi

1 Introduction   1

2 The Varying Requirements and Pathways for
   Completing High School   20

   The Conflicting Goals of High School   21

   The Requirements for Completing High School   28
       Diploma Requirements   28
       Alternative Credentials   35

   Alternative Pathways to High School Completion   36
       Tracking   36
       Segregation   39
       Alternative Schools   42
       Other Options   45

3 The Nature and Extent of the Dropout Crisis   47

   What Does It Mean to Drop Out of School?   47
       The Difficulty of Identifying Dropouts   49
       Student Mobility   52
       Reenrollment   54

   The Debate over Dropout and Graduation Rates   55

   Measuring Dropout and Graduation Rates   59
       Alternative Definitions   59
       The Need for Accurate Data   60
       Competing Measures   66
       The Promise and Reality of Longitudinal Data   73

Contents

The Vast Differences in Dropout and Graduation Rates   78
   Demographic Differences   78
   Differences among Schools, Districts, and States   78
   Trends in Dropout and Graduation Rates   81
   International Comparisons   84

4 The Individual Consequences of Dropping Out   86
   Labor Market Outcomes   88
   Crime   95
   Family Formation   101
   Health   110
   Civic Engagement   117
   Well-Being   119
   Intergenerational Mobility   120

5 The Social Consequences of Dropping Out   130
   Consequences for the Economy   132
   Consequences for the Larger Society   134
      Crime   134
      Welfare   136
      Health   137
      Civic Engagement   138
   Total Economic Losses from Dropouts   139

6 Understanding Why Students Drop Out   143
   The Process of Dropping Out   145
      Alternative Models of Dropping Out   145
      The Role of Engagement   151
      The Role of Context   153
      A Conceptual Framework of the Dropout Process   154
   The Reasons Students Report for Dropping Out   156

7 Predictors of Dropping Out   159
   Individual Predictors of Dropping Out   160
      Educational Performance   160
      Behaviors   169
      Attitudes   178
      Background   181
      Combining Factors   185

Institutional Predictors of Dropping Out   187

     Families   188

     Schools   193

     Communities   199

Explaining Racial and Ethnic Differences in

   Dropout Rates   201

8 Learning from Past Efforts to Solve the Dropout Crisis   207

Alternative Approaches to Improving Dropout

   and Graduation Rates   208

     Targeted Approaches   208

     Comprehensive Approaches   210

     Systemic Approaches   214

What Works?   215

     Judging Scientific Evidence   217

     Identifying Effective Strategies   221

     Early Inverventions   228

     Systemic Interventions   229

     Costs and Benefits   233

What Have We Learned from Large-Scale Reform Efforts?   234

     High School Graduation Initiative   235

     Comprehensive School Reform (CSR)

       Program   236

     California's High Priority Schools

       Grant Program   237

     New American Schools   238

     Gates High School Grants Initiative   240

     New Futures   242

     New York City's Small School Initiative   243

     Lessons Learned   244

     Implications   252

9 What Should Be Done to Solve the Dropout Crisis   255

Current Efforts   256

     National   256

     State   261

     Local   264

     Are Current Efforts Enough?   266

Moving Beyond Current Efforts   269

     Redefining High School Success   269

Contents

Changing Accountability Systems to Provide Incentives
     to Educate All Students   272
Building Capacity of the Educational System   273
Desegregating Schools   274
Strengthening Families and Communities   274

Notes   279
Index   371

ACKNOWLEDGMENTS

M any people—colleagues, educational leaders, government officials, educators, family, and friends—had a hand in this book.

I owe a great deal of gratitude to several persons who shaped my career as a scholar and helped me get to a position where I could write this book. During my undergraduate years as an electrical engineering student at Carnegie-Mellon University, I had a course that opened my eyes to the study of higher education taught by Professor James Korn, who also influenced my decision to go to graduate school in education at Stanford University. When I entered Stanford, I started working on a research project with two professors, Henry Levin and Martin Carnoy, both of whom are economists and influenced my decision to pursue a Ph.D. in education with a focus on economics. Professor Levin became my advisor and, more than any other single individual, has shaped my work and commitment to the field. He embodies all that we value in academia—hard work, dedication, research that informs the important issues of the day, and loyalty to friends and colleagues. I truly would not be the scholar I am today had it not been for his time and devotion to my career and my work. Another valuable colleague whom I got to know when I returned to Stanford as a research associate is Professor Edwin Bridges. I cherish the time we spent together during those six years over coffee and at happy hour discussing a wide range of ideas and of work in the academy. Professor Bridges is one of the most respected professors I have had the privilege of knowing, perhaps best evidenced by the fierce loyalty and appreciation of all his former students. We remain close friends, and I still benefit from his sharp insights and candid observations of the world around us.

Since my entry into the academy, I have also benefited from many good colleagues who have shaped my ideas and understanding of a range of topics. They include Patricia Gándara, whom I had the privilege of working with while directing the University of California Linguistic Minority Research

Institute for ten years; and Jim Connell, Catherine Cooper, Jeremy Finn, Bruce Fuller, Ron Galimore, Michael Gerber, Margaret Gibson, Norm Gold, Claude Goldenberg, Norton Grubb, Kenji Hakuta, Stephen Lamb, Katherine Larson, Robert Linquanti, Dan Losen, Julie Maxwell-Jolly, Lorraine McDonnell, Bud Mehan, Roslyn Mickelson, Jeannie Oakes, Gary Orfield, Greg Palardy, David Plank, Steve Raudenbush, Robert Ream, David Stern, Tom Timar, Doug Willms, and Jules Zimmer.

A number of colleagues contributed directly to this book by giving me ideas and feedback on earlier chapters or papers, which made the book better than I could have done on my own. They include Clive Belefield, Mindy Bingham, Jeremy Finn, Jack Jennings, Judith Koenig, Henry Levin, Lorraine McDonnell, and Robert Warren. I have also benefited greatly from my ongoing discussions of dropout issues with Susanna Cooper, consultant to California senator Darrell Steinberg. I would especially like to thank Beverly Bavaro for her editing, the best I've experienced in my professional life, providing valuable feedback both on my ideas and on how they are presented. Finally, I would like to thank my editor at Harvard University Press, Elizabeth Knoll, who believed in me and the book from the very beginning, and Wendy Muto for her assistance in copyediting.

Last, I want the acknowledge the support and encouragement from my family: my three lovely and wonderful daughters, Anne, Emily, and Jenna, and my loving wife, Sharon, whose support, encouragement, and love throughout our more than thirty years together have enabled me to become who I am, both as a person and as a scholar.

DROPPING OUT

1

INTRODUCTION

Cesar entered Hacienda Middle School in the Los Angeles School District in the sixth grade.[1] He lived with his mother and three younger siblings in a garage that was divided into sleeping quarters and a makeshift kitchen with no running water. His mother, who spoke only Spanish, supported the family by working long hours at a minimum-wage job.

During the first semester of seventh grade, Cesar failed every class, in part due to poor attendance and not completing assignments. But by the end of seventh grade, with the assistance of a dropout prevention project at the school, Cesar was able to pass two of his six classes.

With the support of the dropout prevention project, his grades continued to improve. Yet, as he entered eighth grade, Cesar was spending more time after school away from home and on the streets. He began to wear gang-related attire and hairstyles, although he denied gang involvement.

Teachers began to respond to him more positively as his grades improved, but because he did not change his "appearance," school administrators did not seem to change their earlier negative perceptions about him.

Two weeks into his last semester of eighth grade, Cesar got into a fight and kicked a younger student. Because of this incident, Cesar was given what the school district called an "opportunity transfer." However, no apparent effort was made by the school to see that Cesar actually enrolled in the new school, nor that he attended.

Cesar stopped attending school in eighth grade. He became a school dropout.

Public high schools in the United States reported that 607,789 students dropped out in 2008–09.[2] An even higher number fails to graduate. *Education Week*, the nation's leading education periodical, estimates that 1.3 million students from the high school class of 2010 failed to graduate.[3] This means that the nation's schools are losing more than 7,000 students each school day. And these figures do not count students like Cesar who drop out *before* reaching ninth grade. Altogether, the U.S. Census estimates that in October 2010 there were almost 28 million dropouts age eighteen and over in the United States.[4]

While these figures are sizeable, the magnitude of the problem is better understood when expressed as a rate that reflects the proportion of students who drop out of high school. The 607,789 students who dropped out of high school in 2008–09 represent more than 4 percent of all students enrolled in grades 9–12.[5] The 1.3 million students from the high school class of 2010 who failed to graduate represent 30 percent of the 4.3 million students enrolled in the ninth grade in 2006.[6]

Yet dropout rates tell only part of the story. It is also important to consider *graduation rates*, which reflect the proportion of students who actually graduate from high school. The two rates are not directly related. Students who drop out can still graduate at a later time, while students who never quit school still may not graduate. To graduate, students must earn a high school diploma, but some students earn alternative diplomas by taking state or national examinations. Students who earn these alternative diplomas are not considered graduates, but they also are not considered dropouts.

Dropout and graduation rates vary widely among various populations of students. For example, *Education Week* estimates that in the nation as a whole, 69 percent of all students who entered high school in the fall of 2003 graduated in 2007. But only 56 percent of Hispanics and 54 percent of blacks from that class graduated in 2007, compared to 81 percent of Asians and 77 percent of whites.[7] Among the almost 400,000 students with disabilities who left school in 2006–07, only 56 percent graduated with a diploma.[8] Dropout rates in the two-year period from 2002 to 2004 were twice as high for tenth-grade students whose native language was not English, compared to native English speakers.[9]

Similar disparities exist among districts and schools. *Education Week* estimates that the high school graduation rate for the class of 2007 among the nation's fifty largest school districts ranged from 40 percent in Clark County, Nevada, to 83 percent in Montgomery County, Maryland.[10] One study of Chicago's eighty-six public high schools found that the graduation rates over a four-year period for students who entered the ninth grade in 2000 varied from a low of 27 percent to a high of 90 percent![11]

Not only is the graduation rate in the United States generally low and highly variable, but it also appears to be getting worse. Nobel economist

James Heckman examined the various sources of data used to calculate dropout and graduation rates and, after correcting for errors in previous calculations, concluded that:

- The high school graduation rate is lower than the federal government reports.
- It is lower today than it was forty years ago.
- Disparities in graduation rates among racial and ethnic minorities have not improved over the past thirty-five years.[12]

Reducing the number of dropouts has become a national policy concern both inside and outside of the government:

- In February 2005, the nation's governors held a two-day summit on high schools where Microsoft CEO Bill Gates called American high schools "obsolete," noting that only 68 out of every 100 ninth graders graduate, and six philanthropies pledged $42 million to raise high school graduation rates.[13]
- The April 9, 2006, cover of *Time* magazine was titled "Dropout Nation" and featured a number of stories about the dropout crisis in America.
- Oprah Winfrey dedicated her television show on April 11, 2006, to the nation's dropout crisis.[14]
- On March 1, 2010 America's Promise Alliance brought together government, business, and community leaders to launch the "Grad Nation campaign" with a goal of a 90 percent national graduation rate by 2020.[15] At this event, President Barack Obama stated, "This is a problem we cannot afford to accept and we cannot afford to ignore. The stakes are too high—for our children, for our economy, and for our country. It's time for all of us to come together—parents, students, principals and teachers, business leaders and elected officials from across the political spectrum—to end America's dropout crisis."[16]

Such concern is not new. In 1990, twenty years before the launch of the Grad Nation campaign, the nation's governors and President George H. W. Bush adopted six National Education Goals for the year 2000.[17] One of these goals was to increase the high school graduation rate to 90 percent and to eliminate the gap in high school graduation rates between minority and nonminority students. Sadly, as the figures above demonstrate, the nation fell well short of that goal.

Going back even further, in 1963 President John F. Kennedy initiated a national "Summer Dropout Campaign" to increase publicity about the problem and to assist local school districts in identifying potential dropouts and helping to return these students to school in the fall.[18] Kennedy's efforts were part of a growing nationwide concern over the plight of adolescents who failed to finish high school—a concern that historian Sherman Dorn argues was the beginning of the identification of dropping out as an important social problem worthy of widespread public attention.[19]

The national concern for dropouts is reflected in numerous studies and programs focusing on this issue at the national, state, and local levels. Since 1988, the federal government alone has spent more than $300 million on dropout prevention programs.[20] Many states have enacted their own programs to assist local schools and districts in addressing this issue. And research on school dropouts has increased dramatically over the past decade.

But why is there so much concern?

There are a number of reasons. One is economic. Dropping out of school is costly both for dropouts themselves and for society as a whole. First, dropouts have difficulty finding jobs. Government data show that only 31 percent of students who dropped out of school in the 2009–10 school year were employed the following October.[21] America's recent economic recession has been particularly hard on dropouts: in December 2010 only 44 percent of high school dropouts sixteen to twenty-four years of age were employed, compared to 60 percent of high school completers who were not enrolled in school.[22]

Second, even if they find a job, dropouts earn substantially less than high school graduates. In 2008, the median annual earnings of high school dropouts working full-time over an entire year were 22 percent less than those of high school graduates.[23] Over their working lives, dropouts earn $260,000 less than high school graduates.[24]

Dropouts' poor economic outcomes are due in part to their low levels of education; yet dropouts can, and sometimes do, return to school. Almost two-thirds of eighth-grade students who dropped out of school before their originally scheduled graduation date in 1992 completed either a regular high school diploma (19 percent) or a GED or alternative certificate (43 percent) by the year 2000.[25] And dropouts who earned a high school diploma were more likely to enroll in postsecondary education than students who did not complete high school (60 percent versus 15 percent).[26] Nonetheless, dropouts as a group are much less likely to enroll in postsecondary education than high school graduates, even though most states allow dropouts to enroll in community colleges without a high school diploma. Thus, dropouts' poor economic prospects are due not simply to the fact that they fail to finish high school, but also to their continued underinvestment in education over their lifetime.

Dropouts experience other negative outcomes.[27] They have poorer health and higher rates of mortality than high school graduates; they are more likely than graduates to engage in criminal behavior and be incarcerated over their lifetimes. For instance, black male dropouts have a 60 percent probability of being incarcerated over their lifetime, a rate three times higher than for black male graduates.[28] Dropouts are also more likely to require public assistance and are less likely to vote. Although the observed relationship between dropping out and these economic and social outcomes does not necessarily imply a causal relationship, a growing body of research evidence has demonstrated one. This suggests that efforts to reduce dropout rates would, in fact, reduce these negative economic and social outcomes.

The negative outcomes from dropouts generate huge social costs to citizens and taxpayers. Federal, state, and local governments collect fewer taxes from dropouts. The government also subsidizes the poorer health, higher criminal activity, and increased public assistance of dropouts. One recent study estimated that each new high school graduate would generate more than $200,000 in government savings, and that cutting in half the dropout rate from a single group of twenty-year-olds would save taxpayers more than $45 billion.[29]

A second reason for the growing concern about the dropout problem is demographic. The proportion of students who are racial, ethnic, and linguistic minorities, who come from poor families, and who live in single-parent households—all factors that research has shown are associated with school failure and dropping out—is increasing in the nation's schools.[30] The most profound change is the growth of the Hispanic school-age population, which is projected to grow from 11 million in 2006 to 28 million in 2050, an increase of 166 percent, while the non-Hispanic school-age population is projected to increase by just 4 percent over this same period.[31] Because the rate of high school failure is higher among Hispanics and it improved more slowly in the 1990s than for whites and blacks, the increasing proportion of Hispanics in the school-age population could increase the overall number of dropouts even with marginal improvements in the dropout rate.

A third reason is the growing push for accountability in the nation's public schools that has produced policies to end social promotion (the

practice of promoting a student to the next grade level despite low achievement) and to institute high school exit exams that could increase the
number of students who fail to complete high school.[32]

A final reason for widespread concern over dropping out is that it is related to a host of other social problems facing adolescents today. As noted
by the Forum on Adolescence, created by the National Institute of Medicine and the National Research Council to bring authoritative, nonpartisan research to bear on policy issues facing adolescents and their families:

> One of the important insights to emerge from scientific inquiry
> into adolescence in the past two decades is that problem behav-
> iors, as well as health-enhancing ones, tend to cluster in the same
> individual, and these behaviors tend to reinforce one another.
> Crime, dropping out of school, teenage pregnancy and childbear-
> ing, and drug abuse typically are considered separately, but in the
> real world they often occur together. Teenagers who drink and
> smoke are more likely to initiate sex earlier than their peers; those
> who engage in these behavior patterns often have a history of dif-
> ficulties in school.[33]

If students face such a bleak future by dropping out of school, why do they
do it? The question defies an easy answer.

Dropouts themselves report a wide variety of reasons for leaving school,
including those related to school, family, and work.[34] The most specific
reasons cited by tenth graders who dropped out in 2002 were "missed too
many school days" (44 percent); "thought it would be easier to get a GED"
(41 percent); "getting poor grades/failing school" (38 percent); "did not
like school" (37 percent); and "could not keep up with schoolwork" (32 percent). But these reasons do not reveal the underlying causes of why students
quit school, particularly those causes or factors in elementary or middle
school that may have contributed to students' attitudes, behaviors, and
school performance immediately preceding their decision to leave school.
Moreover, if many factors contribute to this phenomenon over a long period of time, it is virtually impossible to demonstrate a causal connection
between any single factor and the decision to quit school.

Although for the most part existing research is unable to identify unique
causes, a vast empirical research literature has examined numerous predictors of dropping out of and graduating from high school. The empiri-

cal research comes from a number of social science disciplines and has identified two types of factors: (1) individual factors associated with students themselves, such as their attitudes, behaviors, school performance, and prior experiences; and (2) contextual factors found in students' families, schools, and communities.

INDIVIDUAL FACTORS.   The research has identified a wide variety of individual factors that are associated with dropping out. Attitudes and behaviors during high school predict dropping out. Dropout rates are higher among students who have low educational and occupational aspirations. Absenteeism, misbehavior in school, and pregnancy are also related to dropping out. Finally, poor academic achievement is a strong predictor of dropping out. Together, these factors support the idea that dropping out is influenced by both the social and the academic experiences of students in high school.

In addition to these proximal factors, a number of distal factors prior to entering high school are associated with dropping out. One is student mobility. Both *residential* mobility (changing residences) and *school* mobility (changing schools) increase the risk of dropping out of high school.[35] Student mobility may represent a less severe form of student disengagement or withdrawal from school. That is, students may change schools in an attempt to find a more suitable or supportive school environment before quitting school altogether. For example, one study found that students typically attend two or more high schools before dropping out.[36]

Another distal factor is retention, or being held back a grade in school. Although retention may have some positive impact on academic achievement in the short run, numerous studies have found that it greatly increases the likelihood that students will drop out of school. Finally, a number of long-term studies have found that lack of early academic achievement and engagement (e.g., failing courses, absenteeism, misbehavior) in elementary and middle school predicts withdrawal from high school.

While a large array of individual attitudes, behaviors, and aspects of educational performance influence dropping out and graduating, these individual factors are shaped by the institutional settings where children live. As noted by the Forum on Adolescence, "Another important insight of scientific inquiry is the profound influence of settings on adolescents' behavior and development."[37] This perspective is common in such social science disciplines as economics, sociology, and anthropology, and more recently

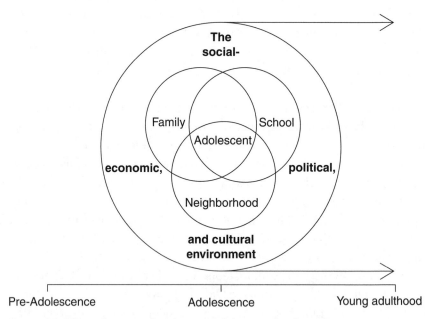

Figure 1.1. The influence of context on adolescent development over time.
Source: Richard Jessor, "Successful Adolescent Development among Youth in High-Risk Settings," *American Psychologist* 48 (1993): figure 2.

has been incorporated in an emerging paradigm in developmental psychology called *developmental behavioral science*.[38] This paradigm recognizes that the various settings or contexts in which children live—families, schools, and communities—all shape their attitudes, behaviors, and experiences (see Figure 1.1). For example, the National Research Council Panel on High-Risk Youth (1993) concluded that too much emphasis has been placed on "high-risk" youth and not enough on the high-risk settings in which they live and go to school.[39] Similarly, a 2004 review of the literature on childhood poverty identified a wide variety of family, school, and community environmental factors that impede the development of poor children.[40] Both reviews reflect the growing emphasis on understanding how these contexts shape educational outcomes.

This new perspective has important implications for studying and understanding the problem of school dropouts. By studying the experiences of dropouts in particular settings, anthropologists have long illustrated the importance of the family, school, and community contexts in understanding dropouts.[41] Recent developments in statistics have also allowed quantitative researchers to study the influence of context, particularly the school setting, on academic performance across large numbers of schools.[42] Relatively little of this work, however, has specifically focused on dropouts.

Nonetheless, there is a growing body of research that has identified an array of factors in families, schools, and communities that affect a child's likelihood of dropping out of school.[43]

CONTEXTUAL FACTORS. Among the three types of contextual factors, families are the most critical. Family background is widely recognized as the single most important contributor to success in school. Socioeconomic status, most commonly measured by *parental education* and *family income*, is a powerful predictor of school achievement and dropout behavior. Parental education influences students' aspirations and educational support (e.g, help with homework), while family income provides resources to support their children's education, including access to better quality schools, after-school and summer school programs, and support for learning within the home (e.g, computers). In addition, students whose parents monitor and regulate their activities, provide emotional support, encourage independent decision-making (practicing what is known as *authoritative parenting style*), and are generally more involved in their schooling are less likely to drop out.[44] Additionally, students living in single-parent homes and with stepfamilies are more likely to drop out of school than students in two-parent families.

Schools are a second contextual factor. It is widely acknowledged that schools exert powerful influences on student achievement, including dropout rates. Four types of school characteristics influence student performance, including the propensity to drop out or to graduate:

1. *Social composition*, such as the characteristics of students attending the schools, particularly the socioeconomic composition of the student body.
2. *Structural characteristics*, such as size, location, and school control (public traditional, public charter, private).
3. *School resources*, such as funding, teacher quality, and the student–teacher.
4. *Policies and practices*, such as the academic and social climate.

School characteristics influence dropout behavior in two ways. One way is indirectly, by creating conditions that influence student engagement, which can lead to students' *voluntarily* withdrawing from school due to boredom, poor attendance, or low achievement. Another way is directly, through explicit policies and conscious decisions by school personnel that lead to students' *involuntarily* withdrawing from school. Schools may enact rules and/or take actions in response to low grades, poor attendance, misbehavior (such as zero-tolerance policies), or exceeding the compulsory schooling age that lead to suspensions, expulsions, or forced transfers. This form of withdrawal is school-initiated and contrasts with the student-initiated form mentioned previously. Some schools, for example, contribute to students' involuntary departure from school by systematically excluding and discharging "troublemakers" and other problematic students.[45]

In addition to families and schools, communities and peer groups can influence students' withdrawal from school. Differences in neighborhood characteristics help explain disparities in dropout rates among communities, apart from the influence of families.[46] Some neighborhoods, particularly those with high concentrations of African-Americans, are communities of concentrated disadvantage with extremely high levels of joblessness, family instability, poor health, substance abuse, poverty, welfare dependency, and crime.[47] Disadvantaged communities may influence child and adolescent development through the lack of resources (playgrounds and parks, after-school programs) or negative peer influences.[48] Community residents may also influence parenting practices over and above parental education and income. Students living in poor communities may also be more likely to have dropouts as friends, which increases the likelihood of dropping out of school.

Settings are important in influencing dropout behavior, but similar settings also affect individuals differently. Why is it that some students persist in school while living in poor families or attending "bad" schools? These different outcomes arise not only because of so-called objective differences in individuals—intelligence, race, or family situation—but also because of how individuals view or interpret their conditions. Thus, dropping out of school cannot be understood simply by studying the conditions of families and schools, or even the behaviors of students, but must also be understood by studying the views and interpretations of those conditions and behaviors by dropouts themselves. Anthropological studies of dropouts are based on this premise.

Finally, understanding why students drop out requires looking at school experiences and performance over a long period of time. Dropping out is more of a process than an event. Students don't suddenly drop out of school. Many dropouts show patterns of early school failure—disruptive behavior, failing grades, repeating a grade—that eventually lead them to give up or be pushed out, like Cesar was.[49]

Knowledge about why students drop out suggests several things about what can be done to design effective dropout intervention strategies. First, because dropping out is influenced by both individual and institutional factors, intervention strategies can focus on either or both sets of factors. That is, intervention strategies can address the individual values, attitudes, and behaviors associated with dropping out, without attempting to alter the characteristics of families, schools, and communities that may contribute to those individual factors. Alternatively, intervention strategies can attempt to improve the environmental contexts of potential dropouts by providing resources and supports to strengthen or restructure their families, schools, and communities.

Second, because dropping out is associated with both academic and social problems, effective prevention strategies must focus on both areas.[50] That is, if dropout prevention strategies are going to be effective, they must be *comprehensive*, providing resources and supports in all areas of students' lives. Because dropouts leave school for a variety of reasons, services provided to them must be flexible and tailored to their individual needs.

Third, because the problematic attitudes and behaviors of students at risk of dropping out appear as early as elementary school, dropout prevention strategies can and should begin early in a child's educational career. Dropout prevention programs often target high school or middle school students who may have already experienced years of educational failure or unsolved problems. Instead, early intervention may be the most powerful and cost-effective approach to dropout prevention.[51]

There are three alternative approaches for improving dropout and graduation rates:

1. *Programmatic approaches* involve creating programs that target a subset of students who are most at risk of dropping out (or have already done

so), by providing either supplemental services to students within an existing school program or a complete alternative school program within a comprehensive high school (school-within-a-school, such as an academy) or in a separate facility (alternative school).

2. *Comprehensive approaches* involve schoolwide reforms that attempt to change school environments to improve outcomes for all students. The most common approach is to reform existing schools by developing a comprehensive set of practices and programs locally or by adopting an externally developed comprehensive school reform (CSR) model. A second approach is to create new schools, by either establishing a new school locally or adopting an externally developed whole school model. The most popular type of new schools are charters—public schools that are established and managed outside the regular public education system, and that are freed from most regulations and requirements of regular public schools. The number of charter schools—half of which include high school grades—and charter school students more than tripled over the ten-year period from 1999–2000 to 2009–10.[52] The third approach—which can be combined with the other two—is to create collaborative relationships between schools and outside government agencies and local community organizations to provide services and programs for students and their families.

3. *Systemic approaches* involve making changes to the entire educational system—what some scholars have labeled "systemic school reform"—under the assumption that such changes can transform how all schools function in the system and therefore have widespread impact.[53] Systemic reform can occur at the federal, state, or local level of government.

All three approaches have a limited record of success.

The U.S. Department of Education established the What Works Clearinghouse (WWC) in 2002 to review scientific evidence on the effectiveness of a variety of educational interventions, including dropout programs. In 2008, the WWC reviewed eighty-four studies of twenty-two dropout prevention (and recovery) programs and found only twenty-three studies of sixteen interventions that met their evidence standards—twelve of the programs were student-support or alternative education programs and four were CSR or new school models—and assessed their effectiveness in improving three student outcomes: (1) staying in school, (2) progressing in school, and (3) completing school.[54] Of the twelve student support programs, five were judged to be effective in keeping students in school, four were effective in helping students progress in school, and four were effective in helping students to complete school. Of the four CSR or new school models, only one was effective at keeping students in school, two were effective in helping students progress in school, and none was effective in helping students to complete school. Moreover, none of these four programs was effective in helping students earn a regular high school diploma; rather, they helped students earn an equivalent diploma by passing the General Educational Development (GED) test. This distinction is important for two reasons: first, research has demonstrated that students who earn a GED do not enjoy the same economic benefits as students who earn a regular high school diploma,[55] and second, most educational accountability systems reward schools and districts only when students earn regular diplomas.[56] Three other reviews of the research evidence on dropout interventions also found a limited number of effective programs.[57]

Evidence on the effectiveness of systemic interventions is also mixed. Increasing the compulsory schooling age to eighteen helps to improve graduation rates, but increasing high school graduation requirements—such as adopting exit exams or a college preparatory curriculum for all students—does not. Creating alternative pathways in either the public or private sector for students to earn a high school diploma also shows mixed outcomes. In particular, several recent large-scale studies found that some charter schools outpace their traditional counterparts, while other charter schools trail behind.

There is more consistent and compelling evidence for two early interventions: preschool programs and class-size reduction in early elementary school. Both produce significant improvements in high school graduation rates.

Studies have examined not only the effectiveness of dropout prevention strategies but also their costs and economic benefits. One recent study found that five specific interventions—from preschool programs to a high school reform model—produced economic benefits that were two to three times their costs.[58] These findings document the economic benefits of investing in proven dropout prevention interventions.

The remainder of this book explores the four dimensions of the dropout problem—the nature, consequences, causes, and solutions—in greater detail. In doing so, I uncover a number of dilemmas and complexities that make understanding and solving America's dropout crisis more difficult than it might seem.

I begin by providing a brief history of high schools and the varying requirements and pathways for graduating. Beginning with their inception in the nineteenth century, I examine the long-standing debate over the purposes and goals of high schools in the United States, from a selective institution preparing advantaged students for entry to college to a comprehensive institution preparing all students for college, careers, and citizenship. I also investigate an ongoing dilemma: What should the graduation requirements be for all students, even those who do not want to go to college? Under the mantra of "college for all," states have been raising the academic requirements for earning a high school diploma to those required for entry into four-year colleges despite evidence that more than one-third of future jobs will require no training beyond high school.[59]

The next chapter examines the nature of the dropout problem. What does it mean to drop out and what is the relationship between dropping out and graduating? The relationship is more complex than it may seem—a student can drop out several times over his or her educational career but can graduate only once. Also, just because a student never withdraws from school doesn't mean that he or she will eventually graduate. So dropping out and graduating are not opposite sides of the same coin. Another issue we'll explore in the chapter is how to measure dropout and graduation rates. The topic is important—it is valuable to know how many students who enter a high school eventually graduate—yet measuring such a graduation rate accurately is actually quite difficult and has generated considerable controversy. The difficulty is due in part to inaccurate or incomplete data as well as to how the statistics are calculated. Accurate dropout and graduation statistics are also important for determining whether the problem is getting better or worse and which students and schools are doing better or worse.

The subsequent two chapters examine the economic and social consequences of dropping out, both for dropouts and for the larger society. It may seem more logical to examine the causes of dropping out before examining the consequences. But it is important first to document the impact of dropping out in order to show its widespread effect and the impact on society if the problem is not sufficiently addressed.

Dropouts suffer in a number of ways—they are less likely to find a job and, once employed, are less likely to earn enough money to live, compared to more educated workers; they have poorer health; they are more likely to commit crimes and to be incarcerated; and they are less likely to vote. These consequences yield huge social costs. Yet while these disadvantages are well documented, the evidence is less clear that dropping out of school actually "causes" these outcomes. Some of the characteristics of dropouts that lead them to quit school—such as poor work habits or lack of motivation—may contribute to these poor outcomes outside of school. So it is often difficult to determine the causal connection between dropping out and subsequent outcomes. Nonetheless, a growing body of research evidence does find a causal connection, which supports the notion that reducing dropout rates and raising graduation rates may in fact improve the economic and social outcomes for dropouts.

The next two chapters examine the causes of dropping out. Here, too, the problem is complex. Research reveals a broad array of factors that influence a student's likelihood of staying in school. Some immediately precede the decision to quit school, such as failing courses or skipping school. But others are more distant. For example, research shows that poor academic performance in middle school and even elementary school can decrease a student's motivation in high school, which can lead to failing courses and skipping school, the more immediate precursors to dropping out. One important issue to consider is the extent to which factors that influence dropping out are similar to those that influence other forms of student achievement, such as test performance. Such information is critical in determining whether common reform strategies can be used to improve both graduation rates and test scores, or whether different reform strategies are required.

The next chapter examines past efforts to address the problem and why they have largely failed. Since the causes of dropping out are complex, so must the solutions be. In other words, there is no simple prescription for solving the nation's dropout crisis. Like other educational outcomes, dropping out is only partially a result of what takes place in school. Consequently, the solution must involve more than schools. Yet most attempts to address the problem of school dropouts in the United States have focused on schools, and most of those attempts have relied on two strategies—mandating sanctions for students and schools to do better, and providing more money for dropout programs. And both strategies have largely been unsuccessful at solving the problem.

The final chapter discusses current efforts to address the nation's dropout crisis, including the Obama administration's efforts to turn around the nation's persistently lowest-achieving schools, and why those efforts are insufficient. I argue that substantially improving the nation's graduation rate will require more fundamental reforms, such as redefining high school success to include a broader array of skills and abilities that have been shown to improve labor-market performance and adult well-being.

The book draws on a variety of evidence to examine these four dimensions of the dropout problem. Statistical data are used to provide a broad, factual overview, and research articles and reports provide evidence on the consequences, causes, and solutions.

The book also draws on my own experiences in conducting research on dropouts over the past thirty years, and two specific efforts to do something about it.

The first was a dropout intervention project in a Los Angeles middle school in the first half of the 1990s.[60] The intervention was designed and implemented by a colleague, with funding from the U.S. Department of Education. The school was probably similar to many other urban schools across America. The students were mostly poor and predominantly Latino. Over the four years we worked there, we found it to be a place of little learning, much rejection, and senseless cruelty.

Our intervention project attempted to counter this environment for a small group of the most problematic and lowest-achieving youngsters in the school, including Cesar. Although originally designed to focus on problem solving, monitoring, and training, over time our intervention expanded to become more involved in support and advocacy for students and their families. We also worked much more with people in the community and came to realize that helping students succeed in school required us to work with them in all the arenas of their lives—schools, families, and communities. Through our own experiences, we "discovered" what notable academics were saying about how contexts shaped dropout behavior.

A rigorous evaluation of our intervention project showed that it was highly successful—that is, a much higher proportion of "our" students stayed in school than a comparable group of other students.[61] More important, it gave us a chance to become closely acquainted with the more than one hundred students and their families whom we worked with over the four years of the project, and we gained valuable insights into how schools and community organizations often fail to provide the support and nurturing "at-risk" students need, or worse yet, how they actively push students out. We also discovered that the highest-risk students we were working with required constant support to succeed in school, something we were unable to provide past the ninth grade. Consequently, only a third of the students we worked with in middle school ever completed high school.

A second effort to address the dropout problem is a current project I am directing, the California Dropout Research Project (CDRP). The project, which began in December 2006, was designed to synthesize existing research and undertake new research to inform policy makers and the larger public about the nature of—and effective solutions to—the dropout problem in California. To date, the project commissioned seventeen research studies and produced thirteen statistical briefs to investigate four facets of the issue: (1) the measurement and incidence of dropping out; (2) the educational, social, and economic costs of dropouts for individuals and the state; (3) the short-term and long-term causes of dropping out; and (4) possible solutions.[62] The project also established the Policy Committee, composed of researchers, practitioners, policy makers, and a community activist. This committee issued a report on February 27, 2008, with a series of recommendations on what schools, districts, and the state should do to improve California's high school graduation rate. I discuss these recommendations in the final chapter.

This project also yielded a valuable lesson: simply producing timely and useful information is insufficient to influence policy change. It is also necessary to disseminate the information and work with policy makers to enact legislation based on the policy recommendations. So the project undertook a multifaceted dissemination strategy. One facet was to make the research findings understandable and accessible to a large number of people—policy makers, educators, and a variety of stakeholders in this widespread problem. To reach this audience, we produced policy briefs—1,500-word summaries written for a lay audience—from each of the research reports. These briefs were distributed in print to all superintendents and legislators in California.

A second facet of the dissemination strategy was to create a website where project publications and other information on dropout efforts from across the United States were available. The project website currently attracts about 2,000 visitors a month, and to date the sixty-six project publications have been downloaded more than 50,000 times.

A third facet is to generate media exposure to publicize the work of the project and maintain a sense of urgency among the larger public about the need to address the problem. Through press releases, op-ed articles, and media events, the project has generated more than twenty television clips on major California news channels, thirty articles and editorials in the state's major newspapers, and three op-ed articles.

Another lesson learned from this project was that to effect policy change involves working with individuals and organizations on the issue over an extended period of time. A key individual in California is Darrell Steinberg, who made high school dropouts the central focus of his legislative agenda after his election to the California Senate in November 2008. After his election he created the Senate Select Committee on High School Graduation to serve as a forum to educate fellow senators and the public about the dropout problem in California. Over the course of twelve months, the committee held five hearings that featured the work of CDRP. The senator also sponsored a series of bills addressing the dropout problem in California, three of which incorporated recommendations from CDRP's Policy Committee, where the senator served as a member.

My personal experiences in these two efforts provide valuable insights into the challenges and difficulties in effecting change in both practice and policy designed to keep students from dropping out of school.

Finally, these sources are augmented with personal accounts and quotations from students and dropouts themselves. These accounts are drawn from a number of in-depth case studies that describe the ordeals and challenges facing young dropouts or would-be dropouts in America, including:

- Angela Valenzuela's account of students in a Houston high school, Nilda Flores-González's account of students in a Chicago high school and Michelle Fine's account of students in a New York City high school.[63]
- Harriet Romo and Toni Falbo's study of one hundred Latino students in Austin, Texas, as they progress through high school.[64]
- Deirdre Kelly's story of students in two continuation high schools in California.[65]
- Mark Fleisher's account of female gang members in Kansas City, Missouri.[66]

- Kathryn Edin and Maria Kefalas's study of poor single mothers in Philadelphia.[67]
- Mercer Sullivan's study of youth crime and work in three Brooklyn neighborhoods.[68]

The real story of dropouts is the story of individual young people, like Cesar. It is a story of their personal lives and histories, and, ultimately, their struggle to succeed.

2

THE VARYING REQUIREMENTS AND PATHWAYS
FOR COMPLETING HIGH SCHOOL

High schools play a unique role in the American education system. Unlike other industrialized countries where students receive a credential after completing lower secondary (middle) or two years of upper secondary (high) school, U.S. high schools award the lowest credential—a diploma—only after completing four years.[1] More important, the diploma serves different purposes. For some students, it serves as the foundation for entry into higher education, where they will acquire more advanced skills and training that will lead to more advanced credentials. For other students, however, it represents the terminal credential. Not all high school graduates want or should be expected to attend college, at least not immediately after high school. For those students, the knowledge and skills acquired in high school should adequately prepare them to enter the workforce and become responsible, productive citizens.

Because high schools prepare students for different roles and destinations, over their history they have provided vastly different experiences for students depending on their social class and ethnic background, and where they attend school. U.S. high schools are still highly stratified, with some providing a rigorous, college-preparatory curriculum taught by well-trained teachers in a safe, supportive setting, with others providing a watered-down curriculum taught by poorly trained teachers in an unsafe, impersonal setting.

To understand what it means to drop out of American high schools, it is first necessary to understand the goals and requirements for high school graduation as well as the vastly different pathways and experiences students face in trying to fulfill those requirements. This chapter addresses these issues.

The Conflicting Goals of High School

Since their inception in the nineteenth century, there has been a long-standing debate over the purposes and goals of high schools in the United States. The debate has concerned who should attend high schools—whether access and attendance should be universal or selective—and a related issue of what is studied—whether the curriculum should be common (the same for everyone) or differentiated based on the students' background, perceived ability, and likely destination.

High schools were established in the nineteenth century as selective institutions, catering to the relatively few students who had the interest and means to attend school past the primary grades. As historian Sherman Dorn points out:

> The advocates of high schools consistently defended them not for their coverage [access] but their fairness. Thus, high schools had a different purpose from elementary schools. While free public schooling was to be common for younger children, it was important for high schools to be available, not necessarily widespread. This difference provided a critical wedge that separated the politics of elementary schooling from secondary schooling.[2]

Drawing on other historians' accounts, Dorn goes on to point out how high schools were not immediately popular in many communities in America, whereas support for elementary schools was widespread. Yet some reformers viewed selective high schools as a way to improve elementary education, as schools sought to better prepare their students to meet the requirements for high school admission. The same mechanism operates today, with high schools preparing their students to meet the requirements of the more selective higher education system.

At the turn of the twentieth century, enrollment in public high schools exploded, increasing from 200,000 to 2.2 million students in the three decades from 1889–90 to 1919–20, a tenfold increase.[3] Accompanying this increase was the emergence of the second great tension in American high schools—the differentiated curriculum. As long as high schools catered to relatively few, elite clients, they could provide a common academic curriculum to prepare those students for entry into higher education or professional occupations, such as teaching. But with the expansion of enrollment came the idea of creating a differentiated curriculum, since no longer could high schools be expected to simply prepare students for higher schooling. Instead, high schools were seen as a vehicle to prepare working-class youth and immigrants for working-class jobs and citizenship:

> Whereas nineteenth-century debates focused on the fairness of access and the problems in public support of selective institutions, twentieth-century high schools became known as mass institutions with the mission of socializing a growing proportion of teenagers. This shifted the focus of secondary education from the question of democratic support to that of utilitarian purpose, and the differentiated curriculum made the change seem natural.[4]

The most prominent aspect of the differentiated curriculum was found in vocational education. In detailing the history of what they term "vocationalism" in American high schools, Marvin Lazerson and Norton Grubb argue that the origins can be traced to some early, prominent reformers of the emerging high schools who sought to make learning more meaningful and for students to learn by doing.[5] The movement to incorporate vocational education into American high schools grew rapidly between 1890 and 1910, and attracted the support of the business community, labor unions, and government officials. The business community viewed vocational education as a way of providing skilled labor for the growing industrial workforce. The labor movement viewed vocational education as a way to improve workers' standard of living, and to keep vocational education in the public education system rather than as a separate system of training facilities controlled by the business community. And educators viewed vocational education as a way to help solve the dropout problem by providing a more relevant curriculum that would prepare them for future employment. The growing support for vocational education led Congress to appoint the Commission on National Aid to Vocational Education, whose recommendations led to the passage of the federal Smith-Hughes Act in 1917, providing federal aid to vocational education.

The transformation of the American high school from a selective institution offering a common, academic curriculum to a mass institution offering a differentiated, academic and nonacademic curriculum is illustrated in the case study of "Middletown" high school by sociologists Robert and Helen Lynd.[6] In 1890, the high school enrolled 170 students and offered two subjects, Latin and English. By 1924, the school enrolled 1,849 students and had twelve tracks, including a college-preparatory track, a "general" track, and eight applied tracks: shorthand, bookkeeping, applied electricity, mechanical drafting, printing, machine shop, manual arts, and home economics. Students took about half of their classes in common areas, such as English, and the rest in elective classes within their tracks.

The idea of differentiated schooling was championed by influential professors at Columbia University, the University of Chicago, and Stanford University, who established training programs for school superintendents around the turn of the twentieth century. Historian David Tyack has labeled these and other educational leaders of the time as "administrative progressives."[7] Differentiated schooling was rooted in the idea of "social efficiency," that the role of schools was to prepare different students for different positions that they would assume in adult life.[8] Professor Ellwood Cubberly of Stanford University wrote in 1909 that schools should "give up on the exceedingly democratic idea that all are equal, and that our society is devoid of classes. . . . Increasing specialization . . . has divided the people into dozens of more or less clearly defined classes."[9]

The twin tensions between universal versus selective access and common versus differentiated curriculum were evident in two influential reports issued during this period by the National Education Association (NEA). At the time, the NEA was a quasi-governmental organization that brought elementary and secondary administrators together with college professors and administrators and education policy makers to issue reports, often commissioned by the federal government.[10] The Committee of Ten, chaired by Harvard President Charles Eliot, issued the first report in 1893. The report argued for selective high schools serving few students and offering a common academic curriculum to prepare all students for college:

> The main function is to prepare for the duties of life that small proportion of all the children in the country—a proportion small in number, but very important to the welfare of the nation—who show themselves able to profit by an education prolonged to the eighteenth year, and whose parents are able to support them while they remain so long at school.[11]

With the explosive growth of high school enrollment at the turn of the twentieth century, the federal government commissioned a new report in 1918, *The Cardinal Principles of Secondary Education.* Whereas the first report emphasized academics over other outcomes of schooling, the second report emphasized the practical: health, "command of fundamental processes," "worthy home-membership," vocation, citizenship, leisure, and ethics.[12] Moreover, the report argued for different curricula for different students based on "a system of educational supervision and guidance." This report envisioned a larger, more inclusive role for high schools, claiming, "an extended education for every boy and girl is essential to the welfare, and even to the existence, of democratic society," and recommending the extension of at least part-time compulsory attendance until age eighteen. The recommendations in the report were prompted by the recognition that the demographics of the high school population "has been modified by the entrance of large numbers of pupils of widely varying capacities, aptitudes, social heredity, and destinies in life."

Both the idea and practice of different curricula for different students were greatly bolstered by the growth of group intelligence tests. These tests were developed during World War I as a way for the armed forces to better "fit" recruits into specific jobs based on their assessed intelligence. Soon the use of tests became widespread in many institutions and had great consequences, as Tyack points out:

> They seemed to provide that the social order was close to a meritocracy since the fittest seemed mostly on top. They leaped to fix on the mass institutions of education, civil service, and business narrow standards of what constituted ability. All this was no malevolent plot. In the war the psychologists were men trying to make a democracy work more efficiently in what they believed was a great cause. They saw themselves as scientists and on occasion changed their minds when evidence proved them wrong in their assertions and assumptions. They even had their moments of utopian dreaming of a smoothly running, conflict-free society where talent rose and ruled benignly.[13]

School personnel seized on the use of group intelligence tests as a means of sorting students for instruction. At the elementary level, the tests were primarily to classify students into homogeneous groups for instruction and to diagnose causes of student failure; at the secondary level, they were used to guide students in choosing courses and careers.[14]

The tension between competing goals for high schools continued in the twentieth century. Supported by the NEA and the American Association of School Administrators, the Educational Policies Commission issued a series of volumes in the 1940s about postwar education, with one, *Education for All American Youth* (1944), focusing on secondary education. The report recommended compulsory attendance until age eighteen or high school graduation, in part, to keep young people out of the labor market to avoid competing with soldiers returning from the war:

> It was thought better by far, for both youth and society, to have young people in attendance at schools in which they could secure occupational training, work experience, and a well-rounded general education than to have them enter an already oversupplied labor market without training, experience, or adequate educational training.[15]

In reaction to the growth of dictatorships in Germany, Italy, the Soviet Union, and Japan, all the reports the commission issued emphasized the democratic goals of schooling.

In 1959, James Bryant Conant, former president of Harvard University, published a widely cited book, *The American High School Today*, where he argued for the comprehensive high school for all to attend, but one that provided a differentiated curriculum that prepared students for different positions—some for advanced schooling and some for the workplace. To reconcile the competing goals, he advocated the use of guidance counselors to select students for the "appropriate" curriculum. As Dorn points out:

> Conant's conception of the comprehensive high school was therefore not a substantial deviation from what educators had proposed for decades. His starting assumptions—that everyone should attend a comprehensive high school, that some should take an academic curriculum but most would not, and that the schools had the responsibility to guide students into the proper curriculum—were, in outline, what the Cardinal Principals report had described.[16]

The competing goals for high schools were part of a larger debate about the goals of public schooling more generally. In their book, *Grading Education: Getting Accountability Right*, authors Richard Rothstein, Rebecca Jacobsen, and Tamara Wilder document the debate over the goals of education over America's 200-year history.[17] They demonstrate that American leaders, beginning with Thomas Jefferson, have long believed that public education should have a range of goals to successfully prepare future citizens for adulthood. In 1818, Jefferson stated that the purpose of public education was:

- To give every citizen the information he needs for the transaction of his own business.
- To enable him to calculate for himself, and to express and preserve his ideas, his contracts, and accounts, in writing.
- To improve, by reading, his morals and faculties.
- To understand his duties to his neighbors and country, and to discharge with competence the functions confided to him by either.
- To know his rights; to exercise order and justice those he retains; and to choose with discretion the fiduciary of those he delegates; and to notice their conduct with diligence, with candor, and judgment.
- In general, to observe with intelligence and faithfulness all the social relations under which he shall be placed.[18]

Support for broad educational goals has continued ever since. Rothstein and his colleagues note that in the early 1950s President Dwight Eisenhower helped secure funds from Congress for states to host conferences on the goals of education. A resulting 1955 national meeting that brought civil and business leaders together with educators recommended a list of fifteen goals for public education that included:

- A general education, with increased emphasis on the physical and social sciences.
- Patriotism and good citizenship.
- Moral, ethical, and spiritual values.
- Vocational education, tailored to the abilities of each pupil and to the needs of the community and nation.
- Domestic skills.
- Health services for all children, including physical and dental inspections, and instruction aimed at bettering health knowledge and habits.[19]

Support for a broad range of educational goals continues to this day. After viewing the historical documents on education goals, Rothstein and his colleagues developed a list of eight goals and commissioned a survey of the general public, elected officials, and state legislators to judge their relative importance. The survey, designed so that all eight percentages added

Table 2.1   Relative importance of eight goals of public education (percent)

	General public	School board members	State legislators
Basic academic skills	19	22	24
Critical thinking	15	18	18
The arts and literature	8	9	9
Preparation for skilled work	11	11	11
Social skills and work ethic	14	12	11
Citizenship	10	11	12
Physical health	12	9	9
Emotional health	11	8	7
Total	100	100	101*

Source: Richard Rothstein, Rebecca Jacobsen, and Tamara Wilder, *Grading Education: Getting Accountability Right* (Washington, DC, and New York: Economic Policy Institute and Teachers College Press, 2008), Table 1.

*Figure adds to 101 because of rounding.

up to 100 percent, demonstrates continued support for broad educational goals (Table 2.1). Although "basic academic skills" was the highest rated goal among all three groups of respondents, it still garnered no more than one-quarter of the votes. Overall, there was relative agreement among all three groups of respondents that public education should meet a wide array of goals, not unlike those expressed by Thomas Jefferson almost 200 years ago.

Although there appears to be a broad, ongoing consensus that public education should meet a wide array of goals, Rothstein and his colleagues document a fundamental contradiction between such a consensus and the federal and state accountability systems that are increasingly used to judge the performance of both students and schools. They review the history of the federal government's accountability system, the National Assessment of Educational Progress (NAEP), and how early versions of the test were designed to measure a broad array of behaviors and abilities, not simply academic skills, reflecting the view of the committee and especially its chair, Ralph Tyler, that NAEP should assess any goal area to which schools devote "15–20% of their time . . . the less tangible areas, as well as the customary areas, in a fashion the public can grasp and understand."[20] But soon after its first administration in 1969, due to political pressure and budget constraints, NAEP focused almost exclusively on academic skills in reading, math, science, and history as assessed with paper-and-pencil tests.

There were repeated criticisms of this narrow focus. In 1987, the National Academy of Education established a committee to evaluate NAEP because of concern that it was too narrowly focused on literacy and math skills that "could have a distorted impact on our schools."[21] The report identified a fundamental contradiction between the goals of public education and the accountability system designed to assess it:

> At root here is a fundamental dilemma. Those personal qualities that we hold dear—resilience and courage in the face of stress, a sense of craft in our work, a commitment to justice and caring in our social relationships, a dedication to advancing the public good in our communal life—are exceedingly difficult to assess. And so, unfortunately, we are apt to measure what we can, and eventually come to value what is measured over what is left unmeasured. The shift is subtle, and occurs gradually. It first invades our language and then slowly begins to dominate our thinking. It is all around us, and we too are part of it. In neither academic nor popular discourse about schools does one find nowadays much reference to the important qualities noted above. The language of academic achievement tests has become the primary rhetoric of schooling.[22]

The Requirements for Completing High School

The goals of public education are codified in graduation requirements. Just as states have the constitutional authority to provide public education, they also have the constitutional authority to determine the requirements for completing high school. The most common way is by earning a high school diploma, which requires completing a specified number of credits in specified subject areas, similar to the system colleges use to award degrees. In addition, some states and districts require students to pass a high school exit examination. States can also award equivalency credentials, typically by passing a state or national examination, or other credentials, such as certificates of completion.

Diploma Requirements

Most states specify both a minimum number and a specific set of course requirements for students to earn a diploma. School districts can add other requirements, which vary among states and over time, as shown in

Table 2.2. In 2010, among states that specified course requirements, the number of course credits varied from a low of thirteen in such states as California, Wisconsin, and Wyoming, to a high of twenty-four in such states as Alabama, Florida, and South Carolina. Alabama appears to have the most rigorous requirements: four yearlong courses in each of four subjects: English, social studies, science, and mathematics, together with eight additional courses. This translates into four academic and two additional courses for each of the four years of high school. Such requirements leave very little room for error—students who fail to earn six credits per year would not progress in school and run the risk of not graduating in the expected four years.

In fact, a recent national study of course credits earned by on-time graduates and dropouts from the class of 2004 found exactly such a pattern.[23] On-time graduates earned an average of almost 26 credits over their four years of high school, or about 6.6 credits per year. Students who dropped out of tenth grade had earned only 3.9 credits in their freshman year, which means they were most likely behind in their credits. Similarly, students who dropped out in eleventh grade had earned only 4.4 credits in their first year of high school, and only 8.5 credits by the end of tenth grade. This means that if their state or district required more than 17 credits to graduate, they, too, were behind in their credits by the end of their sophomore year. Similar patterns were observed for students who dropped out of twelfth grade. Overall, the results show that the fewer credits students earn in high school, the earlier they are likely to drop out. These results are confirmed by a number of studies reviewed in Chapter 6 that find that failing courses in ninth grade is a powerful predictor of dropping out.

Course requirements have also increased over time. Between 1980 and 2010, thirty-six of the thirty-seven states with state-specified course requirements in both years increased them during this period, with only California keeping them the same (see Table 2.2). Many states have established higher requirements for future graduating classes.[24] Furthermore, there is a growing movement in many states to specify not only the number and types of courses needed for high school graduation, but also the content standards and sequence of courses needed to become "college and workplace ready." This effort is being led by the American Diploma Project (ADP), a joint initiative of three prominent national organizations—Achieve, the Education Trust, and the Thomas B. Fordham Foundation. In its report, *Ready or Not: Creating a High School Diploma that Counts* (2004), the

Table 2.2 Compulsory schooling age and diploma requirements by state, 2010

	Compulsory schooling age		Diploma requirements				
	All students	Special ed. services	Credits (1980/2010)	Exit exam subjects	Alt. route	Advanced recognition	Alternative credential
Alabama	7–17	6–21	20/24	EMSH	✓	✓	✓
Alaska	7–16	3–22	19/21	EM	✓		✓
Arizona	6–16	3–21	16/20	EM	✓	✓	
Arkansas	5–17	5–21	16/22	M	✓		
California	6–18	Birth–21	13/13	EM	✓	✓	✓
Colorado	6–17	3–21	†				
Connecticut	5–18	3–21	†/20				
Delaware	5–16	Birth–20	18/22				✓
DC	5–18	–	18/24				✓
Florida	6–16	3–21	†/18 or 24	EM	✓		✓
Georgia	6–16	Birth–21	20/23	EMSH	✓	✓	✓
Hawaii	6–18	Birth–19	20/22			✓	✓
Idaho	7–16	3–21	18/21	EM	✓		
Illinois	7–17	3–21	16/18				
Indiana	7–18	3–22	16/20	EM	✓	✓	
Iowa	6–16	Birth–21	†				
Kansas	7–18	3–21	17/21				
Kentucky	6–16	Birth–21	18/22		✓	✓	✓
Louisiana	7–18	3–21	20/23	EMSH	✓	✓	✓
Maine	7–17	5–19	†/16				✓
Maryland	5–16	Birth–21	20/21	EMSH	✓	✓	✓
Massachusetts	6–16	3–21	†	EMS	✓		✓
Michigan	6–18	Birth–25	†				✓
Minnesota	7–16	Birth–21	15/21.5	EM	✓		
Mississippi	6–17	Birth–20	16/20	EMSH	✓	✓	
Missouri	7–17	Birth–201	20/22	EMSH		✓	✓

State						
Montana	7–16	3–18	16/20			✓
Nebraska	6–18	Birth–20	†/200 hrs.			✓
Nevada	7–18	Birth–21	19/22.5	EMS	✓	✓
New Hampshire	6–16	3–21	16/20		✓	
New Jersey	6–16	5–21	†/22	EM	✓	✓
New Mexico	5–18	3–21	20/24	EMSH	✓	✓
New York	6–16	Birth–20	16/22	EMSH	✓	✓
North Carolina	7–16	5–20	16/20	EMSH	✓	✓
North Dakota	7–16	3–21	17/21			
Ohio	6–18	3–21	17/20	EMSH	✓	✓
Oklahoma	5–18	Birth–21	18/23	2012	✓	✓
Oregon	7–18	3–20	21/22			✓
Pennsylvania	8–17	6–21	13/†		✓	
Rhode Island	6–16	3–21	16/20			✓
South Carolina	5–17	3–21	18/24	EM	✓	✓
South Dakota	6–18	Birth–21	16/22		✓	✓
Tennessee	6–17	3–21	18/20	EMS	✓	✓
Texas	6–18	3–21	18/24	EMSH	✓	✓
Utah	6–18	3–22	15/24			✓
Vermont	6–16	3–21	†/20			
Virginia	5–18	2–21	18/22	EMSH	✓	✓
Washington	8–18	3–21	†/20	E	✓	✓
West Virginia	6–17	5–21	18/24		✓	✓
Wisconsin	6–18	3–21	†/21.5		✓	✓
Wyoming	7–16	3–21	18/22		✓	✓

Source: Thomas D. Snyder and Sally A. Dillow, *Digest of Education Statistics 2010* (NCES 2011-015) (Washington, DC: National Center for Education Statistics, U.S. Department of Education, 2011), http://nces.ed.gov/Pubsearch/Pubsinfo.Asp?Pubid=2011015 (accessed May 14, 2011), Tables 174, 176; Thomas D. Snyder and Charlene M. Hoffman, *Digest of Education Statistics 1990* (NCES 19660) (Washington, DC: National Center for Education Statistics, U.S. Department of Education, 1991), http://nces.ed.gov/Pubsearch/Pubsinfo.Asp?Pubid=91660 (accessed January 17, 2011), Table 142.

Note: Credit hours converted to Carnegie units (2 credit hours = 1 Carnegie unit).

† Graduation requirements determined locally.

project argues that all students, no matter their future destination, should take the same academic curriculum in high school:

> Successful preparation for both postsecondary education and employment requires learning the same rigorous English and mathematics content and skills. No longer do students planning to go to work after high school need a different and less rigorous curriculum than those planning to go to college. In fact, nearly all students will require some postsecondary education, including on-the-job training, after completing high school. Therefore, a college and workplace readiness curriculum should be a graduation requirement, not an option, for all high school students.[25]

The report goes on to suggest that states should support and encourage different approaches, or "multiple pathways," to help students meet these standards, including vocational programs, project-based learning, charter schools, and advanced coursework, such as Advanced Placement and International Baccalaureate Programs. More recently, the National Governors Association Center for Best Practices (NGA Center) and the Council of Chief State School Officers (CCSSO) are leading an effort to develop and adopt common, state-level education standards in English-language arts and mathematics.[26] Some states have gone further, mandating a broader curriculum that includes career and technical education for all students.[27]

Some large urban districts have already moved in this direction, adopting more rigorous requirements in the form of a college-preparatory curriculum for all students. For example, in 2008 the Los Angeles Unified School District—which enrolls more than 700,000, mostly low-income, minority students—began to require all graduates to complete the academic curriculum required for entry into the state's four-year colleges, the University of California and the California State University.[28] The San Francisco Unified School District recently adopted the same requirement. Interestingly, some districts have begun to ease their graduation requirements to improve their high school graduation rates. The Santa Ana school district in Southern California, which had one of the highest high school graduation requirements at twenty-four units, recently reduced its requirements to twenty-two units.[29] Does adopting a college-preparatory curriculum for all students lead to higher academic achievement and improved college prospects? Research reviewed in Chapter 7 suggests not.

In addition to earning the required number and type of course credits, students in many states must also pass a high school exit exam. In the 1970s, several states began using minimum competency tests, typically in a multiple-choice format, to ensure that students had mastered basic skills before receiving a high school diploma. With the growth of the accountability movement and standards-based reform in the 1990s, assessments were used to ensure that students had mastered more rigorous, grade-level content standards. In 1979, New York became the first state to require an examination to receive a diploma.[30] In the 1980s, twelve states added exam requirements, and in the 1990s, four more followed suit. By 2010, twenty-five states required that students pass some sort of exit exam before being awarded a diploma, with Oklahoma adopting an exam in 2012 (see Table 2.2).

Exit exams vary by type and by the subjects tested. Three types are currently used: those based on specially designed, comprehensive exams aligned with state content standards (fifteen states), those based on end-of-course (EOC) exams that test students after completing specific courses (four states), and those based on minimum competency (MC) tests that generally measure skills and knowledge below the state standards (three states).[31] All of the exams are limited to core academic subjects, such as English and math, with some states also including science and history. Most states require students to obtain a minimum score on each subject exam, while some states, such as Maryland, allow students the option of obtaining a minimum level of the combined scores.[32] Finally, some states allow alternative pathways to graduation for general education students and/or special populations (students with disabilities, English-language learners), such as alternative assessments (SAT, ACT, AP), portfolio assessment, or grade comparison.[33]

As of 2010, twenty-five states also awarded advance recognition for exceeding the standard requirements (see Table 2.2). New York, for example, awards three levels of high school diplomas based on the types of course credits earned (all diplomas require twenty-two yearlong credits), and on the number and scores on the Regents Exam, from a minimum score of 55 in five subjects for a Local Diploma, to a minimum score of 65 in eight subjects for a Regents Diploma with advanced designation.[34]

The growing practice of using exit exams as the basis of awarding a high school diploma is not without controversy. The National Research Council report, *High Stakes: Testing for Tracking, Promotion, and Graduation*, describes high school graduation decisions as "certification decisions" in which "the diploma certifies that the student has attained an acceptable level of learning."[35] Exams represent one form of evidence in that decision. Like all high-stakes exams, the use of the tests assumes that:

1. The curriculum and instruction are aligned with what the test measures.
2. The test taps the knowledge, skills, or other attributes it is interpreted to measure.
3. The cutoff score is an accurate discriminator of mastery or nonmastery in the domain.[36]

These assumptions have been challenged in court. In one of the first court cases in Florida, *Debra P. v. Turlington* (1981), a U.S. court of appeals ruled that:

1. Students have a legally recognized proprietary interest in receiving a high school diploma.
2. The graduation test must be a fair measure of what students have been taught.
3. Students must have adequate advance notice of the high-stakes test requirement.[37]

More recent cases have questioned the validity of the tests for certain populations, particularly English-language learners and students with disabilities, whether suitable alternatives to the exam have been explored and offered, and whether students have been taught the subjects being tested and with qualified teachers.[38] In the case of English-language learners, for example, tests administered in English may not provide valid measures of the area assessed, as pointed out in the National Research Council report on testing: "When students are not proficient in the language of assessment (English), their scores on a test given in English will not accurately reflect their knowledge of the subject being assessed (except for a test that measures only English proficiency)."[39] Some states, such as New York, allow English-language learners to demonstrate proficiency in subject areas by taking alternative-language editions of the exit exam.[40]

The minimum graduation requirements based on coursework and exams set by states and local districts dictate the level of performance that all students must meet to earn a high school diploma. Those requirements have increased over the past couple of decades, and many states have established higher requirements for future graduating classes. High school graduation requirements provide an answer to a fundamental question: What knowledge and skills should *all* high school graduates possess in order to receive a diploma?

The American Diploma Project and the thirty-four states that support it argue that all students need rigorous levels of English and math because such courses are "prerequisites for success in college and well-paying jobs."[41] Yet the English and math skills for some of the jobs profiled do not require such rigorous skills. For example, the job of events manager requires a number of English skills, but no rigorous math skills are identified.[42] If such jobs do not, in fact, require such rigorous levels of academic coursework, why require all students to meet those levels to receive a diploma? Similarly, the suggested math curriculum in the American Diploma Project— four years of math with coursework beyond the level of Algebra II—exceeds the math requirement for entrance into the University of California.[43] Should all students meet this requirement before they are awarded a high school diploma, even if they do not wish to attend a four-year college? Although students who complete more rigorous coursework may have access to better jobs and be more likely to complete postsecondary degrees, again the fundamental question is: What level of performance should *all* students be required to meet in order to graduate from high school?

Alternative Credentials

In addition to awarding regular diplomas, states also award alternative credentials for completing high school. The most common alternative credential is the high school equivalency, which is awarded based on the results of a state or national examination. The most widely used national examination is the General Educational Development (GED) test administered by the GED Testing Service, a program of the American Council of Education.[44] The GED is a series of five subject exams in which, beginning in 2002, test-takers had to exceed the performance of at least 40 percent of traditional graduating high school seniors to pass the test.[45] However, states establish their own criteria for using the GED results to issue a high school certificate. Some states award regular diplomas, while other states award "equivalency" diplomas or certificates based on either the GED or state-designed examinations.[46] States also establish eligibility for taking the exam. Although the GED Testing Service specifies that test-takers must be at least sixteen years of age, most states set age requirements at eighteen or higher. But states can grant exceptions. Also, although GED test-takers typically must not be enrolled in secondary education programs, the GED Testing Service has established a GED Option program in eleven states that allows high-risk students to enroll in a GED program while still in high school.[47] Increases in these exceptions have raised the percentage of high school-age test-takers over time, with sixteen- to nineteen-year-old test-takers accounting for virtually all of the growth in GED testing over the past three decades.[48]

The distinction between completing high school by earning a regular diploma and completing high school by earning an equivalency diploma is important for at least three reasons. First, research reviewed in Chapter 4 suggests that the economic benefits are not equivalent. Second, research reviewed in Chapter 7 suggests that increased availability of the GED for high-school-age students may actually increase dropout rates. Third, the two types of credentials can distort the calculation of both high school dropout and completion rates, as discussed in the next chapter.

Alternative Pathways to High School Completion

While the goals and graduation requirements represent the common aspects of high schools—what all students are supposed to learn—a more important issue that has confronted high schools from their inception is their differentiated aspects—what is different in the intended as well as the actual experiences of students within high schools. Students pursue different pathways to high school graduation, some by choice and some by mandate. These alternative pathways operate both within and between schools, and result in very different opportunities, experiences, and outcomes. Within-school differences are most commonly referred to as *tracking*, whereas between-school differences are most commonly referred to as *segregation*.

Tracking

The growth of comprehensive high schools was accompanied by the growth of alternative programs—or tracks—to serve students of different perceived abilities, interests, and likely positions after high school. In her seminal book, *Keeping Track*, Jeannie Oakes studied the process and impact of tracking in twenty-five secondary schools throughout the United States as part of a larger study of American schools led by John Goodlad, then dean of the Graduate School of Education at the University of California, Los Angeles.[49] One of the central findings from the study was that despite the many differences in school features, location, and practices, virtually all secondary schools sorted their students in some fashion.[50] Perhaps even more interesting is that only two of the schools documented the practices they used to sort students; the rest used a variety of means that the researchers had to piece together from other information. Oakes also found that tracking took place in two forms: one was the division of the total school program into academic, vocational, and sometimes other explicit tracks; the other was the division within core academic subjects— English, math, science, and social studies—into different levels appropriate for homogeneous groups of students.[51]

Both forms of tracking are still widespread today, as evidenced by national studies of high school transcripts. One recent study that analyzed the course-taking patterns of high school graduates in 2004 found that about 26 percent had completed a college-preparatory program, 18 percent had completed a vocational program, and the remaining 56 percent had completed a general curriculum.[52] Moreover, the percentage of students completing the various programs and more advanced coursework in particular academic subjects, such as math and science, varied widely by demographic characteristics, with Asians, whites, and students from high social class backgrounds more likely to complete a college-preparatory program and to complete advanced coursework than blacks, Hispanics, and students from low- and middle-class backgrounds.[53]

Oakes provides a detailed account of the characteristics of sorting, its consequences, and how sorting is played out in students' day-to-day experiences. In terms of characteristics, Oakes found:

1. Students are identified in a rather public way as to their intellectual capabilities and accomplishments and separated into a hierarchal system of groups for instruction.
2. These groups are labeled quite openly and characterized in the minds of teachers and others as being of a certain type—high ability, low achieving, slow, average, etc.
3. Individuals in these groups come to be defined by others—both adults and their peers—in terms of these group types.
4. On the basis of these sorting decisions—the groups of students that result, and the way educators see the students in these groups— teenagers are treated by and experience schools very differently.[54]

A considerable part of Oakes's study focuses on the last point—how students are treated differently within the various tracked classes. Oakes studied 300 classes in the 25 schools, most of them tracked into high, middle, and low levels. The research team observed classes, analyzed teacher assignments and instructional materials, and interviewed students and teachers. They found that high-track and low-track classrooms differed in some important ways: students in high-track classes were exposed to more "high status" knowledge than students in low-track classes;[55] teachers in high-track classes emphasized different non-subject-related learning behaviors more suited for university work (critical thinking, independent work, active participation) than teachers in low-track classes (working quietly, being punctual, conforming to classroom rules);[56] high-track teachers reported spending more time on instructional activities (80 percent) than low-track teachers (67 percent) and required more homework (40 minutes per night versus 20 minutes per night);[57] the quality of instruction was higher in high-track compared to low-track classes;[58] and finally, the classroom climate—as evidenced by the relationships between students and teachers and among students, and which influence classroom learning—was markedly different between high- and low-track classrooms.[59]

In terms of consequences, Oakes found that tracking:

- Seems to retard the academic progress of many students—those in the average and low groups.
- Seems to foster low self-esteem among those same students and to promote school misbehavior and dropping out.
- Also appears to lower aspirations of students who are not in the top groups.
- Separates students along socioeconomic lines, separating rich from poor, whites from nonwhites.[60]

The causes and consequences of tracking that Oakes found in her study of twenty-five secondary schools in the 1970s have been confirmed in numerous subsequent studies.[61] In the second edition of her book, published in 2005, Oakes notes that tracking has changed in some respects, with tracking into specific vocational and academic programs largely disappearing, and sorting into different levels of academic courses done more by student choice. Yet she notes:

> However, the deep structure of tracking remains uncannily robust.
> Most middle and high schools still sort students into classes at

different levels based on judgments of students' "ability." This sorting continues to disadvantage those in lower-track classes. Such students have less access to high-status knowledge, fewer opportunities to engage in stimulating learning activities, and classroom relationships less likely to foster engagement with teachers, peers, and learning. The sorting and differentiated opportunities promote gaps in outcomes of every sort: achievement, graduation rates, college going, and so on. Low-income students and students of color still suffer disproportionately into the lowest classes in racially mixed schools and also because they are more likely to attend racially isolated schools where lower-level classes predominate. Thus, through tracking, schools continue to replicate existing inequality along lines of race and social class and contribute to the intergenerational transmission of social and economic inequality.[62]

Segregation

Between-school segregation has been a salient feature of American high schools since their inception. Nowhere is this more evident than in the education of black students. Historian David Tyack documents the growth of segregated schools for black children in the nineteenth century and notes a high degree of variability from community to community

> depending in part on the density of the black population, the nature of black leadership, and degree of white prejudice. In some cities, blacks argued for separate but equal schools, maintaining that such systems offered opportunities for Negroes to obtain good jobs and claiming that black children in mixed schools suffered from the insults of white children and the cruelty and bias of white teachers. . . . In other communities, activists pressed for integrated schools, arguing that separate schools were inherently unequal.[63]

The segregation of blacks between and within schools continued in the twentieth century, aided by the growth of group intelligence testing that identified blacks as inferior "when educators were increasingly empowered to make classifications of pupils according to their notion of what was best for the client, when the results of biased tests were commonly accepted as proof of native ability, when those in control of schooling generally agreed that the function of schools was to sort and train students to fit into the existing order."[64]

As their enrollment soared, so did blacks' aspirations for professional jobs, including those of teachers and counselors. Yet most school districts hired few black teachers, in part because of protests by whites. As a result, many black parents and black leaders were ambivalent about having black students attend integrated schools taught by predominantly white teachers. This ambivalence was voiced by famed activist W. E. B. Du Bois, who first argued that separate schools were inexorably lesser in numerous respects, yet later concluded that "race prejudice in the United States today is such that most Negroes cannot receive proper education in white institutions."[65]

Racial segregation in American schools has persisted even after the Supreme Court outlawed de jure segregation in 1954, and the Civil Rights Act of 1964 forbade discrimination in all institutions receiving federal funds. It also has persisted in the face of continued increases in black high school enrollment. By 1947, 72 percent of blacks ages fourteen through seventeen were enrolled in school, approaching the 81 percent rate for whites.[66] Although blacks have always represented a minority of public school students—from 14 percent in 1968 to 17 percent in 2004—they have continued to attend segregated schools where the majority of their fellow students are nonwhite. As political scientist Gary Orfield documents, the percentage of blacks attending white-majority schools in the Southern states jumped from 2 percent in 1964, when the Civil Rights Act was passed, to 33 percent in 1970, at the peak of the civil rights era.[67] It peaked at 44 percent in the late 1980s, when the South was the most integrated region in the United States, and declined to 30 percent in 2005 as the Supreme Court relaxed desegregation standards. The segregation of Hispanic students has grown the most since the civil rights period and now surpasses that of black students.[68]

Racial and ethnic segregation is closely related to socioeconomic segregation. In 2007–08, 70 percent of black and Latino elementary school students attended schools where more than 50 percent of the students were poor (eligible for free or reduced-price lunch based on federal guidelines), compared to 15 percent of Asians/Pacific Islanders and 5 percent of whites. Forty-six percent of black and Hispanic secondary school students attended schools where more than 50 percent of the students were poor, compared to 5 percent of Asians/Pacific Islanders and 1 percent of whites.[69]

The concern over segregation is fueled, in part, by its association with student achievement. More than forty years ago, sociologist James Coleman conducted the largest and most comprehensive study of American schooling, known as the Coleman report.[70] Coleman's was the first major national study to demonstrate that a student's achievement is more highly related to the characteristics of other students in the school than any other school characteristic. He further found that as the educational aspirations and socioeconomic standings of their fellow students improved, the academic achievement of minority students increased.[71] Subsequent studies have confirmed the finding that the social composition of the school affects student outcomes.[72] Chapter 7 reviews this literature in greater detail.

The story of differentiated schooling in segregated schools can only partly be told with numbers. It must also be told with in-depth accounts of the lived experiences of minority students attending segregated schools—what does or does not happen in their schools that contributes to their dropping out. A number of excellent case studies of urban high schools have been conducted over the past several decades: Michelle Fine's account of a predominantly black high school in New York City in the 1980s where only 13 percent of the incoming ninth-grade class graduated; Angela Valenzuela's study of a predominantly Latino high school in Houston in the early 1990s where 30 percent of the students graduated; and Nilda Flores's study of a predominantly Latino high school in Chicago in the early 1990s where 39 percent of students graduated.[73] All of these schools could be considered "dropout factories." And all of these accounts describe, in depth, how the schools either failed to provide an environment to ensure student success or, worse, actively sought to discharge students who were viewed as troublemakers or misfits. One example is from Valenzuela's study:

> Social relationships at Seguín typically are often fragile, incomplete, or nonexistent. Teachers fail to forge meaningful connections with their students; students are alienated from their teachers, and are often (especially between groups of first-generation immigrants and U.S.-born) hostile toward one another, as well; and administrators routinely disregard even the most basic needs of both students and staff. The feeling that "no one cares" is pervasive—and corrosive. Real learning is difficult to sustain in an atmosphere rife with mistrust. Over even comparatively short periods of time, the divisions and misunderstandings that

characterize daily life at the school exact high costs in academic, social, and motivational currency.[74]

Alternative Schools

Another form of differentiated schooling can be found in alternative education. Although early in the twentieth century philanthropists in some urban areas had attempted to establish separate schools, such as commercial and technical schools, these were mostly absorbed into the public system.[75] Yet a system of specialized and alternative schools did develop within the public system.

In her book *Last Chance High: How Girls and Boys Drop In and Out of Alternative Schools*, Deirdre Kelly documents the history of one type of alternative school, the continuation high school. The origins of the continuation high school go back to expansion of the comprehensive high school and educators' desire to provide a high school education to an increasingly diverse student body that included recent immigrants, school-age mothers, students with disabilities, students who needed to work, truants, and students with discipline problems. The original continuation high schools were designed to provide a part-time education to students who were working. They were closely tied to the vocational education movement to provide skilled labor for local factories. Kelly documents how some businessmen favored creating continuation schools inside factories where students could learn basic education along with vocational skills. But many educational reformers fought against having a dual school system, and they eventually won over the support of the business community in supporting vocational education within the public system, including continuation schools. The first federal legislation in the area of vocational education, the Smith-Hughes Vocational Education Act of 1917, stipulated that "at least one-third of the sum appropriated to any State . . . shall, if expended, be applied to part-time schools or classes for workers over fourteen years of age [and less than eighteen]."[76] As vocational programs expanded in the regular comprehensive high school, they superseded the need for separate continuation high schools, and the Vocational Education Act of 1963 eliminated funding.

But at least in some states continuation high schools took on a new role in "adjustment" education for students considered to be too "ill- or maladjusted" for full-time school.[77] One of the students in Kelly's study described continuation schools in this way: "This is a place for people between school and the street, or between school and no school."[78] Kelly characterizes them in broader terms:

> Any alternative program—in the context of a competitive struggle for, and hierarchical distribution of, status and resources—tends to get stigmatized almost by definition because it exists in opposition to the traditional program. Insofar as the continuation school acts as a dumping ground for students who pose a problem to mainstream schools, it reinforces the idea that the problem rests with a minority who can and should be segregated.[79]

California was a leader in this movement when a coalition of educators, probation and truant officers, youth advocates, and university leaders formed the California Continuation Education Association (CCEA).[80] Working with a California legislative committee, the CCEA helped pass a law requiring all school systems in the state to provide continuation education (or transfers to county-run schools) for youths who were suspended for ten days or more.

Today continuation schools are just one type of school within an increasingly wide array of educational options for high school students. The federal government, which collects a variety of data from states on public schools, defines alternative education as:

> A public elementary/secondary school that (1) addresses needs of students that typically cannot be met in a regular school, (2) provides nontraditional education, (3) serves as an adjunct to a regular school, or (4) falls outside the categories of regular, special education, or vocational education.[81]

In 2007–08, there were 6,293 alternative schools in the U.S. public school system, representing 6 percent of 98,817 public schools, and enrolling only about 1 percent of the students.[82] But alternative schools enroll 3 percent of all high school students, with the percentage varying widely among states.[83] In several states—Arkansas, California, Idaho, Minnesota, Mississippi, Utah, and Washington—more than 5 percent of high school students attend alternative schools. A 2002 study found that forty-eight states had legislation on alternative education, schools, or programs,[84] although the latest federal government survey found only forty states that reported high school students enrolled in alternative education schools.

California has an extensive array of alternative schools, including 522 continuation schools, 203 community day schools, and 178 other alternative schools. In total, there were 1,154 alternative high schools in California in 2005–06, more than the 1,037 regular, comprehensive high schools.[85] Despite the large number of alternative high schools, they enrolled only 8 percent of all students, yet they accounted for one-third of all the state's dropouts. Charter schools are another form of nontraditional schools that are run independently from regular schools through a charter granted by a designated authority. In California, there were 271 charter high schools in 2005–06 that enrolled 4 percent of the students but accounted for 17 percent of the dropouts. Altogether, nontraditional high schools in California enrolled fewer than 12 percent of all high school students but accounted for 49 percent of all dropouts.

Kelly documents the experiences of students, teachers, and administrators in the continuation high schools within three California districts in the late 1980s. One of the themes in her study is that the principals all believed that "their districts used the continuation high school as the 'ultimate scare tactic,' as one put it, to maintain discipline at the comprehensive high schools."[86]

Another major theme in her study was the notion of choice—students either transferred to continuation schools voluntarily or involuntarily—with girls more than twice as likely than boys to report that they transferred to the school voluntarily. But the distinction between transferring voluntarily and involuntarily was not always so clear-cut. In some cases, students in the comprehensive high school engaged in behaviors that they knew would get them involuntarily transferred to the continuation school. In other cases, students—such as pregnant girls—voluntarily transferred after being "strongly counseled" to do so because the continuation school was described as a more appropriate setting.

Whether they were there voluntarily or involuntarily, students attending continuation schools were typically behind on credits. The school therefore served as a place where students could make up credits, either as a bridge back to the regular high school or as a way to earn a diploma through an alternative route. Yet while all three schools offered students a way to make up credits quickly, to do so required high levels of motivation and self-discipline, something most students did not possess. Instead, there was often little effort put forth. As one student noted:

Like the first time you come to this school, you work hard 'cause that's how you were doing at a normal high school, and then you look at other students: they're always kicking back, and you get irritated with that 'cause they're not working. . . . Then the next year, you'll be slowly kind of slacking off. Then later on, you'll be talking the whole period, and you won't even recognize it.[87]

As a result, relatively few students transferred back to their regular schools and many dropped out. In addition, the schools actively sought to rid themselves of the most difficult and disengaged students, much the way comprehensive high schools did—by threatening to send or actually sending them to even less desirable alternatives: adult education, GED programs, or independent study.

Other Options

States, districts and schools, and nonprofit agencies are creating a number of options for students to complete high school, apart from the alternative education system. The oldest and largest of these is Adult Education, a state-administered grant program authorized under the Adult Education and Family Literacy Act (AEFLA), enacted as Title II of the Workforce Investment Act (WIA) of 1998, to support local education agencies, higher education institutions, and community agencies to provide adult basic education, adult secondary education, and English literacy instruction for adult learners age sixteen and older.[88] The secondary education component, which provides high school–level instruction for adults seeking a regular or equivalency diploma, enrolled 336,521 students in 2008–09 (97,008 were age sixteen to eighteen) and awarded 165,690 regular or equivalency diplomas.[89] Job Corps, which is also authorized by the WIA, offers comprehensive career development services for at-risk youth sixteen to twenty-four years of age. The program served 60,896 students in 2008 and awarded 10,893 regular diplomas and 8,403 equivalency diplomas.[90] Newer options include the Gateway to College, a dual-credit community college program serving at-risk youth, ages sixteen to twenty-one, which allows students to earn a high school diploma while progressing to a college degree or certificate.[91]

One major question is whether these alternative programs, as well as the vast array of school-based programs and school reform models, are effective in getting students to complete high school. This is particularly important as the number and variety of educational options for completing high school increase. Chapter 8 addresses this question by reviewing both the costs and effectiveness of the various approaches to dropout prevention and recovery.

3

THE NATURE AND EXTENT
OF THE DROPOUT CRISIS

Not every student who starts high school finishes high school. Students who fail to complete high school are called high school dropouts. It would seem straightforward to determine who is a dropout and who is not. It would also seem straightforward to determine how many students drop out or graduate from high school. Yet determining who is a dropout and how many students drop out or graduate is far more difficult than it would appear. In fact, measuring dropout and graduation rates has sparked widespread debate among scholars, policy makers, and educators and has resulted in conflicting indicators of the severity of the dropout crisis and whether the problem is getting better or worse.

This chapter examines the nature and extent of the dropout crisis. It starts with describing different ways of defining a high school dropout and the difficulty of actually determining who is a dropout. Then it examines the debate on dropout and graduation rates, reviewing alternative definitions and sources of data that yield vastly different measures. Finally, it examines levels and trends in dropout and graduation rates that reveal vast differences among demographic groups and among states and countries.

What Does It Mean to Drop Out of School?

There are several ways to define a high school dropout. One way is to consider dropout as a *status*. Dropouts are individuals who are not enrolled in school and have not graduated. Of course, this status can change: dropouts can reenroll in school and subsequently graduate. So, dropout can be considered a current status—the same way employment or marriage can be considered as such—that could change over time.

Another way to consider dropping out is as an *event*. Some students decide to quit school before they graduate—they drop out. The event may occur at a specific time and be well documented, such as when a student and/or his parents formally fill out paperwork indicating they are withdrawing from school. Students can legally quit school prior to completion if they are above the maximum schooling age dictated by their state of residence. But the event may be less formal and undocumented: students may simply stop attending school, or they may indicate to their current school that they are moving or transferring to another school, but they never enroll again.

Yet a third way to consider dropping out is as a *process*. Most dropouts do not suddenly withdraw from school or stop attending. Many display patterns of poor attendance and school failure that appear long before they formally or informally withdraw from school. As early as elementary school, some dropouts experience academic or social difficulties that may lead to further difficulties in middle and high school: they may have poor attendance and have difficulty getting along with fellow students and with adults in the school; they may become frustrated and unmotivated; they may lose interest in school and in learning; and they may develop poor views of themselves and their abilities.

Better understanding the nature of the crisis requires examining dropping out in all of these ways—as a *status* that affects a group of individuals, as an *event* that occurs at particular places and times, and as a *process* that develops over a long period of time. Each reveals something important and unique about the phenomenon.

Viewing dropout as a *status* reveals how many individuals at some point are dropouts and whether that status is more prevalent in some groups—males or females; Asians, blacks, Hispanics, Native Americans, or whites—or in some locations—inner cities or rural communities; Southern states or western states—than in others.

Evaluating dropout as an *event* reveals how many individuals, over a particular period of time or at a particular grade level, quit school before graduating, and whether those events are more prevalent among some groups of individuals, types of schools, or geographic locations than others.

Considering dropout as a *process* reveals what types of attitudes, behaviors, and school performance indicators precede the decision to quit school and when they occur, providing guidance for developing intervention strategies to keep more students in school.

The Difficulty of Identifying Dropouts

Identifying dropouts is difficult, no matter the type. To understand drop-out as a status—that is, whether someone is a dropout—it is necessary to know two things: whether someone is currently enrolled in school and whether that person has already completed high school. Individuals who are not enrolled or have not completed high school are considered high school dropouts. But determining whether someone is enrolled or has completed school is less straightforward than it may appear.

Consider school enrollment. Students must formally be enrolled in school. Initial enrollment occurs when a student's parents or guardians fill out some sort of paperwork requesting that their child be enrolled in a school or district. Public schools may require proof of residency. They may also require proof of vaccination and other information. After students are initially enrolled, schools will assume they are still enrolled from year to year unless they (1) are promoted to another school—such as from elementary school to middle school, or middle school to high school; (2) formally withdraw; or (3) are absent for an extended period of time, at which point the school classifies them as a dropout.

But there may be periods of time when students are not formally enrolled in school. For example, students may not show up on the first day of the new school year. Until they do show up, the school may not know whether they are still enrolled at the school site or have moved or transferred to an-other school. A study of a Los Angeles middle school (grades seven through nine) found that 19 percent of its seventh-grade students entered *after* the first day of school.[1]

Students may also have spells of not being enrolled when they transfer schools in the middle of the school year. For example, students may for-mally withdraw because their parents move, and it may take several days or more for the family to formally enroll the child in a new school. Technically speaking, any day a child without a diploma is not enrolled in school, that child could be considered a dropout. Yet they rarely are, partly because it would be difficult to know, on any particular day, how many school-age youth have not graduated and are not enrolled in school, and thus could be considered dropouts. But more important, if such persons are not enrolled for a small number of days and intend to reenroll, then it may be unreason-able to consider them dropouts.

And yet, how many days should pass before nonenrolled students are considered to be dropouts? One study of a group of young men twenty-five to thirty-two years old found that 37 percent had quit high school for at least a three-month period, although only 14 percent were classified as high school dropouts at the time of the study.[2] Government data collection procedures allow students to be out of school for months at a time without being considered dropouts. The federal government, which collects dropout and graduation data from all fifty states, defines a dropout as someone who:

- Was enrolled in school at some time during the previous school year.
- Was not enrolled at the beginning (October 1) of the current school year.
- Has not graduated from high school or completed a state- or district-approved education program (including special education and General Educational Development preparation).
- Does not meet any of the following exclusionary conditions: transferred to another public school district, private school, or state- or district-approved education program; temporary absence due to suspension or school-approved education program; or death.[3]

This definition means that students could drop out of school sometime during one school year but not be reported as a dropout so long as they reenrolled by October 1 of the following year.

But even more accurate school enrollment information may be insufficient to identify dropouts. Just because students are enrolled, they do not necessarily attend school. Chronic absenteeism is one of the strongest predictors of dropping out. Also, many dropouts may not formally withdraw from school, so often the only way a school can determine whether a former student is a dropout is by a spell of unexcused absences, sometimes referred to as truancy. How many absences should be allowed before students are considered as not enrolled, and therefore a dropout? Ignoring long periods of nonenrollment and absenteeism means the number of dropouts in many schools, districts, and even states is underreported, as is the number of dropouts in the country as a whole.

The other piece of information needed to identify dropouts is whether students who are no longer enrolled in school have completed high school. Defining what *completing* high school means is also less than straightforward because there are different ways of completing high school. As described in the last chapter, students can earn a regular high school diploma, a high school equivalency certificate, or some other form of alternative credential.

In collecting dropout and graduation statistics from the states, the federal government defines dropouts as previously enrolled students who "have not graduated from high school or completed a state- or district-approved education program."[4] The U.S. Census Bureau, which collects national population data, also defines a dropout as someone who has not completed high school by earning a high school diploma or alternative credential.[5] In other words, completing high school by any type of credential precludes someone from being considered a dropout by the federal government and by virtually all states. In fact, it is not even necessary to earn any type of high school credential to avoid being labeled a dropout; in California, for example, a student is not considered a dropout if the student has "transferred to and is attending a college offering a baccalaureate or associate degree program."[6]

And yet, not dropping out of school is not the same as graduating. The federal government also defines a high school graduate as someone who earns "a regular high school diploma."[7] Similarly, in 2005 all of the nation's governors signed an agreement to voluntarily implement a common formula for calculating their state's high school graduation rate, where graduation is defined as earning a diploma.[8] Hence, keeping students from dropping out is not the same as getting more students to graduate. It is the latter that is most important to states and to the federal government, and may be more lucrative for students.

To understand dropout as an event, it is necessary to know not only *whether* a student is enrolled and has completed high school, but also *when* this change in status occurs. That is, one must consider the element of time. Whereas dropout status can be measured by one point in time, dropout as an event is measured over a specified period, from one point in time to another. For example, a federally defined dropout, as noted above, is a student who was enrolled on October 1 in one school year but was not enrolled (or had not completed school) on October 1 in the following school year. However, that period of time is arbitrary.

It may also be useful to know *when* students drop out of school. If it is early in a student's career, say, in middle school or in the ninth grade, then it may require more attention to the problems or issues confronting students in those earlier grades. If it is later—for those students staying on until grade twelve—then it may demand another type of assistance, such as passing a high school exit exam in the increasing number of states that require it. It may also be useful to know how many students drop out over their entire secondary careers and even how many spells of dropping out students may experience.

A simple schematic illustrates the several facets of dropping out and its relationship to graduation:

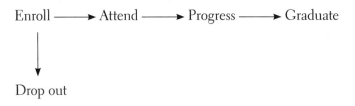

The pathway to graduation starts when students enroll in school. But once enrolled, students must attend school. They also have to progress in school, which means they have to pass their classes and earn enough credits to get promoted from one grade to the next. Finally, after progressing through school and meeting all the requirements, students earn a diploma and graduate. Many students, whether they find schoolwork difficult or uninspiring, progress through school in a straightforward manner and graduate from high school in the normal four-year time frame. Other students, however, experience interrupted enrollment, spotty attendance, and/or slow progress that make graduating from high school much less certain.

Student Mobility

The problem of dropping out is inextricably linked to the phenomenon of student mobility—the practice of students' moving from one school to another. One reason is simply that students are highly mobile in the United States, and this fact makes it difficult to identify whether or when students are enrolled in school and, therefore, whether or when they should be considered dropouts. The other reason is that student mobility itself may be both a precursor and a cause of dropping out of school.

As a society, Americans are highly mobile. According to the U.S. Census, more than 37 million people changed residences between 2008 and 2009, representing 12 percent of the population.[9] Among the 53 million school-age children age five to seventeen, 12 percent changed residences in that one-year period. Although most residential moves are within the same county, they often lead to changes in schools. Yet residential changes and school changes are not strictly linked. Not every child who changes residences changes schools, and not every child who changes schools changes residences. A national study of residential and school changes found that 50 percent of residential changes between grades eight and twelve were not associated with changing schools, and 30 percent of school changes were not associated with changing residences.[10] Nonetheless, the study found that residential mobility was the single biggest predictor of school mobility.

Unfortunately, there are no comprehensive data on student mobility in the United States. Yet sufficient data at the national and local levels suggest that student mobility is commonplace. The national student assessment program, known as the National Assessment of Educational Progress (NAEP), collects survey information from students that includes a question about how many times the student has changed schools in the past two years. According to data from the 2000 assessment (the last year the question was asked), 34 percent of all fourth-grade students reported changing schools over the past two years, with 18 percent reporting one change, 7 percent reporting two changes, and 8 percent reporting three or more changes.[11] A longitudinal study that tracked a cohort of kindergarten students through the eighth grade found that 95 percent changed schools at least once and 13 percent changed schools four or more times.[12] An earlier longitudinal study that tracked a cohort of eighth-grade students through high school found that 61 percent of students changed schools (other than promotion from elementary to middle and middle to high school) between the first and twelfth grades, with 27 percent changing schools between grades eight and twelve.[13]

Longitudinal data from local school districts reveal that student mobility is widespread. A recent study that tracked more than 86,000 students enrolled in the New York City (NYC) school district for eight years—from the fall of 1995, when they were in first grade, to the spring of 2003, when they expected to complete the eighth grade—found that 37 percent had exited the NYC public schools.[14] A recent study in the Los Angeles Unified School District found that 18 percent of ninth-grade students who remained in the district had attended more than one high school.[15]

Widespread student mobility makes it difficult to track students, especially when they leave a school district, and to determine whether they reenroll in another school or educational program—and hence are not dropouts— or whether they quit school and should be considered dropouts. All states in the United States are implementing longitudinal student data systems that use unique student identifiers to better track students who change schools within the state's public school system.[16] Such systems can help provide more accurate counts of dropouts by helping to verify whether mobile students actually reenroll in another school. California, which just implemented its system in 2006, found that 46,652 students who were reported by their original schools as transfers to other California public schools in 2008–09 did not show up as enrolled in the state's data system, so they were reclassified as dropouts.[17] Yet such systems are unable to track students who transfer to private schools or schools in other states, or those who leave the country.

Mobile students are less likely to graduate than students who remain in the same school. In the previously cited study of eighth-graders, dropout rates were three times higher among students who changed schools two or more times between eighth and twelfth grades than among students who remained in the same high school over that four-year period.[18] The Los Angeles study cited earlier found that students who attended more than one high school were half as likely to graduate on time as students who attended a single high school.[19] This does not necessarily mean that mobility causes students to drop out, as we discuss in a later chapter, but it does mean they are related.

Reenrollment

Students who drop out of school may reenroll and earn either a regular high school diploma or an alternative diploma. How many dropouts eventually complete high school?

One national study followed a group of students from the end of eighth grade in 1988, to 2000, eight years after their expected high school graduation in 1992.[20] The study found that 20 percent of the students had dropped out of high school at least once. Among the students who had dropped out, 43 percent had completed high school by the spring of 1994, two years after their expected graduation—14 percent had earned a regular diploma and 29 percent had earned a GED or alternative certificate. An additional 20 percent of the students completed high school between the spring of 1994 and the spring of 2000—5 percent had earned a regular diploma and 15 percent had earned a GED or alternative diploma. Altogether, two-thirds of all dropouts had completed some form of high school. A more recent study followed a group of students from the end of tenth grade in 2002 to 2006, two years after their expected graduation in 2004.[21] The study found that of the 13 percent who had dropped out, 53 percent had either completed high school (21 percent had earned a diploma and 16 percent had earned an equivalent diploma) or were pursuing either a diploma or GED.

The Debate over Dropout and Graduation Rates

Although it is clearly important to define dropouts and to know the number of dropouts from a school or in a community, it is also important to know the percentage of dropouts—known as *dropout rates*—within any given population. Similarly, it is useful to know the percentage of the population that completes or graduates from high school, known as *completion* or *graduation rates.*

One reason for measuring dropout and graduation rates is to gauge the degree to which those rates are considered problematic. While it is likely and even acceptable that some percentage of the population may not complete high school, when that percentage is sufficiently large, the issue may be considered serious and warrants public and government attention. At that point, the situation may even be labeled a "crisis." The same has been said of unemployment. Some unemployment in a population may be likely and even acceptable (some economists call this "natural" unemployment), but when a sufficiently large percentage of the population is unemployed, it is considered problematic and worthy of public and government action.

The issue of measuring dropout and graduation rates has generated considerable discussion and debate in the United States, particularly over the past decade, because of a series of reports that showed the country's dropout rate was unacceptably high. Some of the first studies were commissioned by The Civil Rights Project, a university-based research center focused on the civil rights movement, and Achieve, a leading education reform organization, and presented at a conference at Harvard University on January 13, 2001.[22] The press release for the conference read:

DROPOUTS CONCENTRATED IN 35 CITIES, WHILE FEDERAL DATA ON DROPOUTS UNDERESTIMATES PROBLEM

New Studies Shed Light on Dropout Crisis

The nation's dropout problem is most severe in a few hundred schools in the 35 largest cities in the U.S., where nearly half of schools graduate less than 50% of their freshman class,

according to a new study presented at a national conference at
the Harvard Graduate School of Education on January 13, 2001.
New research also revealed that federally reported data on dropouts is inaccurate and underestimates the dropout problem nationally, particularly among minority students.[23]

The Civil Rights Project then held a series of regional conferences
around the United States in which the organization released additional
studies and reports showing low graduation rates. Each conference garnered considerable media attention. Researchers associated with the organization also published opinion articles highlighting the crisis, such as:

- "The New Math on Graduation Rates," by Christopher B. Swanson
  (*Education Week*, July 28, 2004).[24]
- "Other View: Under NCLB, State Tinkers with Dropouts," by
  Russell W. Rumberger and Daniel J. Losen (*Sacramento Bee*, April
  29, 2005).[25]

A series of reports were also released by Jay Greene and his colleagues
at the Manhattan Institute, a conservative think tank, beginning in November 2001.[26] These reports used federal data sources to calculate national graduation rates, beginning with a rate of 74 percent for the high
school class of 1988, as well as rates for racial minorities, males and females,
states, and major cities.[27] These rates were considerably lower than the official government rates generated by the National Center for Education
Statistics (NCES), a branch of the U.S. Department of Education. These
reports also garnered considerable media attention.

Other educational organizations fueled the national debate about the
problem of high school dropouts and the issue of accurate measures of
rates. The Education Trust, one of the most influential educational organizations, released a report in December 2003, *Telling the Whole Truth (or
Not) about High School Graduation,* in which it stated, "Differences in
the ways states define 'graduation rate' not only result in wide variations in
the data but, in many cases, significantly understate the problems that
schools and students are facing."[28] A liberal think tank, the Economic
Policy Institute, further fueled the debate when it released a report in
2006, *Rethinking High School Graduation Rates and Trends,* in which the
authors argued that graduation rates in the United States were actually
higher than many of the previously released reports were showing.[29] The

Economic Policy Institute report prompted a series of exchanges in the national education newspaper, *Education Week*, over the issue of how best to compute accurate dropout and graduation rates and the limitations of existing data and methods.[30] An article reporting on the conflict began:

> Depending on which of a pair of new think-tank estimates you believe, the nation's high schools are graduating only seven out of 10 of their students or as large a share as 82 percent.[31]

Education Week itself entered the debate when it released the first in a series of annual reports titled, "Diplomas Count," on June 22, 2006:

> Starting with this special issue of *Education Week*, the Editorial Projects in Education Research Center and the newspaper plan to shed light on the crucial subject of high school graduation rates through the Graduation Project, an annual report produced with support from the Seattle-based Bill & Melinda Gates Foundation.
>
> *Diplomas Count: An Essential Guide to Graduation Policy and Rates*, the first edition, provides detailed data on graduation rates across the 50 states and the District of Columbia, and in the nation's 50 largest school districts. The analysis is based on the Cumulative Promotion Index developed by Christopher B. Swanson, the director of the EPE Research Center and a prominent expert on graduation data.[32]

The nation's graduation rate for the high school class of 2002–03, using Swanson's formula, was estimated at 69.6 percent.[33]

The federal government attempted to provide guidance to its agencies, such as the Census Bureau and the National Center for Education Statistics. In October 2003, NCES asked one of its subcontractors to "convene a task force of measurement and policy experts to examine current high school graduation, completion, and dropout indicators (GCD) and recommend improvements in the measures."[34] The task force report, released in November 2004, complicated rather than clarified the issue by detailing a series of indicators, their uses, and the data requirements associated with each.[35] The report appeared to have little influence, as evidenced by the fact that beginning in 2006, NCES began using a new graduation indicator—one not included in the task force report—in its annual report, *Dropout Rates in the United States*. That report showed a graduation rate of 72.6 percent for public high school students in 2001–02, and a graduation rate of 73.9 percent in 2002–03.[36]

The debate over accurate dropout and graduation rates and how best to compute them was further complicated by federal and state systems that allowed varying methods for federal accountability purposes. This resulted in wide variations across states in reported rates, making it hard to compare one state to another.[37] The National Governors Association (NGA), an organization that influences state and national policy, created a task force to address the issue. The resulting report, *Graduation Counts*, was issued in 2005 and recommended that the states begin using a common four-year graduation rate once their data systems could provide the longitudinal data necessary to compute the rate accurately.[38] The governors signed a compact adopting the recommendations in December 2005,[39] and the federal government has issued guidelines adopting the definition, requiring all states to begin reporting the rate in the 2010–11 school year.[40]

Scholars also weighed in.[41] The most notable was James Heckman, a Nobel economist at the University of Chicago, who published a paper in 2010 examining why estimates of the U.S. graduation rate—the most highly contentious indicator—varied so widely.[42] He and his coauthor analyzed a variety of different data sources that other investigators and organizations had used to produce disparate estimates. They found that when comparable measures of graduation rates were computed on comparable samples of the population, the rates were also quite comparable, with the most recent estimated graduation rate at 77 percent.[43] They further pointed out that the disparities were most pronounced for blacks and Hispanics, whose graduation rates the authors estimated to both be at 65 percent, or about 15 percentage points higher than other estimates.

The National Research Council, a part of the National Academy of Sciences that provides policy makers with expert advice based on sound scientific evidence, along with the National Academy of Education, also took an interest in the issue. In 2008, they formed the Committee for Improved Measurement of High School Dropout and Completion Rates, which issued a final report in early 2011.[44] The Committee report details the challenges in computing accurate dropout, graduation, and completion rates and finds shortcomings in many of the rates now widely reported.

Measuring Dropout and Graduation Rates

Accurately measuring dropout and graduation rates requires three things: (1) a suitable definition, (2) accurate data, and (3) an appropriate formula for estimating the defined rate using the selected data. Both the choice of data and the specific formula can result in very different estimates of even the same rate due to various biases or inaccuracies in the estimates. Because there is no consensus among government agencies, outside organizations, and scholars measuring dropout and graduation rates, a number of specific formulas have been proposed and used, accompanied by extensive debates over the accuracy of the various approaches.

Alternative Definitions

Just as there are several ways of looking at the issue of dropouts, there are several ways of defining dropout and graduation rates. Each definition can reveal useful information about the nature and extent of the problem. There are three basic types of rates:

- *Status* rates measure the percentage of people in a population, such as sixteen- to twenty-four-year-olds, who have a specific status (dropout, graduate, completer) at a specific point in time.
- *Event* rates measure the percentage of people in a population, such as ninth to twelfth graders, who achieve a specific status (dropout, graduate, completer) over a specified period of time, often one year.
- *Cohort* rates measure the percentage of people in a population, such as entering ninth graders, who achieve a specific status (dropout, graduate, completer) over a longer period of time, such as the four years from the beginning of ninth grade to the end of twelfth grade.

Each of these types of rates can be applied to measure a person's status as a dropout, graduate, or completer (diploma or alternative certificate).

One of the major distinctions in these various definitions is the population of interest, which for calculating event dropout rates is typically a population of students identified by grade level or age. For example, the federal government reported that the 2007–08 event dropout rate—defined as the percentage of ninth to twelfth-graders from public schools who dropped out during the 2007–08 academic year—averaged 4.1 percent in the United States and ranged from 1.7 percent in Indiana and New Jersey to 7.5 percent in Louisiana.[45]

The population of interest for calculating cohort dropout, completion, and graduation rates is typically a group of students identified by their age or grade level. One particular group of interest, identified by the NGA and the federal government, is the group of ninth-grade students who first enter high school in a particular year. Because most high schools enroll students from grades nine through twelve, it is useful to know what percentage of those students graduate or complete high school in the expected four-year period.[46] For example, as noted earlier, the federal government will require all states to report four-year graduation rates for the high school graduating class of 2010–11, representing students who first entered ninth grade in the fall of 2007.

Although the definitions of the various dropout and graduation rates are rather straightforward, the actual calculations of the rates can become quite complex and contested. This is especially true in calculating cohort graduation rates. One area of contention revolves around which students are removed from the cohort prior to the calculation of the rate. In its new guidelines for calculating what it calls "The Four-Year Adjusted Cohort Graduation Rate," the federal government states: "To remove a student from a cohort, a school or district must confirm in writing that a student has transferred out, emigrated to another country, or is deceased."[47] Although these guidelines may seem appropriate, should students who move out of the country after attending high school for several years with the intention of earning a high school diploma be removed from the cohort? Shouldn't schools be accountable for such students? There is at least some anecdotal evidence of Mexican-American students moving back to Mexico after attending high school in California and failing to pass the state high school exit exam. The Houston Unified School District received national attention in 2003 when it reported very low dropout rates along with relatively low graduation rates because it excluded large numbers of students who moved out of the state or returned to their home country.[48]

The Need for Accurate Data

Calculating accurate dropout and graduation rates requires not only a suitable definition, but also accurate data. This issue, too, is quite complex and has generated considerable discussion and debate. Two basic types of data are used to calculate dropout and completion rates:

- *Cross-sectional data,* collected on a population at a single point in time.
- *Longitudinal data,* collected on a population over a period of time.

Cross-sectional data are most appropriate for calculating status dropout, completion, and graduation rates, while longitudinal data are most appropriate for calculating event and cohort dropout, completion, and graduation rates. Longitudinal data are more difficult and costly to collect, especially over extended periods of time. They are also subject to attrition—losing track of participants over time. As a consequence, cross-sectional data sometimes are used to calculate event and cohort dropout, completion, and graduation rates, which can yield inaccurate estimates, a topic discussed below. Whether the data are cross-sectional or longitudinal, it is important that the data provide *suitable coverage* of the population of interest and provide *accurate information* about the population, particularly their enrollment and completion status.

Data used to calculate dropout, completion, and graduation rates are collected by both federal and state government agencies as part of broadly focused, ongoing data collection efforts. At the federal level, there are several sources of data on dropouts and graduates:

1. *Decennial Census.* A complete census of every household in the country conducted by the U.S. Census Bureau every ten years since 1790, with most households receiving a "short" form containing seven basic questions and a small sample (about one in six) of households completing a "long form" with additional questions, including education questions.[49]

2. *The Current Population Survey (CPS).* The CPS is a monthly survey of about 50,000 individuals that has been conducted since 1940 by the U.S. Census Bureau for the Bureau of Labor Statistics.[50] Data on educational attainment are collected annually in March, and data on school enrollment are collected every October.

3. *American Community Survey (ACS).* A new ongoing household survey of about 3 million housing units per year conducted by the U.S. Census Bureau since 2000 that collects a wide range of demographic and housing information, including school enrollment and educational attainment, and beginning in 2010 replaced the "long form" from the decennial census.[51]

4. *Common Core of Data (CCD).* Annual data collected from state education agencies on the characteristics of public schools, districts, and state education agencies, including descriptive information on

students and staff, conducted by the National Center for Education Statistics.[52]

In addition to these ongoing data collection activities, the federal government also conducts longitudinal surveys of specific populations. NCES, for instance, since 1972 has conducted a number of longitudinal surveys of high school students, with the most recent being:

1. *High School Longitudinal Study of 2009.* A nationally representative study of more than 23,000 ninth graders in 944 schools who will be followed through their secondary and postsecondary years.[53]
2. *Education Longitudinal Study of 2002.* A study of a sample of tenth-grade students started in the spring of 2002, with additional data collections in 2004 and 2006, and scheduled for 2012.[54]
3. *National Education Longitudinal Study of 1988 (NELS).* A study of a sample of eighth-grade students started in the spring of 1988, with additional data collections in 1990, 1992, 1994, and 2000.

Since the 1960s, the Bureau of Labor Statistics also has been conducting longitudinal surveys of age-based samples of the population.[55] The most recent is:

4. *National Longitudinal Survey of Youth 1997 (NLS97).* A survey started in 1997 of young men and women who were twelve to sixteen as of December 31, 1996, with additional surveys conducted annually and with parent data collected in the first round and school data collected in rounds one and five.[56]

While all of these data can and have been used to compute dropout, completion, and graduation rates, two sources of bias can affect estimated rates based on these data: one having to do with the population coverage, and the other with the accuracy of the information on educational attainment. Economists James Heckman and Paul LaFontaine, in their study of high school graduation rates using national data sets, examine both of these issues in depth.[57]

POPULATION COVERAGE. Dropout, completion, and graduation rates are computed for specific populations. The U.S. Census Bureau, for example, computes dropout and completion rates from three surveys (as noted above): the annual CPS, the decennial census, and the annual ACS. Yet they cover different populations. The CPS collects data on the civilian, noninstitutional population, while the decennial census and the ACS include the military and institutional population, including incarcerated persons. These differences are important because education levels of the prison population—now in excess of 2 million—are much lower than those of the noninstitutional population. As a result, excluding the prison population will overstate or cause an upward bias for estimates of graduation rates in the adult population, as Heckman and LaFontaine document.[58] These exclusions are particularly important when computing rates for males and minorities, because they are more likely to be incarcerated than females and whites; one study estimated that 21 percent of all black male high school dropouts ages twenty to thirty-four were in prison in 1999, compared with 3 percent of white high school dropouts.[59] The differences are less problematic for the military, since they have education levels similar to those of the civilian population.[60]

The population of recent immigrants should also be considered when computing graduation rates. A high percentage of young Hispanics are born outside the United States. In October 2007, 40 percent of all Hispanics sixteen to twenty-four years old were foreign born and only 62 percent of them had completed high school; in contrast, only 7 percent of non-Hispanics were foreign born and 91 percent of them had completed high school.[61] An earlier study found that almost half of all foreign-born youth who had not completed high school had never attended high school in the United States.[62] So, including recent immigrants in the population will understate or bias downward the estimated graduation rate for students who attended U.S. high schools. If the goal is to identify the percentage of the population who has or has not graduated from high school, then this may not be important; however, if the goal is to measure the educational performance of students attending high schools in the United States, then excluding immigrants who never attended U.S. schools is appropriate. Heckman and LaFontaine estimated that including immigrants biases the overall high school graduation rate in the adult population downward by almost 3 percentage points, while the graduation rate for Hispanics is biased downward by nearly 11 percentage points.[63]

Two other populations are potential sources of bias in estimating dropout and graduation rates: English-language learners and students with disabilities. These populations may be excluded from surveys if they find it difficult to participate and are offered no accommodations, such as foreign-language translations. But since these populations tend to have higher dropout rates and lower graduation rates than other students, excluding them can bias estimated rates upward. For example, the initial round of data collection for NELS excluded about 5 percent of the targeted population of eighth-grade students who were deemed unable to complete the surveys; 2 percent because of language problems and 3 percent because of disabilities.[64] These so-called base-year ineligible students were added back in subsequent rounds of the survey, and including them lowers the estimated graduation rate.[65]

In addition to the issue of specific populations that may or may not be included in the data is the issue of general population coverage. Surveys such as the CPS and ACS draw samples of individuals from an identified population, and the sample data are weighted to provide estimates of the entire population from which the sample is drawn. The population estimated from the sample can be compared to other, independent estimates of the population to find the extent to which the sample accurately represents the population. To the extent that the survey samples fail to cover certain groups in the population, particularly those with low levels of education, the sample surveys may provide biased estimates of dropout and graduation rates. Heckman and LaFontaine found that the so-called coverage rate for the 2000 CPS, especially for minority males, was indeed lower than for the 2000 decennial census, resulting in CPS high school completion rates that were 3 percentage points higher than those using census data.[66]

ACCURATE DATA ON EDUCATIONAL ATTAINMENT. Bias in estimating graduation, completion, and dropout rates can also arise from inaccurate data. In particular, many surveys rely on respondents to report their level of educational attainment. But the means used to collect this information can produce inaccurate data. For example, a recent study identifies two major differences in the means for collecting information on educational attainment between the CPS survey and the ACS and decennial census surveys.[67] First, the study reports that CPS data is collected primarily through telephone interviews, while the ACS and decennial survey data are collected primarily through mail questionnaires.[68]

People completing the mail questionnaire—where all the response categories are shown on the paper—were better able to distinguish between one response category for completing twelfth grade without a diploma versus finishing twelfth grade with a diploma, than persons responding to a telephone operator providing all the choices over the phone. Second, in the CPS, one survey respondent provides the educational information for all members of the household, while in the ACS and census, each person in the household is instructed to fill out the questionnaire.

Institutional data such as the CCD can also produce inaccurate estimates of high school graduates. The CCD collects data on three types of high school completers:

- *Diploma recipients.* These are students who earn a regular high school diploma.
- *High school equivalency recipients.* These are individuals who are awarded a diploma by passing a state or national equivalency exam, such as the GED. These data are collected only at the state level. As mentioned earlier, some states award regular diplomas based on the GED, while other states award "equivalency" diplomas or certificates, so this makes it difficult to make comparisons across states.[69]
- *Other high school completers.* These are students who receive some other form of high school certificate, such as a certificate of attendance, in lieu of a regular diploma.

As Heckman and LaFontaine point out, one problem with the CCD is that it excludes credentials awarded outside the regular K–12 system, such as adult education and the Job Corps, two government programs that provide basic and secondary education services to adults sixteen and over without diplomas or with poor language skills.[70] Those two programs alone awarded more than 176,000 regular and equivalency diplomas in 2010, so excluding these figures understates graduation rates based on the CCD.[71] Another problem, as mentioned earlier, is that some states award regular diplomas based on the GED, while other states award "equivalency" diplomas or certificates.[72]

Differences in how high school credentials are counted make comparisons across states difficult. To illustrate, Table 3.1 shows figures for each type of certificate from the 2007–08 data collection of the CCD for the United States and for selected states. Of all the high school completion

Table 3.1   Types of high school completion certificates awarded, selected states, 2007–08

	Diploma		Equivalency		Other		Total
	Number	Percent	Number	Percent	Number	Percent	number
U.S.	3,001337	93.3%	157,243	4.9%	56,982	1.8%	3,215,562
California	374,561	97.5%	9,543	2.5%		0.0%	384,104
Florida	149,046	85.3%	16,266	9.3%	9,324	5.3%	174,636
Mississippi	24,795	80.0%	3,368	10.9%	2,823	9.1%	30,986
Nevada	18,815	81.7%	1,784	7.7%	2,421	10.5%	23,020

Source: Common Core Data, http://nces.ed.gov/ccd/bat (accessed December 29, 2010).

certificates awarded in the United States that year, almost 94 percent were regular diplomas, 5 percent were equivalency diplomas, and fewer than 2 percent were other types of certificates. But those percentages varied widely among states; some states, such as California, primarily awarded diplomas, while other states, such as Mississippi and Nevada, awarded much higher percentages of equivalency and other certificates.

Competing Measures

The federal government computes and reports a number of different dropout, graduation, and complete rates, shown in Table 3.2.[73]

Three dropout rates are reported. The *status dropout rate*, which measures the percentage of civilian, noninstitutional population sixteen to twenty-four years old who have not completed high school and are not currently enrolled in school, was 8 percent in 2008. The *event dropout rate*, which measures the percentage of the population fifteen to twenty-four years old who dropped out of grades ten through twelve the previous year, was 3.5 percent in 2008. The *public school event dropout rate*, which measures the percentage of public school students who dropped out of grades nine through twelve the previous year, was 4.1 percent for the 2007–08 school year. Each of these rates does not count as dropouts students who earn a high school equivalency credential The census also does not count as dropouts persons who complete at least some higher education.

The three measures also convey different information about dropouts. The status rate provides information about the percentage of youth who have not completed high school. The two event rates provide information about the percentage of youth who drop out of school over the course of

Table 3.2   Measures of dropout, graduation, and completion rates reported by the federal government

Rate	Population (data source)	Definition	Level	Years	National rate (year)
Status dropout rate	Civilian, noninstitutionalized population 16- to 24-year-olds (CPS)	Percentage who have are not enrolled in school and have not completed high school	Nation	Annually 1972–present	8.0% (2008)
Event dropout rate	Civilian, noninstitutionalized population 15- to 24-year-olds (CPS)	Percentage who dropped out of grades 10–12 in previous year	Nation, states	Annually 1972–present	3.5% (2008)
Public school event dropout rate	Public high school students (CCD)	Percentage who dropped out of grades 9–12 in previous year	Nation, states	Annually 2002–03 to present (nation)	4.1% (2007–8)
Public school averaged freshman graduation rate	Public high school students (CCD)	Percentage who graduate with a regular diploma 4 years after starting 9th grade	Nation, states, districts	Annually 1970–present	75.6%* (2009–10)
Graduate/population ratio	Civilian, noninstitutionalized population 17-year-olds (CPS)	Percentage who hold a regular diploma	Nation	Annually 1870–present	76.7%* (2009–10)
Status completion rate	Civilian, noninstitutionalized population 18- to 24-year-olds (CPS)	Percentage who are not enrolled in school and hold a diploma or equivalent credential	Nation	Annually 1972–present	89.9% (2008)

Source: Chris Chapman, Jennifer Laird, and Angelina KewalRamani, *Trends in High School Dropout and Completion Rates in the United States: 1972–2008* (NCES 2011-012) (Washington, DC: National Center for Education Statistics, Institute of Education Sciences, U.S. Department of Education, 2010), http://nces.ed.gov/ pubsearch/pubsinfo.asp?pubid=2011012 (accessed January 17, 2011), table A-1; Thomas D. Snyder and Sally A. Dillow, *Digest of Education Statistics 2010* (NCES 2011-015) (Washington, DC: U.S. Department of Education, National Center for Education Statistics, U.S. Government Printing Office, 2011), http://nces.ed.gov/ pubsearch/pubsinfo.asp?pubid=2001015 (accessed May 15, 2011), table 110.

*Projected by NCES.

one year. Because students can drop out over a number of years of high school, the event rates are lower than the status rate. The overall event rate of 3.5 percent, which includes both public and private school students, is smaller than the public school rate of 4.1 percent, which reflects the generally lower dropout rate from private schools.[74]

The federal government also reports two graduation rates and one completion rate, with each rate conveying different information about completing high school. The *Averaged Freshman Graduation Rate*, which estimates the percentage of entering ninth-grade public school students who graduate within four years, was projected at 75 percent in 2008–09. The *graduate/ population ratio*, which measures the percentage of seventeen-year-olds with regular high school diplomas, was projected to be 77.1 percent in 2008–09. This rate provides a measure of the overall graduation rate for the population, including students who earned their diplomas from private schools. Because private school graduation rates are generally higher than public school graduation rates, this rate unsurprisingly is about 2 percentage points higher than the public school graduation rate. The *status completion rate*, which measures the percentage of eighteen- to twenty-four-year-olds who have left school and hold a high school credential, was 89 percent in 2007.[75] This rate provides a measure of the proportion of the young adult population who hold any sort of secondary credential, including an equivalency (GED-based) credential; hence, this percentage is significantly higher than the percentage of the population with regular high school diplomas.

Most of the attention and debate about high school graduation rates has focused on measuring the cohort graduation rate, because this is the rate used for federal and state accountability purposes, which we discuss in more detail below. Many different methods have been proposed for measuring the cohort graduation rate, since it measures the educational progress of a group of students over a period of time, from when students begin high school as ninth graders to when they are expected to graduate from high school four years later. The best way to measure this rate would be to follow the same students over the four-year period and simply calculate the percentage who graduate. But because there is no federal longitudinal data system for tracking students and only some states have longitudinal student data systems, the federal government currently uses cross-sectional data from the Common Core of Data (CCD) to estimate cohort graduation rates.

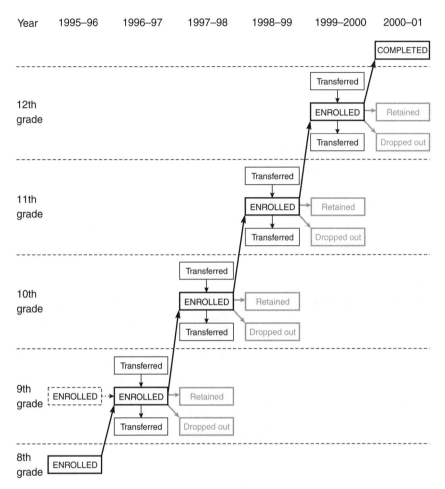

Figure 3.1. A pictorial view of the high school graduating class of 2000.
Note: Black solid lines represent normal trajectory of 2000 cohort. Gray solid lines represent students who leave normal trajectory by dropping out or being retained. Dashed lines represent 1999 cohort.

The challenge of estimating a cohort graduation rate from the CCD data is illustrated in Figure 3.1 for the graduating class of 2000. These students first entered high school as ninth graders in the fall of 1996. If they progressed normally through high school, they were promoted to the tenth grade in the fall of 1997–98, the eleventh grade in the fall of 1998–99, and the twelfth grade in the fall of 1999. They then would have graduated in the spring of 2000, although that data would not have been reported until the fall of 2000. So, data for tracking that cohort of students was reported over a five-year period.

But to compute an accurate cohort graduation rate requires adjusting for two important phenomena: retention and migration. The CCD collects enrollment data only on day one, near the beginning of the school year (usually October 1), for all students enrolled in each grade. However, some students are retained in their grade level, typically because they do not earn enough credits toward high school graduation to be promoted to the next grade level. Retention is particularly high in ninth grade. One way to estimate the percentage of retained ninth graders is to compare ninth-grade enrollment with eighth-grade enrollment a year earlier.[76] In 2000, there were 13 percent more ninth graders than there were eighth graders one year earlier.[77] The bias is even greater for minority students, where ninth-grade enrollment was found to be 20–26 percent higher. States with longitudinal data systems also show high retention rates in ninth grade. In Texas, for example, 12.3 percent of ninth graders were retained in 2008–09, compared to only 1.5 percent of eighth grade students, with ninth-grade retention rates at 16.2 percent for Hispanic students and 15 percent for African-American students.[78] The CCD data do not distinguish between first-time ninth graders and repeat ninth graders, so estimates of cohort graduation rates using CCD enrollment data are biased downward.

Migration is another problem. The CCD enrollment figures do not account for students who transfer in or out of a school during the course of the school year. This is particularly problematic when trying to estimate cohort graduation rates for schools, districts, and even states because enrollment figures can change over time due to transfers. For example, a school could be located in a community that is experiencing rapid population growth, causing increased enrollment over time. As a result, more students would be added to the cohort and the estimated graduation rate would be biased upward. On the other hand, a school could be located in a community that suffers from an economic downturn, causing decreased enrollment over time. As a result, these students would be removed from the cohort and the estimated graduation rate would be biased downward.

Researchers have proposed varied methods for computing a cohort graduation rate using the CCD, including augmenting it with other data. Comparisons among eight measures for the 2000 graduation rate, shown in Figure 3.2, reveal substantial differences among the rates.[79]

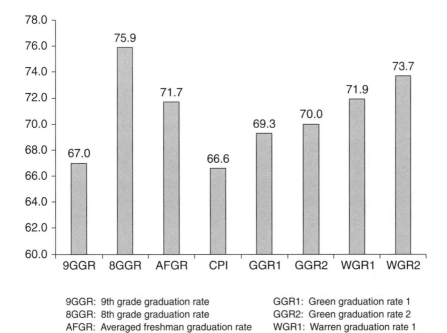

Figure 3.2. Alternative estimates of the cohort graduation rate for 1999–2000.

One of the largest differences is between eighth- and ninth-grade graduation rates. The *ninth-grade graduation rate* (9GGR) is simply the number of diploma recipients in 2000 divided by ninth-grade enrollment in 1996. Based on this formula, the estimated graduation rate for the 2000 high school graduating class was 67 percent. This rate is intuitively appealing because it appears to provide a direct calculation of the number of graduates in 2000 who were enrolled as ninth graders four years earlier. Yet one of the major problems with this rate is that ninth-grade enrollment, as pointed out earlier, includes both first-time and repeat ninth graders. As a result, using total ninth-grade enrollment produces an estimated cohort graduation rate that is too low (biased downward).

Because retention rates are much smaller in eighth grade, the *eighth-grade graduation rate* (8GGR), based on eighth-grade enrollment from 1995, provides a more accurate estimate of the graduation rate for the class of 2000, at 75.9 percent. The estimate is almost 9 percentage points higher than the ninth-grade graduation rate. To the extent that eighth-grade enrollment is a good proxy for beginning ninth-grade enrollment, the difference verifies that using ninth-grade enrollment biases the estimated graduation rate downward significantly.

The averaged freshman graduation rate (AFGR), used by the National Center for Education Statistics in its annual *Dropout Report,* estimates first-time ninth-grade enrollment by averaging the enrollment for grade eight in 1995, grade nine in 1996, and grade ten in 1997. As a result, the estimated value of 71.7 percent is about midway between the eighth- and ninth-grade graduation rates, which suggests it helps to reduce, but does not eliminate, the estimated bias from ninth-grade retention.

Another formula, the Cumulative Promotion Index (CPI), was created by two researchers from the Urban Institute and is now used by the Editorial Projects in Education Research Center to provide annual graduation rate estimates for the nation, states, and school districts published in the national education newspaper, *Education Week,* in its June supplement, *Diplomas Count.*[80] It is designed to simulate the probability of a ninth-grade student's being promoted through each grade level and finally receiving a diploma. The advantage of this measure is that it requires data from only two adjacent years instead of the usual five years most of the other measures require. But it assumes that promotion rates in more recent years reflect the promotion rates for students in the graduating class, which may not be the case. In other words, it is not a true cohort graduation rate for students who entered ninth grade in the fall of 1996 and were expected to graduate in the spring of 2000. It also does not adjust for the bias from ninth-grade retention. As a result, the estimated rate of 66.6 percent is quite similar to the ninth-grade graduation rate, which makes sense because neither adjusts for ninth-grade retention.

Some researchers have proposed more complex graduation measures to account for migration and transfers. Jay Greene and Marcus Winters estimated two alternative rates. The first (GGR1) uses the same technique for averaging freshman enrollment as the AFGR, but it adjusts for migration by including enrollment growth for grades nine through twelve. Because that growth was positive, it estimates a lower graduation rate than the AFGR: 69.3 percent versus 71.7 percent. The second rate (GGR2) uses CPS data to adjust for population growth and produces a somewhat larger estimate: 70 percent.

The two rates calculated by Rob Warren are higher than the Greene rates because Warren used eighth-grade enrollment as a proxy for entering ninth-grade enrollment, which results in a lower estimate for the size of the entering ninth-grade class, and a larger estimated graduation rate (WGR1) of 71.9 percent. The second rate (WGR2) also adjusts for immigration by removing some of the population who may have not attended school in the United States. This raises the estimated graduation rate by 1.8 percentage points to 73.9 percent.

Whether the differences in these rates are meaningful is a matter of interpretation. In the current era of accountability, where states, districts, and schools are compared to one another and are expected to make improvements from year to year, the choice of measures can make a huge difference.[81] For example, under the federal No Child Left Behind Act, schools and districts can meet the requirements of the law by increasing their graduation rates by a scant 0.1 percentage point per year.[82] Moreover, states can use other measures that may be even more biased and result in even larger differences among estimates.

Table 3.3 shows the graduation rates in all fifty states and the District of Columbia for 2007 using three rates that are computed and reported regularly: the Cumulative Promotion Index (CPI), published by *Education Week* every June; the averaged freshman graduation rate (AFGR), published by the National Center for Education Statistics, and the graduation rate computed and reported by states to the federal government under No Child Left Behind. As the previous discussion pointed out, the AFGR is generally a better measure than the CPI because it adjusts, at least in part, for ninth-grade retention, while the CPI does not.[83] Consequently, forty-seven of the fifty-one AFGR estimates were higher than the CPI estimates. In addition, eleven of the state-reported graduation rates were more than 10 percentage points higher than the AFGR estimates (shown in bold in the last column), with New Mexico 27 percentage points higher. Because states can use different measures for computing their graduation rates, resulting in vastly different results, the National Governors Association proposed—and the federal government adopted—a common measure for computing high school graduation rates as soon as the data allow.

The Promise and Reality of Longitudinal Data

Because national longitudinal data are not available on a regular basis, researchers, organizations, and government agencies have been forced to rely on cross-sectional data to estimate cohort graduation rates. But there are a few national longitudinal studies, based on nationally representative

Table 3.3 Alternative graduation rates by state (percent)

	Education Week (CPI)			U.S. Department of Education (AFGR)			State-reported
	1997	2007	Change	1997	2007	Change	2007
Alabama	56.9	62.5	+5.7	62.4	67.1	+4.7	**83.1**
Alaska	66.4	65.2	-1.2	67.9	69.0	+1.1	63.0
Arizona	59.8	68.2	+8.4	65.3	69.6	+4.3	73.0
Arkansas	68.6	69.3	+0.6	70.6	74.4	+3.8	**86.0**
California	67.4	62.7	-4.7	68.8	70.7	+1.9	80.6
Colorado	69.4	73.2	+3.9	74.7	76.6	-1.9	75.0
Connecticut	75.1	77.7	+2.6	76.7	81.8	+5.1	**92.4**
Delaware	59.2	65.0	+5.7	71.7	71.9	+0.3	81.0
DC	52.9	59.5	+6.6	54.6	54.8	+0.2	**75.5**
Florida	54.2	62.1	+7.8	62.7	65.0	+2.3	69.8
Georgia	55.1	57.8	+2.7	62.0	64.1	+2.1	72.3
Hawaii	58.4	65.1	+6.7	69.1	75.4	+6.3	79.2
Idaho	73.2	73.5	+0.3	80.1	80.4	+0.3	88.3
Illinois	71.3	74.6	+3.3	76.1	79.5	+3.4	85.9
Indiana	69.2	72.4	+3.2	74.0	73.9	-0.1	76.5
Iowa	78.9	80.2	+1.3	84.6	86.5	+1.9	90.5
Kansas	73.8	75.1	+1.3	76.9	78.8	+1.9	**89.7**
Kentucky	69.6	71.8	+2.2	71.1	76.4	+5.3	837
Louisiana	52.1	57.4	+5.3	59.3	61.3	+2.0	–
Maine	74.8	77.6	+2.8	75.2	78.5	+3.3	82.0
Maryland	74.5	73.7	-0.8	76.6	80.0	+3.4	85.2
Massachusetts	74.4	77.3	+3.0	78.4	80.8	+2.4	80.9
Michigan	72.0	77.8	+5.7	73.5	77.0	+3.5	75.5
Minnesota	77.3	77.2	-0.1	78.6	86.5	+7.9	91.2
Mississippi	56.1	62.5	+6.4	59.6	63.5	+7.2	**87.0**
Missouri	70.6	75.3	+4.6	74.7	81.9	+7.2	86.2

Montana	76.7	75.2	−1.5	83.2	81.5	−1.7	84.6
Nebraska	79.7	74.3	−5.5	84.8	86.3	+1.5	88.4
Nevada	65.7	41.8	−23.9	73.2	52.0	−21.2	**67.5**
New Hampshire	66.4	76.2	+9.8	77.3	81.7	+4.4	85.8
New Jersey	80.6	83.3	+2.6	83.9	84.4	−0.7	92.8
New Mexico	56.3	54.9	−1.4	62.5	59.1	−3.4	**86.8**
New York	60.3	70.6	+10.3	65.3	68.9	+3.6	75.0
North Carolina	58.3	57.8	−0.5	65.5	68.6	+3.1	69.4
North Dakota	58.3	57.8	−0.5	87.8	83.1	−4.7	87.7
Ohio	68.3	74.6	+6.3	76.4	78.7	+2.3	86.9
Oklahoma	68.9	71.8	+2.9	74.8	77.8	+3.0	76.6
Oregon	69.0	74.1	+5.1	69.1	73.8	+4.7	81.4
Pennsylvania	74.7	77.6	+2.9	79.8	83.0	+3.2	89.9
Rhode Island	67.1	71.1	+4.0	72.9	78.4	+5.5	**89.2**
South Carolina	53.5	54.9	+1.5	59.6	58.9	−0.7	**71.2**
South Dakota	79.5	75.4	−4.1	84.2	82.5	−1.7	88.4
Tennessee	52.6	65.8	+13.2	61.6	72.6	+11.0	818
Texas	59.3	65.1	+5.8	67.0	71.9	+4.9	78.0
Utah	79.0	77.1	−1.9	81.1	76.6	−4.5	**88.2**
Vermont	76.4	82.3	+5.9	83.6	88.5	+4.9	86.0
Virginia	72.3	69.9	−2.3	76.6	75.5	−1.1	79.4
Washington	70.6	67.9	−2.3	74.0	74.8	+0.8	72.5
West Virginia	75.5	71.6	−3.9	76.7	78.2	+1.5	84.7
Wisconsin	76.9	81.0	+4.1	83.7	88.5	+4.8	89.6
Wyoming	74.4	72.6	−1.8	78.4	75.8	−2.6	79.5
U.S.	65.7	68.8	+3.1	71.3	73.9	+2.6	79.5

Sources: Editorial Projects in Education Research Center, *Diplomas count 2010: Graduation by the numbers* (Bethesda, MD: Author, 2010), www.edweek.org/ew/toc/2010/06/10/index.html (Accessed January 17, 2011), 24; Thomas D. Snyder and Sally A. Dillow, *Digest of Education Statistics 2009* (NCES 2010–013) (Washington, DC: National Center for Education Statistics, U.S. Department of Education, 2010), http://nces.ed.gov/Pubsearch/Pubsinfo.Asp?Pubid=2010013 (accessed January 17, 2011), table 105; U.S. Department of Education, SY 2007-2008 *Consolidated State Performance Reports* (Washington, DC: Author, 2010) www2.ed.gov/admins/lead/account/consolidated/sy07-08part1/index.html (accessed July 21, 2010).

samples, that can and have been used to estimate cohort graduation rates. Do those data produce vastly different estimates than those produced with cross-sectional data, especially the ones attempting to correct for several of the known biases? Of course, longitudinal studies have their own biases, with probably the most serious one being attrition—participants who move or simply "disappear." Because participants who leave a study tend to have different characteristics than those who remain, national longitudinal studies use weighting schemes to adjust for the changing sample characteristics so that the data can be used to generate accurate population estimates. Scholars who have compared cross-sectional estimates with those from longitudinal studies have found, after adjusting for differences in population coverage, that they are generally comparable. For example, scholars found that the estimated cross-sectional cohort graduation rate for 1992 public school students using the CCD at 79 percent was almost identical to the rate estimated with data from the NELS.[84] In fact, Heckman and LaFontaine found that estimated graduation rates from a number of longitudinal studies were comparable to cross-sectional estimates based on the CCD, the CPS, and the decennial census, once appropriate adjustments were made for population coverage and information on educational attainment.[85]

Despite the apparent comparability of cross-sectional and longitudinal estimates of cohort graduation rates at the national level, there is a wide consensus in the education community that the best way to create more accurate measures of cohort graduation rates at the state and local levels is through the use of state longitudinal data systems that track all public school students. As mentioned earlier, the National Governors Association (NGA) report, *Graduation Counts*, recommended that states begin using a common four-year graduation rate once their data systems could provide the longitudinal data necessary to compute the rate accurately.

There is a growing recognition among educators, policy makers, and researchers that state longitudinal data systems can and should be used to improve educational performance. The Data Quality Campaign, a national, collaborative effort to encourage and support the development and use of state longitudinal data systems, argues that such systems can be used to answer important questions on the educational effectiveness of programs and schools by measuring student performance over time. The campaign has identified ten essential elements to such a system, including student-level dropout and graduation data:

A majority of states currently collect annual records on individual graduates and dropouts, but to calculate the graduation rates defined in the new National Governors Association compact, states need to be able to track individual students over time. The calculation of accurate graduation rates also requires the ability to accurately account for what happens to students who leave public education. For example, states must be able to distinguish correctly between departing students who drop out or get a GED and students who transfer to another school.[86]

Each year the Data Quality Campaign surveys all fifty states to determine how many of the ten elements have been implemented. By 2010 all fifty states reported that they had the capacity to calculate the NGA longitudinal graduation rate.[87]

Yet the information collected in the survey may not be accurate. For example, California reported to the Data Quality Campaign that it has student-level graduation and dropout data, but the California Department of Education website in early 2011 reported otherwise: "Since student level data are not collected, cohort graduation rates that account for incoming and outgoing transfers cannot be calculated."[88]

Even longitudinal data do not ensure accurate dropout and graduation statistics. Students who leave the state education system—by moving to another state or country, or by transferring to a private school—can be excluded from the analysis, thereby boosting the estimated rates. For example, Texas has had a statewide longitudinal data system for some time, yet in calculating longitudinal completion rates for the graduating class of 2007, it excluded almost 20 percent of the sample because they either left the Texas public school system or could not be followed because of student identification problems.[89] Such practices have been challenged for producing more favorable graduation rates. As reported earlier, the Houston school district was subject to national attention when it reported very low dropout rates, in part because the Texas student data system allows schools to place students into a number of "leaver" categories that exclude them in computing dropout and graduation statistics.[90]

Longitudinal data systems can also produce inaccurate estimates if they fail to track students into other programs offering secondary school credentials, such as adult education and government programs such as Job Corps and the National Guard ChalleNGe program, all of which grant both regular and equivalency diplomas. Incorporating such data is particularly difficult for adult education because there are so many providers, including local education agencies, community-based organizations, and institutions of higher education.[91] Until those data are incorporated, students who transfer into adult education and other credential programs may be counted as dropouts—as they are in California—even though some of them may earn diplomas or equivalency credentials.[92]

The Vast Differences in Dropout and Graduation Rates

The growing concern for the dropout crisis is fueled, in part, by significant disparities in dropout and graduation rates among demographic groups, among schools and communities, and even among countries. Adding to the concern are trends showing that the problem has not improved over the past four decades.

Demographic Differences

As do other aspects of educational achievement, dropout and graduation rates vary widely among demographic groups, as illustrated in Table 3.4. First, dropout and completion rates vary by gender. Males are more likely to drop out and less likely to complete high school than females. Second, blacks and Hispanics are more likely to drop out and less likely to complete high school than whites and Asians. Third, low-income students are more likely to drop out of school than high-income students. Fourth, among Hispanics, foreign-born students have the highest dropout rates and the lowest completion rates, while those students who are second generation and higher have the lowest dropout rates and the highest completion rates. Among non-Hispanics, the picture is more complicated; first-generation students appear to have the highest event dropout rates, as well as the highest completion rates, but the lowest status dropout rates.

Differences among Schools, Districts, and States

Dropout and graduation rates vary widely among educational jurisdictions. Despite the great interest in dropout and graduation rates of individual schools, no national data exist on school-level rates. To get around this problem, Bob Balfanz and Nettie Legters developed a Promoting Power (PP) indicator, which is simply the ratio of twelfth-grade students in a school to ninth-grade students three years earlier.[93] Although the indicator is not

Table 3.4   Dropout and completion rates by demographic characteristics, October 2008

	Event dropout rates of 15- to 24-year-olds	Status dropout rates of 16- to 24-year olds	Status completion rates of 18- to 24-year-olds
Total	3.5	8.0	89.9
Sex			
Male	3.1	8.5	89.3
Female	4.0	7.5	90.5
Race/ethnicity			
White, non-Hispanic	2.3	4.8	94.2
Black, non-Hispanic	6.4	9.9	86.9
Hispanic	5.3	18.3	75.5
Asian/Pacific Islander, non-Hispanic	4.0*	4.4	95.5
American Indian/Alaska native, non-Hispanic		14.6	82.5
Family income			
Low income	8.7		
Middle income	3.0		
High income	2.0		
Immigration status			
Foreign born			
Hispanic	8.1	32.8	59.6
Non-Hispanic	4.6	5.5	93.7
First generation			
Hispanic	3.7	10.5	85.1
Non-Hispanic	1.4*	3.1	96.2
Second generation or more			
Hispanic	5.5	10.8	85.8
Non-Hispanic	3.3	6.0	92.6

Source: Chris Chapman, Jennifer Laird, and Angelina KewalRamani, *Trends in High School Dropout and Completion Rates in the United States: 1972–2008* (NCES 2011-012) (Washington, DC: National Center for Education Statistics, Institute of Education Sciences, U.S. Department of Education, 2010), http://nces.ed.gov/pubsearch/pubsinfo.asp?pubid=2011012 (accessed January 17, 2011), tables 1, 6, 9.
    *Interpret data with caution due to small sample size.

a direct measure of either dropout or graduation rates, they argue that by measuring persistence from ninth to twelfth grade, the indicator can be used to judge how well schools are succeeding in getting their students to graduate.[94] In their analysis of data for the class of 2002, Balfanz and Legters found that 18 percent, or 2,007 of the nation's 11,129 regular and vocational high schools, had 60 percent fewer seniors than freshmen, and produced more than half of the dropouts; the authors therefore labeled these schools "dropout factories."[95] These and more recent results have been widely cited in the national discourse on the dropout crisis, including remarks by President Barack Obama.[96]

Despite its appeal and widespread use, the PP indicator suffers from the same biases in graduation rates discussed earlier, and a recent study found that it underestimates persistence rates in low-persistence and high-minority schools.[97] Another limitation is that it ignores more than 6,000 alternative schools and programs (discussed in more detail below), the majority of which enroll secondary students.[98] A recent study in California found that nontraditional high schools, which included both alternative-education and charter schools, enrolled only 12 percent of all high school students but accounted for half of all dropouts.[99] These data reveal that the dropout crisis is not simply confined to so-called dropout factories, although reducing attrition in comprehensive high schools may reduce, but probably would not eliminate, the need for alternative schools.

Data on dropout and graduation rates for school districts are more readily available, but graduation rates are based on the same biased indicators we reviewed earlier. The National Center for Education Statistics compiles CCD data on dropout rates for all districts in the country and computes graduation rates from CCD data using its AFGR formula. Graduation rates vary widely across districts, ranging from below 50 percent in such large, urban school districts as Los Angeles, Cleveland, Detroit, and Atlanta, to over 90 percent in such affluent suburban districts as Fort Bend Independent and Katy Independent School Districts (Texas) and Howard County Public Schools (Maryland).[100] *Education Week* also computes graduation rates for all school districts using its CPI formula and makes them available on its website. As shown earlier, the CPI rate is generally lower than the AFGR, so school districts can be judged differently depending on what measure is used.

Similar disparities result for state graduation rates, as shown in Table 3.3, again leading to different conclusions about the severity of the problem and whether the problem is getting better or worse. For example, the 2010 report by *Education Week* showed that California's high school graduation rate had declined from 1997 to 2007 by 4.7 percentage points, prompting widespread media coverage of California's worsening graduation rate.[101] Yet graduation figures from the U.S. Department of Education show that California's graduation rate *improved* over that period.

Trends in Dropout and Graduation Rates

It is important to know not only the number and proportion of students who are dropping out and graduating, but also whether dropout and graduation rates are improving over time. Trends in dropout and graduation rates paint two pictures: one based on long-term trends and one on short-term trends. Long-term trends show that high school graduation rates have improved dramatically over the past century. But short-term trends, over the past four decades, show a slight decline or at best a leveling in graduation rates, even in the face of declining dropout rates.

Long-term trends in high school enrollment and graduation rates over the past century show impressive gains, especially in the first half of the twentieth century (Figure 3.3). In the three decades between 1909–10 and 1939–40, the percentage of fourteen- to seventeen-year-olds enrolled in high school (grades nine through twelve) increased from 14 percent to 73 percent, and the percentage of seventeen-year-olds with a high school diploma increased from 9 percent to 51 percent. The next three decades witnessed continued improvements, but at a slower pace. Enrollment rates increased from 73 percent to 92 percent, and graduation rates increased from 51 percent to 77 percent. But the last three decades of the twentieth century saw stagnating or declining growth. High school graduates, as a proportion of the seventeen-year-old population, saw similar trends, with rapid increases in the first four decades of the twentieth century and a peak rate of 77 percent, reached in 1969–70.

More recent trends paint a more sobering picture about improving the nation's high school graduation rate and some seemingly contradictory trends: while enrollment rates, dropout rates, and completion rates have all improved, graduation rates have not. Over the past forty years, enrollment rates have continued to rise, from 92 percent in 1970 to 97 percent in 2010 (Figure 3.4). Over the same period, dropout rates declined, from 15 percent in 1970 to 8 percent in 2008. This means that more and more young people are staying in school.

More young people are also completing high school. The high school completion rate—which includes students who earn GED and alternative credentials—increased from 83 percent in 1972 to 90 percent in 2008 (Figure 3.5). Yet high school graduation rates, which include only students who complete high school by earning a diploma, are no higher today than forty years ago.[102] The public school graduation rate, in fact,

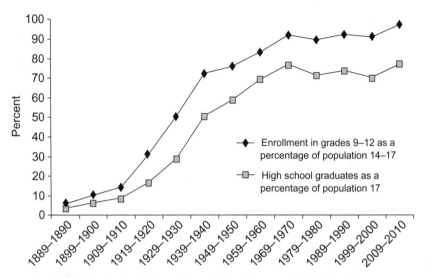

Figure 3.3. Enrollment and graduation rates, 1889–1890 to 2009–2010. *Source:* Thomas D. Snyder and Sally A. Dillow, *Digest of Education Statistics 2010* (NCES 2011-015) (Washington, DC: National Center for Education Statistics, U.S. Department of Education, 2011), http://nces.ed.gov/Pubsearch/Pubsinfo.Asp?Pubid= 2011015 (accessed May 9, 2011), tables 50 and 110.

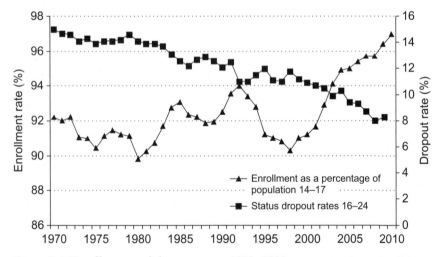

Figure 3.4. Enrollment and dropout rates, 1970–2010. *Source:* Snyder and Dillow, *Digest of Education Statistics 2010*, tables 50 and 115.

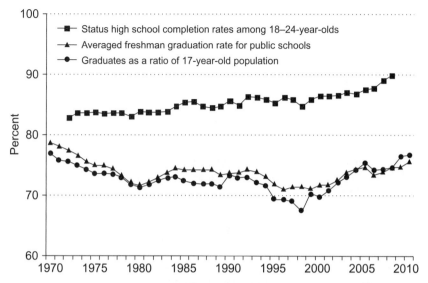

Figure 3.5. Graduation and completion rates, 1970–2010. *Source:* Snyder and Dillow, *Digest of Education Statistics 2010,* table 110; Chris Chapman, Jennifer Laird, and Angelina KewalRamani, *Trends in High School Dropout and Completion Rates in the United States: 1972–2008* (NCES 2011-012) (Washington, DC: National Center for Education Statistics, U.S. Department of Education, 2010), http://nces.ed.gov/pub-search/pubsinfo.asp?pubid=2011012 (accessed January 17, 2011), table 10.

is lower: as measured by the AFGR, it peaked in 1970 at 79 percent, declined to a low of 71 percent in 1996, and has since increased to 76 percent in 2010. The overall public and private school graduation rate, as measured by the ratio of graduates to all seventeen-year-olds, paints a slightly better picture: it stood at slightly less than 77 percent in 1970, declined to a low of 68 percent in 1998, and increased back to 77 percent in 2010.

The diverging trends between the high school completion rate and the graduation rate can be explained, in part, by the increasing number of students who take and pass the GED. The number of persons passing the GED doubled between 1971 and 2008, with the majority less than twenty-five years of age.[103]

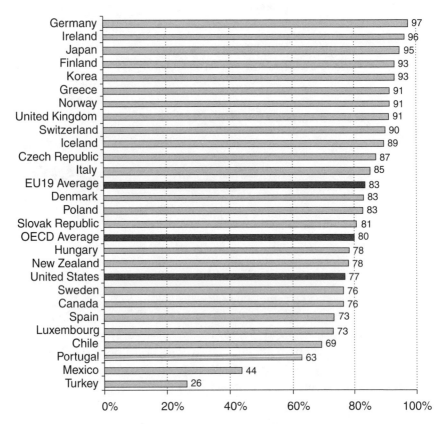

Figure 3.6. High school graduation rates in OECD countries, 1995 and 2008.
Source: Education at a Glance 2010 (Paris: Organisation for Economic
Co-operation and Development, 2010), www.oecd.org/edu/eag2010 (accessed January
17, 2011), table A.21.

International Comparisons

Not only is stagnating growth in high school graduation rates problematic
domestically, but it also reflects the relative status of the United States in
the global labor market. In his best-selling book, *The World Is Flat*, *New
York Times* columnist Thomas Friedman argues that new developments
in telecommunications have "flattened" the world, allowing entrepreneurs
from large, growing economies, such as India and China, to compete with
the United States for a variety of highly skilled jobs in telecommunications, accounting, computer programming, and engineering.[104] According

to a 2009 report from the Information Technology and Innovation Foundation, although the United States ranked sixth out of forty countries and regions in innovation-based global competitiveness, it ranked last in improvements made in international competition and innovation capacity over the decade from 1999 to 2009.[105]

Increasingly, other countries that have greatly expanded their education systems are challenging the historical comparative advantage of the United States. This is evidenced at both the lower and upper ends of the educational distribution. According to data collected by the Organisation for Economic and Co-operative Development (OECD), the United States ranked eighteenth among OECD countries in the percentage of students who graduated from high school in 2008, with a graduation rate of 77 percent (see Figure 3.6).[106] The average among all OECD countries in 2008 was 80 percent, and the average among the nineteen OECD countries in the European Union (EU)—those countries that represent our closest economic competitors—was 83 percent. The gap between the United States and EU countries has remained fairly constant over the past thirteen years: from 1995 to 2008, the average graduation rate in OECD countries improved by 6 percentage points, from 77 percent to 83 percent, while the average graduation rate in the United States improved by 8 percentage points, from 69 percent to 77 percent.[107]

Despite differences and disagreements on how to measure dropout and graduation rates, there is widespread consensus that far too many students fail to graduate from high school in the United States. The seriousness of the problem becomes more vivid by examining the array of individual and social consequences from dropping out, the topic of the next two chapters.

4

THE INDIVIDUAL CONSEQUENCES
OF DROPPING OUT

Students who drop out of school suffer a range of consequences for the rest of their lives. Dropouts face bleak economic futures—they are the least educated workers in the labor market and thus have the poorest job prospects compared to more educated workers. This means they are less likely to find jobs, and when they do find them, the jobs generally pay the lowest wages. Dropouts are also less likely than more educated workers to invest in additional education and training, further limiting their prospects for securing well-paying jobs over their entire working lives. As a result, dropouts are more likely to live in poverty and require public assistance throughout their lifetimes.

The consequences of dropping out are not just economic. Dropouts are more likely to engage in crime and, consequently, are more likely to be arrested and incarcerated. They also have poorer health and, as a result, have shorter life spans than persons with more education. Finally, dropouts are less likely to vote and to participate in local community activities.

This chapter documents the individual impacts of dropping out. Yet documenting the impacts of dropping out on these various outcomes is problematic for a couple of reasons. First, these outcomes are both interrelated and spatially concentrated. In his landmark 1965 study, *The Negro Family: The Case for National Action*, Daniel Patrick Moynihan documented how a host of social problems—joblessness, family instability, poor health, substance abuse, poverty, welfare dependency, and crime—were not only interconnected but also concentrated within certain urban neighborhoods, particularly those with high concentrations of blacks, in what he labeled a "tangle of pathology."[1] Moreover, these neighborhoods of concentrated disadvantage are highly durable, creating a cycle of poverty and disadvantage that continues to repeat itself; what some scholars have more recently labeled "poverty traps."[2] Since that time, a number of comprehensive studies have documented how little has changed—that while some specific neighborhoods have shifted, the spatial concentration of disadvantage and racial segregation in America remains.[3] In fact, a study of concentrated disadvantage in Chicago found that only blacks lived in the most disadvantaged neighborhoods, calling into question the general practice of attempting to identify a single causal effect of disadvantage that can apply to all racial groups.[4]

The second challenge is distinguishing the observed association between dropping out and these various outcomes from its causal impact. Both theory and empirical research suggest that similar factors may influence both the likelihood of dropping out and various adult outcomes. For example, children from poor, dysfunctional families may be more inclined to drop out of school and to engage in crime, which makes it difficult to determine the extent to which dropping out of high school exerts an independent, causal impact on crime. While theories can be used to explain why dropping out may exert an independent effect, demonstrating the causal connection empirically is more difficult. Nonetheless, recent advances in statistical modeling have allowed social scientists to establish such causal connections. Doing so is important, in part, to justify interventions designed to improve high school graduation as a strategy to improve adult outcomes, particularly for at-risk students and disadvantaged neighborhoods.

It is also important to point out that not all dropouts experience negative consequences. Some dropouts can be quite successful with respect to any of these outcomes, while some high school graduates are not. For example, here are some famous millionaire dropouts, outstanding because of unusual talents that are rare in the population:

- Quentin Tarantino (writer and film director).
- Dave Thomas (founder of Wendy's fast food restaurants).
- Johnny Depp (actor).
- Nicolas Cage (actor).
- Christina Aguilera (singer/artist).
- John Travolta (actor).[5]

Nonetheless, completing high school increases the odds of achieving more positive outcomes as an adult for most of the population.

Differences in outcomes between high school dropouts and completers can also vary among subpopulations, such as between males and females, or among racial and ethnic groups. But in general, although the size of the difference may vary, the relative differences tend to be consistent across groups. That is, female high school graduates fare better in the labor market than female dropouts, just as male high school graduates fare better in the labor market than male dropouts, even if the size of the earnings gap varies across groups.

Labor Market Outcomes

One of the most apparent and lasting impacts of dropping out is observed in the labor market. Dropouts are the least competitive workers in the job market because they have the least education. Even if they have skills and abilities, their lack of a credential makes it more difficult to demonstrate those skills and abilities to a would-be employer. As a result, they are the least likely to get a job, and the jobs they do get pay the lowest wages and are less likely to offer benefits.

Dropouts soon realize the benefits of education and their disadvantaged position in the job market. In a 2005 survey of recent dropouts, four out of five respondents said that graduating from high school was important to success in life, and half said that not having a diploma made it hard to find a job.[6] The severe economic recession that started in 2009 was particularly hard on dropouts. In a story from the *Denver Post* from March 31, 2009, one dropout noted, "I used to get a job so easy. I worked at a salon, I worked at movie theaters, at the mall, but they're gone."[7]

So what happens to high school dropouts in the labor market? The statistics are sobering. Both in the short term, when dropouts first leave school, and in the long term, over their entire working lives, dropouts are severely disadvantaged relative to students who complete high school.

The federal government surveys recent high school graduates and dropouts each fall. The survey identifies sixteen- to twenty-four-year-olds who either completed school (by earning a diploma or alternative credential) or dropped out of school between October the previous year and October of the current year. The October 2010 survey results show that 68 percent of students who completed high school in the 2009–10 school year were enrolled in college the following October, with an additional 16 percent working (see Figure 4.1, left column). Altogether, 84 percent of completers were engaged in at least one of two productive activities

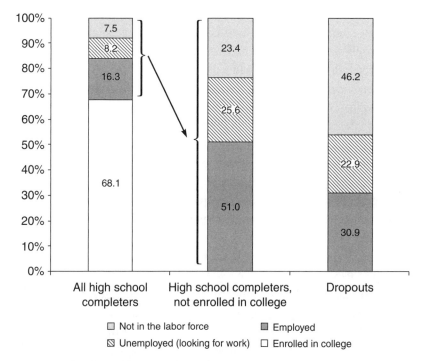

Figure 4.1. School enrollment and employment for 2009–10 high school dropouts and completers, October 2010. *Source: College Enrollment and Work Activity of 2010 High School Graduates* (Washington, DC: Bureau of Labor Statistics, U.S. Department of Labor, 2011), www.bls.gov/news.release/archives/hsgec_04082011. htm (accessed May 9, 2011).

that would likely improve their future economic prospects—going to college or working. Economists characterize both activities as investing in human capital through formal (college) or informal (working) learning. Even among the 32 percent of high school completers who were not enrolled in college, more than half were employed and an additional 26 percent were unemployed but actively looking for work (Figure 4.1, middle column). In contrast, only 31 percent of high school dropouts were employed in the October following the year they left school, with an additional 23 percent unemployed (looking for work) and almost 50 percent not in the labor force—what some observers refer to as "idle youth" (Figure 4.1, right column). More recent data from December 2010 show only 44 percent of high school dropouts sixteen to twenty-four years of age were employed, compared to 60 percent of high school completers who were not enrolled in school.[8]

Labor market prospects for both completers and dropouts vary by race. Among high school completers sixteen to twenty-four years of age who were not enrolled in school in December 2010, 62 percent of whites and 61 percent of Hispanics were employed, compared to 54 percent of blacks.[9] Among high school dropouts sixteen to twenty-four years of age, only 46 percent of whites and 52 percent of Hispanics were employed, whereas fewer than 33 percent of blacks were employed. The unemployment rate—the percentage of persons in the civilian labor force looking for work—among high school completers was 20 percent for whites, 21 percent for Hispanics, and 27 percent for blacks. The unemployment rate for high school dropouts was 25 percent for whites and 24 percent for Hispanics, but a staggering 47 percent for blacks.

The low employment and high unemployment rates among high school completers, especially blacks, who were not enrolled in college raises questions about the employment incentives for non-college-bound youth to complete high school. If young people who complete high school have such difficulty finding a job, it could make would-be dropouts wonder how completing high school will improve their prospects in the labor market. Even if they find a job, it may pay so poorly that it provides little incentive to graduate. This may be especially true in disadvantaged neighborhoods with few employment prospects. A study of inner-city youth in three neighborhoods of New York City found that would-be dropouts were skeptical of the value of a diploma. As one student noted, "I know this friend of mine. He graduated from Fillmore. He's working in a factory making $3.10 a hour. A guy with a high school diploma he don't know nothing, so what trade's he got?"[10]

As dropouts get older, their labor market prospects improve, but they still remain greatly disadvantaged relative to high school graduates. A government longitudinal survey known as the National Longitudinal Survey of Youth 1997 (NLSY97) tracked a sample of 9,000 young men and women born between 1980 and 1984.[11] Respondents were first interviewed in 1997, when they were ages twelve to seventeen. Data released in 2011 examined the school enrollment and employment experiences of respondents when they were age twenty-three in October, from 2003 to 2008. Among young adults not enrolled in school at age twenty-two, 75 percent of high school graduates who were never enrolled in college were employed, 5 percent were serving in the armed forces, 5 percent were unemployed (looking for work), and 14 percent were not in the labor force (not working or looking for work).[12] In contrast, 60 percent of high school dropouts were employed— a much higher rate than reported earlier for December 2010, when the United States was in a severe recession—while 8 percent were unemployed and 32 percent were not in the labor force. Overall, twenty-three-year-old dropouts in this survey were twice as likely to be "idle" as high school graduates who were never enrolled in college (40 percent versus 20 percent). The data further reveal that the rates of dropouts' being "idle" were much higher for young women than young men (50 percent versus 32 percent) and much higher for blacks (46 percent) than for Hispanics (31 percent) and whites (35 percent).

Another study using the NLSY97 data found four distinct patterns of how youth connect to work and school between the ages of eighteen and twenty-four:

- *Consistently connected youth*, who were connected to school or a job over 90 percent of the time for most weeks in the study period (60 percent of the population).
- *Later-connected youth*, who were equally likely to be connected or disconnected at age eighteen but who increased their rate of connectedness to approximately 90 percent by age twenty-four (15 percent of the population).
- *Initially connected youth*, who were highly connected at age eighteen but became disconnected over the next six years (15 percent of the population).
- *Never-connected youth*, who were persistently disconnected from either school or employment between the ages of eighteen and twenty-four (10 percent of the population).[13]

Students who completed high school were much more likely to be in the consistently connected group, while students who failed to complete high school were much more likely to be in the other three groups, even after controlling for other predictive factors.

Even when they find work, dropouts are more likely to work part-time (fewer than thirty-five hours per week) compared to high school graduates. In November 2010, 36 percent of dropouts who were employed were working part-time, compared to 30 percent for nonenrolled high school completers.[14] But the prospects for part-time work vary by race. Whereas 35 percent of white and 39 percent of black dropouts were working part-time in November 2010, 51 percent of Asian and 50 percent of Hispanic dropouts were working part-time.[15]

Dropouts continue to be disadvantaged in the labor market as adults. First, they are less likely to participate in the labor market at all: in 2009, only 40 percent of all dropouts were in the labor market, compared to 56 percent for high school graduates who never attended college.[16] Second, once in the labor market, dropouts are less likely to find work: in 2009, the unemployment rate for dropouts was 15 percent, compared to 10 percent for high school graduates with no college.[17] Third, they are less likely to find steady work: through age thirty-five, only 36 percent of dropouts held a job for five years or longer, compared to 56 percent for high school completers.[18] Fourth, even when they find full-time work, they earn less: the median annual earnings of dropouts working full-time over an entire year (fifty weeks or more) were 22 percent less in 2008 than full-time, full-year high school graduates—$23,500 versus $30,000.[19] In addition to lower earnings, dropouts are half as likely to hold jobs offering pensions and health insurance. For example, among all adult workers in 2003–04, only 29 percent of dropouts held jobs offering pension plans, compared to 50 percent of high school graduates.[20]

As a result of their lower earnings, dropouts are more than twice as likely as graduates to be employed at or below the minimum wage, and more than twice as likely to be classified as the working poor, meaning they spent at least twenty-seven weeks in the labor force (working or looking for work) but had incomes below the official poverty level.[21] Dropouts are almost twice as likely to be poor—in 2009, 25 percent of high school dropouts had incomes below the poverty level compared to 14 percent for high school graduates with no college.[22] Finally, dropouts are more likely to participate in government assistance programs—in 2003, almost one-third of high school dropouts received benefits from government assistance programs (e.g., Medicaid, housing assistance, food stamps, Temporary Assistance for Needy Families), compared to 16 percent for high school graduates with no college; and dropouts were three times as likely as high school graduates to receive benefits for thirty-six consecutive months from January 2001 to December 2003.[23]

The economic disadvantages of not completing high school have grown more sizeable over time as the availability of low-skilled jobs has declined. The median annual earnings of full-time, full-year dropouts were 15 percent less than those of high school completers in 1980, but increased to 21 percent less by 2008.[24] The earnings of dropouts in constant (2008) dollars declined by 25 percent over this period, with males suffering a larger decline than females (28 percent versus 22 percent).

Over their entire working lives, the economic disadvantage to not completing high school is sizeable. Using U.S. Census data from 2003 and 2004, economist Cecilia Rouse estimated the lifetime earnings of high school dropouts from age eighteen to sixty-seven and compared them to the lifetime earnings of high school completers who never attended college and all high school completers, including those who attended college.[25] The difference in lifetime earnings between dropouts and completers who never attended college exceeds $260,000, and the difference in lifetime earnings between dropouts and all high school completers—assuming that if dropouts were to complete high school, they would attend college at rates similar to high school graduates—exceeds $550,000.[26] Another study using similar methodology found that over their working lives, dropouts earned about 75 percent of what high school graduates earn.[27]

Do Dropouts Benefit from Completing High School?   One way for dropouts to improve their economic prospects is by completing high school. Some dropouts eventually complete high school, either by reenrolling in high school and earning a regular diploma or by passing a high school equivalency exam, such as the GED, and earning an alternative diploma. According to the NLSY97 data, 11 percent of respondents who were high school dropouts in October when age eighteen had completed high school when age nineteen;[28] similarly, 11 percent of respondents who were high school dropouts in October when age nineteen had completed high school when age twenty,[29] and 8 percent of respondents who were high school dropouts in October when age twenty had completed high school when age twenty-one.[30] Data from a national study that tracked high school sophomores from 2002 through 2006 found that 18 percent of dropouts earned a diploma within two years of their scheduled graduation, and an additional 31 percent earned a GED credential.[31] Data from an earlier longitudinal study of eighth-grade students found that 19 percent of all students who have ever dropped out of high school earned a diploma, and an additional 43 percent earned a GED credential by age twenty-six.[32]

But do dropouts garner any economic benefits from completing high school, either by earning a diploma or a GED? If they do, then they should be encouraged to do so, but if they do not, then there may be little advantage. The answer to this question has generated considerable debate among economists, beginning when Nobel economist James Heckman and a colleague, Stephen Cameron, published an academic article, "The Nonequivalence of High School Equivalents," which found that males who earned a GED had no better labor market prospects than high school dropouts.[33] Since that time, a large number of studies have been conducted that generally confirm that finding, although some studies have shown that the GED generates positive economic benefits for some groups, such as students who drop out with low skills and therefore must increase their skills to pass the GED.[34]

The reason for the lack of economic benefits from the GED involves what economists call "noncognitive" skills. It is widely acknowledged that schooling helps to develop cognitive skills in reading, math, and other areas that directly contribute to higher earnings. But increasingly economists have come to realize that noncognitive skills and abilities—perseverance, motivation, self-esteem, and self-control, among others—also contribute to higher earnings (as well as other outcomes, such as health, crime, etc., which I discuss below).[35] So while persons who pass the GED have to achieve a reasonably high level of cognitive performance, GED holders generally have lower levels of noncognitive skills that suppress their earnings relative to those of high school graduates.[36] The deficit in noncognitive skills of GED holders also helps explain their continued lack of investment in postsecondary education and training.[37]

This is illustrated with data from the Nation Longitudinal Survey of Youth 1997 (NLSY97), which obtains information on formal training activities outside of regular school, including vocational, technical or trade training, nursing programs, apprenticeship programs, basic adult education and GED programs, formal company training or seminars, and government training. Among respondents who were dropouts in October when age twenty, only 3.6 percent were enrolled in any sort of training program during the October when age twenty-one, compared to 5.6 percent for high school graduates not enrolled in college.[38]

Dropouts are also less likely to serve in the armed forces. Among respondents in the NLSY97 who were dropouts in October at age twenty-one, only 0.6 percent were serving in the armed forces, compared to 6.4 percent for high school graduates never enrolled in college.[39] The armed forces generally does not recruit high school dropouts, but in 2006, when the wars in Iraq and Afghanistan increased the need for new recruits, the armed forces did admit recruits without diplomas if they could pass the GED and a composite quality indicator that measured motivation, cognitive skills, and physical fitness.[40] In our current recession, with an adequate supply of recruits among the more educated, dropouts are no longer being recruited.

Crime

While dropouts are less likely to participate in further education and training or to work, perhaps not surprisingly they are more likely to engage in crime, get arrested, and be incarcerated. In fact, as shown below, there is a causal connection between employment prospects for dropouts and criminal activity.

Criminal activity can be measured by type of crime, number of arrests, and length of incarceration. The government routinely collects information on arrests and incarceration, but data on criminal activity are much harder to come by and are generally collected from self-reports on surveys. Researchers estimate that the incidence of crime is up to seven times more frequent than arrests.[41]

Criminal activity is dominated by males: of the 2.3 million inmates in federal or state prisons, or in local jails, on June 30, 2009, more than 90 percent were male.[42] Prisoners are also disproportionately minorities: while there were 708 white male inmates per 100,000 white males in the larger population, there were 4,749 black males and 1,822 Hispanic males per 100,000 in their respective populations.[43] In other words, Hispanic males were more than twice as likely to be incarcerated and black males were more than six times as likely to be incarcerated as white males.

Research has consistently found that rates of crime, arrests, and incarceration are higher for dropouts than for high school graduates.[44] For example, one recent study found that dropouts were twice as likely to report committing crimes and having been arrested than high school graduates.[45] Another study found that sixteen- to twenty-four-year-old high school dropouts were 50 percent more likely than high school graduates to report having ever been arrested, even after accounting for differences in family background disadvantage that might also contribute to criminal activity.[46] Still another recent study found that dropouts ages sixteen to twenty-four were six times more likely than high school graduates to be institutionalized in 2006–07, with the vast majority (93 percent) in correctional institutions.[47] Rates of imprisonment were profoundly higher for black dropouts, with 23 percent incarcerated in 2006–07, compared to 6–7 percent of Asian, Hispanic, and white high school dropouts.[48]

Dropouts also face higher risks of imprisonment over time. Figures not only show higher risks of incarceration than simple imprisonment statistics, but also reveal startling differences by education levels and race. One recent study estimated the cumulative risks of imprisonment by age thirty to thirty-four for a series of five-year birth cohorts of white and black males born from 1945 to 1979.[49] The risk of imprisonment by age thirty to thirty-four of white males born between 1945 and 1949 was 4.2 percent for high school dropouts, compared to 0.7 percent for high school graduates who never attended college.[50] For the latest cohort, born between 1975 and 1979, the risk of imprisonment for high school dropouts had increased to 15.3 percent, compared to 4.1 percent for high school graduates who never attended college. In contrast, the risk of imprisonment by age thirty to thirty-four of black males born between 1945 and 1949 was 14.7 percent for high school dropouts, compared to 10.2 percent for high school graduates who never attended college. For the latest cohort, born between 1975 and 1979, the risk of imprisonment for high school dropouts had increased to an astonishing 69 percent, compared to 18 percent for high school graduates who never attended college.

By 1999, imprisonment for black males, especially high school dropouts, had become the norm, a phenomenon sociologist David Garland has labeled "mass imprisonment."[51] Indeed, recent incarceration rates in the United States for the population as a whole have reached unprecedented levels—seven times the rate in the United States from 1925 to 1973, and seven times the current rate in Western Europe.[52] The growth of aggregate incarceration rates has been traced to declining economic opportunities for low-educated and low-skilled workers, especially in large urban centers with high concentrations of minority youth, and to changing criminal sentencing laws, especially for drug-related offenses.

But why is crime so much higher among dropouts than among the more educated? Is it causally related to education itself, or is it due to other factors that may be related to both educational attainment and the propensity to commit crimes?

These questions are important to address, both to better understand the role that education plays in crime and to inform policy makers about the role that education could play in reducing crime. If education has a causal connection to crime, then reducing dropout rates could reduce crime, but if there is no causal connection, then reducing dropout rates may have little effect on reducing crime and incarceration rates.

Theoretical perspectives rooted within several social science disciplines have been used to explain the relationship between education and crime. Economists have offered a number of theoretical reasons why raising educational attainment should reduce crime.[53] One is that cognitive and noncognitive skills developed in school improve the prospects of finding a job and of receiving a higher wage, both of which increase what economists call the "opportunity cost" of crime and incarceration—more educated criminals have more to lose than less educated criminals. Schooling can also influence a person's time horizon—more educated persons attach more value to future prospects of imprisonment, and hence would be less inclined to commit crimes and risk imprisonment. Schooling can also affect one's values for not engaging in crime. Of course, many disadvantaged students attend schools where dropping out and criminal activity—both in school and in the surrounding community—are the norm, so attending such schools may actually *induce* criminal activity. Indeed, two studies found that increasing the amount of time students spent in school increased the rate of violent crimes, especially among repeat juvenile offenders, even while the rate of property crimes decreased.[54]

An in-depth study of a youth gang called the Freemont Hustlers in Kansas City, Missouri, provides a vivid illustration of the economic perspective:

> Freemont research shows that a youth gang's social life is an intricate set of economic transactions which have social effects. The underlying economic principle is this: When kids perceived a gain by doing one thing instead of another, they move in the direction of the gain. When there's a perception of greater gain in selling drugs than in doing school work, drug selling wins. The principle operates in purely social transactions. When there's greater gain in hanging out with a gang than in avoiding it, the gang wins. When a girl perceives greater gain in having a

relationship with an abusive boy than in having no boyfriend, there's victimization of teenage girls.[55]

This perspective is further illustrated in Mercer Sullivan's in-depth study of crime and employment in three neighborhoods of New York City, where youth equated crime with work, in an ironic and less-than-serious fashion, through their use of the expression "getting paid."[56]

Theories of criminology offer a more complex picture of the relationship between dropping out and crime. Two dominant criminological theories explain why dropping out may either increase or decrease criminal activity.[57] The first, strain theory, suggests that students at risk for dropping out—those who experience academic and social failure in school and feel frustrated and dissatisfied—may be less inclined to commit crimes once they leave school and the source of the strain is removed. But other scholars argue that it depends on the reasons for leaving school and hence the source of strain—students who leave a negative source of strain, such as doing poorly or being taunted by classmates, may be less inclined to commit crimes, while students who leave a positive school experience because of family obligations or financial reasons may experience increased strain and hence be more likely to engage in crime.

The second theory, social control theory, suggests that schools serve as an important social institution that transmits positive values and goals through the bonds students have with teachers and other students, so that dropouts would be more inclined to commit crimes once those bonds are severed. But other scholars argue that the effect depends on the bonds, roles, and identities that dropouts assume once they leave school—those who adopt positive roles as worker or parents may have positive experiences that reduce crime, while those who experience unemployment or hanging around with idle friends may be more inclined to commit crimes.

Because boys and girls leave school for different reasons and assume different roles when they do, the effects of dropping out on crime generally differ as well. Girls who assume more positive roles as mothers and wives may be less inclined to commit crimes, while boys who assume roles as fathers, husbands, and workers may also be less inclined to commit crimes.[58]

The age-related nature of crime further complicates the relationship between dropping out and crime. Criminal activity increases during adolescence, peaks in late adolescence (age eighteen to nineteen), and then declines into adulthood. Developmental theories of crime consider the interaction between individuals and their environment over the life course, from childhood through adolescence to adulthood. While childhood antisocial behavior predicts delinquency in adolescence and crime in adulthood—supporting the notion of stability in antisocial behavior over the life course—each developmental period has its own environmental influences that can alter the likely trajectory. As two leading authors of this so-called life-course criminology, Robert Sampson and John Laub, conclude from their long-term longitudinal studies of male delinquents:

> A fundamental thesis of our age-graded theory of informal social control was that whereas individual traits and childhood experiences are important for understanding behavioral stability, experiences in adolescence and adulthood can redirect criminal trajectories in either a more positive or more negative manner. In this sense, we argue that all stages of the life course matter and that "turning points" are crucial for understanding processes of adult change.[59]

Turning points are new institutional or structural situations—such as work, school, military, marriage, residential change—that provide new opportunities for social support, individual growth, and identity transformation, among other things.[60] Turning points help explain why most juvenile delinquents do not become adult offenders, as well as why all criminal activity tends to decline with age. Completing high school can serve as a turning point for youth, helping to reduce the propensity to commit crimes. The notion of turning points also illustrates how criminologists see work, school, marriage, and other activities as interrelated—each could provide a situation that could alter the individual propensity to engage in crime. As Laub notes, "Good things can happen to bad actors and when they happen, desistance [withdrawal from crime] has a chance."[61]

A developmental perspective of crime also helps explain why youth who engage in antisocial and criminal activity at younger ages are more likely to engage in criminal activity as adults. Either through a higher level of individual propensity (e.g., lack of self-control) or exposure to a more criminogenic family environment (or both), such youth are more likely to engage in criminal activity throughout their life course.[62] Such youth have been called "life-course persistent" offenders, although there is an ongoing debate over whether they constitute a unique group or are simply the highest-rate offenders.[63]

It also remains unclear from the theoretical literature whether completing high school should have the same protective effect on early starters as later starters. In their longitudinal study of more than 2,000 youth offenders in California, Misaki Natsuaki, Xiaojia Ge, and Ernst Wenk test two competing hypotheses: completing high school should have a greater effect on early starters because they have fewer protective factors than late starters; and that completing high school should have greater effect on later starters because early starters have more cumulative disadvantages to overcome.[64] While they found that completing high school benefited both groups, lending support to the value of turning points, they found a greater impact on late starters.

It is difficult to establish the causal connection between education and crime because similar—sometimes other observed or unobserved factors—may account for both phenomena. For example, students who misbehave in elementary or middle school may be less likely to complete high school (as demonstrated in the next chapter) and are subsequently more likely to engage in crime as adolescents and adults. Or students who interact with peers who are more likely to drop out and engage in crime may be more likely themselves to drop out and engage in crime. In fact, longitudinal studies have found numerous differences between dropouts and graduates that can explain the higher rates of crime exhibited by dropouts, including poor school performance as early as elementary school, more impoverished family environments, and early criminal activity.[65]

After accounting for such differences, two recent studies failed to find a causal connection between dropping out and crime, at least in the aggregate. But both studies found significant impacts for some students. One study found that the pace of offending was slowed for adolescents who first committed crimes after age fifteen.[66] The other study found some support for the idea that the impact depends on the reason for leaving school and whether the subsequent role contributed to a more positive identity, such as that of a worker or mother.[67] Males who dropped out for economic reasons were less likely to become delinquent, at least in the short run. But females who dropped out to get married or to have a child did not exhibit less violence, perhaps because becoming a teenage parent could provide more obstacles and stressors for young mothers. Mark Fleisher's account of female adolescents who were members of a youth gang in Kansas City in the early 1990s illustrates such a situation: girls became pregnant by gang boys who provided no financial and little emotional support or, worse yet, abused them and were incarcerated.[68] Results from the Fragile Families study, discussed below, provide additional illustrations.

Recent advances in statistical analysis have helped researchers establish a stronger causal connection between dropping out and crime. One such study found that education was causally related to crime, arrests, and incarceration rates. For example, it estimated that a 10 percentage point increase in the high school graduation rate would reduce arrest rates by 20 percent for murder and assault, 13 percent for motor vehicle theft, and 10 percent for rape.[69] It also found that increasing the high school graduation rate would decrease the incarceration rate, with a greater reduction among black males than among white males.[70] Finally, the study found that about 25 percent of the difference in incarceration rates between black and white males could be explained by differences in high school completion rates. Further evidence on the causal connection between education and crime comes from studies showing that unemployment and wages are causally related to crime.[71] Since other studies have shown the causal connection between education and unemployment and crime, one can infer a causal connection between education and crime.

Family Formation

One of the major impacts of dropping out of school is related to childbearing and marriage. Patterns of childbearing and marriage vary widely by education, with dropouts more likely than graduates to become teen parents and have children outside of marriage. Yet the relationship between education and childbearing, as well as the relationship between childbearing and marriage, is far from simple, as a number of both statistical and in-depth case studies reveal. In particular, it is not always clear to what extent dropping out of school is causally connected to early and nonmarital childbearing, or whether dropping out is more of a mediator in which other factors account for both dropping out and subsequent patterns of childbearing and marriage.

Research shows a strong connection between dropping out and three types of childbearing patterns that have been shown to lead to adverse consequences for both children and their parents: childbearing during adolescence (teenage childbearing), unplanned childbearing, and non-marital childbearing. These patterns are interrelated, as the story of Millie Acevedo clearly illustrates.[72]

> Millie moved in with her boyfriend, Carlos, when she was fourteen. They were both eager to have children, but agreed to wait so that she could stay in school. Despite using birth control, Millie had a child before her sixteenth birthday. Though the conception was not planned, the prospect of becoming parents delighted them both. The pair shared old-fashioned, Puerto Rican family values, and she willingly dropped out of school to care for their child full time. A year later they conceived a second child, this one planned, reasoning that as long as they had started a family, they might as well finish the job.
>
> Millie and Carlos enjoyed a fairly stable relationship until she became pregnant a third time, a "total accident" in Millie's words, three months after the second child was born. When she told Carlos about the pregnancy, he "totally flipped. . . . He couldn't deal with [having another child], and he left . . . then, after [I went through] the whole pregnancy by myself, he came back after the baby was born. He wanted to be with me again. . . . We tried to stay together for like a whole year after the baby was born."
>
> But during this year, which Millie recalls as the worst in her life, Carlos "had so many jobs it wasn't even funny." His frequent conflicts with supervisors led to violent confrontations at home. "And when it got to that point, I was like, 'This is not good for my kids, this is no good for me, either he's gonna hurt me, I'm gonna hurt him, one of us is gonna be dead, one of us is gonna be in jail, and what's gonna happen to my kids then?' That's when I put an end to it," she says. "I got a restraining order on him, I got him out of the house, and that was the end of it. I never took him back."

Teenage childbearing has been a long-standing concern because children born to teenage mothers have a higher risk of poor health outcomes, including low birth weight, preterm births, and infant mortality.[73] Teenage mothers are also more likely to experience depression, lower levels of marital stability, additional nonmarital births with multiple partners, less stable employment, higher rates of poverty, and greater welfare use.

Birthrates for teenage females, especially minority females, remain stubbornly high, despite long-term declines. Birthrates for teenage females ages fifteen to nineteen declined by 34 percent from 1991 to 2005 (from 61.8 births per 1,000 females in 1991 to 40.5 births per 1,000 females in 2005), although birthrates increased to 41.5 in 2008.[74] Teenage birthrates also remain quite high among minority teens—whereas birthrates among teens were 27 (per 1,000 females) for non-Hispanic whites and 17 for Asians, they were 63 for non-Hispanic blacks, 78 for Hispanics, and 58 for American Indian or Alaska Natives.[75]

Although a substantial body of research has shown that high school dropouts, both males and females, are more likely to become teen parents, the causal relationship is less clear. Does teenage childbearing cause students, especially girls, to drop out of school, or does dropping out cause teenagers to become parents? Similarly, is teenage childbearing a cause of these adverse outcomes for children and parents, or are these outcomes related to other factors that cause students to become teen parents?

Earlier research studies generally concluded that girls who had children as teenagers were much less likely to complete high school.[76] A recent study also found that only 68 percent of young women who had a child before age eighteen had completed high school by age twenty-two, compared to 94 percent of young women who did not experience a teen birth.[77] But recent studies based on more innovative techniques that control for both observed and unobserved differences between teen moms and other teens have found that girls who become teen moms were more likely to drop out of school anyway because of poverty, poor academic performance, reduced educational expectations, and declining engagement in school.[78] Thus, teen pregnancy was less of a causal factor in dropping out.

But teen pregnancy does not always precede the decision to drop out of school—one study found that almost the same percentage of teen mothers dropped out before becoming pregnant as dropped out after becoming pregnant (28 percent versus 30 percent), although these percentages varied widely among whites, blacks, and Hispanics.[79] Among whites and Hispanics, more students dropped out before pregnancy, while almost four times as many black teens dropped out after pregnancy as before. The effect of dropping out on childbearing also varies by racial and ethnic groups. Two studies using the same national data set found that—after controlling for individual, family, classroom, and school characteristics—dropping out of school increased the risk for teenage pregnancy among white and Hispanic students, but not black students.[80] Also, staying in school longer reduced the odds of teen pregnancy for whites and Hispanics, but not blacks. A number of individual, family, and school characteristics also influenced teen pregnancy, with high educational performance and school involvement reducing the risk of pregnancy among all three groups. Having a child reduces the odds of graduating—one study found that women who had a baby after dropping out of school were half as likely to eventually graduate as women who did not have a baby.[81]

One reason teenage births are problematic is that they are more likely to be unintended—either unwanted or mistimed (occurring before they are desired). Like teenage births, unintended births are associated with a host of negative outcomes for both children and their mothers, including higher rates of complications during pregnancy, birth, and the postpartum period, as well as negative consequences for the mothers' mental well-being and the quality of their relationships.[82] One recent study found, for example, that unintended and mistimed children received fewer cognitive resources (learning materials and opportunities in the home) and emotional resources (positive mother-child interactions) from their mothers than their intended siblings, even after controlling for the effects of education, ability, and other personal characteristics of the mother.[83]

In 2002, only 22 percent of all births to teen mothers were intended, with 22 percent unwanted and 57 percent mistimed, whereas 76 percent of all births to mothers ages twenty-five to forty-four were intended.[84] The percentage of unwanted births among women less than twenty-five years of age was higher for Hispanics and non-Hispanic blacks than among non-Hispanic whites, and higher for second or more births than for first births.[85]

High school dropouts not only are more likely to become teen parents and have unintended children, but they are also more likely to have children out of wedlock, what is generally referred to as nonmarital childbearing. In 2007, almost 40 percent of all registered births in the United States were to unmarried women, more than double those from 1980.[86] Nonmarital birthrates vary widely by race and Hispanic origin: in 2006, nonmarital birth rates for blacks were twice as high, and nonmarital birth rates for Hispanics were three times as high, as for non-Hispanic whites and Asian or Pacific Islanders.[87] The proportion of births to unmarried women varies widely by age: in 2007, 93 percent of all births to fifteen- to seventeen-year-olds were nonmarital, 82 percent of births to eighteen- to nineteen-year-olds were nonmarital, and 60 percent of births to twenty- to twenty-four-year-olds were nonmarital.[88] Yet over time the proportion of total nonmarital births to teenagers has declined from 50 percent in 1970 to 23 percent in 2007.[89]

Dropouts are much more likely than high school graduates to have children out of wedlock. A longitudinal study of almost 5,000 newborn children and their parents from seventy-five hospitals in twenty-five large cities throughout the United States, known as the Fragile Families and Child Wellbeing Study, found that almost half of single mothers had not completed high school, compared to fewer than 18 percent of married mothers.[90] Similarly, 44 percent of the fathers of the children born to single mothers had not completed high school, compared to 22 percent of the married fathers.[91]

The Fragile Families study also measured the family resources and parents' capabilities for raising their children. The lower education levels of both parents were directly related to family income, with more than 50 percent of single mothers reporting incomes below the poverty level, four times the rate reported by married families.[92] In addition to lower financial and human resources, single parents also had poorer mental health and health behaviors, which the study considered indicators of parents' social-emotional skills and ability to form stable relationships. For example, unmarried parents—both those who were cohabitating and those who lived apart—were more likely to suffer from depression and report heavy drinking and illegal drug use than married parents.[93] Unmarried fathers were also three times as likely to be violent, and nearly seven times as likely to have been incarcerated, as married fathers.[94] Finally, more than one-third of unmarried parents had a child with another partner, double the rate reported by married parents.[95]

The study also examined the nature of the parental relationships in these families, particularly whether there was stability in these relationships over the first five years of the children's lives, as well as whether there were other relationships and children during this period. At the time of their child's birth, most unmarried parents held positive views about the benefits of marriage for their children and the chances that they would eventually get married. Pro-marriage attitudes were much stronger among black and Hispanic mothers than among white mothers, although single, white mothers reported higher chances of marriage.[96] Yet five years after the birth of their child, only 22 percent of unmarried parents had wed, and only 16 percent were still married.[97] Instead, two-thirds of unmarried mothers had entered into at least one new partnership over this period, and more than a third had experienced two or more partnership changes.[98] In addition, only one-third of fathers were living with their children five years later, while one-third had no contact.[99]

Finally, the study examined how the parents and children fared over the first five years of the child's life.[100] Both parents benefited from marriage—either remaining married or marrying after the birth of the child—in terms of earnings growth and changes in mental health. Fathers who remained married had the highest earnings and the highest earnings growth, followed by fathers who married after their child's birth. Married fathers and fathers who later married also reported fewer mental health problems at the time of their child's birth, although all groups experienced an increase in mental health problems during the first five years, with no change in disparities among groups.

Married mothers reported the highest incomes at birth, but all mothers, except those who divorced, reported similar income gains during the first five years of their child's life. Married mothers also reported the fewest health problems at the time of their child's birth, and while mental health problems increased for all women during this period, partnership changes had short-term negative effects on mothers' mental health. Unmarried mothers were also less likely to report material and emotional assistance from family and friends because they were more likely to live in impoverished neighborhoods and to experience residential mobility. Partnership changes also contributed to more maternal mental stress among women with a high school degree or less.

Finally, the study found that children who lived with stable single mothers or mothers who experienced multiple partnership changes were more likely to show higher levels of aggression, anxiety, and depression than children who lived with married or stable cohabitating parents. The study concludes that nonmarital childbearing reduces children's life chances by lowering parental resources and the quality of parenting through two primary mechanisms: partnership instability and childbearing with multiple partners.

Why are less educated women, especially high school dropouts, more likely to have children out of wedlock, especially if they can perceive that it may diminish their opportunities for further education and employment?

As they do with males' behavior with respect to crime, economists use the concept of "opportunity cost" to explain women's behavior with respect to childbearing and marriage. More educated women have better economic opportunities, particularly higher earnings, than less educated women, so they have more to lose by childbearing. Similarly, adolescent females who have the ability and aspirations to go to college are less inclined to have children as adolescents while pursuing their education.

Communities shape economic opportunities and educational aspirations in multiple ways.[101] One is through the economic and institutional resources available in the community—communities with more resources provide more opportunities for employment and access to medical facilities and community organizations that provide incentives for teens to avoid pregnancy or to seek abortions or adoptions if they become pregnant. Another is through parental relationships—the social support available to parents through family and friends can help family functioning by helping to monitor children and reducing parental stress. Still another is through community-wide formal and informal institutions—adults and institutions in the larger community can also help supervise and monitor youth and provide informal social control, whereas peers can provide a form of collective socialization. Supportive and beneficial relationships in families, schools, and communities are known as social capital.[102]

The role of distressed communities in shaping dropout behavior, childbearing, and motherhood is illustrated in Kathryn Edin and Maria Kefalas's study of 172 poor, single mothers in Philadelphia:

> In an America that is profoundly unequal, the poor and the rich alike are supposed to wait to bear children until they can complete their schooling, find stable employment, and marry a man who has done the same. Yet poor women realize they may never have children if they hold to this standard. Middle-class taxpayers see the children born to a young, poor, and unmarried mother as barriers to her future achievement, short-circuiting her changes for what might have been a better life, while the mother herself sees children as the best of what life offers. Though some do

express regret that an untimely birth robbed them of chances to improve their lot in life, most do not. Instead, they credit their children for virtually all that they see as positive in their lives. Even those who say they might have achieved more if they hadn't become parents when and how they did almost always believe the benefits of children far exceed the costs. As Celeste, a twenty-one year old white mother of a five-month-old, explains, "I'd have no direction [if I hadn't had a child]. I could sit here and say, 'Oh, I would have . . . gone to a four-year college,' [but] I probably wouldn't have." Like Celeste, many unmarried teens bear children that are conceived only after they've already experienced difficulties or dropped out of school.

What outsiders do not understand is that early childbearing does not actually have much effect on a low-skilled woman's future prospects in the labor market. In fact, her life chances are so limited already that a child or two makes little difference. . . . What is even less understood, though, are the rewards that poor women garner from becoming mothers. These women rely on their children to bring validation, purpose, companionship, and order to their lives—things they find hard to come by in other ways. The absolute centrality of children in the lives of low-income mothers is the reason that so many poor women place motherhood before marriage, even in the face of harsh economic and personal circumstances.[103]

The women Edin and Kefalas interview characterize motherhood as a "turning point" in their lives that gives them a reason to get up in the morning and calms their wild behavior. Edin and Kefalas themselves characterize motherhood as a primary vocation for young women living in decaying, inner-city neighborhoods.[104] National data further show that childbearing reduces smoking and marijuana use, further underscoring its moderating influence.[105] Elizabeth Zachry's study of nine teenage mothers enrolled in a Boston welfare-required GED program also found that their children gave them a reason to improve their situation and get off welfare.[106] Nonetheless, national data show that having a child out of wedlock tends to reduce educational expectations.[107]

But why do these women have children out of wedlock? Similar to the unmarried women in the Fragile Families study, the single moms in

Edin and Kefalas's study aspire to marriage. But their environment limits their prospects, particularly by the lack of what sociologist William Julius Wilson describes as "marriageable men" in inner-city neighborhoods. In Wilson's Chicago study, inner-city black women "argued that Black males are hopeless as either husbands or fathers and that more of their time is spent on the streets than at home."[108] Similarly, the single moms in Edin and Kefalas's Philadelphia study report that the men who father their children are not suitable for marriage or even stable relationships because of infidelity, domestic violence, substance abuse, and criminal activity.

So instead of maintaining relationships with such men, these women attempt to become economically self-sufficient and some, like Jen, succeed.

> Right now, Jen—once an aimless high school dropout with a depressed air—is not exactly on top of the world, but she is close. Monday through Thursday she enters data at a warehouse distribution center, earning an astonishing $10.25 an hour. She has held the job for three years now, and has shown high aptitude for the task and a strong work ethic. . . .
>
> Since her son has started school, she's been faithfully attending a high school completion program offering evening and weekend class, and a single test—in her least favorite subject—is all that stands between her and her diploma. . . .
>
> Ambition is now Jen's middle name, but the passion to succeed—to make a better life for herself and her son—only began after Rick's dramatic exit from the scene about three and a half years ago on the night of his twenty-second birthday. "You know that bar [down the street]? It happened in that bar. I was at my dad's. I was supposed to meet [Rick and his friends] there [to celebrate], but I was sick. . . . They were in the bar, and this guy was like bad-mouthing [Rick's friend] Mikey, talking stuff to him or whatever. So Rick had to go get involved in it and start with this guy. . . . Then he goes outside and fights the guy, [and] the guy dies of head trauma. . . . They were all on drugs, they were all drinking, and things just got out of control, and that's what happened. He got fourteen to thirty years.
>
> While Rick was in jail, Jen embarked on a radically different future. "That's when I really started [to get better], because I

didn't have to worry about what *he* was doing, didn't have to worry about him *cheating* on me, all this stuff. [It was] then I realized that I had to do what I had to do to take care of my son."[109]

What about men? Why do they father children out of wedlock? It is widely believed that unmarried men, especially low-income unmarried men, are uninterested in fatherhood and marriage.[110] For example, in Wilson's Chicago study, black males demonstrated a weak support for the institution of marriage because they reported that marriage tied them down, resulting in a loss of freedom.[111] Even fathering a child did not create a sense of obligation to marry, with little pressure from either his or his partner's family to marry.[112]

But data from the Fragile Families study show that the majority of both cohabiting and non-cohabiting fathers provided some type of support during pregnancy and told the mothers that they wanted to help raise the child.[113] Five years later, just over half of nonresident fathers provided some sort of financial support.[114]

Both parents and children tend to thrive more in married households than in households with cohabiting parents or single parents. Education not only affects the likelihood of teenage childbearing, unintended childbearing, and nonmarital childbearing, it also affects the likelihood of marriage for similar reasons: going to school precludes time for marriage and childbearing, while increasing schooling—which leads to increased skills and labor market earnings—increases the opportunity costs of marriage and childbearing. Research bears this out: the number of years of schooling increases the rates of marriage and decreases the rates of cohabitation, especially among young adults.[115]

Health

There is a well-documented relationship between education and health. Persons with more schooling report being healthier. The National Center for Health Statistics conducts an annual National Health Interview Survey where respondents are asked to rate their own health. Results from the 2009 survey show that only 38 percent of high school dropouts reported being in excellent or very good health, compared to 52 percent of high school graduates and 75 percent of four-year college graduates.[116] A more comprehensive study of data from several years of the same survey found that more educated persons reported having lower morbidity from the most common and acute diseases (heart condition, stroke hypertension, cholesterol, emphysema, diabetes, asthma attacks, and ulcers), were less likely to report anxiety or depression, and reported spending fewer days in bed or away from work due to illness.[117] Another study of twenty-five- to forty-five-year olds born after 1969, based on data from the General Social Surveys, found that high school graduates were 50 percent more likely to report being in very good health compared to high school dropouts even after accounting for differences in family background that might also contribute to better health.[118] Still another study that used two other national surveys found that more educated persons reported higher levels of physical health, physical functioning, and psychological well-being (absence of depression).[119] There is also evidence that differences in health across levels of education increase with age and that the relationship between health and education has grown over time.[120]

Death rates are also higher for dropouts. Death rates in 2007 for persons twenty-five to sixty-four years old were 14–39 percent higher (depending on how death rates were measured) for high school dropouts than for persons who completed high school.[121] Finally, life expectancy is much lower for dropouts. A study of mortality from major diseases found that the life expectancy of high school dropouts was nine years less than for persons who graduated from high school, with heart disease, lung cancer, and stroke the diseases that most contributed to those differences.[122] Another study found that each additional year of schooling increases life expectancy at age 35 by 1.7 years.[123]

What explains the relationship between education and health? Is it causal—that is, does more education cause better health? Or is it spurious— do some underlying factors contribute to both higher school completion and better health?

Economists, sociologists, psychologists, and epidemiologists together offer a number of different theories and explanations that support a causal relationship. In a major review of the research literature, sociologists Ross and Wu document three major theoretical explanations that are supported by empirical research:[124]

1. *Work and economic conditions.* The first explanation is based on the economic outcomes of schooling reviewed earlier. More educated persons

are more likely to be employed, to be employed full-time, and to earn more money when they are employed than persons with less education. Greater income from regular employment and higher-paying jobs contributes to better health outcomes, in part because financial resources provide access to health care. In contrast, job loss, economic hardship, and poverty not only limit economic resources, but also impose psychological strain and stress, which can make one more susceptible to disease.[125]

Yet income alone does not account for all of the positive association between education and health. Results from the National Health Interview Survey show that differences in income explain only about half of the differences in self-reported health between high school dropouts and high school graduates. For example, among respondents with family incomes between $35,000 and $55,000, 62 percent of high school graduates reported being in excellent or good health, compared to 49 percent of high school dropouts, about half of the overall differences reported above.[126] Even among the poor, the differences between high school graduates and dropouts in those reporting excellent and good health were 10 percentage points. The national study of twenty-five- to forty-five-year-olds found that income accounted for only one-quarter of the reported differences in health between high school graduates and high school dropouts.[127]

The health benefits from work are due not only to income, but also to the types of jobs that more educated workers secure. The national survey of twenty-five- to forty-five-year-olds found that, independent of income, persons with more schooling had jobs that offered more sense of accomplishment, more autonomy, and more opportunity for social interaction.[128] More educated workers also reported being more satisfied with the job, with income having little to do with job satisfaction.[129] These nonpecuniary aspects of work can contribute to better health, although the relationship is not well established in the research literature.[130]

2. *Psychosocial resources.* A second mechanism that explains the relationship between education and health is through the psychosocial resources that schooling develops.

One of those resources is a sense of personal control over one's life. The cognitive and noncognitive skills and abilities that schooling develops increase a person's sense of control over events and outcomes in one's future life. In contrast, students who experience educational failure develop a sense of perceived powerlessness and a lack of control, believing that outside forces and powerful individuals control their lives. The sense of personal control improves health both directly, through its effect on the immune system and, indirectly, through its effect on health-related behaviors, such as smoking and drug use. Personal control can also improve health outcomes through its positive association with job satisfaction, pay, and occupational status.[131] On the other hand, personal control can be undermined by living in poor communities with limited employment opportunities and high levels of violence, as Mercer Sullivan's study of New York City vividly portrayed.

Another resource is social support (social capital)—being part of a social network of mutual obligation in which others can be counted on—which provides a sense of being cared for, loved, and esteemed.[132] Schooling increases one's sense of social support. As we noted earlier, dropouts are more likely to have children outside of marriage, denying them the social support often found in marriage. They are also more likely to live in impoverished communities that lack positive social support. Social support improves health and decreases mortality, both directly, through its effect on mental health, and indirectly, through its effect on health-related behaviors.

Two recent reviews of the research literature further support the findings from the earlier Ross and Wu review. One study identified an array of psychosocial factors contributing to coronary heart disease that were related to socioeconomic status (e.g., low education and low income): depression, hostility and anger, lack of social support, lack of optimism, perceived stress.[133] Another study identified eight factors that were moderate predictors of positive health practices, such as exercise and relaxation: loneliness, social support, perceived health status, self-efficacy, future time perspective, self-esteem, hope, and depression.[134]

3. Health lifestyle. A third mechanism that explains the relationship between education and health is through health-related behaviors—smoking, illegal drug use, exercise, diet, and health checkups.

More educated individuals are less likely to smoke and use illegal drugs. In the 2008 National Survey on Drug Use and Health, 49 percent of high school dropouts reported using cigarettes in the previous thirty days, compared to 42 percent of high school graduates and 29 percent of college graduates.[135] In the same survey, 22 percent of high school dropouts reported using illicit drugs (marijuana, cocaine, etc.), compared to 20 percent of high school graduates and 15 percent of college graduates. And although the survey results show that increased education is associated with increased alcohol consumption, dropping out of high school has been shown to increase the long-term risk for alcohol dependence.[136]

Smoking has a well-documented effect on health. As noted by the Centers for Disease Control and Prevention, smoking harms nearly every organ of the body and causes many diseases. It accounts for an estimated 438,000 deaths, or nearly 1 of every 5 deaths, in the United States.[137] Drug and alcohol use has been linked to unintentional injuries, physical fights, academic and occupational problems, and illegal behavior among youth.[138] Drug use is also linked to the HIV epidemic, and alcohol and drug use also contribute to infant morbidity and mortality.

More educated individuals are also more likely to exercise, which leads to better health outcomes. In the 2009 Health Interview Survey, 31 percent of high school graduates reported engaging in moderate or rigorous exercise at least once a week, compared to 20 percent of high school dropouts.[139] According to the Centers for Disease Control and Prevention, regular physical activity can help control weight, reduce the risk of cardiovascular disease, reduce risk for type 2 diabetes, reduce risk of some cancers, strengthen bones and muscles, improve mental health and mood, improve the ability to do daily activities and prevent falls for older Americans, and increase the chances of living longer.[140]

Finally, more educated persons are more likely to have access to health care. The more educated are more likely to be employed in jobs that offer health benefits: census data reveal that high school graduates were almost twice as likely as high school dropouts to be covered by employer-provided health insurance in 2009.[141] The more educated also have higher incomes that allow them to purchase health insurance. In 2009, persons in households with incomes above $75,000 were three times more likely to have health insurance than households with incomes below $25,000.[142]

Health insurance has a direct effect on health care and health outcomes for children and adults. A 2009 report from the National Institute of Medicine, *America's Uninsured Crisis: Consequences for Health and Health Care*, found that adults without health insurance face serious harm and grave consequences. They are much less likely to receive preventive health care—annual physical exams, immunizations, and screenings—that can reduce unnecessary morbidity and premature death.[143] The chronically ill are also more likely to delay or forgo doctor visits and treatments. Similarly, children with health insurance have access to well-child care (and immunizations that can prevent future illness), prescription medications, and basic dental services.

The comprehensive study of health based on the National Health Interview Surveys, cited earlier, confirms that the better educated have healthier behaviors with respect to smoking, drinking, diet and exercise, use of illegal drugs, household safety, use of preventive medical care, and care for hypertension and diabetes.[144] The same study found that the effect of education on mortality was reduced by only 30 percent after controlling for health behaviors, which suggests that other factors play an important part.

Economists offer three explanations for how education improves health outcomes apart from the role of income and resources.[145] More educated persons have more health knowledge than less educated persons, such as information about the health benefits or dangers of smoking, nutrition, and exercise. They are also more likely to believe the information. Further, based on the concept of productive efficiency, more educated individuals are more likely to support good health because they act on the information, such as by following a doctor's advice. For example, a recent review of risk factors for stroke found that low education is a risk factor through its effects on high-risk behaviors such as smoking, poor diet, diminished health care utilization, and noncompliance with medical treatment of risk factors.[146] To illustrate, a study found that more educated mothers immediately reduced their smoking after publication of the 1964 surgeon general's report documenting the negative effects of smoking on health, while less educated women did not.[147] Finally, the better educated are more likely to recognize and value future benefits versus present ones, including the value of making current investments in preventive health practices that improve the likelihood of future health benefits. As Nobel economist Gary Becker argues:

> Schooling focuses students' attention on the future. Schooling can communicate images of the situations and difficulties of adult life, which are the future of childhood and adolescence. In addition, through repeated practice at problem solving, schooling helps children learn the art of scenario simulation. Thus

educated people should be more productive at reducing the re-
moteness of future pleasures.[148]

Supporting evidence comes from the national study of twenty-five-
to forty-five-year-olds, which found that more than 50 percent of dropouts
agreed with the statement "Nowadays, a person has to live pretty much for
today and let tomorrow take care of itself," compared to fewer than 30 percent for college graduates.[149] Time preferences can directly affect health
behavior. A recent study found that individuals with higher life expectancy
and lower time preference (more concern for the future than for the present) were more likely to undergo cancer screening.[150]

Epidemiologists have more recently examined the role that environmental conditions play in producing and maintaining health disparities.
Education and income affect health outcomes through their relationship
to various dimensions of environmental quality—hazardous waste, air pollution, water pollution, ambient noise, residential crowding, housing quality, educational facilities, work environments, neighborhood quality—that
all contribute to health.[151] More educated persons live in neighborhoods
with better environmental quality than less educated persons. They are
also associated with more educated peers who can positively influence their
health behaviors and, as a result, their health outcomes.[152]

As with other consequences of education, one important question is
whether education has a causal impact on health, because only if it does
so would a reduction in dropout rates improve health outcomes for persons at-risk of dropping out. Alternatively, poor health in childhood
could contribute to dropping out and to poor health in adulthood. For
example, low birth weight lowers educational attainment and predicts
poor health in adulthood.[153] Other factors, such as family background,
genetic traits, or other individual differences, could also contribute to
both educational attainment and adult health. Yet, the comprehensive
health study cited earlier found that controlling for family background,
current employment, marital status, and health insurance coverage reduced the effect of education by less than 40 percent, suggesting that education has a direct effect on health outcomes.[154] Other, quasi-experimental
studies further support the notion that education has a causal effect on
adult health.[155]

Civic Engagement

Another consequence of education is civic engagement. As documented in an earlier chapter, among the many goals of public education identified by Thomas Jefferson were several related not to the individual or private benefits of education, but the public ones, including "to understand his duties to his neighbors and country, and to discharge with competence the functions confided to him by either."[156]

Two types of civic engagement—political participation and civic participation—are crucial to a well-functioning society. Political participation is critical to maintaining a healthy democracy where all citizens are afforded the right to vote. Civic participation is critical to supporting one's community, including participating in the vast array of public religious and nonreligious institutions that represent the social fabric of society. Dropouts are less likely to participate in either activity.

In the 2008 presidential election, for example, only 37 percent of high school dropouts twenty-five to fifty-five years of age voted, compared to 52 percent of high school graduates and 76 percent of four-year college graduates.[157] The national study of twenty-five- to forty-five-year-olds found that fewer than 40 percent of high school dropouts reported that they had *ever* voted, compared to 55 percent of high school graduates and more than 80 percent of college graduates.[158] The same study found that only about one-third of dropouts reported that they volunteered, compared to more than half of high school graduates and two-thirds of college graduates. In both cases, controlling for differences in income did little to change the findings, suggesting that material resources cannot explain the relationship. Other national surveys find that dropouts are half as likely as high school graduates to volunteer and to donate blood.[159]

One mechanism that explains the relationship between education and civic engagement is trust. Political scientist Eric Uslaner refers to trust as the "chicken soup of social life. It reputedly brings all sorts of good things—from a willingness to get involved in our communities to higher rates of economic growth, to satisfaction with government performance, to making daily life more pleasant."[160] While there are different kinds of trust, it is trust in people we don't know and who are likely to be different from us—what Uslaner calls "moralist trust" and particularly a generalized trust in most people (as opposed to trusting only in people like us)—that leads people to get involved in their communities.[161] He finds that education increases levels of generalized trust and that increasing levels of general-ized trust are associated with greater levels of charitable donations and volunteering.[162] Trust also contributes to a sense of well-being.[163] The study of twenty-five- to forty-five-year-olds also found that high school graduates were more likely than high school dropouts to report that people can be trusted.[164]

Interestingly, trust did not predict political participation as measured by turnout in presidential elections, working for political parties, and signing petitions. In fact, Uslaner argues that political engagement is fueled by mistrust: "People will be more likely to get involved in political life when they get mad and believe that some others, be they other people or political leaders, cannot be trusted."[165] Yet education can help bridge political dif-ferences by helping people become more open to differing opinions. For example, in a national survey of individuals age twenty-five and older, only 59 percent of high school dropouts reported that it was important to under-stand others' opinions, compared to 64 percent of high school graduates and 73 percent of four-year college graduates.[166]

Economists, such as Thomas Dee, offer other explanations of how edu-cation influences civic participation.[167] First, the increased cognitive skills from schooling may facilitate civic participation by making it easier to pro-cess and comprehend complex political information. Second, schooling may shape individual preferences for civic activities.[168] Yet Dee also sug-gests that increased schooling could decrease civic participation by increas-ing the opportunity costs of an individual's time, which may be especially consequential for volunteering.

As Dee and others have pointed out, the observed associations between education levels and various aspects of civic engagement, such as voting and volunteering, may not be causal. For example, the same family back-ground characteristics that influence educational attainment—such as valuing education—may also promote increased civic participation. Also, more educated and civic-minded families may live in neighborhoods with high-quality schools that improve educational outcomes. By using sophis-ticated statistical models, Dee was able to demonstrate an arguably stron-ger causal connection between education (both secondary and postsecond-ary) and several measures of civic engagement: voting, newspaper readership, group memberships (e.g., fraternal and community-service groups, politi-cal clubs, church-service groups) and attitudes toward free speech for particular groups (e.g., anti-religionists, communists, homosexuals). Another rigorous study also found strong causal effects in that better educated adults are not only more likely to vote, but also "more likely to follow election campaigns in the media, discuss politics with others, associate with a political group, and work on community issues."[169]

Well-Being

In addition to the economic and health benefits of education, social scientists have increasingly focused on a broader concept of well-being. Although there is no set definition of well-being, it generally comprises a broad array of economic, social, and individual dimensions that contribute to a successful life.[170] These dimensions include economic positions and resources, political rights and power, intellectual resources, housing and infrastructure, personal health and security, social capital, leisure and cultural activities, personal satisfaction, and autonomy.[171] Measuring well-being, especially its subjective aspects, is challenging.[172] An international group of economists commissioned by the United Nations first developed the human development index in 1990 that is used annually to measure three basic ingredients of human well-being—health, education, and income—in all the countries of the world.[173] Several organizations—the OECD, the Annie Casey Foundation, and the Foundation for Child Development—issue annual reports on child well-being based on indicators of economic well-being, housing and environment, educational well-being, health, risk behaviors, and quality of school life.[174]

The U.S. Census Bureau collects a variety of information on the economic well-being of people in the United States through its ongoing Survey of Income and Program Participation.[175] Information is collected on cash and non-cash income as well as child care, health insurance, program participation, assets (e.g., appliances, computers, cell phones), and wealth. In the most recent survey for 2005, 18 percent of households reported that they had trouble paying rent or mortgage, paying utilities, or affording medical or dental care in the previous twelve months. But 26 percent of households headed by dropouts reported such difficulties, compared to 20 percent of households headed by high school graduates and 8 percent of households headed by four-year college graduates.[176]

One broad measure of well-being is self-reported happiness. In the national survey of twenty-four- to forty-five-year-olds, high school graduates with no additional schooling were more likely to report being happy or very happy with life than high school dropouts (89 percent versus 81 percent).[177] Adjusting for differences in family income, high school graduates still reported being happy about 4 percentage points more than high school dropouts. Thus, income accounts for only about half of the differences in happiness, suggesting that schooling affects well-being through other, non-economic means. The effect on health and civic engagement suggests two possible factors. High school graduates are also more likely to report being very satisfied with their jobs.[178]

Three mechanisms can be used to explain the relationship between education and well-being.[179] The first is an *absolute* mechanism, where education develops the skills, competencies, values, attitudes, beliefs, and motivations that contribute directly to adult well-being. The second is a *relative* mechanism, where education improves a person's relative position in society through its credentialing function rather than through the skills and abilities it develops. The absolute mechanism implies that improving education will improve outcomes for everyone, while the relative mechanism may improve outcomes only for some at the expense of others, because the overall distribution of opportunity and well-being may remain the same. The third is the *cumulative* mechanism, where education may have an absolute effect, but its effect is conditioned on the average level of education of those in the same vicinity. This is what economists refer to as externalities. For example, one study estimated that the earnings of high school dropouts are 10 percent higher in communities where the percentage of four-year college graduates is 5 percentage points above the national average (28 percent versus 33 percent).[180] In other words, even though high school dropouts are economically disadvantaged relative to high school graduates in all communities, they are more disadvantaged in absolute terms in communities with fewer college-educated workers. These are the communities of concentrated disadvantaged discussed earlier, contributing to the intergenerational reproduction of poverty that we now discuss.

Intergenerational Mobility

One of the most far-reaching and lasting impacts of education is the role it plays in intergenerational mobility. Social scientists have long debated the degree to which economic privilege and well-being are transmitted from one generation to another. Economists tend to focus on mobility in terms of income and wages, while sociologists tend to focus on mobility in terms of occupational status and prestige.

In an economic essay on the role of families in transmitting economic inequality across generations, Nobel economist Gary Becker notes:

> In every country with data that I have seen . . . earnings regress strongly to the mean between fathers and sons. Probably much less than 40% of the earnings advantages or disadvantages survive three generations. Evidently, abilities and other endowments that generate earnings are only weakly transmitted from parents to children.[181]

Other economists dispute this claim:

> Recent evidence points to a much higher level of intergenerational transmission of economic position than was previously thought to be the case. America may still be the land of opportunity by some measures, but parental income and wealth are strong predictors of the likely economic status of the next generation.[182]

Although another review of the research found that about 40 percent of the differences in family incomes in one generation continued into the next, a more recent study using more extensive data and more sophisticated methods found that 60 percent of the differences in income continued into the next.[183]

Poverty is also transmitted from one generation to the next. One study found that children who were poor at birth were five times more likely to be poor at least half of their years in young adulthood (ages twenty-five to thirty) than children who were not poor at birth.[184] An earlier study found that black children raised in poor families were more than twice as likely to be poor in early adulthood compared to black children raised in non-poor families, while white children raised in poor families were more than seven times more likely to be poor as adults than children raised in non-poor families.[185] Because dropouts are twice as likely to be poor as high school graduates, children of dropouts are also more likely to become poor adults.[186] Another study found that 55 percent of young adults who came from the poorest 20 percent of households as children were themselves in the poorest 20 percent of households as adults, while 45 percent of those who came from the wealthiest 20 percent of households as children were in the wealthiest 20 percent of households as young adults.[187]

Finally, occupational status is transmitted from one generation to another. Using national representative data from men and women born after 1950, Emily Beller and Michael Hout found that among men, 32 percent were immobile (meaning that their occupational category was the same as their father's), 37 percent were upwardly mobile, and 32 percent were downwardly mobile.[188] Among women, 27 percent were immobile, 46 percent were upwardly mobile, and 28 percent were downwardly mobile.

There is also disagreement on the mechanisms that contribute to the intergenerational transmission of well-being and privilege. One major source of contention is the role of heredity. In their controversial book, *The Bell Curve*, Richard Herrnstein and Charles Murray argue that the reproduction of poverty from one generation to the next is due largely to poor children inheriting their parents' cognitive deficits, which leads to poor adult outcomes.[189] Yet critics argue that the evidence they provide cannot disentangle the effects of heredity from those of the environment, in part because they are unable to adequately measure many aspects of the environment that may contribute to adult outcomes.[190] Similarly, a recent study of children adopted from South Korea who were randomly assigned to U.S. adoptive families found that only 16 percent of the variation in years of educational attainment was accounted for by shared family environment, whereas 44 percent was accounted for by nature and 40 percent to nonshared environment.[191] Yet another recent study of 320 pairs of twins tracked from birth to age seven found that the inheritability of IQ (intelligence) depended on social class origins: among the most impoverished families, all of whom were living below the poverty level, the inheritability of IQ was essentially zero, while shared environmental factors accounted for almost 60 percent of variability in IQ at age seven; among the most affluent families, it was almost exactly the opposite—60 percent of the variability in IQ was attributable to genes and none of the variability was due to shared environment.[192] An even larger study of 829 adolescent youths found the same differential effects.[193]

So, if the transmission of poverty from one generation to the next is largely due to the environment, which environmental factors contribute to this effect and through what mechanisms do they operate? Political scientist Mary Corcoran reviews four theoretical perspectives that explain the intergenerational transmission of socioeconomic mobility and the evidence to support them.[194]

The first explanation focuses on the lack of material resources. Poor families have fewer material resources—money, time, or energy—to invest in their children's human capital at home, through school, and in the community. They have less money to purchase learning materials and services outside of school, less time to read to their children and help with homework, and less energy to devote to parenting their children. For example, in 2005, children of high school graduates were three times as likely to participate in any after-school activities—such as academic activities, arts, clubs, religious activities, Scouts, and sports—as children of high school dropouts.[195] The primary mechanism for transmitting family background to adult outcomes is schooling. Although numerous studies have demonstrated that poor children acquire less schooling than advantaged children, studies also find that the effect of parental poverty on children's economic outcomes is largely independent of schooling.[196] Yet other studies find it is the quality rather than the amount of schooling that matters. Studies find, for example, that poor children are less likely to enroll in high-quality, intensive preschool programs that have been shown to improve high school graduation, college access, and health, and to reduce teen pregnancy, drug use, and crime.[197] Poor children also attend poorer quality elementary and secondary schools with poorer facilities, less qualified teachers, and less academically qualified classmates.[198]

The second explanation focuses on family structure, particularly female-headed households. Although poor families are more likely to be headed by a female than nonpoor families, other factors besides income and material resources may matter. In a recent review of the literature, demographers Sara McLanahan and Christine Percheski found that living apart from one biological parent (usually the father) is associated with a large number of negative child and adult outcomes. Such children score lower on standardized tests, report poorer grades, and are more likely to drop out of high school and less likely to graduate from college; they are also more likely to experience behavioral and psychological problems, to have sex at an early age, and to begin childbearing at an early age.[199] The authors examine the issue of selection bias—whether other, underlying and perhaps unobserved factors (e.g., interpersonal skills) could explain these relationships—and conclude that the effects are at least partly causal.[200] They go on to identify two primary mechanisms that link family structure to child outcomes—parental resources and parenting.[201] Parental resources include economic resources, noneconomic resources (e.g., time spent with mothers and fathers, parental help with homework, parental supervision), and community resources (support from friends and institutions). In addition to these mechanisms, the Fragile Families study discussed earlier identified two others—partnership instability and multipartner fertility—both of which reduce the mother's prospects for forming a stable union and receiving child support, while also producing considerable stress for mothers and children.[202]

The third explanation focuses on the role of welfare and the culture of poverty that it creates and is transmitted from one generation to another. According to this perspective, parents who rely on welfare develop poor attitudes and work habits that are passed on to their children.[203] Parents and their neighbors also provide poor role models regarding work and marriage. Although research documents that children raised in welfare-dependent homes are more likely to become teen parents out of wedlock, to drop out of school, and to end up on welfare themselves, in general the research is unable to determine whether these are effects of welfare or poverty.[204]

The last explanation focuses on the role of communities. As noted in the beginning of the chapter, in 1965 Daniel Patrick Moynihan pointed out how a wide range of social problems—joblessness, family instability, poor health, substance abuse, poverty, welfare dependency, and crime—were not only interconnected, but also concentrated within certain urban neighborhoods, particularly those with high concentrations of blacks. He also documented how these neighborhoods of concentrated disadvantage are highly durable and create a cycle of poverty and disadvantage that continues from one generation to the next. Analyzing more recent longitudinal data from Chicago and the United States, sociologist Robert Sampson found that these conditions continued to exist.

In a series of books based on ethnographic fieldwork in Chicago during the 1980s, sociologist Julius William Wilson provides a more complex picture of how neighborhoods reproduce economic and social inequality, especially for African-Americans. First, he argues that a series of both political actions of government beginning in the 1930s—such as those pertaining to housing and highway construction—and economic forces—such as the movement of middle-class jobs from the inner cities to the suburbs—led to the creation of highly impoverished neighbors, particularly in the Midwest and Northeast. Such neighborhoods are characterized by high rates of male unemployment, concentrated poverty, and low proportions of middle-class residents who weakened important socializing institutions like churches and community organizations, forcing residents to live in "social isolation."[205] He then argues that a combination of structural and cultural factors together shape outcomes—such as joblessness and the fragmentation of families—in these neighborhoods:

> We have seen that some cultural patterns in the inner-city ghetto reflect informal rules that shape how people interact or engage one another and make decisions. The decision making is often related to perceptions about how the world works—what we call meaning making. The meaning-making and decision-making processes evolve over time in situations imposed by racial segregation and poverty; situations that severely hamper social mobility. To state this process in formal sociological terms, culture *mediates* the impact of structural forces such as racial segregation and poverty. In other words, residents of the ghetto develop ways, often quite creative, to adjust and respond to chronic racial and economic subordination, as reflected in meaning-making and decision-making processes, including those resulting in the development of informal codes that regulate behavior.[206]

He further argues that the ongoing debate over the role of social structure versus culture in shaping outcomes for African-Americans fuels a political divide, with liberals focusing on structural factors and conservatives focusing on cultural factors.[207]

While a large body of research evidence supports the ideas that neighborhoods influence child and adult outcome, as with other factors, it is hard to determine the causal effects of neighborhoods and the underlying processes through which neighborhoods exert their influence.[208]

Education is widely viewed as the single most important mechanism transmitting economic privilege from one generation to another. Indeed, many studies have demonstrated a strong connection between social origins and educational attainment. For example, one recent study found that while 97 percent of youth from the top quarter of families, based on a family-income-to-needs ratio, graduated from high school, only 64 percent of youth from the bottom quarter graduated from high school; similarly, while 42 percent of youth from the top quarter graduated from college, only 6 percent of youth from the bottom quarter did so.[209] A recent review of this literature also found that the association between social origins and educational attainment has remained fairly stable in the United States, while it has declined in a number of European countries.[210]

While there is widespread agreement on the importance of education in reproducing inequality from one generation to the next, there is less agreement on whether education largely affects adult outcomes through its effect on cognitive skills or noncognitive skills. The human capital framework that underlies much of the research in this area tends to focus on cognitive skills. Indeed, cognitive skills of young children are highly related to maternal education. For example, children three to five years of age with mothers who were high school graduates were twice as likely to recognize all their letters and to count to twenty as children with mothers who were high school dropouts.[211] In a longitudinal study of more than 2,000 children ages six to twelve living in Chicago, Robert Sampson, Patrick Sharkey, and Stephen Raudenbush found that living in a severely disadvantaged neighborhood (defined as living in the bottom quartile of a six-item composite measure of neighborhood characteristics) reduced the later verbal ability of African-American children by the equivalent of a year or more of schooling.[212]

A growing number of scholars have come to recognize the importance of noncognitive skills, such as motivation, tenacity, trustworthiness, and perseverance.[213] In a recent review of the research on the determinants of earnings, economists Samuel Bowles, Herbert Gintis, and Melissa Osborne found that less than one-fifth of economic returns to schooling were attributable to cognitive effects as measured by test scores.[214] Instead, research shows that a number of psychological and behavioral variables, such as self-esteem and a belief that outcomes are a result of hard work or luck (known as an externality scale), exert a strong, independent influence on earnings. And while education may develop some of those traits, these characteristics also contribute directly to the transmission of well-being from one generation to the next.

Health may also play an important role. In a recent review of the research evidence, economist Janet Currie found that parental education, income, and health have a causal impact on child health and that child health has a causal impact on adult education, income, and health.[215] She examined several aspects of health—overall, self-reported health; fetal health at birth (due to external shocks such as wars, epidemics, etc.); low birth weight; poor nutrition; mental health, including children with attention-deficit/

hyperactivity disorder (ADHD); chronic physical conditions, including asthma; acute conditions, such as dental cavities and ear infections; and toxic exposures, such as lead paint. Overall, poor children had poorer health in all these areas than non-poor children. For example, data from the 2009 National Health Interview Survey show that 71 percent of poor children were reported to be in excellent or very good health compared to 90 percent of non-poor children.[216] And while the incidence of asthma is only 20 percent higher among poor versus non-poor children, poor children are more than three times more likely to be limited by asthma. Because dropouts are twice as likely as high school graduates to be poor, one can conclude that the children of dropouts are also more likely to suffer from poor health.

As with other outcomes, it is difficult to demonstrate a causal connection between parental socioeconomic status and child health. Yet some recent studies based on more sophisticated techniques have demonstrated a causal connection. For example, one study demonstrated that higher maternal education improves infant health, as measured by birth weight and gestational age, by increasing the use of prenatal care and reducing smoking.[217] Overall, the research evidence is still relatively small, but expanding.

Similarly, there is a good deal of evidence linking child health to adult health and other outcomes such as educational attainment and workplace productivity. For example, children born during the influenza epidemic of 1918 were 15 percent less likely to graduate from high school, and males earned 5 percent to 9 percent less than individuals born just before or just after the epidemic.[218] They were also more likely to suffer from diabetes, stroke, activity limitations, cancer, hypertension, and heart problems and reported poorer general health status as older adults.[219] Respondents from a survey of fifteen- to fifty-four-year-olds who reported early onset of psychiatric problems were also less likely to have graduated from high school or attended college.[220] And children who had emotional and behavior problems at ages six to eight were less likely to graduate from high school even after controlling for socioeconomic background.[221] But similar to the literature linking family background to children's health, the literature demonstrating strong causal effects is limited.

Overall, the research literature finds that the transmission of well-being from one generation to another can largely be explained by three mechanisms: cognitive and noncognitive skills, educational attainment and quality, and physical and mental health. Yet one study suggests the lingering effects of poverty may be the hardest to explain. The study found that while the effects of family origins on adult mental and physical health could be explained in large part by respondents' education, current employment, and economic conditions, there was still a persistent negative effect of childhood poverty, especially on adult mental health.[222]

The history of one family in Mark Fleisher's study of gang girls in Kansas City provides a vivid, human face to intergenerational mobility:

> Fourth youngest in a family of 13 children, Cathy escaped home at age 16 by telling her mother she was pregnant and had to get married. She married a 21-year-old fellow named Michael.
>
> "In third grade I started doing all the cooking and cleaning, because my mother was sick and my older sister, well, she was drunk and didn't help."
>
> Cathy told me her mother became abusive when Cathy was a young teenager. She claimed that her mother broke both her arms and legs just before she left home. "She beat me with a broom handle and punched and kicked me, and she'd get angry and throw [kitchen] glasses at me. I refused to let her know she got to me. She was just horrible to me. . . ."
>
> Hours of conversations with Cathy didn't reveal anything about her four daughters' three fathers. Melanie and Mary had one father, Cara another, April a third. Cara's father and April's, too, were prison inmates. . . .
>
> I'd watched April slowly pull herself out of school over the 1995–96 academic year. She said she got into too much trouble and didn't like the "black girls" because they picked on her, and in turn, she had to fight to protect herself. Cara encouraged April's return to school, at least when I was in earshot, offering to buy her a pair of $100 Nikes as a reward for staying in or returning to school, as the case may be. April didn't want Cara's gift.
>
> April stopped going to school at age 16 and hid from the aggression there, as she did from Cara's bullying. April worked as a waitress at Pizza Hut and then took a second job as an evening janitor; Cara worked with April as a janitor for a few weeks, then quit.[223]
>
> Cathy's family history shows that destructive life courses permeate a family's future generations deeply and invisibly. Cathy's

life course and her daughters' too were foretold 40 years ago, when Cathy's mother made bad decisions. Families are rivers of good and bad decisions flowing from one generation to the next.[224]

This chapter has documented a wide range of negative consequences from dropping out. Although it is difficult to demonstrate a causal connection between dropping out for all of these consequences, the research evidence is sufficiently extensive to make a convincing case. Yet, as we show in the next chapter, the impacts of dropping out affect not just dropouts themselves, but the rest of society as well.

5

THE SOCIAL CONSEQUENCES
OF DROPPING OUT

Dropping out has not only consequences for individuals, but also far-reaching consequences for the larger society. The low human capital of high school dropouts robs the economy of skills needed to fuel economic growth and enhance U.S. competitiveness in the global economy. The increased criminal activities from dropouts—arson, robbery, theft, rape, murder, family violence—exact tremendous economic, physical, and emotional harm on victims. The low voter and civic engagement of dropouts undermines our democratic way of life. The higher rates of teenage pregnancy and nonmarital births among dropouts have lasting consequences on their children.

The social consequences from dropping out also translate into huge financial losses for the country, for states, and for local communities. Drawing on myriad data sources and research studies that have examined the impact of dropping out on these various outcomes, economists have estimated the overall economic losses to society from high school dropouts. Henry Levin conducted the first comprehensive study in 1972 for the Select Committee on Equal Educational Opportunity of the U.S Senate, chaired by Senator Walter Mondale.[1] Levin identified seven social consequences of inadequate education, which he defined as the failure to complete high school:

1. Forgone national income.
2. Forgone tax revenues for the support of government services.
3. Increased demand for social services.
4. Increased crime.
5. Reduced political participation.
6. Reduced intergenerational mobility.
7. Poorer levels of health.

He reviewed and summarized the research literature on the relationship between education and each consequence. He then estimated the social costs associated with the first four consequences. For a cohort of males twenty-four to thirty-four years of age in 1969, over their lifetimes the forgone income amounted to $237 billion, forgone tax revenues amounted to $71 billion, and the social costs of providing social services and fighting crime amounted to $6 billion.[2]

Thirty-three years later, in 2005, Levin organized a symposium, "The Social Costs of Inadequate Education," at Teachers College to kick off its new Campaign for Educational Equity.[3] He commissioned a series of papers that examined the social consequences of dropping out on earnings and taxes, health, crime, and public assistance, which were eventually published in an edited volume, *The Price We Pay: Economic and Social Consequences of Inadequate Education*.[4] He and a colleague, Clive Belfield, then used the results of these new studies to estimate the lifetime economic benefits to taxpayers of getting each dropout to graduate from high school. I review the results of this analysis below. He also compared these benefits with the costs of providing a number of proven educational interventions to improve high school graduation rates. I review the results of this part of his analysis in Chapter 8.

In 2009, two economists from the Rand Corporation, Stephen Carroll and Emre Erkut, released a similar study, *The Benefits to Taxpayers from Increases in Students' Educational Attainment*, which estimated the economic benefits to taxpayers of not only raising the educational attainment of dropouts to high school graduates but also raising the educational attainment of high school graduates to college graduates, and even the unlikely event of raising the educational attainment of high school dropouts to college graduates.[5] Although they focused on areas similar to those of Levin and his colleagues—tax payments, social program spending (including health), and crime—they derived substantially lower estimates of social benefits. The differences are attributable to different sources of data and different assumptions about expected earnings and government spending.[6] The biggest difference is due to the assumption of Levin and his colleagues that some portion of dropouts who complete high school will attend and complete college, thereby raising their earnings and their tax payments.[7] They also assumed that earnings would increase in the future due to productivity increases, whereas Carroll and Erkut made no such assumption.[8]

This chapter draws on these and other studies to examine the severe consequences of dropping out on the U.S. economy and on the country.

Consequences for the Economy

One of the most important consequences of dropping out is the effect on the economy. As documented earlier, dropouts have higher rates of unemployment, work fewer hours when they are employed, and have lower earnings than high school graduates. As a result, they pay fewer taxes that support public spending. Several studies estimate that dropouts pay one-half to two-thirds of the taxes paid by high school graduates.[9]

These lower economic outcomes continue throughout their working lives. Also reported in the previous chapter, economist Cecilia Rouse calculated the expected earnings of high school dropouts over their working lives from eighteen to sixty-seven and compared them to the expected earnings of high school completers (including those who earned a GED) and all high school completers, including those who attended college. The difference in lifetime earnings between dropouts and those who were only high school completers exceeded $260,000. The difference in lifetime earnings between dropouts and *all* high school completers, including those who attended college, exceeded $552,000.[10] She also estimated that dropouts pay $97,000 less in federal income taxes, state income taxes, and Social Security taxes over their lifetimes compared to high school completers only, and $225,000 less in taxes compared to all high school completers, including those who attended college. She then calculated that there were about 600,000 dropouts in a single age cohort of twenty-year-olds in the United States in 2004. Using the estimates of lifetime earnings and lifetime taxes, Rouse then estimated that over their lifetimes, this single group of twenty-year-old dropouts would account for at least $165 billion in forgone economic income for the country, and $58 billion in lost tax revenues.[11] Comparisons with all high school graduates, including those with some college, yielded estimates of $330 billion in economic losses and $135 billion in lost tax revenues.

Both earnings and tax payments vary widely by race, ethnicity, and gender. Levin and Belfield used Rouse's data and similar procedures to estimate the extra tax payments for increasing high school graduation rates of dropouts for white, Asian, black, and Hispanic males and females. In this case, they included only income, sales, and property taxes (not Social Security taxes). The increased taxes ranged from $85,000 for Hispanic females to $202,700 for white males, with an average figure of $139,100.[12] Carroll and Erkut estimated much lower tax increases, ranging from $38,000 for black women to $54,000 for white males.[13]

Similar estimates have been made for states and cities. Using the same data and methods as in their national study, Belfield and Levin estimated that each twenty-year-old dropout in California generated $289,820 in economic losses from earnings over his or her working lifetime, $75,350 in lost federal income tax revenue, and $25,830 in lost state and local taxes.[14] They calculated that there were 118,496 twenty-year-old dropouts in the state in 2005.[15] Over their lifetimes, this cohort of dropouts would account for $46 billion in total economic losses for the state and $6 billion in lost state and local tax revenues.

The economic losses from dropouts are also felt at the local level. The California Dropout Research Project applied Belfield and Levin's estimates to seventeen of the largest cities in California to dramatize the local impact and to support local efforts to address the problem.[16] For example, in the city of Los Angeles, there were 12,367 dropouts from grades seven through twelve in the 2006–07 school year. Even if half of the dropouts eventually graduated from high school, as some studies suggest, the remaining half would still deprive the city of $1.2 billion in lost earnings.

In November 2009, the Alliance for Excellent Education, a national policy and advocacy organization promoting high school transformation, released a series of reports estimating the economic benefits of reducing high school dropouts in the fifty largest U.S. cities.[17] The analysis examined benefits only in terms of earnings and taxes. In all fifty cities and metropolitan areas, they estimated that 600,000 students from the high school class of 2008 dropped out of school. If half of those dropouts would have graduated, the group estimated, they would earn over $4.1 billion in additional wages in an average year of their working lives and pay an additional $536 million in state and local property, income, and sales taxes.[18] In the Los Angeles–Long Beach metropolitan area, they estimated that if half of the 70,000 dropouts had graduated, they would earn over $575 million in additional wages in an average year of their working lives and pay an additional $79 million in taxes. In June 2010, the Alliance added estimates of the benefits of reducing dropout rates for students of color.[19]

The low education and skill levels of dropouts threaten the future economy, which will increasingly require a more educated workforce. On the White House website, President Barack Obama states that "all Americans should be prepared to enroll in at least one year of higher education or job training to better prepare our workforce for a 21st century economy."[20] He further says that he is committed to ensuring that the United States has the highest proportion of students graduating from college in the world by 2020.

The country has a long way to go: based on data from the Organisation for Economic and Co-operative Development (OECD), the United States was fourteenth in the world in the percentage of the population who had completed four-year college degrees in 2008, below the average among OECD nations.[21] More disturbing, over the period from 1995 to 2008, the average percentage of college graduates among OECD countries increased from 20 percent to 38 percent, while it increased only from 33 percent to 37 percent in the United States.[22] In an analysis of historical trends in high school graduation, college access, and college completion rates, Nobel economist James Heckman attributes a substantial portion of the slowdown in college-educated workers to a slowdown in the high school graduation rate in the United States.[23] He concludes, "To increase the skill levels of the future workforce, America needs to confront a large and growing dropout problem."[24] Yet college completion rates have also declined over the past few decades due to both changes in the preparedness of entering students and declining resources per student.[25]

States and local communities are also at risk for having an insufficiently educated workforce in the future. In a major study of California's future economy, the Public Policy Institute of California estimated that if current demographic and economic trends continue, in 2020 the state will have fewer college-educated workers than the economy requires and twice the number of high school dropouts than the economy can employ.[26]

Consequences for the Larger Society

The social consequences of dropouts are not confined to the economy. Dropouts also affect the welfare of the larger society.

Crime

One such area is crime, which has a number of consequences. First, there are consequences for the victims of the various crimes—murder, rape, assault, theft, and arson, among others—due to lost wages, medical costs, and reductions in quality of life. Crime also affects other citizens who may decide where and how to live—for instance, having to keep their doors locked and their lights on, and purchasing insurance and home security systems to protect themselves from crime. There are also effects on government agencies and the taxpayers who fund them, from the criminal justice system (policing, prosecution, sentencing, incarceration, parole) to crime prevention agencies (e.g., Drug Enforcement Agency and the Bureau of Alcohol, Tobacco, Firearms, and Explosives).

Economists have estimated the economic losses associated with these various consequences and how much of those losses can be attributed to dropouts. The losses vary greatly by the type of crime. One study estimated the victim costs alone per crime range from $370 for larceny and theft to $2.9 million for murder, and the incarceration costs per crime range from $44 for larceny and theft to $845,455 for murder.[27] The study then estimated that increasing the high school graduation rate by 1 percent would reduce the total number of crimes by 94,310 and the total number of arrests by 11,750, generating $1.4 billion in savings from victim and incarceration costs. Finally, the study estimated that the social benefit for each additional male high school graduate ranges from $1,187 to $2,100 per year, which is about 14–25 percent of the private benefits in terms of higher earnings, and would generate social benefits far in excess of the additional costs of providing additional schooling.[28]

As part of their study on the economic costs of dropping out, Levin and Belfield, along with colleagues Peter Muennig and Cecilia Rouse, examined a wider range of costs associated with crime, including all the government costs associated with policing, judicial activities, corrections, and crime prevention, as well as government-funded victim costs, for five major crimes—murder, rape, violent crime (robbery and aggravated assault), property crime (burglary, larceny-theft, motor vehicle theft, arson), and drug offenses.[29] The estimated savings for each twenty-year-old high school graduate was $2,440 per year and $26,566 over a lifetime, with lifetime cost savings varying widely by race and gender, from $8,300 for Hispanic females to $55,500 for black males.[30] The criminal losses generated from the 709,000 twenty-year-old dropouts in 2004 over their lifetimes would amount to $18.8 billion in lifetime losses.[31] Carroll and Erkut's estimates for crime, which account only for state and local incarceration spending, range from zero for Asian females to $123,000 for black males.[32]

A similar analysis conducted for California found that the lifetime fiscal losses from crime for each twenty-year-old high school dropout were $10,580 for the federal government, $21,370 for state and local governments, and

$79,890 for the victims of crime.[33] The total economic losses to the state for the 118,496 twenty-year-old dropouts in 2005 amounted to almost $12 billion.[34]

All of these studies examined the economic losses from crimes committed by adults. But juveniles ten to seventeen years of age commit a sizeable fraction of crimes, and those crimes also generate economic losses for the larger society. Belfield and Levin recently completed another study, in which they estimated the economic losses from juvenile crime in California attributable to dropouts.[35] First, they found that in 2007, juveniles were arrested for about one-sixth of all violent crimes and one-quarter of all property crimes.[36] They estimated that the total costs of juvenile crime due to government spending on all crime-related activities (policing, prosecution, sentencing, etc.), victim costs, and school expenditures on crime prevention and safety (e.g., school-based police officers) amounted to $8.9 billion per year.[37] Next, they averaged the results of three studies that examined the relationship between education and juvenile crime to estimate that $1.13 billion of the $8.9 billion in total costs of juvenile crime, or about 13 percent, could be attributed to dropouts. Finally, they estimated that for a single cohort of twelve-year-olds, the economic losses from juvenile crime amounts to $1.13 billion, and the economic losses from adult crime amounts to an additional $10.5 billion over their lifetimes.[38] Since each year there is another cohort of twelve-year-olds, these figures represent the annual economic losses from juvenile crime attributable to high school dropouts and rise substantially as one considers successive cohorts of youth.

Welfare

Another social consequence of dropping out concerns welfare. As discussed earlier, dropouts are more likely to qualify for and receive government welfare benefits.[39] Those benefits include Temporary Assistance for Needy Families (TANF), food stamps, and housing assistance from the federal government, and state welfare assistance. Because these programs generally serve low-income individuals and dropouts are more likely to be low-income, a disproportionate share of these programs serves dropouts. For example, 45 percent of TANF and housing assistance went to high school dropouts, which is roughly double their representation in the population.[40]

As they did with crime, Belfield, Levin, Muennig, and Rouse estimated the social costs of welfare programs attributable to high school dropouts.

First, drawing on other studies, they estimated the annual costs of the three federal assistance programs—TANF, food stamps, and housing assistance—and state welfare assistance. Next, they estimated the proportion of those costs that can be attributed to the lack of a high school education. They then estimated the lifetime costs per dropout for each program. The sum of those costs came to $2,963 for an "average" dropout, with estimates ranging from $1,200 for white and Hispanic males to $9,000 for black females.[41] For a single cohort of 709,000 twenty-year-old dropouts, the total costs to taxpayers would amount to $2.1 billion over the lifetime of these dropouts.

Health

Still another social consequence of dropping out is related to health. The poorer health outcomes for high school dropouts documented in the previous chapter also generate huge social costs because dropouts are more likely to qualify for the two federal government–funded health insurance programs: Medicaid, which serves low-income residents, and Medicare. Because dropouts are more likely to be poor, they are more likely to qualify for and receive Medicaid benefits. Belfield, Levin, Muennig, and Rouse estimate that dropouts are two to three times more likely to receive Medicaid benefits than high school graduates (with differences varying among race and gender groups).[42] Medicare mostly serves elderly Americans sixty-five years and over, but persons under the age of sixty-five with disabilities can qualify for Medicare. To the extent that education reduces the incidence of disabilities, dropouts are more likely than high school graduates to receive Medicare benefits under the age of sixty-five. Indeed, Belfield, Levin, Muennig, and Rouse show that to be the case, with dropouts twice as likely to receive Medicare benefits as dropouts.[43] Based on these figures, Belfield, Levin, Muennig, and Rouse then estimated that the lifetime costs of public health insurance for each twenty-year-old high school dropout was $40,500 on average, with costs ranging from $27,900 for white males to $62,700 for black females.[44] This amounts to $28.7 billion in public health care expenditures associated with a cohort of 709,000 dropouts.

Carroll and Erkut examined the costs to taxpayers of eight government social support and insurance programs in the areas of health and public assistance:

1. Welfare programs (TANF, general assistance, and other welfare).
2. Subsidized housing (public housing and rental assistance).

3. Food stamps (the Supplemental Nutrition Assistance Program).
4. Supplemental Security Income.
5. Medicaid.
6. Medicare.
7. Unemployment insurance.
8. Social Security (retirement, disability, and survivor programs).[45]

Their estimated costs to taxpayers per dropout for these programs range from $22,000 for white males to $64,000 for black females.[46] Despite considering a wider range of assistance programs, their estimates are quite similar to those of Levin and his colleagues.

Civic Engagement

As discussed earlier, dropouts are less likely to vote and engage in other civic activities. Society is clearly worse off when fewer of its citizens participate in the democratic process. But are there social repercussions beyond simply a lower voter turnout and less participatory democracy?

In his book *Unequal Democracy: The Political Economy of the New Gilded Age*, political scientist Larry Bartels suggests there are.[47] He argues that economic inequality threatens our democracy, particularly regarding the welfare of the poorest Americans. Drawing on a variety of economic sources, Bartels documents the rising economic inequality in the United States over the past thirty years that has greatly increased the wealth of the richest Americans relative to the poorest ones, especially the richest 1 percent. He then reviews and discounts a number of economic explanations for rising economic inequality and instead offers a political explanation based not simply on the unequal voter turnout, knowledge, contacting their representatives, and even political campaign contributions and lobbying activities between rich and poor voters, but also on the increasing partisan ideologies and actions of Republican and Democratic congressional representatives, as well as those of the president. The unequal political representation produces policies—such as tax cuts for the wealthy, along with a declining real minimum wage for the poor—that further perpetuate economic inequality:

> These disparities in representation are especially troubling because they suggest the potential for a debilitating feedback cycle linking the economic and political realms: increasing economic inequality may produce increasing inequality in political respon-

siveness, which in turn produces public policies that are increasingly detrimental to the interests of poor citizens, which in turn produces even greater inequality, and so on. If that is the case, shifts in the income distribution triggered by technological change, demographic shifts, or global economic development may in time become augmented, entrenched, and immutable.[48]

He further argues that this cycle threatens not only the welfare of the poorest Americans, but also democracy itself, as Aristotle warned: "Where the possession of political power is due to the possession of economic power or wealth, whether the number of persons be large or small, that is oligarchy, and when the unpropertied class have power, that is democracy."[49]

Dropouts are disadvantaged not only because they are more likely to be poor and less likely to vote; Bartels's analysis demonstrates that their interests and future welfare are less likely to be addressed through a political system that favors the more educated and wealthy.

Total Economic Losses from Dropouts

Both Levin and his colleagues and Carroll and Erkut estimate the total costs to taxpayers of high school dropouts by adding the reduced tax revenues and increased public expenditures for crime, welfare, and health. Levin and his colleagues estimated that an "average" twenty-year-old dropout generates $209,210 in economic losses over his or her working lifetime, with the losses ranging from $143,000 for Hispanic females to $268,500 for black males.[50] For the entire cohort of 709,000 twenty-year-old dropouts, this amounts to a total loss of $148 billion (see Table 5.1).

Carroll and Erkut's estimates of the total social costs of dropouts are generally lower than those of Levin and his colleagues, ranging from $89,000 for white and Asian males to $201,000 for black males.[51] Another recent study estimated $292,000 in lifetime economic losses from each dropout, a figure substantially higher than those from the other two studies.[52]

Belfield and Levin conducted a similar analysis for California.[53] In this case, they estimated not simply the "public" economic losses to taxpayers, but also the economic losses to the economy from reduced lifetime earnings and from total victim costs, not simply those compensated by the government. They also estimated the losses from what economists call "externalities"—the fact that more educated workers make their coworkers

Table 5.1 Lifetime economic losses for U.S. taxpayers per cohort of twenty-year-old dropouts, 2004

	Losses per dropout	Losses per cohort (billions)
Taxes	$139,100	$98
Crime	$26,600	$19
Welfare	$3,000	$2
Health	$40,500	$29
Total	$209,200	$148

Source: Henry Levin et al., *The Costs and Benefits of an Excellent Education for All of America's Children* (New York: Teachers College, Columbia University, 2007), www.cbcse.org/Media/Download_Gallery/Leeds_Report_Final_Jan2007.pdf (accessed January 17, 2011), table 7.1.

more productive and attract investment into the state that also contributes to economic growth. The economic losses from all these sources for each twenty-year-old dropout in the state amounted to $391,910 in 2005, almost twice the taxpayer costs they estimated nationally, and the total economic losses for the entire cohort of 118,496 (adjusting for the resources needed to keep students in school) amount to over $46 billion.[54]

The figures were also used to estimate the economic losses from dropouts in the 2006–07 academic year for each of seventeen major cities in California. For example, in Los Angeles, there were 12,367 dropouts from grades seven through twelve in the 2006–07 school year. Even if half of the graduates eventually graduated from high school, as some studies suggest, the remaining half would still deprive the city of $2.1 billion in economic losses over their lifetimes. If a similar number of students drop out each year, it means that the City of Los Angeles is losing over $2 billion each year from dropouts.[55]

The poor prospects for high school dropouts threatens not just the American economy or even the political system, but also America itself, a country known for the opportunity it affords all its citizens. President Obama, who made three references to the problem in his first year in office, clearly recognized the importance of this issue. In his most recent remarks before the U.S. Chamber of Commerce on March 1, 2010, Obama stated:

> For America to compete and to win in the 21st century, we know that we will need a highly educated workforce that is second to

none. And we know that the success of every American will be tied more closely than ever before to the level of education that they achieve. The jobs will go to the people with the knowledge and the skills to do them—it's that simple. In this kind of knowledge economy, giving up on your education and dropping out of school means not only giving up on your future, but it's also giving up on your family's future and giving up on your country's future.

Graduating from high school is an economic imperative. That might be the best reason to get a diploma, but it's not the only reason to get a high school diploma . . . high school dropouts are more likely to be teen parents, more likely to commit crime, more likely to rely on public assistance, more likely to lead shattered lives. What's more, they cost our economy hundreds of billions of dollars over the course of a lifetime in lower wages and higher public expenses.

So this is a problem we cannot afford to accept and we cannot afford to ignore. The stakes are too high—for our children, for our economy, and for our country. It's time for all of us to come together—parents, students, principals and teachers, business leaders and elected officials from across the political spectrum—to end America's dropout crisis.[56]

The president speaks for many Americans, educators, and leaders in their belief that improving the U.S. educational system will improve economic and social outcomes of American youth and the international competitiveness of the U.S. economy. But a word of caution is in order. As economist Henry Levin noted in his 1994 essay, *Can Education Do It Alone?* past politicians, academics, and citizens have also viewed education as the key to improving America's economy and international competitiveness.[57] Yet, he argues, the impacts of education on labor market outcomes, public assistance, and crime are overstated because they ignore important complementary conditions or inputs that influence education's payoff and must be in place if future benefits are to be realized, such as employment opportunities for more productive workers. He points out that in the past, a few noted academics expressed similar skepticism about the simple connection many politicians made between education and America's competitiveness. One of them, noted scholar and University of California President Clark Kerr, stated in 1991, "Seldom in the course of policymaking in the United States have so many firm convictions held by so many been based on so little convincing proof."[58]

Despite this caution that the benefits of addressing America's dropout crisis depend on other actions, no one doubts the need to solve it, and to do so requires understanding its causes, a topic I address in the next two chapters.

6

UNDERSTANDING WHY STUDENTS DROP OUT

Why do students drop out of school? Are they unaware of the many benefits of completing high school and the severe consequences of not doing so? Or are they aware, but are uninfluenced by them? Instead, are they influenced by more immediate concerns, such as getting a job, having a baby, or escaping a dull and perhaps threatening school environment? Or are they effectively pushed out of school by boring and irrelevant classes, uncaring teachers and administrators, and unreasonable requirements and policies?

Understanding why students drop out of school is the key to designing effective interventions to help solve this critical and costly problem. Yet identifying the causes of dropping out is extremely difficult. Like other forms of educational achievement, such as test scores and grades, dropping out of school is likely influenced by an array of factors, some immediately preceding departure from high school and others occurring years earlier in middle and even elementary school. These factors may be related to the characteristics and experiences of the students themselves as well as the characteristics and features of their environment—their families, their schools, and the communities in which they live.

One way to identify the causes of dropping out is by examining theories and conceptual models used to explain educational achievement. Scholars from a number of disciplines—psychology, anthropology, sociology, and economics among them—have developed theories and conceptual models to explain why some students are more successful in school than other students, where student success may be measured by grades, test scores, educational attainment, or dropping out. Some theories focus especially on dropping out, while others explain dropping out as part of a larger phenomenon of student achievement. Some theories focus on an individual perspective that considers the role that individual characteristics—such as demographics, school experiences, attitudes, and behaviors—play in dropping out. Other theories focus on the role played by institutional characteristics—families, school, and communities. As we demonstrate below, both perspectives are useful and, indeed, necessary to understand this complex phenomenon.

Another way to identify the causes of dropping out is by examining empirical studies, in which researchers employ two primary methods. One method is to simply ask students who have already dropped out the reasons they did so. Researchers can either present dropouts with a list of reasons and ask them to identify all the reasons that contributed to their decision to quit school, or they can simply ask them why and then develop a list of reasons for the many responses they receive. Although the reasons dropouts report for leaving school may be illuminating, they typically focus on the more immediate and recent factors relating to their experiences in high school, not the more distant factors that may underlie or contribute to those more immediate experiences. Also, the stated reasons frequently ignore factors in the students' environment that may have also contributed to those more immediate experiences. And because respondents are recalling events from the past, their recollections may be faded or inaccurate. Finally, since students often report many reasons for quitting school, it is hard to sort out the relative importance of any specific factor, which would be useful in designing interventions.

The other method is to use data sets, typically containing a large number of variables about students and their families, schools, and communities, to estimate statistical models that predict whether students drop out or graduate. This method allows researchers to isolate the effects of each variable in the model while controlling for the effects of the other variables, generating an estimate of the independent influence of a particular variable. Such variables are sometimes called *predictors* because they can be shown to predict the likelihood of dropping out or of graduating. Yet this method is also limited because it cannot control for all of the possible factors or variables that may affect the outcome of dropping out or graduating. It also cannot determine a causal relationship between any factor and the outcome. Nonetheless, the method does allow researchers to identify *potentially* causal factors that could be considered in designing interventions.

This chapter reviews alternative models that have been developed to explain why students drop out. From existing models I then develop a new conceptual model of the dropout process and use this framework to review the empirical literature. I first review studies that have examined the reasons dropouts report for leaving school. In the next chapter, I then review studies that have identified the salient factors that predict whether students drop out or graduate from high school. The discussion is augmented with in-depth case studies that document the experiences of actual students.

The Process of Dropping Out

In Chapter 3, dropping out was characterized as a status, an event, and a process. To understand why students drop out, it is most useful to consider dropping out as a process that culminates in students' either quitting or finishing high school. Researchers have developed a number of models to explain the process of dropping out and the underlying factors that contribute to it. In fact, some scholars have also characterized dropping out as a "symptom," in recognition of the role and importance of these underlying factors: "Dropping out of high school is overrated as a *problem* in its own right—it is far more appropriately viewed as the end result or *symptom* of other problems which have their origin much earlier in life."[1] Researchers have also developed models to explain some of the factors that figure prominently into the process of dropping out, particularly school engagement. Finally, researchers have examined the role of context or settings in shaping various aspects of adolescent development, including dropping out.

Alternative Models of Dropping Out

Scholars have proposed a number of models to explain the process of dropping out of school. The models differ with respect to the specific constructs they employ and the relationship among them in portraying the process of dropping out. Some models focus specifically on dropping out, while others attempt to explain student outcomes in general, with dropping out representing only one. Most of the models focus on the individual perspective and identify a number of general types of factors: prior school experiences, particularly academic performance (grades, test scores, etc.); behaviors, including academic (e.g., doing homework), cognitive (exerting effort), and social (getting along with teachers and classmates); and psychological conditions, such as self-esteem and identification with school. While there is a fair amount of overlap in the models, they differ with respect to the specific factors (italicized in the discussion below) that are thought to exert the most influence on dropping out and the specific process that leads to that outcome.

FINN'S MODELS. In a widely cited review of the literature published in 1989, psychologist Jeremy Finn proposes two alternative, developmental models to explain dropping out.[2] The first, which he labels the "frustration-self-esteem" model, posits that the initial antecedent to school withdrawal is early *school failure*, which in turn leads to low *self-esteem* and then *problem behaviors* (skipping class, truancy, disruptive behavior, and juvenile delinquency). Over time, problem behaviors further erode school performance, which leads to further declines in self-esteem and increases in problem behaviors. Eventually, students either voluntarily quit school or are removed from school because of their problematic behavior.

The second model Finn labels the "participation-identification" model. In this model, the initial antecedent to withdrawal is the lack of *participation* in school activities (classroom participation, homework, and participation in the social, extracurricular, athletic, and governance aspects of the school), which in turn leads to *poor school performance* and then to less *identification* (a sense of "belonging" and "valuing") with school. Over time, the lack of identification with school leads to less participation, poorer school performance, less identification with school, and eventually dropping out of school.

Both of Finn's models include three types of factors: school performance, behaviors, and psychological conditions. The models differ in the specific behavioral and psychological factors they highlight: the "frustration-self-esteem" model focuses on problem behaviors and self-esteem, while the "participation-identification" model focuses on participation and identification.

LIFE-COURSE MODELS. A number of long-term longitudinal studies have been conducted in the United States to track the educational experiences and outcomes of small, local samples of children. These studies have developed and tested empirical models of the dropout process to determine the direct and indirect effects of various early and late factors on whether students dropped out or completed high school. Because of their long-term perspective, some scholars refer to these studies as life-course models.

In their study of 1,242 children enrolled as first graders in public and parochial schools in the poor, black community of Woodlawn in Chicago in the 1966–67 school year, Margaret Ensminger and Anita Slusarcick examined how variables within five domains—family background, family educational expectations and values, parent-child interaction concerning school, the social integration of the family in terms of school, and the child's cognitive and behavioral performance in school—predicted whether children dropped out or graduated from high school.[3]

In their study of 205 Euro-American families with varied living arrangements (two-parent families, single mothers, cohabitating couples, and communal and group living arrangements) from California that started in 1974–75, Helen Garnier, Judith Stein, and Jennifer Jacobs examined the direct and indirect influence of nonconventional family lifestyles and values, cumulative family stresses, and family socioeconomic status on school performance and motivation, adolescent stress and substance use, and, ultimately, school dropout.[4]

In their study based on data from the Baltimore Beginning School Study—a panel study of 661 children who entered first grade in twenty Baltimore city schools in the fall of 1982—Karl Alexander, Doris Entwisle, and Nader Kabbini present and test a model of dropping out from a life-course perspective that views dropping out as a long-term "process of progressive academic disengagement."[5] Their model focuses on three types of factors— students' school experiences (school performance, grade retention, and track-like placements), students' personal resources (what they label "engagement behaviors" and "engagement attitudes"), and parental attitudes, behaviors, and support—in several developmental periods of students' school careers: first grade, elementary years (grades two through five), middle school (grades six through eight), and early high school (grade nine).

In two studies based on data from the Chicago Longitudinal Study—an ongoing investigation of 1,569 low-income, minority children born in 1979 or 1980 who grew up in high-poverty neighborhoods of Chicago—Arthur Reynolds, Suh-Ruu Ou, and James Topitzes develop a conceptual model designed to test five hypotheses of the various pathways that preschool participation affects such long-term outcomes as educational attainment and juvenile delinquency.[6] In their model, preschool participation is hypothesized to directly affect school performance (cognitive ability, retention), social adjustment, and family support, which in turn affect school support and motivation in middle grades, which in turn affect educational attainment and delinquency in later adolescence.

TINTO MODEL.   Another useful theoretical perspective in explaining dropout behavior is a widely acknowledged theory of institutional departure at the postsecondary level developed by sociologist Vincent Tinto.[7]

Tinto focuses on the role of the institutional environment in influencing students' adjustment and ultimately their departure decision. The process of departure is first influenced by a series of personal attributes, which predispose students to respond to different situations or conditions in particular ways. These personal attributes include *family background, skills and abilities,* and *prior school experiences,* including *goals* (intentions) and *motivation* (commitments) to continue their schooling. Once students enroll in a particular school, two separate dimensions of the institution influence whether a student remains there: a social dimension that deals with the *social integration* of students with the institution and to the value of schooling, and an academic dimension that deals with the *academic integration* or engagement of students in meaningful learning. Both dimensions are influenced by the informal as well as the formal structure of the institution. For example, academic integration may occur in the formal system of classes and in the informal system of interactions with faculty in other settings.

These two dimensions can have separate and independent influences on whether students leave an institution, depending on the needs and attributes of the student, as well as external factors. To remain in an institution, students must become integrated to some degree in either the social system or the academic system. For example, some students may be highly integrated into the academic system of the institution but not the social system. Yet as long as their social needs are met elsewhere and their goals and commitment remain the same, such students will remain in the same institution. Likewise, some students may be highly integrated into the social system of the institution, but not the academic system. But again, as long as they maintain minimum academic performance and their goals and commitment remain the same, such students will remain in the same institution.

Tinto's model offers several insights into the process of institutional departure, which can involve either transferring to another school or quitting school altogether. First, it distinguishes between the commitment to the goal of finishing school and the commitment to a particular institution, and how these commitments can be influenced by students' experiences in school over time. Some students who are not sufficiently integrated into their current school may simply transfer to another educational setting rather than drop out, if they can maintain their goals and commitment to schooling more generally. Other students, however, may simply drop out rather than transfer to another school if their current school experiences severely diminish their goals and commitment to schooling. Second, it suggests that schools can have multiple communities or sub-cultures to accommodate and support the different needs of students. Third, it acknowledges the importance of external factors that can influence student departure. For example, external communities, including families and friends, can help students better meet the academic and social demands of school by providing necessary support. External events can also change a student's evaluation of the relative costs and benefits of staying in a particular school if other alternatives change (e.g., job prospects).

Drawing on Tinto's model, Katherine Larson and I developed and tested a model that found that higher levels of both academic engagement (e.g., doing homework) and social engagement (e.g., attending school, participating in school activities) reduced the likelihood of dropping out of high school.[8]

WEHLAGE MODEL. Drawing on their research on at-risk students and programs as well as Tinto's model, Gary Wehlage and his colleagues developed a model to explain dropping out and other high school outcomes that focuses on the contribution of school factors.[9] In this model, student outcomes are jointly influenced by two broad factors: *school membership* (or social bonding) and *educational engagement.*

Social bonding, which is critical to connecting students to the school, has four aspects: "A student is socially bonded to the extent that he or she is attached to adults and peers, committed to the norms of the school, involved in school activities and has belief in the legitimacy and efficacy of the institution."[10] Drawing on Tinto's work, they then identify four common impediments to school membership: *adjustment* to a new and often larger and more impersonal school setting; *difficulty* in doing more rigorous academic work; *incongruence* between students' values, experiences, and projected future and the school's goals and rewards; and *isolation* from teachers and peers in both academic and social experiences, something very similar to Tinto's concept of academic and social integration.[11]

Educational engagement refers to the "psychological investment required to comprehend and master knowledge and skills explicitly taught in school."[12] They then identify three impediments to educational engagement: (1) schoolwork is not extrinsically motivating for many students because achievement is not tied to any explicit and valued goal; (2) the dominant learning process pursued in schools is too abstract, verbal, sedentary, individualistic, competitive, and controlled by others (and therefore not intrinsically motivating), as opposed to concrete, problem-oriented, active, kinesthetic, cooperative, and autonomous; (3) classroom learning is often stultifying because educators are obsessed with the "coverage" of the subject matter, which makes school knowledge superficial and intrinsically unsatisfying, preventing students from gaining a sense of competence.[13]

MODELS OF DEVIANCE.   All the models presented thus far have viewed dropping out as a process influenced largely by experiences and conditions occurring within the school. Yet some models did suggest connections to outside influences. In his self-esteem model, Finn acknowledged the negative influence of peers on problem behavior in school. And Tinto identified out-of-school factors, such as working or ties with family and friends outside of school, as influencing students' integration in college. Social scientists in such fields as psychology, sociology, economics, and criminology have focused on a range of deviant behaviors—including juvenile delinquency, drug and alcohol abuse, and teenage parenting and childbearing—during adolescence and their relationship to school dropout.[14]

Sara Battin-Pearson and her colleagues identified five alternative theories of dropout that differently conceptualize the process and the salient influences of dropping out.[15] The first model, *academic mediation theory*, posits that all predictors of dropping out, including deviant behavior, low social bonding, and family background, are mediated by poor academic achievement. In the remaining four models, poor academic achievement only mediates some of the effects of the other predictors, so that at least some predictors also exert a direct influence on dropping out. In the second model, *general deviance theory*, several types of deviant behavior—juvenile delinquency, drug and alcohol use, smoking, and teenage pregnancy—exert a direct influence on dropping out. In the third model, *deviant affiliation theory*, bonding with antisocial or delinquent friends exerts a direct influence on dropping out. In the fourth model, *family socialization theory*, poor family socialization, as related to parental expectations, family stress, and parental control, exerts a direct influence on dropping out. And in the fifth model, *structural strains theory*, demographic factors, such as race, ethnicity, and family socioeconomic status, exert a direct influence on dropping out. In addition to general models of deviance, criminologists have developed a number of alternative theories to explain why involvement with the juvenile justice system may be detrimental or beneficial to subsequent delinquent behavior and school dropout.[16]

The Role of Engagement

Student engagement figures prominently in the process of dropping out. In fact, in an early review of the research literature published in 1987, I suggested, "Dropping out itself might be better viewed as a process of disengagement from school, perhaps for either academic or social reasons, that culminates in the final act of leaving."[17] Similarly, in her study of students in two California continuation high schools, Deirdre Kelly preferred to use the term *disengagement* to either *dropout*, which she argued put inordinate blame on the student's agency, or *pushout*, which put inordinate blame on schools.[18] Student engagement is also an important precursor to other aspects of school performance, particularly academic performance in the classroom. Because of its importance, scholars have proposed a number of models to explain student engagement.

In a follow-up to his work on at-risk students and programs, Gary Wehlage and his colleagues, Fred Newman and Susie Lamborn, developed a model of student engagement in academic work, which they define as "the student's *psychological investment* in and *effort* directed toward learning, understanding, or mastering the knowledge, skills, or crafts that academic work is intended to promote."[19] As they point out, because engagement is an inner quality of concentration and effort, it is not readily observed, so it must be inferred from indirect indicators such as the amount of *participation in academic work* (attendance, amount of time spent on academic work), *interest*, and *enthusiasm*. They further suggest that engagement is related to but differs from motivation, a subject of long-standing concern to educational psychologists:

> Academic motivation usually refers to a general desire or disposition to succeed in academic work and in the more specific tasks of school. Conceivably students can be motivated to perform well in a general sense without being engaged in the specific tasks of school. Engagement in specific tasks may either precede or presume general motivation to succeed. By focusing on the extent to which students demonstrate active interest, effort, and concentrations in the specific work that teachers design, engagement calls special attention to the contexts that help activate

underlying motivation, and also to the conditions that may generate new motivation.[20]

They posit that engagement in academic work is largely influenced by three major factors: "students' underlying *need for competence,* the extent to which students experience *membership* in the school, and the *authenticity* of the work they are asked to complete."[21] They identify a number of factors that influence school membership and authentic work similar to those identified by Wehlage and his colleagues in their model of student dropout.

In 2004, the National Research Council issued a report, *Engaging Schools: Fostering High School Students' Motivation to Learn,* which similarly made the distinction between motivation and engagement in schoolwork.[22] The committee that issued the report stated that engagement involved both observable behaviors (actively participating in class, completing work, taking challenging classes) and unobservable behaviors (effort, attention, problem solving, and the use of metacognitive strategies) as well as emotions (such as interest, enthusiasm, and pride in success), similar to how Newman, Wehlage, and Lamborn characterized it. But unlike Newman and his colleagues, the committee developed a model in which the effect of the educational context (such as instruction, school climate, school organization, school composition, and school size) on engagement is mediated by three psychological variables: students' beliefs about their *competence* and *control (I can),* their *values* and *goals (I want to),* and their sense of *social connectedness* or *belonging (I belong).* This model incorporates more explicit aspects of student motivation, although other theories of motivation include additional psychological factors.[23] James Connell and James Wellborn, for example, developed a model that postulates that children are motivated to engage in learning activities that meet three psychological needs for *autonomy, competence,* and *relatedness.*[24]

Both the Wehlage and National Research Council models focus on engagement in academic work. But as Tinto and Finn suggest in their models, participation and integration in school can take place in other arenas besides the classroom. So while academic engagement may be sufficient to improve academic achievement, engagement in other areas of the school may be equally valuable in getting students to stay in school.

In their extensive review of research literature, Jennifer Fredericks, Phyllis Blumenfeld, and Alison Paris identify three dimensions of this broader concept of engagement: (1) *behavioral engagement,* which represents behaviors that demonstrate students' attachment and involvement in both the academic and social aspects of school, such as doing homework and participating in extracurricular activities like athletics or student government; (2) *emotional engagement,* which refers to students' affective reactions to their experiences in school and in their classes, such as whether they are happy or bored; and (3) *cognitive engagement,* which represents mental behaviors that contribute to learning, such as trying hard and expending effort on academic tasks.[25] In a more recent review, James Appleton, Sandra Christenson, and Michael Furlong identify a myriad of definitions and measures of engagement that help illuminate the various dimensions of the concept, but also make it difficult to collect and use consistent information on engagement to design interventions.[26]

The Role of Context

The models presented thus far focus largely on dropping out as a process influenced by a broad array of individual factors including attitudes, behaviors, and school performance. Yet these factors and students' experiences more generally are shaped by three settings or contexts where youths spend their time: families, schools, and communities. Increasingly, social scientists have come to realize the importance of these settings in shaping child and adolescent development. In psychology, for example, Urie Bronfenbrenner's influential book, *The Ecology of Human Development,* helped to focus the attention of psychologists on how the various contexts of the family, schools, peer groups, and communities shape all aspects of adolescent development—physical, psychological, cognitive, and social—as well as how relationships between context and development change over time.[27]

The importance of context was further emphasized by the National Research Council Panel on High-Risk Youth in its 1993 report, *Losing Generations: Adolescents in High-Risk Settings,* which argued that too much emphasis had been placed on high-risk youth and their families, and not enough on the high-risk settings in which they live and go to school:

> The work of this panel began as an attempt to better understand why some adolescents are drawn to risky life-styles while others, similarly situated, engage in only normal adolescent experimentation. As our work progressed, however, we become convinced that a focus on individual characteristics of adolescents would

contribute to the overemphasis of the last two decades on the personal attributes of adolescents and their families at the expense of attention to the effects of settings or context. We concluded that it was important to right the balance by focusing on the profound influence that settings have on the behavior and development of adolescents.[28]

Social scientists have long recognized the critical role that context plays in understanding such phenomena as poverty, racial inequality, gang behavior, and unwed motherhood.[29] Context also plays an important role in understanding why students drop out of school.

A Conceptual Framework of the Dropout Process

Drawing on existing theoretical and empirical research, I constructed a conceptual framework for understanding the process of dropping out and graduation, as well as the salient factors underlying that process. The framework, illustrated in Figure 6.1, considers dropping out and graduation as specific aspects of student performance in high school and identifies two types of factors that influence that performance: individual factors associated with students, and institutional factors associated with the three major contexts that influence students—families, schools, and communities.

Individual factors can be grouped into four areas or domains: educational performance, behaviors, attitudes, and background. Although the framework suggests a causal ordering of these factors, from background to attitudes to behaviors to performance, the various models of dropout and engagement discussed earlier indicate a less linear relationship. In particular, the relationship between attitudes and behaviors is generally considered to be more reciprocal; for example, initial attitudes may influence behaviors, which in turn may influence subsequent attitudes (as suggested by Tinto's model). The factors listed within each group represent conceptual categories that may be measured by one or more specific indicators or variables.

The first domain is educational performance. The framework posits three interrelated dimensions of educational performance: (1) academic achievement, as reflected in grades and test scores; (2) educational persistence, which reflects whether students remain in the same school or transfer (school mobility) or remain enrolled in school at all (drop out); and (3) educational attainment, which is reflected by progressing in school (e.g.,

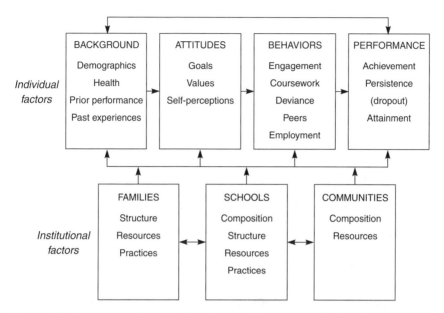

Figure 6.1. A conceptual model of student performance in high school.
Source: Russell W. Rumberger and Sun Ah Lim, *Why Students Drop Out of School: A Review of 25 Years of Research* (Santa Barbara: California Dropout Research Project, 2008), http://Cdrp.Ucsb.Edu/Dropouts/Pubs_Reports.Htm#15 (accessed January 17, 2011).

earning credits and being promoted from one grade to another) and completing school by earning degrees or diplomas. Educational attainment depends on both persistence and achievement. That is, students who either interrupt their schooling by dropping out or changing schools or have poor academic achievement in school are less likely to progress in school and to graduate.

The second domain consists of a range of behaviors associated with educational performance. The first factor is student engagement, which we list in the behavioral group even though some conceptions of engagement, as discussed earlier, can have attitudinal (emotional) as well as behavioral components. Other behaviors that have been identified in the research literature include course-taking, deviance (misbehavior, drug and alcohol use, and childbearing), peer associations, and employment.

The third domain consists of attitudes, which we use as a general label to represent a wide range of psychological factors including expectations, goals, values, and self-perceptions (e.g., perceived competence, perceived autonomy, and perceived sense of belonging).

The last domain consists of student background characteristics, which include demographic characteristics, health, prior performance in school, and past experiences, such as participation in preschool, after-school activities, and summer school.

The framework further posits that these individual-level characteristics are influenced by three institutional contexts—families, schools, and communities—and several key features within them: composition, structure, resources, and practices.

The framework identifies a vast array of factors that influence the decision to drop out of school. Do research studies provide empirical support that any of these factors matter? The answer is yes. Below we review studies of the reasons dropouts report leaving school. In the next chapter we review statistical studies of predictors of dropping out.

The Reasons Students Report for Dropping Out

A number of studies have examined the reasons students report for leaving school. One of the most recent and influential was *The Silent Epidemic*, by John Bridgeland, John DiIulio, and Karen Burke Morison from Civic Enterprises.[30] The report was based on data collected in 2005 from four focus groups of ethnically and racially diverse sixteen- to twenty-four-year-olds in Philadelphia and Baltimore, and interviews (primarily face-to-face) with 467 ethnically and racially diverse dropouts ages sixteen to twenty-five from twenty-five different locations across the United States.[31] As the authors note, the data are not a representative sample of dropouts, "but they do offer reflections from a broad cross-section of the very people who are most affected by the silent epidemic of high school dropouts in America."[32]

The study provides a vivid portrait of dropouts (or at least of those who were interviewed) and why they report dropping out. Among dropouts in the study:

- 88 percent had passing grades and 62 percent had Cs and above.
- 58 percent dropped out with just two years or fewer to complete high school.
- 66 percent said they would have worked harder if expectations had been higher.

- 81 percent recognized that graduating from high school was vital to their success.
- 74 percent would have stayed in school if they had to do it over again.[33]

While respondents reported a wide variety of reasons, and typically more than one reason for dropping out, the top five were:

- Classes were not interesting (47 percent).
- Missed too many days and could not catch up (43 percent).
- Spent time with people who were not interested in school (42 percent).
- Had too much freedom and not enough rules in my life (38 percent).
- Was failing in school (35 percent).[34]

Participants in the focus groups elaborated on these reasons. In discussing their schools and classes, many students reported that high school was "boring, nothing I was interested in," or "it was boring . . . the teacher just stood in front of the room and just talked and didn't really like involve you."[35] Another student reflected, "The work wasn't even hard . . . once I figured I wasn't going to get any learning done in there, there wasn't any need to go."[36] Other students reported that events outside of school interfered with their schooling: 32 percent left to get a job, 26 percent became a parent, and 22 percent had to help their family.[37]

In another report—based on a nationally representative, longitudinal study of high school sophomores—students who dropped out between 2002 and 2004 reported twenty-one specific reasons (they could report more than one), with the top ten being:

- Missed too many school days (44 percent).
- Thought it would be easier to get GED (41 percent).
- Getting poor grades/failing school (38 percent).
- Did not like school (37 percent).
- Could not keep up with schoolwork (32 percent).
- Got a job (28 percent).
- Was pregnant (28 percent among females only).
- Thought couldn't complete course requirements (26 percent).
- Could not get along with teachers (25 percent).
- Could not work at same time (22 percent).[38]

The reasons fell into three major categories: any school reason (83 percent); any family reason (34 percent); and any job reason (35 percent). The study also found that the reasons varied widely by gender: 89 percent of males reported any school reason versus 75 percent of females; 25 percent of males reported any family reason versus 45 percent for females; and 41 percent of males reported any job reason versus 28 percent for females.[39]

Together, these studies identify a wide range of factors that contribute to students' decisions to drop out of school. Some involve students' own attitudes, behaviors, and performance, such as missing school, getting poor grades, or not liking school. Others involve features of schools and classrooms, such as classes not being interesting. Still others involve factors outside of school, such as getting a job or becoming pregnant. The findings underscore the point that dropping out is the result of not simply one specific factor, but an array of factors. They also suggest that different factors may be relevant to different students. The review of predictors of dropping out in the next chapter reinforces that point.

7

PREDICTORS OF DROPPING OUT

Scholars have conducted literally hundreds of studies to understand
how and why students drop out or graduate from high school. They
have also employed a wide range of research methodologies. Some scholars have conducted in-depth case studies of students and schools to understand the process of dropping out and the salient factors that contribute
to that process.[1] Other scholars have used local and national data sets to
develop and test elaborate statistical models to identify the unique contribution of specific factors on whether students drop out or graduate
from high school.[2] Still other scholars have combined both approaches—
so-called mixed-methods studies—to provide a more complete picture
of what factors are most important and how they actually operate in students' lives.[3]

It should be pointed out that, for the most part, scholars are unable to
establish definitively that any specific factor "causes" students to drop out.
Even complex, statistical models with large numbers of variables are often
unable to control for other, unobservable factors that may contribute to
the dropout process and that may mediate the effects of other variables.
However, in recent years, new research designs and statistical models have
allowed stronger, more causal inferences to be made.[4] Yet because most
existing studies do not employ these techniques, it is more accurate to refer to these various factors as "predictors" or "influences" rather than "causes"
of dropping out.

Using the framework developed in the previous chapter, this chapter
reviews the research literature on predictors of dropping out. The discussion below draws heavily on a 2008 review of the research literature I
conducted with Sunah Lim that examined 389 separate analyses found in
203 statistical studies published in academic journals between 1983 and
2007.[5] Findings from the review are augmented with findings from more

recent statistical studies, qualitative and case studies, and published reports from research centers and other organizations. The qualitative studies are particularly important in providing a "human face" to dropping out and showing how these statistical factors appear in students' lives.

Individual Predictors of Dropping Out

Individual predictors of dropping out fall into four broad areas or domains: (1) educational performance, (2) behaviors, (3) attitudes, and (4) background.[6] In keeping with a view of dropping out as a process, scholars have also identified at what point or when in the process of dropping out various factors matter. For instance, at what grade level or how many years prior to dropping out do various aspects of educational performance, behaviors, or attitudes predict whether students are likely to drop out of school? Knowing what and when various factors are most predictive can be used to better design interventions to target students in the right areas and at the right time to improve their chances of staying in school and graduating. Accordingly, I first discuss predictors of dropping out within the four main domains and then by grade level—high school, middle school, elementary school, and preschool.

Educational Performance

Research suggests that educational performance, especially during high school, is the single most important predictor of whether students drop out or graduate from high school. In fact, as the conceptual framework developed in the previous chapter illustrated, dropping out and graduation themselves are two indicators or aspects of educational performance that are related to yet other aspects. At least four of those other aspects of educational performance in high school affect the likelihood of dropping out or graduating: failed courses; retention; poor grades and test scores; and student mobility.

FAILED COURSES. To graduate from high school, students have to earn credits in a specified set of courses determined by the state and the district. Typically, students must pass a certain number of classes—usually one-quarter of the required courses—each year to get promoted to the next grade level. If students fail to earn sufficient credits, they are retained in the same grade until they earn enough credits to be promoted. Although students need to earn credits each year of high school to graduate, research has shown that ninth grade—the first year of high school for most students—is the most critical.

The importance of passing ninth grade as a predictor of high school graduation is well documented by Elaine Allensworth and John Easton in their 2005 research study of the Chicago Public Schools, *The On-Track Indicator as a Predictor of High School Graduation*.[7] They constructed an "on-track" indicator to identify students who earned enough credits in ninth grade to be promoted to tenth grade, and who failed no more than one semester of a core academic course. Among students who entered ninth grade for the first time in 1999, 59 percent were on track and 81 percent of them graduated four years later, whereas only 22 percent of the off-track students graduated four years later.[8] In other words, on-track students were three and a half times more likely to graduate in four years than off-track students.[9] Course failures alone were also highly predictive (although less so than the combined indicator): 83 percent of the students who failed no core classes in ninth grade graduated within four years, compared to 63 percent of students who failed only one class.[10] The study further found that the on-track indicator was a better predictor of high school graduation than students' test scores in eighth grade or their background characteristics, such as socioeconomic status (SES).

Failing classes at any point in a student's high school career can lessen the chances of graduating. A study of students from the graduating class of 2005 in the Los Angeles Unified School District found that over three-quarters of all students failed at least one academic class during high school, with each course failure reducing the likelihood of graduating by 10 percentage points.[11] Passing algebra was especially telling: students who passed algebra by the end of ninth grade—and only 38 percent did so—were twice as likely to graduate as students who failed to do so (70 percent versus 35 percent).[12]

Course failures in middle school also predict high school graduation. In fact, in the Los Angeles study, half the students failed at least one course in middle school, and each course failure reduced the likelihood of graduating by 20 percentage points or double the 10-percentage-point effect of failing courses in high school.[13]

Another study of district graduation rates in three California school districts—Fresno Unified, Long Beach Unified, and San Francisco Unified—found that failing classes in seventh grade (2000–01) was highly predictive of whether students graduated five years later (2005–06).[14] In Long Beach, for example, nearly one-third of all students failed two or more classes and among those, only 37 percent graduated, whereas 75 percent of students with no failed classes graduated.

RETENTION.   Course failure is closely linked to retention. In high school, students who fail to earn enough credits during the academic year are typically retained in their grade level. And ninth grade—the first year of high school for most students—is when the most course failure, and hence retention, occurs. Although no national data exist on retention in high school, comparing ninth grade enrollment with eighth grade enrollment in the previous year suggests a ninth grade retention rate of more than 10 percent.[15] State data show similar rates. Data from Texas show that 12.3 percent of ninth graders were repeating that grade level in 2008–09, compared to 6.8 percent in grade ten, 5.6 percent in grade eleven, and 7.8 percent in grade twelve.[16] Ninth-grade retention rates for black and Hispanic students were significantly higher—15 percent for blacks and 16.2 percent for Hispanics.[17] In some urban school districts, retention rates are even higher. A recent study found that more than one-third of ninth graders from the fall 2001 entering class in the Los Angeles Unified School District failed to get promoted to the tenth grade.[18]

While retention in high school is based on passing classes, retention in elementary and middle school is based on other criteria. Many states and districts have established policies for retaining students in elementary and middle schools based on academic achievement.[19] In Texas, for example, state statute stipulates, "A student may be promoted only on the basis of academic achievement or demonstrated proficiency of the subject matter of the course or grade level."[20] The provisions of the law further stipulate that students in grades three, five, and eight pass the state reading and mathematics tests to be promoted. But promotion and retention decisions can be, and often are, based on teacher and parent input as well. In fact, research indicates there is substantial variation not only in retention criteria among schools, districts, and states, but also in actual practices and impacts.[21] Nationally, about 13 percent of eighth graders in 2007 had been retained at some point since kindergarten.[22] Census data from 1997 indicate that the highest retention rate in elementary school occurs in grade one.[23]

The research literature finds that retention is a consistent predictor of whether students graduate. Most studies have examined the effect of retention in elementary school or the combined effects of retention in elementary and middle school.[24] A review of seventeen studies published between 1970 and 2000 found that retention was associated with higher dropout rates and lower graduation rates.[25] In our review of the dropout literature, thirty-seven of the fifty analyses found that retention in elementary or middle school increased the odds of dropping out of high school. Only two analyses examined the effects of high school retention on dropout, and neither found any significant effects, although both studies controlled for a number of other strong predictors including criminal activity and prior retention.[26] One of those studies, based on data from the Baltimore Beginning School Study (see Chapter 6), found that even after controlling for school performance, parent attitudes, pupil behaviors, and public attitudes in elementary school, middle school, and the first year of high school, retention at all grade levels except ninth grade were significant predictors of dropping out.[27] Interestingly, retention in middle school was the most powerful predictor—students retained in middle school were ten times more likely to drop out than nonretained middle school students, while students retained in first grade were seven times more likely to drop out than nonretained first-grade students.[28]

Of course, just because students who fail courses or are retained in school are more likely to drop out or less likely to graduate does not prove that course failures or retention cause those outcomes. A number of underlying factors—low academic background, poor engagement, a lack of motivation, misbehavior—could contribute to both retention and dropping out.

The interrelationship among factors contributing to retention and dropout can be illustrated from the story of Richard, one of the 100 Latino students in Harriett Romo and Toni Falbo's longitudinal study of high school students in Austin, Texas:

> Richard flunked the seventh grade. This event was brought about largely by the turmoil of his early middle school years. He described his problems as stemming from his drug use, his "drinking problem," and his friends, a group of friends who he claimed got him involved in gang activities, including at least one drive-by shooting. While in middle school, he drank heavily and smoked marijuana with his friends.[29]

To the extent that research studies can control for such underlying factors, the studies can make a stronger causal claim about the impact of retention.

The longitudinal study based on the Baltimore Beginning School Study, described in Chapter 6, is one example. Yet there may be other unobserved differences between retained and nonretained students that could account for differences in dropout and graduation rates. One study that used more sophisticated statistical techniques to model the effect of retention on eventual labor market earnings found that retention could actually lower dropout rates and improve earnings, although the results were not statistically significant.[30] Overall, however, the research evidence finds that retention is a strong predictor of high school dropout and graduation.

A related predictor of dropping out is being over-age. The most common age of students entering the ninth grade is fourteen. According to U.S. Census data, 67 percent of all students enrolled in the ninth grade in October 2008 were fourteen years old or younger, which means about one-third could be considered over-age.[31] However, students in states with late school entry dates could be age fifteen at the time of the census survey and thus not be over-age. Many, but not all, students who are over-age when entering high school have been retained at some point in their school careers, most likely during elementary school. Others may be over-age because they live in a state where the compulsory schooling age begins at age 7 rather than age 5 or 6 (see Table 2.2) or because their parents held them back prior to starting school, a growing practice known as "redshirting."[32]

In the Los Angeles study, about 17 percent of the ninth-grade students were over-age and they were half as likely to graduate as students who were normal age, even after controlling for other academic and demographic factors.[33] In our review of the literature, three of the four analyses found that over-age students in high school were significantly more likely to drop out and less likely to graduate than students who were not over-age.

Many of the statistical studies we reviewed were based on two national longitudinal studies of grade cohorts, such as the National Education Longitudinal Study (NELS), which tracked a cohort of eighth-grade students beginning in the spring of 1988.[34] In such studies, students who are older than other students in their grade level are, in effect, over-age (even if they are not directly identified as such) and could have been retained. At the high school level, thirty-one of the fifty-two studies found that older students were more likely to drop out and less likely to graduate than younger students.

ACADEMIC ACHIEVEMENT. One of the most widely studied predictors of high school dropout and graduation is academic achievement. Two indicators of academic achievement—*test scores* and *grades*—have been shown to predict whether students drop out or graduate from high school. In the Los Angeles study, almost three-quarters of the ninth-grade students scored at the two lowest proficiency levels ("basic" or "far below basic") on either the math or English language arts portions of the California Standards Tests, and only 46 percent of them graduated from high school four years later, compared to 71 percent of the students who scored at the basic, proficient, or advanced levels of the exam.[35]

Middle school achievement also predicts high school graduation. The study of three California districts found that the overall graduation rates were 55 percent for Fresno, 59 percent for Long Beach, and 65 percent for San Francisco.[36] The study then predicted the probability of graduating for a typical student across the three districts (i.e., a student with the same average academic and demographic characteristics) with different GPAs in seventh grade. In all three districts, students with a 4.0 seventh-grade GPA had similar probabilities of graduating—about 80 percent.[37] But the probability of graduating with lower GPAs varied more widely. Students with a 2.0 seventh-grade GPA had only about a 40 percent probability of graduating in Fresno, a 45 percent probability of graduating in San Francisco, and about a 56 percent probability of graduating in Long Beach. Students with a 1.0 seventh-grade GPA had only about a 25 percent probability of graduating in Fresno, a 30 percent probability of graduating in San Francisco, and about a 40 percent probability of graduating in Long Beach.

Because students in California must also pass the state high school exit exam in order to graduate, the study also examined how test scores predicted whether students passed the exam on the first try in tenth grade. A "typical" student with the lowest score at the highest proficiency level (a score of 425) on the English Language Arts California Standards Test (CST) had more than a 95 percent probability of passing the exam on the first try in all three districts.[38] But again the probability of passing the exam with lower scores varied more widely among the three districts. Students with the lowest score at the "basic" proficiency level (a score of 300) had only a 60 percent probability of passing the test on the first try in Fresno but an 85 percent probability of passing in Long Beach and San Francisco. Students with the lowest score at the "below basic" proficiency level (a score of 250) had only a 30 percent probability of passing the test on the first try in Fresno, but a 70–75 percent probability of passing in Long Beach and San Francisco.

In our review of the research literature, we identified more than 200 analyses that examined the effects of test scores and grades on dropout or graduation.[39] A majority of the studies found that academic achievement had a statistically significant effect on the likelihood of dropping out or graduating from high school, although the effects were stronger in middle and high school. At the high school level, thirty of the fifty-one analyses found that higher test scores lowered the risk of dropping out or, conversely, lower test scores increased the risk of dropping out. Of the forty-five analyses that examined grades, thirty found that high grades reduced the risk of dropping out. At the elementary level, the majority of studies did not find a direct effect of grades or test scores on graduation. Yet a 2011 national study of 4,000 students and their parents found that students who were not reading proficiently by third grade were four times greater than proficient readers to not graduate from high school.[40] In general, however, the results of previous studies are more consistent (e.g., a higher proportion of statistically significant effects) for grades than for test scores, which reflects the fact that test scores represent students' ability usually measured on one or two days, whereas grades reflect students' effort as well as their ability throughout the school year. In that sense, grades are a more "robust" measure of academic achievement than test scores.

STUDENT MOBILITY. Another predictor of dropping out is student mobility. Although most students begin and end their high school careers at a single school, some students attend more than one, for varying reasons.[41] Some students voluntarily leave one school to attend another more suited to their needs or interests. Some students are forced to change schools for other reasons, such as behavior problems or expulsion. The large and growing number of alternative high schools generally serves both groups of students. Other students are forced to change schools because their families change residences. And still other students are forced to change schools because of school district, city, and federal policy changes. For example, the Chicago Public School system closed 44 regular high schools and opened 136 new high schools between 1995 and 2007, forcing many students to change schools.[42]

Both dropping out and transferring schools can be considered forms of persistence, with student mobility the less severe form of nonpersistence. In fact, persistence can be considered along a continuum: students may quit school permanently or temporarily—in the latter case, they simply reenroll, often at another school, and the amount of time they are out of school may vary from short to long.

Student mobility during high school is widespread. A national study that tracked a sample of eighth-grade students through high school found that 27 percent of the students attended more than one high school.[43] Another study based on the same data also found that students were twice as likely to change schools during the first two years of high school as during the last two years.[44] In the Los Angeles study, 18 percent of the students who remained in the district attended more than one high school.[45] Assuming that at least some of the students who left the district reenrolled in another school, the total mobility rate was probably much higher.

The research literature shows that student mobility during high school generally increases the odds of dropping out and decreases the odds of graduating. In the Los Angeles study, only 32 percent of the students who attended more than one high school graduated, compared to 57 percent who attended a single high school.[46] The previously referenced national study found, for example, that students who changed high schools once were 50 percent more likely to not graduate, and students who changed high schools two or more times were more than twice as likely to not graduate as students who remained in the same high school, even after controlling for other predictors.[47] Yet the second previously referenced study found that while student mobility during the first two years of high school increased the odds of dropping out by tenth grade, students who were able to remain enrolled until the tenth grade were actually less likely to drop out during the second two years of high school.[48] The study also found that mobility during the last two years of high school did not increase the odds of dropping out.

Mobility is even more widespread during elementary and middle school. Analyzing data from a national longitudinal study of students who entered kindergarten in the fall of 1998, the U.S. Government Accountability Agency found that almost two-thirds had attended two or more schools by eighth grade and that almost one-third had attended three or more.[49] Another national study of high school sophomores in 2002 found that more than half had made one nonpromotional school change since first grade, and almost one in five had made three or more nonpromotional school changes.[50]

The research literature shows that student mobility, at least during middle and high school, affects school dropout and graduation. At the high school level, ten of fourteen analyses in our review of the literature found that student mobility increased the odds of dropping out or decreased the odds of graduating. At the middle school level, nine of thirteen analyses found a positive effect of student mobility.[51] At the elementary level, eight of fourteen analyses found a significant relationship. One possible reason for the stronger impact at the secondary level is that the secondary students are more sensitive to the disruptions to their friendship networks.[52] Of course, the significant association between mobility and dropout may not be causal; instead, it could be due to preexisting, common factors, such as academic achievement or misbehavior, which influence both mobility and dropout. Nonetheless, even studies that control for a host of preexisting factors, such as student achievement, conclude that there is likely at least some causal association between mobility and educational performance.[53]

Research suggests that students suffer psychologically, socially, and academically from mobility. One in-depth study of student mobility in California found that both students and educators reported that transferring to a new school affected students' personality or psychological well-being.[54] Jim, who changed schools twice during high school and twice during middle school, commented:

> Moving and changing schools really shattered my personality. I feel like there's all these little things I picked up from all of the different schools and I feel all disoriented all the time. There's no grounding. I always just feel like I'm floating. It's psychological damage, really . . . because you never feel like a complete person. That's how I feel—I feel fragmented. Every time I moved I felt less and less important.[55]

Students also reported impacts on friendship networks, as a student named Luy stated:

> When I first moved here, I did not know anybody. I was very lonely. Nobody really helped me at school when I first came. Most of my friends are still back at the old high school. I do not have good friends to support me here like back at the old high

school. . . . I just want to get out of here as quickly as possible and go on to something else.[56]

Finally, some students reported that mobility had a direct effect on staying in school. One such student, Alejandra, commented, "During one of the breaks in schooling, I didn't go back to school for about a month-and-a-half. . . . I never got to the 12th grade—that was one consequence of mobility. I didn't finish. It's just the lack of me wanting to go back to school."[57] Interviews with school personnel also revealed some of the reasons mobile students have trouble finishing—they sometimes get placed in classes that do not contribute to high school completion or they get placed in classes where the curriculum differs from their previous school—a condition referred to as "curricular incoherence."

Behaviors

Student behavior is critical to success in school. Students must exhibit positive behaviors and avoid negative behaviors. A number of behaviors have been shown to predict whether students drop out or graduate from high school. Some behaviors reflect what students do in school, while others reflect what students do outside of school.

ENGAGEMENT.   In the earlier discussion about the process of dropping out, engagement emerged as an important part of the educational process and a powerful precursor to dropping out. Students who are engaged in school, whether in the academic arena or the social arena, are more likely to attend, to learn, and eventually to finish high school; students who are disengaged are not. Research studies have measured engagement in several ways, but no matter how it is measured, the level of engagement predicts dropping out.

One of the most direct and visible indicators of engagement is attendance. To graduate, students not only must enroll in school, but they must attend school as well. Yet some students have poor attendance, and such students are more likely to drop out. In our review of the literature, thirteen of the nineteen analyses found that high absenteeism predicted dropping out.[58]

Some students exhibit poor attendance long before they drop out. Kathy, one of the 100 Latino students tracked by Romo and Falbo in their longitudinal study in Austin, Texas, illustrates this pattern:

Kathy did not drop out of high school because she was pregnant. She had not been attending school regularly for years before she became pregnant. From the school's perspective, Kathy had an "attendance problem." Going to school every day and attending all her classes throughout the day was something Kathy did not do, at least from the time she entered this school district, when she was placed in the eighth grade.[59]

Another study that tracked one cohort of seventh-grade students from a small urban school district in Massachusetts in the 1980s found that dropouts exhibited a pattern of deteriorating attendance (as well as academic and behavior grades) as early as fourth grade.[60]

Poor attendance may contribute to dropping out differently for males and females. In Deirdre Kelly's study of two continuation high schools in the San Francisco Bay area, girls' poor attendance was less likely to cause alarm among teachers and administrators, at least among the more quiet, seemingly "nice" girls.[61] At the same time, girls were twice as likely to transfer to continuation high schools because of truancy problems as boys, while boys were much more likely to transfer because of discipline problems. Kelly characterized gender differences this way: "Generally, girls tend to slip in and out of the schooling system, both continuation and conventional high schools, more quietly than boys."[62] Kelly also noted gender differences in the reasons for cutting school, with girls more likely to cut class to be with boyfriends, and boys more likely to cut class to drink and take drugs.[63]

Another indicator of engagement is participation in extracurricular activities. Most, but not all, middle and high school students participate in extracurricular activities. In 2002, more than 50 percent of high school sophomores reported participating in athletics, 11 percent in cheerleading and drill teams, 22 percent in music, and 10 percent in hobby clubs.[64] In 2007, 59 percent of eighth graders reported participating in sports, 40 percent in drama or music, and 32 percent in clubs.[65] In our review of the literature, fourteen of the twenty-six analyses found that participation in extracurricular activities reduced the odds of dropping out. At the middle school level, only two out of seven analyses found that involvement in extracurricular activities reduced the odds of dropping out of high school. Participation in sports, especially among males, shows more consistent effects than participation in other extracurricular activities or participation in extracurricular activities more generally.[66] Yet sports can also help engage girls, as Linda, one of the girls in Romo and Falbo's Austin study, explained: "I think sports have kept me in school a lot, you know, 'cause I'm always, I mean, I try so hard to pass, you know, have passing grades."[67]

Other research studies created multiple indicators of student engagement, often based on information from student and teacher questionnaires. For example, one 2009 study of high school sophomores created an index of academic engagement based on four questions from the student survey:

- How many times during the first semester or term were you late to school?
- How many times during the first semester or term did you cut or skip class?
- How many times during the first semester or term were you absent from school?
- How much do you agree or disagree that the subjects you're taking are interesting and challenging?[68]

The least engaged students (those who ranked in the bottom third of this index) were five times more likely to drop out (12.1 percent versus 2.5 percent) than the most engaged students (those who ranked in the top third).[69] Several recent studies have found that various behavioral, cognitive, and affective aspects of engagement predict dropping out, with students demonstrating different engagement trajectories through their adolescent years.[70]

Of the thirty-five analyses that examined student engagement in high school in our review of the literature, twenty-four found that higher levels of engagement reduced the likelihood of dropping out or increased the likelihood of graduating from high school. Of the thirty-one analyses that examined student engagement in middle school, ten found that engagement reduced dropout and increased graduation from high school. At the elementary level, only one of three analyses found that engagement reduced the odds of dropping out of high school.[71]

COURSE-TAKING. Students must take a prescribed number and specific types of courses to graduate from high school. As pointed out in Chapter 2, students' course-taking patterns determine not only which subjects they will learn, but also the quality of the teachers and the rigor of instruction they receive.

A number of studies have examined the relationship between course-taking, mainly in high school, and the propensity to drop out or graduate from high school. Thirteen analyses examined the impact of being in an academic or college track, and eight of them found that students in an academic track were less likely to drop out and more likely to graduate. Six analyses also examined the impact of taking vocational courses in high school, and two found that students who took vocational courses were less likely to drop out. Thus, the evidence generally finds that by itself, course-taking has little influence on dropping out or graduating.

DEVIANCE.   To remain in school, students must devote their time and attention to their schoolwork and their school activities. They must also get along with their teachers and fellow students. But some students engage in a number of deviant behaviors in and out of school that increase their risk of dropping out. These deviant behaviors include misbehaving in school, delinquent behavior outside of school, drug and alcohol use, and sexual activity and teen childbearing. The research literature finds that engaging in any of these behaviors increases the risk of dropping out of school.

Most research studies have examined the effects of one or two specific indicators of deviant behavior—such as criminal activity or childbearing—on dropping out. Two exceptions are related studies that developed general constructs of deviance based on data from a longitudinal study of 808 fifth-grade students attending eighteen elementary schools from high-crime neighborhoods of Seattle.[72] One study developed three indicators of deviance when the students were age fourteen (with most in eighth grade) based on self-reported items from confidential student interviews about drug use, violent behavior, and nonviolent behavior over the previous year.[73] The other study constructed four indicators of deviance at age fourteen: school problems, delinquency, drug use, and sexual activity.[74] Controlling for a host of other predictors, including prior academic achievement and family background, both studies found that deviant behavior at age fourteen had a significant and direct effect on early school dropout by age sixteen, and later high school failure (dropout and months of missed school) in grade twelve. A third study measured eight types of classroom and school misbehavior, including fighting, alcohol and marijuana use, and gang involvement, and found that students displaying two or three misbehaviors were almost three times as likely to drop out as students displaying none or one, while students who displayed four or more misbehaviors were five times as likely to drop out.[75]

The most common indicator of deviant behavior is *school misbehavior.* Several qualitative studies of adolescents document the relationship between dropout, school misbehavior, and crime. For example, in his study of youth crime and work in three neighborhoods of Brooklyn, Mercer Sullivan noted, "In addition to their general lack of academic success, their gradual estrangement from school was hastened by the involvement of these youth in fighting and crime."[76]

In our review of the research literature, forty-nine analyses examined the relationship between misbehavior and dropping out, with most of the analyses focusing on the high school level. Among the thirty-one analyses at the high school level, fourteen found that misbehavior was significantly associated with higher dropout and lower graduation rates.[77] Of the seventeen analyses at the middle school level, fourteen found that misbehavior in middle school was significantly associated with higher dropout and lower graduation rates in high school. The one analysis that focused on the elementary school level found that misbehavior in elementary school increased the odds of dropping out of high school.[78]

Misbehavior may contribute to dropping out in a number of ways. Students who misbehave may be suspended or even expelled, as Sullivan documents in his study.[79] They also may be transferred to alternative school settings. In Kelly's study of two continuation high schools, two-thirds of the boys were sent to such schools because of discipline problems.[80]

Misbehavior can also take place outside of school, where it is generally referred to as *delinquency* or sometimes as juvenile delinquency. In our review of the research literature, we identified nineteen studies that investigated the relationship between delinquency and dropout. Most of them relied on students' self-reports of delinquent behavior. For example, one recent study asked survey participants to identify six types of delinquent acts: (1) intentional destruction of property, (2) theft of items worth less than $50, (3) theft of items worth more than $50 (including automobiles), (4) other property crimes, (5) attacking someone with intent to seriously hurt them, and (6) selling illegal drugs.[81] The studies also identified whether students were arrested and whether their crimes were adjudicated through the court system. One of the challenges in these and other studies of out-of-school behaviors is whether the behavior, in this case delinquency, is causally related to dropping out, or whether both behaviors are caused by a common set of underlying factors. That is, delinquent adolescents may differ from their non-delinquent peers in ways that may not be easily identified or measured in empirical studies, which could result in biased estimates of the effects of delinquency on dropout behavior. To address this concern, researchers utilized a variety of statistical controls and techniques to derive more accurate estimates. The most rigorous techniques involved using longitudinal data to select non-arrested youth and measure their student characteristics at an initial point in time, to identify delinquent behavior at a later point in time, and then to determine dropout status at a still later point in time.[82] Such a technique establishes a more causal sequencing of the connection between delinquency and dropout. Nonetheless, the technique still cannot control for other, unobserved differences between delinquent and non-delinquent youth.

Eleven of the nineteen analyses in our review of the research found that delinquent youth were more likely to drop out of school than non-delinquent youth.[83] But three of the four studies that examined involvement in the justice system found that being arrested had a separate and generally larger effect on dropping out of school than delinquency.[84] For example, one study found that a first-time arrest during high school doubled the odds of dropping out, while a court appearance nearly quadrupled the odds of dropping out.[85]

While statistical studies can document specific factors linking delinquency to dropping out, they cannot reveal the underlying process and its complexity the way in-depth case studies can. Sullivan documents the developmental nature of criminal activity among youth in all three neighborhoods and the interrelated influences of their neighborhoods, the social life of their communities, and their own agency. Youths in all three neighborhoods demonstrated common patterns of peer-recruited, exploratory theft during the early and middle teens (thirteen through sixteen) that progressed to robbery in middle and late teens and to drug dealing, work-related theft, and adult-related criminal operations in later teens and thereafter.[86] Yet their involvement in these activities developed according to their individual entrepreneurial calculations of the relative worth of engaging in school, work, or crime vis-à-vis their actual opportunities for these activities, opportunities that varied widely among three neighborhoods in terms of employment, crime, and local social control (which was a result of general poverty and joblessness).[87]

Another form of deviant behavior is *drug and alcohol use.* Forty-two analyses examined the relationship between drug and alcohol use and dropout. Of the twenty-three of these analyses that focused on high school behavior, seventeen found that drug or alcohol use during high school was associated with higher dropout rates, whereas eleven of the nineteen middle school analyses found that drug or alcohol use during middle school was associated with higher dropout rates. Since alcohol, drug, and tobacco use are often correlated, some studies have attempted to determine whether some of these activities are more detrimental than others. Two studies found that tobacco use during middle school had a direct effect on the odds of dropping out, while drug (marijuana) use did not.[88] Another study found that both marijuana and tobacco use had direct effects on dropping out, but marijuana use had the stronger effect.[89]

A final indicator of deviant behavior that has been studied in the research literature is *teen parenting and childbearing.* The research literature generally finds that teenage parenthood, and particularly childbearing among adolescent females, is related to a series of negative socioeconomic consequences, including low educational attainment and earnings, and higher rates of poverty and welfare.[90] For example, only 51 percent of teen mothers earned a high school diploma by age twenty-two, compared to 89 percent of young women who had no teen births.[91] The major challenge in this research is to establish a causal connection between teenage childbearing and dropout behavior. In other words, does teenage childbearing cause adolescent females to drop out, or are there other, unobservable factors that contribute to both childbearing and dropping out of school? To try to estimate the causal connection between childbearing and dropout behavior, social scientists have employed a number of innovative techniques, including comparing the educational outcomes of sisters who had children as teenagers with those who did not and comparing the educational outcomes of teen mothers with teens who miscarried.[92]

A number of the studies have examined the effects of parenting and childbearing during high school. Of the sixty-two analyses in our review that focused on high school predictors, fifty found that teenage parenting and childbearing increased the odds of dropping out or reduced the odds of graduating. In studies that compared males and females, teenage parenting had more serious consequences for females than for males.[93] Some studies also found the impact was more detrimental among black females than among white or Hispanic females.[94] Two studies that used more advanced statistical techniques to control for unobserved differences between teen mothers and girls who delayed childbearing until adulthood (age twenty or greater) found smaller, but still significant, effects in at least some of their analyses, compared to studies that controlled only for observed differences.[95] However, two other studies that compared teen mothers with teens who miscarried did not find that teenage childbearing had a statistically significant effect on obtaining a high school diploma.[96] Finally, a more recent 2009 study that took into account the timing of the miscarriage together with other community-level characteristics found that teenage childbirth reduced the probability of receiving a high school diploma by 5 to 10 percentage points. This finding is consistent with an earlier study that found that delaying childbearing from ages sixteen to seventeen until ages twenty to twenty-one would increase the probability that children would graduate from high school by about 10 percent.[97]

PEERS.   Peers exert a powerful influence on adolescents.[98] They influence students' social and academic behaviors, attitudes toward school, and access to resources (social capital) that may benefit their education.[99] Yet research fails to find a direct connect between peers and dropout or graduation. One reason is that studies measure peer relationships in different ways. Some studies examined students' perceived popularity, with one study finding no effect[100] and two other studies finding that students who perceived themselves to be popular and important among their peers in eighth grade were actually *more* likely to drop out of school by tenth grade, after controlling for a host of other factors.[101] Other studies found that generally having friends or having friends who are interested in school reduces the odds of dropping out.[102] The most consistent finding is that having deviant friends—friends who engage in criminal behavior, for instance—or friends who have dropped out increases the odds of dropping out, with such associations appearing as early as seventh grade.[103]

One specific form of peer influence is gangs. Nationally, 5 percent of youth are involved in gangs, with rates exceeding 10 percent in some localities.[104] Gangs are a common feature of American cities and their schools. In a 2005 national survey, 24 percent of students ages twelve to eighteen reported that gangs were present in their school, with the figure jumping to 39 percent for students attending urban public schools.[105] Research has identified numerous risk factors in five developmental domains—individual, family, school, peer group, and community—that predict gang involve-ment.[106] The complexity of gang involvement is well illustrated in Mark Fleisher's in-depth study of a gang known as the Freemont Hustlers in Kansas City, Missouri, in the mid-1990s:

> *Dead End Kids* shows that gang behavior doesn't happen be-cause a 14-year-old is bored after school and needs something to do. A youth gang isn't an after-school play group. Rather, the label "youth gang" is a metaphor for a number of behaviors, in-cluding truancy, school failure, kids' disenfranchisement from parents and the mainstream community, drug use, drug selling, street violence, and teenage pregnancy and parenthood. How-ever, every behavior has a cause and a context, and it was the search for the causes and socioeconomic contexts of youth-gang behavior that was the purpose of the Freemont research. . . . Freemont research shows that the causes of gang behavior are often invisible and run deep inside the social dynamics and eco-nomics of gang kids' families, neighborhoods, and communities.[107]

EMPLOYMENT. Employment during high school is widespread in the United States. A study of 2002 high school sophomores found that 26 per-cent were working, and 6 percent reported working more than twenty hours per week.[108] Employment rates among sixteen- to seventeen-year-olds ex-ceeded 30 percent in 2000.[109] Although working during high school may impart valuable experience as well as provide income to students, working too much can interfere with participating in school and doing homework.[110]

A large body of research has examined the relationship between high school employment and a wide range of outcomes, including work-related outcomes (e.g., work attitudes and motivation), family-related outcomes (e.g., participation in family activities), school-related outcomes (e.g., grades, absenteeism, engagement), and deviancy.[111] One of the challenges in con-ducting this research, as noted previously in studies of other behaviors, is establishing a causal connection between employment and these outcomes. Students who choose to work may differ from their nonworking peers in observed and unobserved ways that make it difficult to establish whether work itself contributes to these outcomes. For example, studies have found that students who work are generally less engaged in school prior to working, so working may be as much a symptom as a cause of subsequent outcomes.[112]

To address this problem, some researchers have used longitudinal designs and statistical techniques to better establish the causal link between working and subsequent outcomes.[113]

Research suggests that working during high school isn't necessarily detrimental to staying in school. In fact, some studies found that students who work fewer than twenty hours consistently throughout their high school careers were actually less likely to drop out of school, compared to students who worked more hours or did not work at all.[114] But a number of research studies also find that students who worked more than twenty hours a week were significantly more likely to drop out.[115] Also, some studies found that the impact of working in high school varies by race, gender, and type of job held, while other studies found similar effects among gender, racial, and academic backgrounds of students and local labor market characteristics.[116]

One recent study examined the impact of work intensity by "matching" students with similar propensities to work more than twenty hours a week using a variety of background characteristics measured before students began working in grades nine and ten.[117] The authors found that the odds of dropping out were 50 percent higher for students who worked more than twenty hours per week than for those who worked less, but working more than twenty hours a week did not affect the odds of dropping out for those students who had a high propensity to work long hours in the first place.

Attitudes

Students' beliefs, values, and attitudes are related to both their behaviors and their performance in school. These psychological factors include motivation, values, goals, and a range of students' self-perceptions about themselves and their abilities. These factors change over time through students' developmental periods and biological transformations, with the period of early adolescence and the emergence of sexuality being one of the most important and often the most difficult period for many students:

> For some children, the early-adolescent years mark the beginning of a downward spiral leading to academic failure and school dropout. Some early adolescents see their school grades decline markedly when they enter junior high school, along with their interest in school, intrinsic motivation, and confidence in their

intellectual abilities. Negative responses to school increase as well, as youngsters become more prone to test anxiety, learned help-lessness, and self-consciousness that impedes concentration on learning tasks.[118]

Although there is a substantial body of research that has explored a wide range of student beliefs, values, and attitudes, far less research has linked them to student dropout.[119]

One exception is a detailed longitudinal study of a cohort of first-grade students from the Baltimore Beginning School Study (BSS) that began in the fall of 1982.[120] That study collected a wide range of attitudinal and behavioral information on students in grades one through nine from student self-reports, teachers' reports, and school report cards. The attitudinal information included self-expectations for upcoming grades, educational attainment, self-ability and competence, and measures of psychological engagement ("likes school") and school commitment.[121] The attitudinal items (as well as the behavioral items) were all combined into a single construct for grade one, grades two through five, grades six through eight, and grade nine. This allowed the researchers to examine not only the relative effects of student attitudes and behaviors overall relative to other predictors, but also their relative effects over different grade levels or stages of schooling. The authors found that while the effects of behavioral engagement on school dropout appear in grade one, even after controlling for the effects of school performance and family background, student attitudes do not demonstrate a separate effect on school dropout until grade nine, with behavioral engagement still showing the stronger effect.[122] Interestingly, the authors also found that the correlation between attitudes and behaviors increases from grade one to grade nine.[123]

GOALS.   To succeed in school, students must value school. That is, they have to believe that it will be instrumental in meeting their short-term or long-term goals.[124] Most students, as well as their parents, believe that education is the key to a better job and a better life. Yet some youths, such as those profiled in Sullivan's study of youth crime and work in Brooklyn, were more ambivalent about whether finishing high school would lead them into better jobs in their neighborhoods where such jobs were scarce and their fathers and older brothers were employed in jobs that did not require educational credentials.[125]

Most students and their parents also expect not only to complete high school, but also to finish college. In 2002, more than 80 percent of high school sophomores (and their parents) expected that they would earn a bachelor's degree or more advanced college degree.[126]

Students who expect to graduate from college are much less likely to drop out of high school than students who expect only to finish high school. Among high school sophomores in 2002 who expected to earn a bachelor's degree, only 4 percent dropped out of high school, compared to 21 percent for students who expected only to complete high school.[127] These findings are confirmed in other research studies. In our review of the research literature, we identified eighty-two analyses that examined the relationship between educational expectations and school dropout. At the high school level, thirty-three of the forty-one analyses found that higher levels of educational expectations were associated with lower drop-out rates. At the middle school level, twenty-three of the thirty-eight analyses found the same relationship. Three analyses examined educational expectations in elementary school and none found a significant effect on high school dropout or graduation.

SELF-PERCEPTIONS.   To be successful in school, not only must students value school, but they also must believe they are capable of achieving success. Students' perceptions of themselves and their abilities are a key component of achievement motivation and an important precursor of student engagement.[128]

Research studies have examined a number of self-perceptions and their relationship to high school dropout and graduation. All of these perceptions are constructed as composite measures based on student responses to a number of questions about themselves. One such construct is *self-concept*, which is basically a person's conception of himself or herself.[129] Although self-concept can be viewed and measured as a general construct, scholars have come to realize that it is multidimensional and should be measured with respect to a particular domain, such as academic self-concept or self-concept with respect to reading. A related construct is *self-esteem*, which measures self-assessments of qualities that are viewed as important.[130] Another construct is *locus of control*, which measures whether students feel they have control over their destiny (internal control) or not (external control).

Poor self-perceptions can undermine motivation, thereby increasing the risk of dropping out, as Alice, one of the students in Romo and Falbo's

Austin study, explained after finding out she had been labeled as "at risk" by her school: "I don't really have too much belief in myself that I can really do it and I am more depressed about it. And then it just draws in my mind. And when I go to school, I mean, I just keep thinking about it."[131]

Although such perceptions are a central component of motivation for remaining in school, relatively few studies have found a direct relationship between any of these self-perceptions and dropping out. The most studied has been locus of control. Of the twenty-two analyses of locus of control in our review, only three analyses in three studies found a significant relationship with dropout, with students who had an external locus of control—the feeling of little control over one's destiny—showing a higher propensity to drop out, even as early as first grade.[132]

Background

A number of student background characteristics are linked to whether students drop out or graduate. They include demographic characteristics and health.

DEMOGRAPHICS.   Dropout and graduation rates vary widely by a number of demographic characteristics of students. As we illustrated in Chapter 3, dropout rates are higher for males than for females, and they are higher for blacks, Hispanics, and Native Americans than for Asians and whites. But what explains these differences? Are they related to differences in the levels or extent of salient factors, such as school performance, that have common effects on all demographic groups? Or do different factors affect dropping out for different demographic groups? Because of the widespread attention paid to racial and ethnic differences in educational achievement, and because some of these differences are related to other demographic and institutional factors that are discussed in the next section, we postpone the discussion of these differences until the end of the chapter. Here we focus on other demographic factors: gender, immigration, linguistic minority, and disability status.

Gender differences in dropout rates can be attributed to both common and different factors. The primary reason for dropping out reported by both males and females in one national study was "missed too many school days."[133] This suggests that poor school performance diminishes the prospects for completing high school for both girls and boys. Yet male and female dropouts also report different reasons. For example, 28 percent of female dropouts cite pregnancy as a reason for leaving school, whereas 34 percent of male dropouts cite getting a job (versus 20 percent for females).[134] Kelly's study of two continuation high schools in California, cited earlier, also suggests that the process of dropping out is different for girls than for boys, with girls demonstrating more "silent" aspects of disengagement, such as truancy, and boys demonstrating more visible aspects, such as fighting. Overall, the research suggests there are both common and unique factors that affect dropout and graduation rates among males and females.

The complexity of the relationship between gender and dropout is illustrated in our review of the statistical research literature. We identified almost 200 analyses that examined the relationship between gender and high school dropout and graduation. At the high school level, twenty-seven analyses found that females had higher dropout rates or lower graduation rates, fifty-five found no significant relationship, and twenty found that females had lower dropout rates or higher graduation rates.

One study I conducted illustrates how the relationship is affected by other factors in the analysis. After controlling for family and academic background, I found no significant relationship between gender and dropout but, after controlling for a variety of attitudes, behaviors, and indicators of educational performance in eighth grade, I found that females had higher dropout rates.[135] In general, studies in which the researchers controlled only for background characteristics showed that females had lower dropout rates or that there was no significant relationship, whereas studies in which the researchers controlled for attitudes, behaviors, and performance in school showed that females had higher dropout rates.

The relationship between gender and dropout behavior sometimes varies among subpopulations of students. For example, a study based on a national, longitudinal data set found that when using the entire sample, and in a subsample of whites, females had lower dropout rates, but in a subsample of blacks, females had significantly higher dropout rates.[136] Another study found that females had lower dropout rates when using the entire sample of census data and among subsamples of persons in central cities and suburbs, but higher dropout rates in rural areas.[137] This latter result illustrates how context may affect dropout rates, a topic we address in more detail later in this chapter.

Another demographic characteristic that has been examined in the research literature is immigration status. Almost 22 percent of elementary and secondary students are foreign-born or have foreign-born parents.[138] Foreign-born students have higher dropout rates than native-born students—among sixteen- to twenty-four-year-olds in 2007, dropout rates were 21 percent among foreign-born compared to 8 percent among native-born.[139]

In our review of the statistical research, twenty-six analyses examined the relationship between immigration status and dropout. Most analyses compared first-generation (foreign-born) and second-generation (at least one parent foreign-born) with third-generation (native-born students and parents) students. Some analyses examined the effects of immigration status on dropout for the entire population of students, while other studies examined its effects on different racial and ethnic subgroups. One study of an entire population of high school sophomores found that second-generation students had lower dropout rates than either first- or third-generation students,[140] while another study of an entire population of eighth-grade students found no differences in dropout rates between grades eight and ten by immigration status, after both studies controlled for family background characteristics.[141]

But the effects of immigration status vary among ethnic and racial groups. Four studies found that second-generation—and, in one study, early first-generation (under age six at arrival)—Hispanics had lower dropout rates than third-generation Hispanics.[142] Two studies found that the effect of nativity varied among Hispanic subgroups—one found that recent Mexican (Chicano) and Puerto Rican immigrants had higher dropout rates, but Cubans had lower dropout rates,[143] while the other found lower graduation rates among foreign-born Mexicans, but not among other Hispanic subgroups.[144] Another study also found lower graduation rates among foreign-born compared to second- and third-generation Mexicans.[145] Yet another study found no differences among Hispanic or nativity subgroups, after controlling for family socioeconomic status and language proficiency.[146]

Scholars have advanced a number of explanations of how and why immigration affects high school completion. Some researchers attribute the higher graduation rates among second-generation students to these students' having higher English skills than immigrant students, but also more optimism and motivation than third-generation students.[147] Others argue that differences in educational outcomes among immigrant groups can be explained by differences in social capital found in families, schools, and communities.[148] Still others, such as Angela Valenzuela in her study of

Mexican-American immigrants in a Houston high school, suggest a much more complex process where schools "fracture students' cultural and ethnic identities."[149]

Closely related to immigration status is English-language proficiency. Most immigrants come from non-English-speaking countries, so not only is proficiency in English an important skill for fully participating in school and the larger society, it is also a marker of acculturation.[150] This is especially true because few schools provide primary language instruction and effective bilingual education programs.[151] A number of studies demonstrate that immigrant students with higher English-language proficiency had lower dropout rates, even after controlling for a wide variety of additional factors.[152] Still another study found that biliterate Hispanics had higher graduation rates than not only other English-proficient and Spanish-dominant Hispanics but also non-Hispanic whites, after controlling for other factors.[153]

A final demographic characteristic is disability status. Students with disabilities have much higher dropout rates than students without disabilities. For example, data from a longitudinal survey of eighth graders found that the dropout rate for students with learning disabilities was 26 percent, and the dropout rate for students with emotional or behavioral disorders was 50 percent, while the dropout rate for students without disabilities was 15 percent.[154] Yet like other demographic factors, the effects of disabilities are mediated by other factors. One study found that test scores and high school grades explained higher dropout rates among students with learning disabilities.[155]

HEALTH.   Poor mental and physical health may be both a cause and a consequence of dropping out. Research viewed in Chapter 4 demonstrated that high school graduates have better health and incur lower health care costs than high school dropouts.

Poor health also contributes to dropping out. One study of more than 15,000 adolescents from the National Household Survey on Drug Abuse found that respondents who reported that they had excellent or very good health were less likely to drop out than respondents who reported good, fair, or poor health, net of other predictors.[156] Yet a 2010 review of the research literature finds that it is difficult to demonstrate a clear, direct connection between health conditions in childhood and adolescence, and high school dropout.[157] For example, the review found few adverse educational consequences to such childhood physical disorders as asthma and type 1 diabetes. There is stronger evidence that conditions such as early-onset psychiatric disorders and overweight may diminish learning and thus contribute to school dropout. For example, one study found that children who had emotional and behavioral problems at ages six to eight were less likely to graduate from high school, even after controlling for socioeconomic background.[158] In our review of the statistical research literature, a number of studies found that adolescents who reported symptoms of depression (feeling helpless, lonely, sad, etc.) were more likely to drop out, even after controlling for a number of other contributing factors, including academic performance and family background.[159]

Combining Factors

While it is useful to identify individual predictors of dropping out, it is also useful to understand how various factors jointly contribute to the process of dropping out. Researchers have used three approaches for combining factors: creating a composite index of risk; creating taxonomies to identify different types of dropouts; and testing structural models that link factors together.

RISK FACTORS.   A number of studies combined a series of factors into a composite index of risk. Some studies included only student factors,[160] while other studies included both student and family factors.[161] For example, one study based on a national longitudinal study of eighth-grade students created an "academic risk" index based on five factors: (1) average middle school grades below C, (2) retained between grades two and eight, (3) educational expectations no greater than high school, (4) sent to the office at least once in the first semester of grade eight; and (5) parents notified at least once of a problem with their child during the first semester of grade eight.[162] The study found that about one-third of the students had at least one risk factor and those students were twice as likely to drop out as students with no academic risk factors. Another study, based on institutional data from the Philadelphia Public Schools, created an index based on four factors measured in sixth grade that indicated whether the student: (1) attended school 80 percent or less of the time, (2) failed math, (3) failed English, and (4) received an out-of-school suspension.[163] This study found that students with at least one risk factor were half as likely to graduate as students with no risk factors. All five studies in our review of the statistical research found that academic (and in some cases academic and family) risk was a significant predictor of whether students graduated or dropped out of high school.[164]

TYPOLOGIES.   Another approach is to use various factors to create a typology that distinguishes different types or profiles of dropouts. One study of high school students in Montreal, Canada, identified four types of dropouts: (1) *quiet* dropouts (40 percent of dropouts), who demonstrated moderate to high levels of commitment and no evidence of school misbehavior; (2) *maladjusted* dropouts (40 percent), who demonstrated low commitment and poor school performance; (3) *disengaged* dropouts (10 percent), who demonstrated low commitment, average performance, and average to low levels of school misbehavior; and (4) *low-achiever* dropouts (10 percent), who demonstrated low commitment, very poor performance, and average to low levels of school misbehavior, but very poor school performance.[165]

STRUCTURAL MODELS.   Another approach for examining how various factors jointly influence the dropout process is to construct and test a structural model using a statistical technique known as structural equation modeling.[166] This technique allows researchers to examine the strength of the direct and indirect relationships among predictors and to estimate how well the resulting model "fits" the data. One recent study estimated a model based on the National Research Council report *Engaging Schools*, which suggested that dropping out is influenced by student engagement and a set of psychological antecedents. The estimated model is shown in Figure 7.1.

The study found that only two factors directly influence dropping out in high school: students with higher grades in tenth grade and students with higher levels of behavioral engagement (not absent, late, skipping classes, or getting into trouble) are less likely to drop out. Both behavioral engagement and cognitive engagement (works hard, puts forth effort) also influence dropping out through their effects on grades. In turn, affective engagement (likes school, finds classes interesting and challenging) affects both cognitive and behavioral engagement. Finally, three psychological antecedents— perceived competence, valuing school, and a sense of belonging—influence the three dimensions of engagement.

A number of other studies have estimated models of dropping out using this technique, including studies that incorporate predictors from early

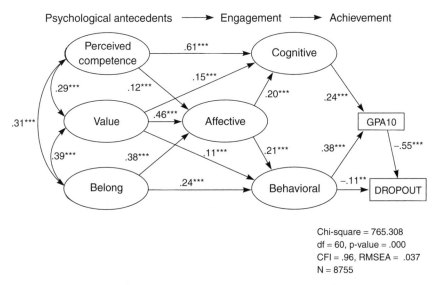

Figure 7.1. A structural model of dropping out. *Source:* Susan L. Rotermund, "The Role of Psychological Antecedents and Student Engagement in a Process Model of High School Dropout" (PhD diss., University of California, Santa Barbara, 2010).

childhood.[167] Together, these studies support the notion that dropping out is indeed a long-term process influenced by a wide variety of background, psychological, behavioral, and achievement factors.

Institutional Predictors of Dropping Out

While a large array of individual attitudes, behaviors, and aspects of educational performance influence dropping out and graduating, these individual factors are shaped by the institutional settings where children live—families, schools, and communities. Research has identified a number of factors within students' families, schools, and communities that influence whether students drop out or graduate from high school. As in the case of individual factors, it is difficult to verify a causal connection between institutional factors and dropping out, but research has demonstrated that a number of factors affect the odds that students will drop out or graduate from high school.

Families

Family background has long been recognized as the single most important contributor to success in school.[168] What is less clear is what aspects of family background matter and how they influence school achievement.[169] Although the research literature has identified a wide array of family factors that contribute to dropping out, three aspects appear to be most important: (1) family structure, (2) family resources, and (3) family practices.

STRUCTURE.   Family structure generally refers to the number and types of individuals in a child's household. In 2009, 71 percent of families in the United States with children under eighteen were married-couple families, 24 percent were female-headed families, and 6 percent were male-headed families.[170] Yet in-depth studies, such as the Fragile Families study discussed in Chapter 4, reveal much more complicated, fluid, and often disruptive family situations for many children in America during the course of their childhood.[171] For example, Salvador, one of the students in Romo and Falbo's Austin study, was born to a single mom who gave him to his sister to raise; then he reentered his mother's life as an adolescent after she had remarried, only to have his mother divorce his new stepfather shortly thereafter.[172] According to the authors, "This trauma, combined with his early history, led him to become deeply involved in gang life while in middle school. Gang behaviors—such as skipping classes, arriving late, not doing homework, and fighting on school grounds—interfered with his school work."[173]

Family structure affects the physical, social, and cognitive development of children through its relationship to other features of families, particularly its resources and parenting practices. For example, single-parent families, particularly ones headed by women, have lower incomes and are more likely to depend on public assistance. In 2009, 44 percent of female-headed families with children under eighteen were living in poverty.[174] Family practices that promote school achievement, such as monitoring and supervision, are also lower in single-parent families and stepfamilies, compared to two-parent families.[175]

The majority of the studies in our review of the statistical research found that students living with both parents had lower dropout rates and higher graduation rates, compared to students in other family living arrangements.[176] Other studies have examined the effects of changes in family structure, which the research literature has shown can have profound and devastating effects on children's economic, emotional, and social needs, as Salvador's story so clearly illustrates.[177] One study found that changes in family structure before the age of four actually increased high school graduation, while changes after that age reduced the high school graduation rate.[178] Another study found that students who had changed from living with both parents as eighth graders to living with only their mother or father four years later were more likely to drop out of high school.[179] Other studies have combined changes in family structure with other potentially stressful events (such as a family move, illness, death, adults entering and leaving the household, and marital disruptions) into a composite family stress index and found that higher levels of family stress increased the odds of dropping out.[180] A related measure of family stress—poor maternal mental health—has also been linked to dropout.[181]

Family structure is related to residential mobility. Not only is residential mobility common in the United States—with 10 percent of all households with school-age children (6 to 17 years of age) changing residences each year—but it is also more common in single-parent families. In 2008–09, female-headed households with school-age children were almost three times as likely to change residences as married-couple families with school-age children.[182] Mobility can be a stressful event for both adults and children, although it is often linked to problematic situations prior to moving itself, making the causal impact of residential mobility hard to detect.[183] Residential mobility is also associated with school mobility, whose effects we reviewed earlier. Both residential and school mobility can disrupt valuable social relationships for adults and children—so-called social capital (see discussion below)—that can impair family functioning and student school success.[184]

The majority of studies in our review of the statistical research found that residential mobility is associated with an increased risk of dropping out of school.[185] A more recent synthesis for thirteen studies found that children who moved three or more times had dropout rates three times higher than stable students, even after controlling for prior achievement and other factors.[186] Residential mobility at any grade level tends to increase the risk of high school dropout, with the risk increasing with each additional move. Even frequent moving before beginning elementary school appears to be detrimental. One study found that three or more residential moves between birth and first grade increased the odds of dropping out by about 70 percent for both girls and boys, independent of other factors.[187]

Another structural feature of families is size. Larger families may have fewer resources per family member to support education. In our literature review, of the 120 analyses that investigated the relationship between family size—measured by the number of siblings or the total number of family members in the household—and high school dropout and graduation, about half found that the odds of dropping out were higher in larger families than in smaller families.

Three specific living situations greatly reduce students' prospects for completing high school—homelessness, foster care, and juvenile justice.[188] Although homeless youth—who are estimated to currently number about 1.6 million—remain in the custody of their families, the families are typically poor and the children may experience stressors above and beyond those experienced by other poor children.[189] Only half of homeless children finish high school.[190] In contrast, children in the foster care and juvenile justice systems are under the legal authority of the government, yet often face myriad problems that impede their educational performance and reduce their prospects for completing high school.[191]

RESOURCES.   Family resources are critical for supporting the emotional, social, and cognitive development of children. Two types of types of family resources have been shown to promote success in school: (1) *financial resources* that can provide a richer home environment (more books, computers) and access to better schools and supplemental learning opportunities (after-school and summer programs, tutors, etc.); (2) *human resources* of parents, as reflected in their own education, that provide the means to directly improve the cognitive development of their children through reading, helping with homework, etc., and to influence their children's motivation and educational aspirations.

Research studies measure family resources in a number of ways. The most widely used indicator of family resources is *socioeconomic status* (SES), which is typically constructed as a composite index based on several measures of financial and human resources, such as both parents' years of education, both parents' occupational status, and family income.[192] A national study of high school sophomores found that students from the lowest quartile of SES were five times more likely to drop out of school (12.4 percent versus 1.8 percent) than students from the highest quartile of SES.[193] In our review of statistical research studies, the majority of analyses found that students from high SES families are less likely to drop out than students from low SES families.[194]

Our review also found that two other indicators of family resources, *parental education* and *family income*, also predicted whether students dropped out or completed high school. Childhood poverty, in particular, is a powerful predictor of adolescent and adult outcomes. A 2010 study that tracked a cohort of children from birth to age thirty found that children who were poor at birth—13 percent of all children, 8 percent of white children, and 40 percent of black children—were three times more likely than children who were not poor at birth to lack a high school diploma as young adults.[195]

Instead of examining the relationship between individual family predictors and school dropout, some studies have created composite measures of several indicators to determine their combined effects. For instance, one study created a social risk index based on five attributes of students and their families: (1) disadvantaged minority (black, Hispanic, or Native American), (2) linguistic minority, (3) household poverty, (4) single-parent household, and (5) mother or father failed to complete high school.[196] The authors found that the odds of dropping out of high school were 66 percent higher for students with at least one risk indicator, compared to students with no risk indicators, even after controlling for both eighth- and tenth-grade achievement and behaviors.

PRACTICES.   Fiscal and human resources simply represent the means or the capacity to improve the development and educational outcomes of children. This capacity is realized through the actual practices and behaviors that parents engage in. These practices, manifested in the relationships parents have with their children, their schools, and the communities, are what sociologist James Coleman labeled *social capital*.[197] Other researchers have labeled such practices *parental involvement* or *parenting style*.[198] Parenting practices include educational expectations (how much schooling they want or expect their children to get), within-home practices (supervision, helping with or monitoring homework), and home-school practices (participation in school activities, communication with the school).

Our review of the statistical research literature did not reveal a consistent, direct relationship between parenting practices and school dropout.

Only about half of the studies found that high parental expectations and positive parenting practices decreased the risk of dropping out of school.

Yet several studies found that multiple indicators of parenting practices at the secondary level reduced the risk of dropping out. One early study of 1980 high school sophomores found that four parenting practices (as reported by the students) during high school had significant effects on whether students dropped out or graduated: (1) whether their mother wanted them to graduate from college, (2) whether their mother monitored their school progress, (3) whether their father monitored their school progress, and (4) whether their parents supervised their schoolwork.[199] A more recent study of eighth graders from 1988 found four parenting practices that predicted whether students dropped out by grade twelve: (1) parental educational aspirations for their child in grade eight, (2) parental participation in school activities in grade eight, (3) parental communication with the school in grade twelve, and (4) a measure of intergenerational closure—how many parents of their children's friends do they know— which is a key component of social capital that provides a source of information, norms, expectations, and standards of behavior.[200]

These findings from large-scale statistical studies correspond very closely with the seven strategies that Romo and Falbo derived from their study of the 100 Latino adolescents and their parents in Austin:

1. *Parent in charge.* Parents of graduates took charge of their adolescent-age children, whereas parents of dropouts typically had no control over their children.
2. *Two-way influence.* Parents of graduates asserted their authority in ways that were respectful of the youths.
3. *Set limits.* Youths who graduated knew some things were non-negotiable, such as completing their schoolwork and staying out too late.
4. *Monitor student.* Youths who graduated knew that their parents "kept an eye on them."
5. *Draw the line with peers.* Parents of graduates made certain that their children were not influenced by peers who did not attend school or take their schoolwork seriously.
6. *Continuous message.* Youths who graduated got the same message, "Stay in school," from all family members often.

7. *Involved in school.* Youths who graduated knew their parents were involved in their schooling.

An indirect indicator of family environment more generally is whether a sibling dropped out. Several studies that examined this indicator found that students were more likely to drop out if they had a sibling who dropped out.[201]

Schools

It is widely acknowledged that schools exert powerful influences on student achievement, including dropout rates. But demonstrating how much influence schools exert and identifying the specific school factors that affect student achievement presents some methodological challenges. The challenge is underscored by the fact that students in the United States are highly segregated by race, ethnicity, family background, and prior achievement, which leads to widespread differences in observed school outcomes.[202] As a result, at least some of these observed differences in school outcomes are due to differences in the background characteristics of students, not the effectiveness of the schools. Fortunately, recent developments in statistical modeling have allowed researchers to more accurately estimate how much schools influence student achievement, after controlling for the individual background characteristics of students.[203] These developments have demonstrated that although student and family characteristics can explain most of the variability in student achievement, about 20–25 percent of the variability in student outcomes can be attributed to the characteristics of the schools students attend.[204] Nonetheless, as in the case of individual factors, it is hard to verify a causal relationship between school factors and dropout rates. Yet some studies employ more sophisticated techniques that can make strong causal inferences.[205]

Four types of school characteristics have been shown to influence student performance, including dropout and graduation rates: (1) student composition or characteristics of the student body, (2) resources, (3) structural characteristics, and (4) processes and practices. The first three factors are sometimes considered as "school inputs" by economists because they are largely "given" to a school and therefore not alterable by the school itself.[206]

STUDENT COMPOSITION.   Student characteristics influence student achievement not only at an individual level but also at an aggregate or social level. That is, the social composition of students in a school can influence student achievement, apart from the effects of student characteristics at an individual level.[207] In fact, famed sociologist James Coleman concluded from his study of American schools in 1966 that "the social composition of the student body is more highly related to achievement, independent of the student's own social background, than is any school factor," including school facilities and attributes of teachers.[208] More recent studies have indeed found that the social composition of schools can have as great an impact on student outcomes as individual background characteristics.[209]

Social composition may affect student achievement in two ways. First, it may simply serve as a proxy for other characteristics of schools, to the extent that those characteristics are correlated with social composition. For example, high-poverty and high-minority schools generally have more inexperienced teachers and suffer from high teacher turnover.[210] Second, student composition may impact student achievement directly—through peer effects that influence student achievement through peer learning, peer motivation, or peer social behavior.[211]

A number of studies have found that several dimensions of social composition—the average socioeconomic status of the students attending the school, the proportion of at-risk students (students who get poor grades, cut classes, have discipline problems, or were retained), the proportion of racial or linguistic minorities, the proportion of students who had changed schools or residences, and the proportion of students from nontraditional (not both parents) families—affect dropout rates above and beyond other school characteristics.[212] These studies support the notion that the effects of social composition operate at least partially through peer effects. However, some studies have shown that when peer groups (e.g., percentage of disadvantaged students in school) are treated as an endogenous factor—that is, unobserved factors both influence peer group membership and dropout— then peer groups do not exert an independent influence on dropping out.[213] Other studies found that after controlling for a number of structural, resource, and school practice variables, all the composition variables became insignificant.[214] Yet school practices themselves may be highly influenced by the school's student body composition, as a number of case studies of high schools point out.[215]

STRUCTURE.   Several structural characteristics of schools contribute to student performance—school location (whether the school is in an urban, suburban, or rural area), school size, and particularly type of school (public versus private). It is difficult to draw a causal connection between structural features of schools and student outcomes because the structural features of schools are highly correlated with each other and with other school inputs, mainly student composition and school resources. For example, in comparison with smaller schools, larger schools are more likely to be: public versus private, located in an urban versus suburban or rural community, and have larger versus smaller concentrations of ethnic and linguistic minorities and poor students.[216]

The research evidence is inconsistent on whether school location influences dropout rates. In our review of the research literature, some studies found that attending an urban school increased the odds of dropping out,[217] some studies found that dropout rates were actually lower in urban schools,[218] and still other studies found no significant effects.[219]

The research evidence is also inconsistent on the relationship between high school size and dropout or graduation rates. Some studies found that students were more inclined to drop out of large (greater than 1,500 students) high schools;[220] other analyses found that students were less likely to drop out of large schools,[221] and still others found that school size had no significant effects.[222] One reason for the mixed effects is that the relationship between school size and student outcomes may be nonlinear, with medium-size schools (500–1,200 students) more effective than either small or large schools.[223] Another reason is that there may be offsetting features of schools associated with size, with large schools offering more curriculum and program options, but also having a poorer social climate.[224] School size may have different and conflicting effects on different school outcomes; one recent study found that larger schools had greater improvement in student learning, perhaps because of curricular benefits, but they also had higher dropout rates, perhaps because of poorer climate.[225]

One structural feature of schools that has generated considerable debate in the United States concerns school control—whether private schools, particularly Catholic schools, produce better student outcomes than public schools. A similar, more recent debate has emerged over whether public charter schools—public schools run by a wide variety of both nonprofit and for-profit organizations that operate largely outside of the constraints imposed on traditional public schools—also produce better student outcomes.

Overall, the evidence finds that Catholic schools are generally more effective than public schools due to their stronger and more egalitarian academic program and their stronger sense of community.[226] The evidence with respect to dropout and graduation rates is also mixed. Some studies have compared public schools with all private schools (including Catholic), while some studies have compared Catholic with public and other private schools. In our review of the statistical literature, about half the studies found that private schools are more effective than public schools or that Catholic schools were more effective than public schools or other private schools. The evidence is somewhat stronger that dropout rates are lower and graduation rates higher in Catholic schools, even after controlling for student background characteristics and other school inputs.[227] Some of those studies also find that the Catholic school effect is mediated by school practices, which further supports the claim that Catholic schools provide a more rigorous and supportive school environment compared to public and other private schools.[228] Yet empirical studies have also found that students from private and Catholic schools typically transfer to public schools instead of or before dropping out, meaning that student turnover rates in private schools are not statistically different than turnover rates in public schools.[229]

Because the charter school movement is relatively recent and premised, in part, on improving high school graduation rates, I review the evidence on the impact of charter schools on dropout and graduation rates in the next chapter.

RESOURCES. Another area of considerable debate concerns the extent to which school resources contribute to school effectiveness. Much of the debate focuses on whether fiscal resources make a difference, with some scholars claiming that schools lack incentives or the knowledge to use resources effectively.[230] There is more agreement that material resources, particularly teachers, contribute to school effectiveness.[231]

A number of studies have examined the relationship between various types of school resources—average expenditures per pupil, teacher salaries, the number of students per teacher, and measures of teacher quality, such as the percentage of teachers with advanced degrees—and dropout or graduation rates. Overall, relatively few studies found significant effects.[232] However, one recent study using sophisticated techniques found that teacher quality had large causal effects on graduation rates in the San Diego school district.[233] Several additional studies that used district- and state-level data, along with more sophisticated statistical techniques to better control for unobserved factors, found that higher per pupil expenditures or higher teacher salaries were associated with lower dropout rates.[234] For example, one study that used a more sophisticated model of teacher salaries, which took into account the nonmonetary job characteristics and alternative employment opportunities in the local job market—what economists refer to as "opportunity costs"—found that raising teacher wages by 10 percent reduced high school dropout rates by 3–4 percent.[235]

PRACTICES.   Despite all the attention and controversy surrounding the previous factors associated with school effectiveness, it is the area of school processes that many people believe holds the most promise for understanding and improving school performance. While many schools, especially public ones, have little control over the characteristics of the students they serve, the school's size and location, and the resources they receive, they do have control over how they are managed, the teaching practices they use, and the climate they create to promote student engagement and learning. In particular, some scholars argue that the social relationships or ties among students, parents, teachers, and administrators—which have been characterized as *social resources* or *social capital*—are a key component of effective and improving schools.[236]

School policies and practices affect student persistence in two ways. One way is through policies and practices that lead to students' disengaging from school and eventual *voluntary* withdrawal—either dropping out or transferring—from school. The other way is through policies and conscious decisions that cause students to *involuntarily* withdraw from school. These rules may concern factors—such as low grades, poor attendance, misbehavior, or being over-age—that can lead to suspensions, expulsions, or forced transfers of "troublemakers" and other problematic students.[237] This form of withdrawal is school-initiated and contrasts with the student-initiated form of voluntary withdrawal. One metaphor that has been used to characterize this process is *discharge*: "students *drop out* of school, schools *discharge* students."[238]

Several in-depth case studies of students and schools provide vivid examples of how numerous school policies and practices promote both forms of withdrawal. The case studies also find that the impact of school policies and practices varies widely among students depending on their identity and affiliation with different cultural peer groups that characterize many large urban schools and are often associated with class, race, ethnicity, and immigration status. In her case study of a Chicago high school, for example, Nilda Flores-González observed two major cultural peer groups, one school-oriented and the other street-oriented.[239] In her study of two continuation high schools, Kelly observed four cultural peer groups: stoners, rappers, punks, and Mexicans.[240]

One practice is that of tracking, where low-achieving students (often racial, ethnic, and linguistic minority students) are placed in non-college-preparatory or remedial classes, some of which yield no credits toward graduation. Romo and Falbo, in their study of Latino students in Austin, documented repeated instances of such practices: "Few students in our sample questioned what courses their counselors assigned them. Their acceptance resulted from neither the students nor their parents understanding the long-term consequences of their being tracked into the non-college-preparatory courses."[241]

A more pervasive and potentially powerful manifestation is in the school's climate. Valenzuela's case study of a Houston high school noted such a climate in the poor relations between teachers and students:

> Teachers fail to forge meaningful connections with their students; students are alienated from their teachers, and are often (especially between groups of first-generation and U.S.-born) hostile to one another, as well; and administrators routinely disrespect even the most basic needs of both students and staff. The feeling that "no one cares" is pervasive—and corrosive. Real learning is difficult to sustain in an atmosphere rife with mistrust Over even comparatively short periods of time, the divisions and misunderstandings that characterize daily life at the school exact high costs in academic, social, and motivational currency.[242]

Michelle Fine, in her case study of a New York City high school, documented various ways that students were discharged from the school: some were allowed to leave because they reached the compulsory school age of seventeen; some were forced to leave because of truancy (which was enforced summarily when parents did not respond to written requests for a school meeting); others were forced to leave because of discipline problems, such as fighting.[243] One guidance counselor admitted the problem: "We do throw students out of here for no good reasons. They feel terrible. We deny them their education. Black kids especially."[244]

In our review of the statistical literature, we identified a number of studies that examined the relationship between a variety of school practices and dropout or graduation rates. The studies differed in what specific practices were examined and how they were measured. One study, which created a single composite indicator of school climate from student responses to questions about various aspects of the school, such as school loyalty and student behavior (e.g., fighting, cutting class), found that a positive school climate reduced the likelihood of dropping out, net of other factors.[245] Another study found that schools with higher attendance rates—another measure of overall school climate—had lower dropout rates.[246]

Most studies examined the effects of a number of indicators of school academic and disciplinary climates. Several studies found that students were less likely to drop out if they attended schools with a stronger academic climate, as measured by more students in the academic track (versus general or vocational) or taking academic courses, and students spending more hours doing homework.[247] Some studies have found that students were more likely to drop out in schools with a poor disciplinary climate, as measured by student reports of student disruptions in class or discipline problems in the school, or in schools where students reported feeling unsafe.[248] Several studies have found that positive relationships between students and teachers—an aspect of school social capital—reduced the risk of dropping out, especially among high-risk students.[249]

In addition to school policies and practices, there are a number of policies that districts, states, and the federal government impose on schools, such as compulsory attendance laws and graduation requirements. I address the impacts of these systemic activities in the next chapter.

Communities

Communities and neighborhoods (subsections of larger communities) play a crucial role in adolescent development along with families, schools, and peers. Neighborhoods influence children and youth through three primary mechanisms: (1) access to *institutional resources* (e.g., child care, medical facilities, employment opportunities); (2) *parental relationships* that can provide access to family and friends as well as social connections with the neighborhood; and (3) *social relationships* (or *social capital*) that arise out of mutual trust and shared values and that can help to supervise and monitor the activities of the residents, particularly youth.[250] Yet there is considerable social inequality among U.S. neighborhoods in terms of poverty, joblessness, and racial segregation, and in the prevalence of such social problems as infant mortality, low birth weight, child maltreatment, adolescent delinquency, school dropout, and crime.[251] Blacks, in particular, are most likely to live in communities of concentrated disadvantage that have endured over the past several decades.

Some of the case studies cited earlier in this and previous chapters documented how neighborhood structural conditions interact with individual factors to influence adolescent behaviors, including school dropout. For example, in his study of economic crime in Brooklyn, Sullivan argues that youth crime must be understood in two economic senses: that of the individual youth as an economic entrepreneur, and that of the inner-city neighborhood as an economic environment.[252] In their study of poor single mothers in Philadelphia, Kathryn Edin and Maria Kefalas argue that poor women have children out of wedlock because of neighborhoods that offer few opportunities for meaningful work or meaningful relationships.[253] And in her study of a Chicago high school, Flores-González documents how "street-oriented" students, including "gang bangers" who keep their gang activities outside of school, are able to replicate street life at school, thereby disrupting the performance of all the students.[254]

A number of statistical studies have examined the relationship between community characteristics and dropping out or graduating. The studies differ widely in how they measured community characteristics—most rely on measures of the social composition of the residents in the community, such as the percentage of people holding white-collar jobs, the percentage of people living in poverty, and the percentage of the population with high or low incomes. A number of studies have found that the population characteristics of communities based on such measures are associated with dropout rates.[255] Yet the relationship may not be linear. Two of the studies found that living in a high-poverty neighborhood was not necessarily detrimental to completing high school but rather that living in an affluent neighborhood was beneficial to school success.[256] These two studies support the notion that affluent neighborhoods provide students more access to community resources and positive role models from affluent neighbors.

Some studies found that community characteristics affected some demographic groups but not others. One study found that whites, but not blacks and Hispanics, had higher dropout rates in counties with a higher percentage of families on welfare,[257] while another study found that the neighborhood dropout rate affected girls' but not boys' dropout rates.[258] Two other studies found that neighborhood violence was associated with higher dropout rates.[259]

Another way that communities can influence dropout rates is by providing employment opportunities both during and after school. Relatively favorable employment opportunities for high school dropouts, as evidenced by low neighborhood unemployment rates, could increase the likelihood that students will drop out, but the majority of the studies we identified in our review of the statistical literature failed to find a statistically significant relationship.[260] Yet two additional studies found that states with higher unemployment rates had lower dropout rates and higher graduation rates.[261]

Explaining Racial and Ethnic Differences in Dropout Rates

One of the most challenging educational issues facing the United States is understanding and solving the persistent disparities in achievement among racial and ethnic groups. While much of the focus on this issue has centered on student achievement as measured by grades and test scores, there also has been considerable attention to understanding and explaining the large observed differences in dropout rates.[262]

Two general approaches have been used to explain differences in dropout rates among racial and ethnic groups. The first approach is based on the idea that differences in dropout rates and other measures of educational achievement can be explained largely by differences in the social contexts of families, schools, and communities, particularly differences in available resources within each of those settings. This approach was adopted by the National Research Council Panel on High-Risk Youth, which focused its study on the high-risk settings of family, school, and community to explain the poor outcomes of high-risk and minority students.[263] In *The Latino Education Crisis*, Patricia Gándara and Frances Contreras detail what they characterize as the cumulative disadvantages of Latino children found in their homes, schools, and communities.[264] Indeed, the family, school, and community conditions for racial and ethnic minorities in the United States are generally much worse than for the white majority. For example, black and Hispanic children are three times more likely than whites to be poor, and eight times as likely as whites to attend high-poverty schools (see Table 7.1).

Several empirical studies of dropouts have found that at least half of the observed differences in dropout rates between racial groups can be attributed to differences in family and community characteristics.[265] Another study found that up to half of the observed differences in dropout rates between whites and minorities would be reduced if racial groups attended schools with similar racial and socioeconomic compositions.[266]

The second approach is based on the idea that differences in resources and material conditions in families, schools, and communities are insufficient to explain differences in achievement among racial and ethnic groups. In particular, critics of the first approach argue that it fails to explain why some minority groups with similar levels of "socioeconomic" background succeed, while other groups do not. Instead, they argue that sociocultural factors—particularly cultural differences in values, attitudes, and behaviors—help explain why some racial and ethnic minorities are successful in American schools and others are not.

Anthropologist John Ogbu, one of the best-known proponents of the sociocultural perspective, argues that minorities can be classified into two groups: (1) voluntary minorities who came to the United States by their own choosing (e.g., European- and Asian-Americans), and (2) involuntary minorities who were brought into the United States against their will, either through immigration or domination (e.g., African-Americans and early Mexican-Americans).[267] Voluntary and involuntary minorities view school success very differently: "Voluntary minorities do not perceive learning the attitudes and behaviors required for school success as threatening their own culture, language, and identities, [while] . . . involuntary minorities do not seem to be able or willing to separate attitudes and behaviors that result in academic success from those that may result in linear acculturation or replacement of their cultural identity with White American cultural identity."[268] Although Ogbu's perspective offers an appealing explanation of minority group differences in achievement, empirical support for this perspective is limited.[269]

Other sociocultural perspectives also suggest that differences in attitudes and behaviors of students, peers, and families help explain racial and ethnic

Table 7.1 Selected individual and institutional characteristics of children and students, by race/ethnicity (percentage)

	Total	White	Black	Hispanic	Asian/Pacific Islander	American Indian/Alaska native
Individual						
Foreign-born (under 18), 2007	5	2	3	11	24*	<1
Language minority, K–12, 2007**	21	6	6	69	64*	16
Disability, 6–21, 2007	9	9	12	8	5	14
NAEP 8th-grade reading at or above proficient, 2007	31	40	13	15	41	18
NAEP 8th-grade math at or above proficient, 2009	34	44	12	17	54	18
Grade retention, K–12, 2007	12	9	21	12	–	–
Suspended, 6–12, 2007	22	16	43	22	11*	14
Live births per 1,000 females 15–19, 2007	42	27	64	82	17	59
Family						
Children under 18 living in poverty, 2007	18	10	34	27	11*	33
Children under 18 living with married parents, 2007	66	75	34	61	82*	47
Mother with bachelor's degree or higher, 2008	28	36	17	11	51	16
School						
Public elementary students attending high-poverty school, 2007–08***	20	5	40	42	15	28

Sources: Susan Aud, Mary Ann Fox, and Angelina KewalRamani, *Status and Trends in the Education of Racial and Ethnic Groups* (NCES 2010-015) (Washington, DC: National Center for Education Statistics, 2010), http://nces.ed.gov/pubsearch/pubsinfo.asp?pubid=2010015 (accessed January 17, 2011), table 2a, 3, 4, 5, 8-1a, 11.1, 11-2, 17a, 17b, 21a; Susan Aud et al., *The Condition of Education 2010* (NCES 2010-028) (Washington, DC: National Center for Education Statistics, 2010), http://nces.ed.gov/pubsearch/pubsinfo.asp?pubid=2010028 (accessed January 17, 2011), table A-25-1.

* Asian only.

** Children ages 5–17 who spoke a language other than English.

*** Schools with more than 75 percent of the students eligible for free or reduced-price lunch.

differences in achievement. For example, Laurence Steinberg, Sanford Dornbusch, and B. Bradford Brown argue that Asians are more successful in school than other ethnic groups because of two cultural beliefs: (1) that not getting a good education will hurt their chances for future success (rather than a belief that a good education will help their chances), and (2) that academic success comes from effort rather than ability or the difficulty of the material.[270] They also find that the contexts of families, schools, and peers influence the achievement of racial and ethnic groups differently. Studies have also shown differences among racial and ethnic groups in salient predictors of school dropout.[271] Psychologist Claude Steele demonstrates that the social stigma of intellectual inferiority among certain cultural minorities—referred to as *stereotype threat*—contributes to their lower academic achievement.[272]

Some scholars argue that youth outcomes are shaped both by structural features of families, schools, and communities and by culture. In fact, they argue that it is impossible to separate one from the other because it is their interaction that matters. As pointed out in an earlier chapter, Julius William Wilson argues for such a perspective in his analysis of neighborhood effects when he states, "Culture mediates the impact of structural forces."[273] And in her study of a San Antonio high school, Angela Valenzuela argues that race and ethnicity "are not mere stock that individuals possess, manipulate, and bring to bear on institutional life," but instead "the latter significantly influences the direction and form that ethnic identities take."[274]

Together, this research suggests that differences both in structural conditions in families, schools, and communities, and in culturally influenced behaviors and attitudes help account for racial and ethnic differences in dropout and graduation rates. Both sets of factors may in turn lead to differences in an array of individual factors that have a demonstrated association with dropping out. Some of those factors are displayed in Table 7.1. Hispanic and Asian students, for example, are much more likely than white and black students to be immigrants and to come from non-English-speaking households that, as demonstrated below, are related to higher dropout rates. Black, Hispanic, and American Indian/Alaska Native students have much lower academic achievement levels than whites and Asians. Black students are much more likely to have repeated a grade and to have been suspended from school than students from other ethnic groups. Finally, rates of teen pregnancy are much higher among black,

Hispanic, and American Indian/Alaska Native female students than among white and Asian female students.

Several conclusions about the causes of dropping out emerge from the theoretical and empirical research literature.

First, dropping out is a complex process that often begins early in a student's academic career. Research based on long-term longitudinal studies has found that some predictors of whether students drop out of high school begin as early as first grade. This supports a view of dropping out as a long-term process of gradual disengagement from school.

Second, dropping out is more than simply a consequence of academic failure, although it figures prominently in the process. Academic failure in high school, as evidenced by failing classes, is the most powerful predictor of whether students eventually graduate from high school. Course failure in ninth grade, which leads to significant numbers of students repeating that grade level, is particularly critical. Course failure in middle school is also predictive, while poor academic performance in elementary school is also predictive. Yet other factors also contribute, including high absenteeism and misbehavior in school. For this reason, composite measures of academic risk based on multiple measures of student behaviors, attitudes, and academic performance are powerful predictors of whether students eventually drop out or graduate.

Third, the individual factors that contribute to students' dropping out are highly influenced by the settings where students live—families, schools, and communities. Families exert the most powerful influence on all aspects of a child's development, including their academic ability, attitudes toward school, and academic and social behavior, all of which directly contributes to their effort and performance in school. But schools and communities are also critical to students' success.

Fourth, all of the factors that contribute to the dropout process, both at the individual and institutional levels, are highly interrelated. Individual factors that place students at risk for dropping out—poor academic performance, disengagement, misbehavior in school, criminal activity outside of school, teen pregnancy—often occur together, compounding their effects on students. Similarly, the quality of a student's home environment is often related to the quality of his or her school and neighborhood, compounding their effects as well. In this sense, it is difficult and may not be particularly helpful to focus on isolated factors at either the individual or institutional level to understand and solve the dropout crisis in this country.

Finally, some groups of students, particularly black students, are more likely to live in settings of concentrated disadvantage and be at the most risk for dropping out of school. As a result, the dropout crisis itself is concentrated in some neighborhoods and schools more than others, and in some demographic groups more than others.

8

LEARNING FROM PAST EFFORTS TO SOLVE
THE DROPOUT CRISIS

America's dropout crisis is not new. High school graduation rates have hovered around 75 percent for the past forty years. Efforts to address the problem are at least as old. In 1963, President John F. Kennedy initiated a national "Summer Dropout Campaign" to increase publicity about the problem and to assist local school districts in identifying potential dropouts and in returning these students to school in the fall.[1] In 1983, the federal government issued its landmark report, A Nation at Risk, which called for more rigorous standards and higher expectations, including more rigorous high school graduation requirements.[2] In 1990, the nation's governors and the U.S. president adopted six national education goals for the year 2000, one of which was to increase the high school graduation rate to 90 percent.[3] And in 2002, President George W. Bush signed into law the No Child Left Behind Act, which holds schools accountable for improving high school graduation rates.[4]

These and other efforts have spawned a variety of government, foundation, and private-sector programs that have funded the development and dissemination of dropout prevention and school improvement projects. The federal government alone has spent more than $300 million on dropout prevention programs since 1988.[5] In 1993, the Annenberg Foundation helped invest more than $1 billion to initiative reform efforts for 2,400 schools in 300 districts in 25 states. And in the ten-year period from 2000 to 2009, the Bill & Melinda Gates Foundation invested more than $2 billion to start new high schools or redesign existing high schools.[6]

Yet despite this long-standing attention and significant investment, the high school graduation rate has failed to improve. Why have past efforts been unsuccessful? Is the problem the lack of effective strategies? Or is it the inability to implement effective strategies widely in the schools and communities with the highest dropout rates? And how can meaningful improvements be made in both the design and the wide-scale implementation of effective strategies? What roles should the federal and state governments, foundations, advocacy organizations, and other groups play in these efforts?

This chapter and the next address each of these questions. In this chapter, I first describe the range of alternative approaches for improving dropout and graduation rates and what we know about their effectiveness. Then I review past efforts to design and implement effective strategies and why these efforts have largely been unsuccessful. Finally, in the final chapter, I discuss current efforts to address the crisis, their limitations, and what I believe needs to be done to solve America's dropout crisis.

Alternative Approaches to Improving Dropout and Graduation Rates

Although countless programs and strategies have been developed to improve dropout and graduation rates, they can be grouped into three basic approaches: targeted, comprehensive, and systemic. The three approaches differ in both scope and focus, and they each have advantages and disadvantages.

Targeted Approaches

The most common approach for improving dropout and graduation rates is to develop a special program targeting students most at risk for dropping out of school. There are two targeted approaches. One is to provide supplemental services to students within an existing school program. The second is to provide an alternative school program, either within an existing school (school within a school) or in a separate facility (alternative school). Neither approach attempts to change existing institutions serving most students; instead the approaches create supplemental or alternative programs that target students who are somehow identified as being at risk of dropping out or who have already dropped out.

Supplemental programs provide services and supports to students within a regular high school setting. In such programs, some mechanism is used to identify those students most at risk of dropping out. Chapter 7 reviewed a number of studies that used school administrative data to identify at-risk students based on such criteria as failed courses, low GPA, high absenteeism, and disruptive behavior. The identified students are then provided a series of academic and social supports to help them become more successful in school. The supports are provided during a specified time during the school day—such as in an elective period, during lunch, or after school—and frequently delivered by specially trained adults within the school (e.g., counselors, teachers) or outside the school (from businesses, churches, or community organizations). The adults may serve as tutors, mentors, and advocates for the students, and as liaisons between students' families and the school.

The other targeted approach to dropout prevention is to create alternative school programs that target only students at risk of dropping out. These programs can either operate within regular schools or as separate, alternative schools. They generally provide a complete education program, but one that represents an alternative to what is offered in regular, comprehensive schools. In addition, they typically provide many of the other support services found in supplemental programs. Stand-alone programs are also the most common approach for reenrolling students who have already dropped out, so-called *dropout recovery* programs.

The most long-standing example of an alternative school program is the continuation high school. As described earlier, continuation high schools were first established during the expansion of public high schools in the early part of the twentieth century to provide a part-time education to students who were working, but gradually they took on a new role in "adjustment" education for students considered to be maladjusted for full-time school.[7] Today there are more than 6,000 alternative schools in the United States.[8] California alone has more than 1,000 alternative high schools, more than the number of traditional comprehensive high schools.[9] In addition to traditional alternative schools, a growing number of charter schools serve students at risk of dropping out or young adults who have already dropped out.

The main advantage of the targeted approach is its simplicity—it is generally easier to develop and implement a dropout prevention program that serves a small number of students than it is to develop and implement a more broadly focused program serving larger numbers of students. In fact, school districts in some states are required to establish continuation high schools or other alternative programs to provide an educational program for all students, even those who may be expelled or otherwise cannot or choose not to attend regular, comprehensive high schools. But there are also disadvantages to this approach. First, even if successful, a dropout prevention program will have limited impact on reducing dropout rates, especially in schools with large numbers of students dropping out. Second, because targeted forms of dropout prevention programs are supplemental to the regular school program and typically require additional resources, they are vulnerable to changing budgets and priorities. Third, both supplemental and alternative dropout prevention programs can struggle to attract students because of negative perceptions by students, parents, and educators that such programs are a dumping ground for "bad" students and that they symbolize the failure of the regular system.[10] Fourth, grouping together at-risk students could exacerbate the risk of dropping out through negative peer influences.[11]

Comprehensive Approaches

A second approach to dropout prevention is through comprehensive or schoolwide reform. This approach is premised on the belief that targeted programs are insufficient to improve dropout or graduation rates either because they are not comprehensive enough or because they do not help enough students. Supplemental programs, for example, typically provide academic and social supports for students but rarely attempt to change the instructional program that may be failing to engage students and to improve their academic achievement. Alternative programs may be effective but typically serve relatively few students and therefore may do little to improve dropout and graduation rates in schools and districts with large numbers of at-risk students. In contrast, comprehensive approaches focus on reforming or creating entire schools that better educate all the students attending them, thereby having the potential to affect many more students.

There are three comprehensive approaches to dropout prevention. One is to reform existing high schools. The most common school reform approach involves developing a comprehensive set of practices and programs locally or by adopting an externally developed comprehensive school reform model. Comprehensive School Reform (CSR) involves multiple strategies to alter all facets of a school and "is built on the premise that unified, coherent, and integrated strategies for improvement, knitted together into a comprehensive design, will work better than the same strategies implemented in isolation from each other."[12] The federal government's comprehensive school reform program identifies eleven required elements:

1. Proven methods and strategies based on scientifically based research.

2. A comprehensive design with aligned components.
3. Ongoing, high-quality professional development for teachers and staff.
4. Measurable goals and benchmarks for student achievement.
5. Support within the school by teachers, administrators, and staff.
6. Support for teachers, administrators, and staff.
7. Meaningful parent and community involvement in planning, implementing, and evaluating school improvement activities.
8. High-quality external technical support and assistance from an external partner with experience and expertise in schoolwide reform and improvement.
9. Evaluation of strategies for the implementation of school reforms and for student results achieved, annually.
10. Resources to support and sustain the school's comprehensive reform effort.
11. Strategies that have been found to significantly improve the academic achievement of students or that have strong evidence to suggest they will significantly improve the academic achievement of students.[13]

Although individual schools may undertake comprehensive school reform, the widespread interest in CSR has come from the development of specific design models that can be replicated or scaled up in other sites. The idea behind this approach is that instead of countless individual schools attempting to identify and implement research-based strategies on their own, external developers design and package a comprehensive set of proven strategies in a coherent model and then assist other schools in implementing their model with financial support from the government or the private sector. A review from 2003 identified thirty-three CSR models that had been replicated in ten or more schools.[14]

Less common school reform approaches involve "reconstituting" an existing school by replacing all or most of the staff—the principal and teachers—or "restarting" the school by converting it to a charter. These two approaches, which have been adopted by the Obama administration as a way to improve America's worst-performing schools, are discussed in Chapter 9.

A second school reform approach is to create new schools, either by establishing a new school locally or by adopting an externally developed whole-school model. This strategy is premised on the idea that it may be easier to create a new school with new people and a new program than to reform an existing school with existing staff, or that creating a new school will create competition for existing schools, thereby causing them to improve or go out of business. The approach is most often carried out by creating a particular type of new school known as a charter school—public schools that are established and managed outside the regular public education system, and that are freed from most of the regulations and requirements of regular public schools. Charter schools were established to provide choice within the public school system, spur educational innovation, create competition as a way to improve non-charter schools, and improve student achievement. The extent to which charter schools have achieved those goals has been the subject of intense and often partisan debate.[15] Nonetheless, their popularity continues to grow. In the ten-year period from 1999–2000 to 2009–10, the number of charter schools increased almost threefold, from 1,524 to 4,952, and enrollment increased almost fivefold, from 340,000 to 1.6 million students.[16] About half of all charter schools include high school grades.[17] Although charter schools can be established by either converting existing schools or creating new schools, more than 90 percent of charters in 2009–10 were new schools.[18] Finally, charter schools can serve general student populations or exclusively at-risk populations, putting them in the category of alternative schools.

The third school reform approach is to create collaborative relationships between schools and outside organizations, such as government agencies and local community organizations.[19] This approach—which can be combined with the other two—is based on the idea that schools do not have the resources or expertise to attend to all the needs of their students and their students' families.

> The primary institutions that serve youth—health, schools, employment, training—are crucial and we must begin with helping them respond more effectively to contemporary adolescent needs. Effective responses will involve pushing the boundaries of these systems, encouraging collaborations between them and reducing the number of adolescents whose specialized problems cannot be met through primary institutions.[20]

Outside groups can provide a range of services, such as medical and counseling services, and after-school and summer-school programs. In some cases the services can be provided on the school campus, such as medical and dental clinics, or after-school programs. Partnerships with the business community can provide computers and other material resources, mentors and tutors, and work-related opportunities.

Comprehensive approaches can be used to improve the performance of all schools, including high schools, but in several respects, reforming high schools is more challenging than reforming elementary and middle schools. For one thing, high schools are generally larger than elementary and middle schools.[21] One reform strategy is to restructure large schools into small learning communities; another is to create new, small schools, but both approaches are difficult to implement. Middle and high schools are also difficult to reform because teachers are trained and credentialed in specific subjects, and many schools have departmental structures, both of which make it difficult for teachers to collaborate on instructional reform.[22] Finally, high school students vary greatly in their academic preparation and are more challenging to teach, which requires a broad array of instructional offerings and student support services. For example, teachers report that student tardiness, absenteeism, and apathy are much more prevalent among secondary students compared to elementary students.[23] These challenges have increased over time, as all levels of schooling have seen an increase in student diversity, particularly second-language learners.[24]

There are at least three advantages of comprehensive approaches to dropout prevention. First, such approaches can improve dropout and graduation rates for more students than dropout prevention programs. Whereas a dropout prevention program may target 100 students, new schools may enroll up to 400 students, while comprehensive school reform models are often adopted by large urban high schools enrolling 2,000 students or more. Second, comprehensive approaches, by their nature, reform more aspects of a school and therefore have the potential to have a greater impact on dropout and graduation rates than programs that typically provide a more limited array of supports. Finally, comprehensive approaches can improve an array of educational outcomes. In addition to improving dropout and graduation rates, effective schools can raise student achievement and better prepare students for college and careers by improving both cognitive and noncognitive outcomes.

Despite these advantages, there is one major disadvantage—comprehensive approaches are difficult. Opening new schools, especially charters, can be difficult because many charter schools face challenges in finding suitable facilities and often have to raise the additional funds to supplement the public funding they receive. Reforming existing comprehensive high schools may be even more difficult, in part because either charter schools select their students or their students select them. And charter schools generally get to select their principals and teachers, even nonunion teachers, while comprehensive high schools are bound by district union contracts. Conversion charters, which may face the same challenges as other comprehensive approaches to reforming existing schools, generally have shown less impact than new charters.[25]

Systemic Approaches

Systemic approaches involve making changes to the entire educational system under the assumption that such changes can transform how all schools function in the system, what some scholars have labeled "systemic school reform."[26] Systemic reform can occur at the federal, state, or local level of government.

Although all systemic reforms may affect dropout and graduation rates by improving school performance, three specific reforms are directly connected to dropout and graduation rates. One is to raise the compulsory schooling age—the age to which students must attend school—to eighteen, as a way to force more students to remain in school.[27] Another is to change high school graduation requirements, both the number and specific array of courses that students must pass to be awarded a diploma, as well as to specify whether students must pass a high school exit exam to earn a diploma. A third reform is to create alternative pathways or options for completing high school coursework and earning diplomas. The federal and state governments are developing and supporting a growing number of alternative pathways for completing high school, including dual enrollment programs that allow high school students to take college courses while still in high school, public charter schools, and vouchers that allow students to attend private high schools.[28]

Another form of systemic reform is that undertaken by the private sector. While only the federal and state governments can effect change in the entire public education system, the private sector has a long history of involvement in educational reform in the United States. Much of this work has been undertaken by several large foundations, including the Ford Foundation, the Carnegie Foundation, and more recently the Bill & Melinda

Gates Foundation. These and other private organizations have largely funded the development and wide-scale adoption of comprehensive school reform models, new forms of alternative schools, and charter schools, all of them representing comprehensive approaches designed to improve student achievement and high school graduation rates. I review some specific foundation initiatives below.

What Works?

Whatever approach is adopted to address the dropout crisis, it is critical to know whether the specific program or strategy that is designed and implemented is effective. Unlike medicine, where research is used to develop new treatments and to evaluate their effectiveness, education has long been criticized because many programs and practices are not based on research, nor are they evaluated to know whether they are truly effective.[29] This is beginning to change. Over the past decade, there has been an increasing awareness of the need to base educational reform efforts on rigorous, scientific evidence.[30] The federal No Child Left Behind (NCLB) Act, for instance, recommends programs and practices "based on scientifically-based research" more than 100 times.[31] One important function for research is to answer the question: What works? In the case of dropout prevention, the question becomes: What specific approaches to dropout prevention are effective? Answering this question requires research knowledge about whether a dropout intervention had a causal impact on dropout or graduation rates. This type of research is known as evaluation research.

Evaluation studies are designed to determine the effectiveness of a wide variety of educational interventions from specific programs implemented in a single school site to systemic policies designed to affect student achievement throughout the educational system. There are a variety of research designs for conducting evaluation studies, and the rigor of the design dictates the ability of determining a causal connection between the intervention and student outcomes. The so-called gold standard in evaluation studies is the randomized experiment, more formally referred to as the *randomized controlled trial* (RCT), where students (or teachers, classrooms, schools) are randomly assigned to either the intervention (experimental group) or the regular or nonreform program (control group).[32] RCTs are used frequently in medical research and increasingly are being advocated for evaluating educational interventions.[33] One well-known, large-scale example is the Tennessee class-size reduction study, where students in kindergarten to third grade were randomly assigned to small (fifteen students) or regular-size (twenty-five students) classes.[34]

Although they are rigorous, RCT designs are difficult to conduct. One difficulty is that some students in the experimental group may move or otherwise leave the intervention before it is completed, so comparing program completers with a control group may no longer represent equivalent groups. A solution to this problem is to compare all students initially assigned to the treatment, regardless of whether they completed it, with the control group, a technique known as "intent-to-treat." This technique judges the ability of the treatment to retain participants as well as the effectiveness of the treatment on those who complete it. Another difficulty is that students in the comparison group could be receiving other dropout services outside of the program, thereby diminishing the measured effects of the treatment program.

RCT designs are also difficult to implement in evaluating school reform models. Because it is virtually impossible to randomly assign students to schools, an alternative design for evaluations of whole-school intervention models is to randomly assign reform models to schools.[35] But this technique is costly and difficult, requiring a large sample of schools to establish strong causal inferences.[36] A more common evaluation design is the quasi-experimental design that is not based on random assignment but instead uses statistical techniques to control for differences in the characteristics of students attending experimental and control schools. Several techniques can be used to estimate causal effects from quasi-experimental studies.[37]

Evaluating the effectiveness of new schools, such as charters, presents special challenges.[38] Randomized evaluations can be conducted only in schools that are oversubscribed and use lotteries to randomly select students, allowing comparisons between admitted and nonadmitted students, but such evaluations can determine only whether those particular charter schools are effective, not whether all charter schools are effective. Alternatively, evaluations that are more rigorous can be conducted by comparing the achievement gains of students who transfer into new schools with students in traditional public schools, using longitudinal achievement data, although this approach requires a number of assumptions to establish a causal connection, particularly that the two groups of students are comparable on both observed (test scores) and unobserved (motivation) characteristics.

Judging Scientific Evidence

Although there is widespread agreement that educational reform should be guided by scientific research evidence, what evidence counts as "scientifically based" is open to question and has led to inconsistent conclusions by the federal and state governments, independent organizations, and individual scholars about the effectiveness of educational interventions and reform strategies.[39] Reviews of the scientific research consistently find a paucity of both the number and quality of existing evaluation studies, rejecting most evaluation studies as insufficient to determine whether a particular intervention is effective. But reviews also employ different standards to determine whether a particular evaluation study should be included in the review and, as a result, reach different conclusions about the effectiveness of specific interventions. This is the case in all types of educational interventions, including those designed to improve dropout and graduation rates. Reviews of dropout prevention programs also judge the programs on different outcomes. Some reviews focus only on outcomes directly related to dropping out—attendance, dropout, progress toward graduation (grade promotion), and high school completion (earning a diploma or alternative credential)—while other reviews focus on a broader array of outcomes, such as achievement (test scores, grades), as well as dropout and graduation rates.

There have been several recent reviews of the research evidence on dropout prevention interventions.[40] The first report was published in 2006 by the Comprehensive School Reform Quality Center, a clearinghouse operated by the American Institutes for Research (AIR) and funded by the federal government.[41] The Center reviewed 197 studies of 18 secondary comprehensive school reform models and found only 28 studies of 16 models that met their standards.[42] The review then judged the programs on a number of outcomes—academic achievement in specific subject areas as well as a wide array of other outcomes, including attendance, dropout rates, graduation rates, student engagement—and on the strength of the evidence of the program's effectiveness in improving those outcomes. The review identified only three comprehensive school reform models that had positive effects on dropout and graduation rates (see Table 8.1).

The second report was published in 2008 by the What Works Clearinghouse (WWC), a program established in 2002 by the U.S. Department of Education to review scientific evidence on the effectiveness of a variety of

Table 8.1   Evidence on dropout prevention and recovery interventions

	CSRQC (2006)	WWC (2008)	AYPF (2009)
Support programs			
After School Matters			S G
ALAS (M)		S+ P+	
Check and Connect		S++ P+	
Financial incentives for teen parents to stay in school		S+ P0 C0	
Hillside Work-Scholarship Connection			G A
Quantum Opportunity Program		P0 C0	
Talent Search		C+	
Twelve Together		S+ P0	
Alternative programs			
Career Academies		S+ P+ C0	S P
Diploma Plus			S P G A
High School Redirection		S± P+ C0	
Job Corps		P0 C+	
Job Start		C+	
Middle College High School		S0 C0	
National Guard Youth ChalleNGe			C
New Chance		C+	
CSR models			
Accelerated Middle Schools (M)		S+ P++	
First Things First	S+ G+ A+	S0	G A
High Schools that Work	0		
Project GRAD	G+ A+	P0 C0	P
Talent Development High School	S+ P+ G+ A+	P+ G0	P A
Collaborative			
Citizen Schools (M)			S P G A
Communities in Schools			S G A
Early College High School			P G A
Systemic			
Dual enrollment			G

S = staying in school (dropout); P = progressing in school; C = completing school; G = graduating from school; A = academic achievement.

++ very strong or moderately strong evidence; + moderate or limited evidence; ± mixed evidence; 0 = no evidence.

educational interventions.[43] The WWC reviewed eighty-four studies of twenty-two dropout prevention (and recovery) programs and found only twenty-three studies of sixteen interventions that met their evidence standards—twelve of the programs were student-support or alternative education programs, and four were CSR or new school models—and assessed their effectiveness in improving three student outcomes: (1) staying in school, (2) progressing in school, and (3) completing school. Of the twelve student support programs, five were judged to be effective in keeping students in school, four were effective in helping students progress in school, and four were effective in helping students to complete school, although none of the four programs was effective in helping students earn a regular high school diploma. Of the four CSR or new school models, only one was effective at keeping students in school, two were effective in helping students progress in school, and none was effective in helping students to complete school (see Table 8.1).

The third report was published in 2009 by the American Youth Policy Forum, a nonprofit, nonpartisan professional development organization working on youth and education issues.[44] This study reviewed external or third-party evaluations of a variety of youth programs and identified twenty-three that met their evidence standards. Only twelve had demonstrated impacts on high school dropout or graduation rates—two were student-support programs, three were alternative education programs, three were comprehensive school reform models, three were collaborative school models, and one was a type of systemic reform (see Table 8.1).

The last report was published in 2009 by the Washington State Institute for Public Policy (WSIPP), which was created by the Washington Legislature in 1983 to carry out practical, nonpartisan research on the state's important issues.[45] The study reviewed 200 studies of truancy reduction and dropout prevention programs and found only 22 that met their evidence standards.[46] This review did not identify all the specific programs that were evaluated but instead grouped programs into six classes: (1) academic remediation, (2) alternative education programs, (3) alternative schools, (4) behavioral programs, (5) mentoring, and (6) youth development. The review found that only alternative educational programs and mentoring programs had statistically significant impacts on reducing dropout rates, while alternative schools actually increased dropout rates, and academic remediation had no statistically significant effects. Only alternative education programs (specifically, the Career Academies program, which they did identify) had statistically positive impacts on graduation rates, while alternative schools and mentoring had no statistical impacts.

Comparing these four reviews reveals several inconsistencies about what works. For example, the WSIPP review concluded that Career Academies was an effective program for improving graduation rates, while the WWC review concluded that there was insufficient evidence to make that determination. The CSRQC review concluded that both First Things First and Talent Development High Schools were effective in improving graduation rates, while the WWC concluded that the evidence was insufficient.

In addition to determining whether a program is effective at improving dropout and graduation rates, it is also useful to determine how effective particular programs are, or the size of the effect. One of the most common ways to measure the magnitude of a program's effect is with a metric known as an effect size (ES).[47] Effect sizes are particularly useful because they allow comparisons of effectiveness across programs and outcomes based on a common metric. Although there are no absolute standards for judging the magnitude of effect sizes, one prominent statistician argues that an ES of at least 0.2 should be considered a small effect (which corresponds to increasing the likelihood of graduating from 50 percent to 58 percent); an ES of at least 0.5 should be considered a medium effect (which corresponds to increasing the likelihood of graduating from 50 percent to 69 percent); and an ES of at least 0.8 should be considered a large effect (which corresponds to increasing the likelihood of graduating from 50 percent to 79 percent).[48]

The WSIPP computed effect sizes for each of the programs that were reviewed and found the average effect size for reducing dropout rates was 0.054, an extremely small effect size and the equivalent of improving retention rates by 2 percentage points.[49] The average effect size for raising graduation rates was 0.158, also a small effect size and equivalent to raising the graduation rate by about 6 percentage points. The WWC constructed a different metric, the improvement index, which corresponds to the percentile increases associated with effect sizes.[50] For example, the program with the largest impact on dropout rates was the ALAS program, with an improvement index of 42, which is equivalent to improving the school retention rate from 50 percent to 92 percent. Among all the programs in the WWC review, the improvement rates for staying in school ranged from −3 to 42, while the average improvement rate for completing school ranged from −3 to 17.[51] So while the WSIPP review found very small average effects of dropout prevention programs for reducing dropout rates, the WWC found some specific dropout programs had large effects on reducing dropout rates. Yet both the WSIPP and WWC found only a few dropout prevention programs that improved high school graduation rates, and no single program demonstrated anything more than a small effect. This suggests that in general, it is harder to design effective programs to get students to complete high school than to design effective programs to keep them in school, and harder still to design programs to get them to graduate.

Identifying Effective Strategies

Although much of the effort to improve dropout and graduation rates has focused on developing, implementing, and evaluating specific programs or school reform models, it is also useful to identify general strategies or approaches that are commonly found in successful programs. Such information could be used to design local interventions or to inform policies designed to promote reforms by ensuring that the policies supported the identified strategies. Several studies have reviewed the research literature on effective programs and derived some common features.

MDRC STUDIES.   Two related reviews were published by the MDRC, a nonpartisan, nonprofit research firm that has conducted a large number of rigorous evaluations of various educational programs, including comprehensive school reform model and dropout prevention programs. The first study was based on the review of three comprehensive school reform models: Career Academies, Talent Development High Schools, and First Things First. The second study added a fourth program, Project Graduation Really Achieves Dreams (GRAD). Together, these interventions have been implemented in more than 2,700 high schools throughout the United States. All of these programs were evaluated by MDRC using rigorous evaluations methods, either RCT or rigorous quasi-experimental methods. The two reviews identified five challenges facing high school reform efforts and some ways that developers of these programs address those challenges.

1. Creating a personalized and orderly learning environment.   One of the key psychological needs of students, identified in the previous two chapters on the causes of dropping out, is a sense of belonging. Dropouts often state that no one noticed or cared whether they came to school. One way that program developers address this need is to create a more personalized learning environment where students and teachers get to know and care for one another, not just as students and teachers, but also as people. Career Academies, Talent Development High Schools, and First Things First all divide large schools into small learning communities of 300–400 students who remain together, with the same group of teachers for most or all of their high school careers. First Things First also creates a Family Advocacy System where every adult in the school, from janitors to the principal, has a small group of ten to fifteen students with whom they interact, monitor, and mentor throughout their four years of high school, further strengthening the bonds between students and the adults in the school. Additional support about the importance of creating a personalized learning environment is evidenced by the fact that most charter schools are designed to be small.

2. Assisting students who enter high school with poor academic skills. Another challenge facing high schools, especially those enrolling large numbers of disadvantaged students, is that entering ninth-grade students often have poor academic skills, particularly in math and reading. As noted in the previous chapter, poor academic performance, particularly failing courses in ninth grade, is highly predictive of whether students drop out or continue on until graduation. These programs employ a number of strategies to raise students' academic skills, including special catch-up classes with specially designed curricula to raise basic skills in math and reading; block scheduling, which allows students to earn more credits over the school year than traditional scheduling; and double periods of math and English language arts.

3. Improving instructional content and practice. Another contributing factor to dropping out identified in the research literature is student engagement. To remain in school, students must be engaged in learning the academic content required to pass their courses and, if required, the high school exit exam. In its final report, the National Research Council Committee on Increasing High School Students' Engagement and Motivation to Learn described effective high school teaching as

> challenging and focused on disciplinary knowledge and conceptual understanding. It needs to be relevant to and build on students' cultural backgrounds and personal experiences, and provide opportunities for students to engage in authentic tasks that have

meaning in the world outside of school. Engaging instruction gives students multiple learning modalities to master material and represent their knowledge, and allows them to draw on their native language and other resources. This kind of teaching is not possible if teachers do not have a deep understanding of their subject matter, of how people learn, and of how to address students' developmental needs.[52]

To develop this expertise, teachers need ongoing ways of expanding their knowledge and improving their skills. Research increasingly suggests that the most effective way is to develop professional learning communities where teachers collaborate on instructional design and provide collective feedback on their teaching, perhaps with the assistance of instructional coaches or mentors.[53] Such communities can be developed through small learning communities that structure collaborative planning time and provide training on how to use this time effectively.[54]

4. Providing work-based learning opportunities and preparing students for the world beyond high school. Another way to engage students is to create connections to the outside world. John Dewey first championed this idea in his conception of public schools as well integrated into their communities.[55] The most frequently used means to do this is through Career and Technical Education (CTE). Although historically CTE was designed as a separate, less rigorous track in high school, serving more disadvantaged students, CTE is now more often integrated into the regular academic program, providing opportunities to simultaneously prepare for college and career, a strategy referred to as "multiple pathways."[56] Career Academies, Talent Development High Schools, and First Things First all organize small learning communities into thematic or career-oriented clusters and provide career-based instruction. Project GRAD provides summer institutes on college campuses and scholarship coordinators in high schools to better prepare students for college.

5. Stimulating change in overstressed high schools. The last challenge is common to any attempt to bring about fundamental and lasting changes to schools: how to successfully implement proven practices and programs in schools and districts. The importance of program implementation was first documented by Jeffrey Pressman and Aaron Wildavsky in their classic 1973 study of a federal public works program, *Implementation: How Great Expectations in Washington Are Dashed in Oakland*.[57] Since then, numerous studies have documented how even well-designed and well-funded programs may have little impact because of problems related to implementation.[58] The review of the high school reform models likewise identified a number of challenges to successfully implementing these models, including the capacity of existing personnel to envision and implement change, the role of external providers, and the adequacy of district support. These and other challenges have been documented widely in studies of large-scale program implementation, which are reviewed in the following section.

IES PRACTICE GUIDE. The federal government has also undertaken numerous research syntheses in education. In part because so few programs met its high standards for what it considers rigorous evaluations, in 2007 the What Works Clearinghouse began issuing practice guides reviewing a broader array of research evidence concerning important educational issues.[59] A select team of experts, including researchers and practitioners, reviews the research evidence and, based on the review, compiles a set of recommendations on effective practices to address the particular education issue. For each recommendation, the guide summarizes the research evidence and rates the strength of the evidence to support it as:

Strong—the same standards as the regular WWC reviews.
Moderate—some evidence, but not as rigorous or numerous as the
   WWC standards.
Weak—little or no evidence, but based on the panel's expertise.

The review also suggests a number of ways to implement the recommendations, identifies potential roadblocks to implementing them and how they may be overcome, and provides examples of programs that utilize the practices. Twelve practice guides were issued through December 2009.

The practice guide *Dropout Prevention* was issued in August 2008.[60] It provides six recommendations for improving dropout and graduation rates, supported by varying levels of evidence. One challenge the panel faced was that virtually all effective dropout prevention programs had multiple components, making it difficult to judge the level of evidence supporting each specific recommendation. So even if the recommended practice was found in several programs that met the rigorous WWC standards, no single recommendation was given more than a moderate level of evidence. This also led the panel to conclude that making a significant and meaningful impact on dropout and graduation rates requires implementing several if not all of the panel's recommendations. The six recommendations range from those designed to target and support the students most at risk for dropping out, to those designed to improve a broader array of educational outcomes, including dropout and graduation rates, for all students in a school.

1. Utilize data systems that support a realistic diagnosis of the number of students who drop out and that help identify individual students at high risk of dropping out (level of evidence: low). Before struggling students can be supported, they first must be identified. All targeted dropout prevention programs include a means for identifying students at risk for dropping out. Chapter 7 reviewed studies that identified a number of early indicators to identify at-risk students, including course failures, disruptive behavior, and poor attendance. These indicators can be constructed from data commonly found in school and district administrative data systems. While the expert panel agreed on the importance of identifying at-risk students, no studies have evaluated the effectiveness of this strategy, so the level of evidence supporting this recommendation was deemed low. Of course, this strategy alone would not be effective unless it was coupled with subsequent recommendations for providing supports to the identified students.

2. Assign adult advocates to students at risk of dropping out (level of evidence: moderate). Students who are at risk of dropping out often face a number of personal, school, and family challenges. They also are often disengaged from school and lack a sense of belonging, two strong precursors to dropping out. Having a close and personal relationship with a caring and supportive adult can help reengage students and develop their sense of belonging. These adults can also help address the students' challenges. A feature found in several dropout prevention programs is an adult who works with a small group of targeted students and acts as a mentor, counselor, and advocate. Some programs utilize existing school personnel, while other programs depend on outside specialists brought into the school. The level of expertise of these adults varies among programs, as does the extent and type of support provided to the students. For example, the First Things First comprehensive school reform model described earlier uses existing school personnel, who meet with their assigned students once a week and function more as mentors, while the ALAS program uses outside, specifically trained adults who meet with their assigned students at least daily and serve more as counselors and advocates. Of course, the First Things First model assigns adult mentors to all students in the school, while the ALAS program targets the highest-risk students, who generally require more support to be successful. Because only two proven dropout prevention programs—ALAS and Check and Connect—assign students to adults in the school, the level of evidence supporting this recommendation was deemed moderate.

3. Provide academic support and enrichment to improve academic performance (level of evidence: moderate).   As in the previous research synthesis of dropout programs, the practice guide panel recognized that the existing research shows that poor academic performance is a strong precursor to dropping out. It also found that virtually all effective dropout prevention programs provide some form of academic support to improve the academic skills and performance of at-risk students. Comprehensive programs tend to do this through specially designed courses, especially for ninth graders with low academic skills, while targeted programs tend to provide academic supports through tutoring or homework help outside of regular classes. Again, because a number of proven dropout prevention programs assign students to adults in the school, the level of evidence supporting this recommendation was deemed moderate.

4. Implement programs to improve students' classroom behavior and social skills (level of evidence: low).   Disruptive behavior is one of the precursors to dropping out. As such, at least some proven dropout prevention programs provide support and enhance the social skills of students to improve their behavior. For example, the ALAS program teaches a specially designed social skills and resilience curriculum to participating students that is then utilized and reinforced by the counselors who work with the students. But because few dropout programs specially target behavior and social skills, the panel rated the level of evidence supporting this recommendation as low.

5. Personalize the learning environment and instructional process (level of evidence: moderate).   Another strategy to improve students' sense of belonging and engagement is to create more personal relationships throughout the school. As the National Research Council Committee on Increasing High School Students' Engagement and Motivation to Learn found, "Evidence suggests that student engagement and learning are fostered by a school climate characterized by an ethic of caring and supportive relationships, respect, fairness, and trust; and teachers' sense of shared responsibility and efficacy related to student learning."[61] One common feature in effective comprehensive school reform strategies, as noted in the earlier synthesis, is to break large high schools into small learning communities so that adults and students can establish closer and more personal relationships. Because this strategy is so widely used in proven comprehensive programs, the panel designated the level of evidence supporting this evidence as moderate.

6. Provide rigorous and relevant instruction to better engage students in learning and provide the skills needed to graduate and to serve them after they leave school (level of evidence: moderate).   Another strategy for improving student engagement and raising academic performance is to provide more rigorous and relevant instruction. This strategy was also identified in the previous review of comprehensive school reform strategies. The dropout expert panel identified a number of interventions that included specific strategies for improving the relevance and rigor of instruction, including Career Academies and Talent Development High Schools that include Career and Technical Education. Other interventions, such as Talent Development and First Things First, include specific strategies for improving academic instruction in core areas of mathematics and literacy. Because this strategy is found in a number of proven programs, the panel judged the evidence supporting this recommendation as moderate.

The American Youth Policy Forum, in its review of twenty-nine effective dropout prevention programs, identified ten elements of success that appeared to contribute to the effectiveness of the programs. Six of these were related to program features:

- Rigor and academic support.
- Relationships.
- College knowledge and access.
- Relevance.
- Youth-centered programs.
- Effective instruction.

The other four were related to structural features of the programs:

- Partnerships and cross-systems collaboration.
- Strategic use of time.
- Leadership and autonomy.
- Effective assessment and use of data.

These features overlap extensively with the MDRC synthesis and the WWC Dropout Prevention Practice Guide.[62] Thus, it is reasonable to conclude from these three reviews that the basic programmatic elements or strategies for reducing dropout rates and improving high school graduation rates are fairly well established. Yet, although identifying effective strategies is one thing, successfully designing and implementing effective programs is another, as discussed below.

Early Interventions

Dropout interventions are designed to improve dropout and graduation rates. And because virtually all dropouts leave school during high school and, to a lesser extent, during middle school, most dropout prevention programs focus on middle and high schools. But a number of early interventions that focus on improving student performance in elementary school and even preschool have also been shown to significantly improve dropout and graduation rates. Evaluations of these programs track students for many years as they progress through the educational system, thus allowing a determination of the long-term impact of these programs, including whether the programs improve dropout and graduation rates.

One such early intervention is preschool. Not only has a growing body of evidence found that high-quality preschool can improve school readiness and early school success, but long-term follow-up studies have found that preschool can also improve a wide range of adolescent and adult outcomes, including high school completion, criminal activity, reliance on welfare, and teen parenthood.[63] One review reported that three "intensive" high-quality preschool programs—two of which were evaluated with randomized designs—improved graduation rates from 15 to 20 percentage points.[64] Another review of seven studies found that, on average, preschool participation improved graduation rates by 22 percentage points.[65]

In our own review of statistical studies, we identified ten studies that examined the effects of preschool participation on high school dropout and graduation rates. All but two of the studies analyzed the same set of data from the Chicago Longitudinal Study (CLS), an ongoing study of children who participated in preschool and early childhood services from ages three through nine beginning in 1986. The CLS-based studies found that, after controlling for differences in gender, an index of family risk factors, and race/ethnicity, students who participated in the preschool portion of the program had graduation rates about 10 percentage points higher than non–program participants.[66] Several of the studies sought to identify what mediating factors accounted for the program effects. Two studies found that about 90 percent of the program effects were explained by cognitive advantage in early elementary school, improved family support, and improved school support.[67] Another study of an intensive home-based intervention program, the Pittsfield Parent-Child Home Program, found that participants were less than half as likely to drop out of school compared to a randomized control group.[68]

Another early intervention that has been shown to improve high school graduation rates is small classes in early elementary school. The evidence comes from a statewide experiment in Tennessee—Project STAR (Student-Teacher Achievement Ratio)—where students were randomly assigned to a small class (thirteen to seventeen students), a full-size class (twenty-two to twenty-six students), or a full-size class with a full-time teacher aid for up to four years from kindergarten through third grade.[69] The experiment began in 1985 and involved more than 6,000 students in 329 classrooms, 79 schools, and 46 school districts. A long-term study that analyzed the high school transcripts of more than 5,000 STAR students found that the odds of graduating were 80 percent higher for students who had spent four years in the small classes compared to students in full-size classes, and the odds were 150 percent higher for low-income students.[70]

Systemic Interventions

There are a number of systemic interventions that states and districts have implemented to improve high school graduation rates or to better prepare high school graduates for employment or further education: (1) raising the compulsory schooling age, (2) increasing the requirements for a high school diploma, and (3) providing the choice of alternative pathways for earning a high school diploma.[71] How effective are these interventions?

COMPULSORY SCHOOLING AGE. States have the authority to determine the age at which students must attend school, which is referred to as the compulsory schooling age. States vary widely in both the minimum and maximum age for attending school. In some states the maximum schooling age—the age at which students no longer have to attend school—is sixteen or seventeen, which means students do not have to stay in school long enough to graduate. One policy recommendation for improving graduation rates is to raise the maximum compulsory schooling age to eighteen.[72] The research evidence supports this action—several studies found that states with higher compulsory schooling ages had lower dropout rates or higher graduation rates.[73]

HIGH SCHOOL GRADUATION REQUIREMENTS. States have the authority to determine the number and types of courses students must complete to earn a diploma, and most states exercise that authority by specifying a set of requirements.[74] Districts and schools can impose additional requirements. The research evidence is inconclusive on whether increasing course requirements affects dropout and graduation rates. One earlier study found that having more course requirements increased dropout rates, while a later study found no significant relationship.[75] Three recent studies of a mandated college-preparatory curriculum for all high school students in the Chicago Public Schools found no effects on dropout or graduation rates, but that course failure rates increased, test scores and grades did not improve, and students were no more likely to enter college.[76]

States and districts can also require students to pass an exit examination to earn a diploma. Again, the research evidence on the effect of such tests is inconclusive, in part because research studies differ in the data and methods they use, as well as the time periods they examine. Some found that such requirements increased the likelihood of dropping out,[77] some found no impact on dropping out,[78] and some found differential effects, one finding that they increased dropout rates only among better students and another finding that they increased dropout rates only among the lowest-ability students.[79] One explanation for this apparent inconsistency is that several earlier analyses that found no or differential effects were conducted with data for high school graduates from 1992, whereas more recent data show the high school exit exams since that time have lowered high school completion rates, especially in states with higher concentrations of racial and ethnic minorities, and low-income students.[80]

SCHOOL CHOICE. The most fundamental and potentially far-reaching systemic reform involves creating alternative pathways for students to earn a high school diploma and allowing students and parents to choose among them. School choice is premised on the idea that students and parents will benefit by being given viable school options and that those options will come about through competition and innovation among school providers, including private schools. The degree to which these premises are true has been the subject of intense and partisan debates among academics, policy makers, and advocates.[81]

School choice takes two forms. One is limited to choice among public school options, which includes charter schools, alternative schools, magnet programs, and new forms of public schools, such as middle college high schools that allow students to earn college credits and even degrees while completing a high school diploma.[82] The other involves providing publicly funded vouchers that allow students to attend private schools. Research evidence on the effectiveness of both types of choice is generally mixed and has focused primarily on student achievement (test scores).[83]

A substantial body of research has been done on charter schools. In 2008, Julian Betts and Emily Tang summarized the findings from fourteen studies of charter schools that used two of the most rigorous evaluation methods: randomization based on lotteries, as in the previous evaluation, or value-added models that take into account students' past academic history.[84] They found some charter schools outpace their traditional counterparts, while other charter schools trail behind.[85] Among high schools, about half of the studies show significantly positive effects and half show significantly negative effects in reading; in math, more than two-thirds show significantly negative effects and only 4 percent show significantly positive effects.[86] Betts and Tang conclude that while elementary and middle charter schools outperform traditional public schools in some areas, "charter high schools seem to lag behind traditional public schools, especially in math."[87]

Several more recent, large-scale studies of charter schools have reached similar conclusions. A 2009 study of 669 charters in five districts and three other studies found achievement gains were generally no better or were even worse than traditional public schools, although in Florida and Chicago "attending a charter high school is associated with statistically significant and substantial increases in the probability of graduating and attending college."[88] Another 2009 study of charter school performance in fifteen states and the District of Columbia found that "charter school students in elementary and middle school grades had significantly higher rates of learning than their peers in TPS [traditional public schools], while students in charter high schools and multilevel schools had significantly worse rates of learning."[89] A third study, in 2010, of thirty-six charter middle schools across fifteen states found that "on average, charter middle schools that hold lotteries are neither more nor less successful than traditional public schools in improving student achievement, behavior, and school progress."[90]

Although large-scale studies of charter schools have found mixed results, evaluations of specific charter school programs have found more consistently positive results. One of the largest and best known is the Knowledge Is Power Program (KIPP), which began in 1994 and now comprises a national network of almost sixty-six public schools (85 percent middle schools) in nineteen states and the District of Columbia.[91] Three rigorous evaluations of KIPP have been conducted to date and all found improvements in math and reading.[92] The largest and most recent evaluation of twenty-two KIPP middle schools found that half of the schools improved math achievement by 0.48 effect size, or the equivalent of 1.2 years of accumulated growth in three years, and improved reading achievement by 0.28 effect size, or 0.9 years of achievement growth.[93] Large effect sizes have also been reported by evaluation of some local charter programs in New York and Boston.[94]

Most of the positive effects from these local charter schools have been achievement in elementary and middle school test scores. Evidence on high school test scores and graduation rates is limited or mixed. A study of charter high schools in Chicago found they improved performance on the ACT college admission test by half a point and improved high school graduation rates by 7 percentage points.[95] Another study in Chicago found that students who chose among a number of optional high schools and programs—selective enrollment, magnet and charter schools, career and military academies, magnet programs—increased their graduation rates by 11.2 percentage points, but by only 3.5 percentage points after controlling for an array of background characteristics.[96] Yet low-achieving students and students from high-poverty neighborhoods had less benefit from exercising choice, suggesting they would be better off in their neighborhood school.[97] A study of charter schools in New York City found that they improved scores on the state's Regents Examination, which is required to graduate, and raised the probability of earning a Regents Diploma (an advanced diploma that requires passing exams in five subjects) by 7 percent for each year attended, although the effect was not statistically significant.[98]

Research evidence on the effects of vouchers is similarly mixed. In a 2008 review of the research evidence on publicly funded voucher programs in Florida, Ohio, Washington, D.C., Milwaukee, and Cleveland, economists Lisa Barrow and Cecilia Rouse conclude:

> The best research to date finds relatively small achievement gains for students offered education vouchers, most of which are not statistically different from zero, meaning that those gains may have arisen by chance. Further, the very little evidence about the potential for public schools to respond to increased competitive pressure generated by vouchers also suggests that one should remain wary that large-scale improvements would result from a more comprehensive voucher system.[99]

As with that of charters, most of the research on vouchers has focused on student achievement. One recent descriptive study of the Milwaukee Parental Choice Program (MPCP), which provides up to $6,442 in tax support for students to attend private schools, found that MPCP had graduation rates in 2007–08 that were 12 percentage points higher than students in the Milwaukee Public Schools.[100] But as the author points out, the study is unable to determine a causal connection between MPCP schools and the higher graduation rates because it did not control for background differences between MPCP students and students attending the public high schools.[101]

Costs and Benefits

The research literature has identified a number of specific interventions—from preschool to high school reform models—that have been proven to improve dropout and graduation rates. Yet for policy makers and practitioners to decide which interventions to support and implement, they must also consider their costs. Economists have developed techniques for examining the costs of implementing educational programs and comparing those costs either to their effectiveness, which is known as cost-effectiveness, or to their benefits, which is known as cost-benefit analysis.[102] Costs are important to consider not just because resources are always a constraint in making educational decisions, but also because educational decision makers should consider both costs and benefits in allocating resources most efficiently. The most effective or the least costly programs are not necessarily the most cost-effective.

A recent study by economists Henry Levin and Clive Belfield compared the costs and benefits of five interventions that were proven to be effective in raising high school graduation rates.[103] The interventions ranged from preschool programs to a high school reform model:

- Perry Preschool Program.
- Chicago Child-Parent Center Program.
- Project STAR: class-size reduction.
- Teacher salary increase.
- First Things First: comprehensive school reform model.

The authors conducted the cost-benefit analysis in several steps. First, they estimated the programs' effectiveness by using each intervention's evaluation to determine the number of extra high school graduates the intervention produced for each 100 students served. Second, they estimated the public benefits associated with those graduates based on lifetime economic savings per expected "new" high school graduate in terms of extra tax payments, public health savings, criminal justice savings, and welfare savings. Those public benefits—as reported in Chapter 5—equaled $209,100 per graduate. Third, they estimated the public costs per additional graduate produced by each intervention, including the actual intervention costs as well as the public costs associated with funding additional years of high school and college, since some of the new graduates would be expected to attend college. Finally, the authors compared the benefits with the costs in two ways: calculating the ratio of benefits to costs and computing the net benefit by subtracting the costs from the benefits. The results of those comparisons, shown in Table 8.2, indicate that all five interventions produced benefits in excess of their costs. In this case, because all the benefits are equal, the least costly intervention—First Things First—also had the highest benefit/cost ratio of more than 3:1. That is, for every dollar invested in the program, the government would earn a benefit of more than three dollars.[104]

What Have We Learned from Large-Scale Reform Efforts?

Past efforts to improve dropout and graduation rates have often been undertaken as part of large-scale reform initiatives from government agencies,

Table 8.2   Costs and public benefits of alternative interventions for raising high school graduation rates

	Benefits	Costs	Benefits/costs	Benefits − costs
First Things First	$209,100	$59,100	3.54	$150,000
Chicago Parent-Child Centers	$209,100	$67,700	3.09	$141,400
Teacher salary increase	$209,100	$82,000	2.55	$127,100
Perry Preschool	$209,100	$90,700	2.31	$118,400
Class-size reduction, grades K–3	$209,100	$143,600	1.46	$65,500

Source: Henry M. Levin and Clive R. Belfield, "Educational Interventions to Raise High School Graduation Rates," in *The Price We Pay: Economic and Social Consequences of Inadequate Education,* ed. C. R. Belfield and H. M. Levin (Washington, DC: Brookings Institution Press, 2007), table 9-6.

foundations, and other nonprofit organizations. These initiatives were designed to promote educational improvement on a grand scale, funding the development of large numbers of new schools and programs as well as the dissemination of successful models on the state or national level. Some of these initiatives were designed specifically to improve high school graduation rates, while others were designed to improve a range of school outcomes, including graduation rates.

I recently completed a review of all large-scale reform efforts involving high schools for the Center on Education Policy (CEP).[105] What I discovered was sobering. Despite extensive and widespread efforts and the huge sums of money spent, evaluations of these initiatives have found that they yielded relatively few significant and lasting improvements in student outcomes. But the evaluations have also identified a number of factors that promote or impede the successful implementation and impact of these efforts. These findings provide useful lessons and insights in how to design more effective initiatives to improve dropout and graduation rates in the future. Below I review only a few of the initiatives; my CEP report reviews other initiatives.

High School Graduation Initiative

This currently funded federal program ($50 million in 2010), also known as the School Dropout Prevention Program, supports dropout prevention and recovery programs in middle and high schools. The program was preceded by two phases of an earlier program, the School Dropout Demonstration Assistance Program (SDDAP), one operating from 1989 to 1991, the other from 1991 to 1996. Mathematica Policy Research conducted an evaluation of twenty programs around the country that were funded in the second phase of the SDDAP program: eight middle school programs, eight high school programs, and five schoolwide restructuring programs.[106] All of the programs shared two features: (1) they provided support to students to overcome personal, family, and social barriers to school success, and (2) they tried to create smaller and more personal settings in which students could feel secure and learn more effectively.[107]

Of the eight high school programs, five were alternative school programs (four were alternative high schools and one was a school within a school) that offered a regular high school diploma. The evaluation found that none of the five alternative school programs lowered the dropout rate. In four of the five sites, more students earned diplomas than did control students, but the differences were not statistically significant. The other three programs prepared students to take the GED, producing high GED and overall (GED plus diploma) completion rates.

The largest and most ambitious programs were the five school restructuring efforts funded by multimillion-dollar grants to reduce the need for alternative schools or programs. The evaluation found that none of these restructured schools significantly reduced dropout rates in relation to comparable schools.

> The evaluation did not observe much change, however, or even signs of it beginning. Restructuring schools found it easier to add dropout-prevention services than to change teaching and learning. Some initiatives managed to change teaching and learning to a degree, but the changes were fragile and easily undone if district leadership changed or local political contexts shifted.[108]

The study found that there was little consensus about the source of the dropout problem and, in particular, how faculty and staff may have contributed to it. Consequently, few faculty and staff members were eager or willing to change what they were doing. Finally, turnover of district administrators undermined support for change.

Comprehensive School Reform (CSR) Program

This federal program, which received $1.6 billion in funding from 2000 to 2008, shares the same premise of all CSR reform strategies outlined earlier: it attempts to provide coherent improvements to all aspects of a school's operation.[109]

The U.S. Department of Education funded two evaluations of the CSR program. The first focused on the CSR demonstration program, where the federal government provided funds for schools to implement an approved list of seventeen specific CSR models or to develop their own models. The second evaluation focused on the reauthorized CSR program that provided funds to implement any CSR program that included the eleven essential components (described earlier), and that was based on proven research and evaluation methods. Both programs focused on schools identified as "high-poverty" under Title I of the federal Elementary and Secondary Education Act (at least 50 percent of the students were eligible for the federal school lunch program).

Unfortunately, because relatively few high schools received grants, neither evaluation studied the implementation and impact of the CSR program in high schools. Nonetheless, the evaluations identified a number of problems in implementing the models that would likely affect high schools, as they found with elementary and middle schools. First, there was widespread variability in the adoption process, as measured by how informative, inclusive, and legitimate it was, which is a common problem in policy implementation.[110] Second, only a small percentage of schools (10–20 percent) actually adopted all the components of the CSR models, although those that did were more likely to see improvement in academic achievement. Third, about one-third of the schools ended their relationships with the CSR model providers after three years, citing a variety of reasons. One of those reasons, which confronted states' efforts to support the reform models, was the common problem of school capacity:

> One of the most common and fundamental challenges states encountered in developing their approaches to CSR was the fact that they were dealing with high-poverty, low-performing schools which often lacked the capacity to develop a comprehensive school reform plan that was (1) compatible with their particular needs and (2) capable of being successfully implemented.[111]

California's High Priority Schools Grant Program

Many state organizations have initiated large-scale efforts to reform their high schools, but few evaluations have been conducted to date.[112] In addition, state governments have initiated school reform efforts as part of their accountability systems, but again, few have been evaluated.

One state effort that has been evaluated was in California, which established a state accountability system in 1999, known as the Public Schools Accountability Act (PSAA). The PSAA created a system of rewards and sanctions for meeting or not meeting specific performance targets, and established assistance programs for low-performing schools. In 2001, the High Priority Schools Grant Program (HPSGP) was established as part of PSAA to provide additional funds to the lowest-performing schools in the state, taking the place of an earlier program. Participating schools were required to develop an action plan (or use one previously developed) to serve as a blueprint for the school and community to focus on improving student achievement and meeting growth targets, and they received $400 per student per year for three years (and a possible fourth year, depending on progress) to use toward implementing improvement strategies. The program allocated almost $1 billion to underperforming California schools.

In 2005, the California Department of Education (CDE) contracted with the American Institutes for Research (AIR) to examine the implementation, impact, costs, and benefits of the HPSGP.[113] The evaluation found that while participating schools demonstrated academic gains over the period of program implementation, their gains were not statistically different from those of the comparison schools.[114] The findings were similar to evaluations of the earlier school improvement program. The study concludes:

> It appears that a short-term categorical approach to school reform is *insufficient* to overcome much larger system inadequacies that fail to provide the kinds of longer term support and assistance needed to substantially and consistently improve student performance in the state's most challenged schools. We suggest terminating categorical interventions like the HPSGP in favor of more comprehensive statewide school reform that provides long-term administrative and resource support to the state's lowest-performing schools enrolling our most academically challenging students.[115]

New American Schools

A number of large-scale school reform efforts have been mounted outside federal and state governments, some focusing on high schools and some on all levels of public schools. One of the most ambitious efforts to reform

American schools was the New American Schools (NAS) program, which "was formed in 1991 to create and develop whole-school designs that would be adopted by schools throughout the country in order to improve student performance."[116] NAS was established as a nonprofit organization and was largely funded by the private sector. The founders shared the premise underlying other CSR efforts—that piecemeal, programmatic approaches were insufficient to improve low-performing schools. Instead, the premise underlying NAS was:

> All high-quality schools possess, de facto, a unifying design that allows all staff to function to the best of their abilities and that integrates research-based practices into a *coherent* and *mutually reinforcing* set of effective approaches to teaching and learning for the entire school. The best way to ensure that lower-performing schools adopted successful designs was to fund design teams to develop "break the mold" school designs that could be readily adopted by communities around the nation. After developing the design, teams would go on to implement their designs in schools throughout the country. This adoption would lead to NAS's primary goal of improving the performance of students.[117]

The NAS approach was systematic and comprehensive, and was carried out in four phases: (1) competition and selection, 1992; (2) development phase of one year, 1992–1993; (3) demonstration phase of two years, 1993–1995; and (4) scale-up phase of three years, 1995–1998.

The Rand Corporation undertook a long-term evaluation of the NAS effort, documenting its implementation and the conditions that promoted or impeded the goal of widespread adoption and use of the NAS models as a means to improve student achievement. In particular, the Rand evaluation documented an evolving *theory of action* underlying the NAS approach, from one that schools would simply adopt effective designs in some unspecified way, to one where design teams would need to provide assistance to schools to successfully implement the designs, to one that recognized the importance of school- and district-level factors. One important finding from the evaluation was: "The causal chain of events leading to strong implementation and outcomes have proven to be more complex than originally considered by NAS and one that remained largely outside of its control and influence . . . in keeping with the literature on implementation indicating the complexity of the change process."[118] Another important finding was that implementation varied widely by jurisdiction, by design, and across schools, consistent with other evaluations reported earlier and with the research literature.[119] These two findings help explain another major finding: the initial hypothesis (that a school could improve its performance by adopting a whole-school design) was largely unproven.[120] The Rand evaluation goes on to suggest: "Interventions need to address systemic issues that can hinder implementation."[121]

Gates High School Grants Initiative

Perhaps the most ambitious effort to reform America's high schools is being conducted by the Bill & Melinda Gates Foundation. The initiative is driven by the view that the U.S. system of public education is fundamentally obsolete, as stated emphatically by Bill Gates at the 2005 National Education Summit on High Schools:

> America's high schools are obsolete. By obsolete, I don't just mean that our high schools are broken, flawed, and under-funded—though a case could be made for every one of those points. By obsolete, I mean that our high schools—even when they're working exactly as designed—cannot teach our kids what they need to know today. . . . This isn't an accident or a flaw in the system; it is the system.[122]

From 2000 to 2009, the foundation invested more than $2 billion to start new high schools or redesign existing high schools.[123]

In 2001, the Gates Foundation funded a five-year evaluation of its initiative that was conducted by the American Institutes for Research and SRI International.[124] The evaluation examined the activities of twenty-two grantee organizations, four model schools that were replicated in a number of locales, and dozens of individual schools collecting both qualitative and quantitative data. Like the evaluation of the NAS initiative, the evaluation of the Gates initiative documented an evolving theory of change, beginning with one that focused simply on creating not only small high schools (with no more than 100 students per grade level), but also schools with a number of essential attributes:

- Common focus by students and teachers on a few important goals.
- High expectations to complete a rigorous course of study to prepare for college, career, and citizenship.

- Personalized relationships between students and teachers.
- Respect and responsibility.
- Time for staff to collaborate.
- Performance-based advancement with adequate student support.
- Technology as a tool.[125]

Over time, the theory changed as a result of experience with initial grantees, external conditions, and the growth of foundation staff and capacity. The new theory emphasized more clearly specified models coupled with extensive support, more attention to curriculum and instruction, and more attention to results-oriented models, regardless of the specific attributes found in the model. The theory was further refined to recognize the importance of working with both school districts and state policy. Finally, the theory emphasized the notion of variety and choice of approaches operated by both districts and outside providers so that families could select schools based on their students' interests and needs.

The evaluation examined student outcomes, instructional quality, and district-level efforts to provide school choices to at least 30 percent of students. Student outcomes in new schools and redesigned schools were compared to district averages. The evaluation found that student achievement levels in both new and redesigned schools were below district averages, although data from a more limited sample showed that more than half of both types of schools made above-average gains in student proficiency levels in English language arts, and somewhat smaller gains in math. As the authors point out, students in both types of foundation-sponsored schools had eighth-grade test scores well below the district average, which means students were often several grade levels behind.[126] The evaluation also found that attendance, engagement, and ninth-to-tenth-grade promotion rates in new schools were higher than district averages, but not higher in redesigned schools. As the authors further point out, students in new schools were self-selected and therefore may have been more motivated to succeed than students in redesigned schools.[127]

With respect to instructional quality, the evaluation found that the rigor and relevance of coursework in both English language arts and math was higher in foundation-sponsored new high schools than in classroom assignments in comprehensive high schools in the same or nearby districts with similar populations, although the levels of rigor and relevance of the math assignments were generally low in all schools.[128]

Finally, the evaluation found that in the seventeen districts where the foundation worked, the average percentage of students attending schools of choice increased from 6 percent in 2001–02 to 33 percent in 2004–05.[129] Districts provided locally developed (four districts), externally provided (four districts), or both types of school models (eight districts).[130]

The authors identify several limitations of the evaluation. One is that the schools included in the evaluation were selected during the initial stage of the foundation's theory of change that focused on models with particular attributes rather than models with proven records.[131] Second, the schools had been in operation for only a few years, so the evaluation was unable to examine longer-term impacts that other research indicates is often necessary to show meaningful results. Despite these limitations, the evaluation yielded some useful insights into the challenges facing school reform:

- New schools faced the challenge of recruiting qualified faculty, especially in mathematics, and in retaining teachers because of stressful working conditions.
- Redesigned schools were less successful than new schools in achieving positive student outcomes because it was harder to change the culture and because redesigned schools often focus more on structural than instructional changes.
- Some redesigned schools also created small learning communities that were stratified by academic ability, creating a form of tracking.
- Grantee organizations varied in their capacity to support their schools, with secondary curriculum being a common weakness.[132]

In 2009, the foundation changed its approach to focusing on improving teacher effectiveness after Bill Gates admitted their initial efforts "fell short."[133]

New Futures

While school-based reform initiatives have produced little widespread impact on high school performance, so too have initiatives focused on collaborative reform strategies. One ambitious initiative was the New Futures Initiative, promoted and funded by the Annie E. Casey Foundation beginning in 1988. New Futures was an attempt to build new collaborative structures among existing public and private institutions in five cities (Dayton, Ohio; Lawrence, Massachusetts; Little Rock, Arkansas; Pittsburgh,

Pennsylvania; and Savannah, Georgia) to address the problems of at-risk youth, including dropping out of school. The key strategy was to establish an oversight collaborative in each city with representation from public and private-sector agencies to "identify youth problems, develop strategies, and set timelines for addressing these problems, coordinate joint agency activities, and restructure educational and social services."[134] The collaboratives also included case managers who (1) brokered services among the disparate agencies serving at-risk youth and their families, (2) served as advocates for at-risk youth, and (3) served as the "eyes and ears" of the collaboratives by providing information and feedback to the group about what reforms were needed.

Evaluations of this ambitious, systemic reform effort found that it did little to reduce dropout rates and other problems of at-risk youth.[135] The evaluations found several generic problems in trying to establish community collaboration:

1. *Slippage between policy and action* because case managers were generally unsuccessful in overcoming the "turf battles" among existing agencies and in getting collaboratives to address them.
2. *Discord over reform policies* because of fundamental disagreements over the definitions of, causes of, and remedies to problems.
3. *Disjuncture between policy and community conditions* because of the top-down organization of the collaboratives that resulted in an incomplete understanding of the problems and hence ineffective policies.

These problems, clearly evident in New Futures school reforms, paralleled those found in the earlier evaluation of restructured schools. In particular, "most educators in New Futures schools believed that the problems that created at-risk students were problems inside the students, not inside the school and its curriculum."[136] Hence, as found in other systemic reform efforts, there was little incentive or support for changing the fundamental functioning of schools.

New York City's Small School Initiative

One of the most ambitious high school reform efforts is under way in the New York City public schools. It began in 2001 as the New Century High Schools Initiative (NCHSI) when New Visions for Public Schools in 2001 was awarded $30 million by the Carnegie Corporation and the Open

Society Initiative to establish seventy-five small schools by 2005.[137] In 2002, when Mayor Michael Bloomberg assumed control of the city's schools and appointed Joel Klein chancellor of the Department of Education, the department launched the "Children First" reform agenda that pledged to close more than 20 underperforming high schools and open more than 200 new secondary schools over the next five years. With $150 million in funding by the Bill & Melinda Gates Foundation, eighteen intermediary organizations were charged with designing, opening, and supporting a range of school designs, from new schools to conversions of existing schools, although all designs were based on a common set of ten principles developed by New Visions from the research literature on school reform.[138] Although some of the intermediary organizations had developed and implemented school reform models for many years, few of the models have been rigorously evaluated.

A number of evaluations have been conducted on the New York City initiative. An early evaluation found that students in ten of the initial group of twelve NCHS high schools had graduation rates 18 percentage points higher than students in comparable schools, although the percentage of students earning state-endorsed (Regents) diplomas were comparable.[139] However, students in subsequent entering classes of NCHS had lower rates of school attendance and credit accrual, and higher rates of school suspension, which may impact subsequent graduation rates. The evaluation also found considerable variation in these qualities among the schools. It should be noted that the WWC reviewed three evaluations of the New Century High Schools and found that none was rigorous enough to meet their evaluation standards.[140]

More recent evaluations have been conducted on the larger initiative, including case studies of the intermediary organizations and six high schools.[141] A recent study of 123 "small schools of choice"—small, academically non-selective, four-year public high schools open to students at all levels of academic achievement and located in historically disadvantaged communities—found that they increased the percentage of students who after their first year of high school were on track to graduate by 10 percentage points and they increased overall graduation rates by 6.8 percentage points.[142]

Lessons Learned

Two major lessons can be drawn from large-scale reform efforts, which can be compared to some lessons drawn from a review of a number of federal reforms efforts of the 1960s, '70s, and '80s conducted by RAND researchers.[143]

1. *Large-scale reform initiatives have generally not been successful in making widespread, significant improvements in classroom teaching or in student outcomes.* Reform initiatives have supported a number of different, largely schoolwide reform strategies: school restructuring, comprehensive school reform, new schools, and school-community collaborations. No single reform initiative—except perhaps the New York City small schools initiative—had an overall impact on classroom teaching or on student outcomes, including improved academic achievement and graduation rates, supporting the conclusion stated earlier that no single reform strategy is inherently better than the others. A similar conclusion was reached in a review of earlier federal programs by Rand researchers, who found that

> educational reform has historically had little effect on teaching and learning in classrooms. In this pessimistic sense, educational reform is "steady work." That is, the rewards are puny, measured by substantial changes in what is taught and how; but the work is steady, because there is a limitless supply of new ideas for how schools should be changed and no shortage of political and social pressure to force those ideas onto the political agenda.[144]

2. *There was widespread variability in both the implementation and impact of the initiatives across the settings of schools, districts, and states.* Evaluations found substantial variability in the implementation and impact of the reforms among schools, districts, and states. For instance, the review of the federal Comprehensive School Reform Program found widespread variability in how many of the eleven components of CSR models schools adopted, with most adopting relatively few of them.[145] The Rand evaluation of earlier reform efforts reached the same conclusion: "Variability is the rule and uniformity is the exception," although it also found that "reforms succeed to the degree that they adapt to and capitalize upon variability."[146]

Although the evaluations of these large-scale school improvement efforts found little impact on either instructional practice or student achievement, they did identify a number of factors that limited their implementation and impact. These factors have also been identified in the growing research literature on the implementation of programs and policies.

WILL AND CAPACITY.   The research literature has identified two broad factors that affect implementation: *will* and *capacity*.[147] *Will* and *capacity* refer to traits of both individuals and institutions. At the individual level, *will* refers to the motivation and commitment of educators—teachers and administrators—to implement reform strategies. Both groups of educators play important, yet different roles in the reform process, and respond to different incentives. Teachers' willingness to engage in reform, which often involves learning new instructional practices, depends on several factors: (1) whether they believe it will benefit their students, (2) whether they believe they have the ability and support to learn new practices, and (3) whether they believe that the requisite effort is professionally rewarding and a district priority.[148] Principals' willingness to engage in reform depends on similar factors: (1) how they perceive the reform to affect the administrative business of the school—whether it may create undue burden to the overall functioning of the school, for example, (2) whether they, too, have the ability and support to implement the reform, and (3) whether they also believe it is professionally rewarding and a district priority.[149]

The individual *capacity* of teachers and administrators to carry out reforms is clearly important. The capacity of teachers to implement reforms, which, again, usually means changing their instructional practices, is a time-consuming, multistage process that includes persuasion over the need for reform. Some scholars refer to this as "sensemaking"[150]—an understanding of the new practice, along with feedback about the development of new roles and skills, time, collegial interaction, and technical assistance.[151]

While the will and capacity of individuals are clearly important in educational reform, equally important are the will and capacity of institutions—particularly schools—where most educators work. Institutional will resides in the incentives, structures, norms, and culture of the organization that influence the will of individual educators to engage in reform efforts: "If you ask teachers to change the way they deal with students and to relate to their colleagues differently, the incentives that operate at the organizational level have to reinforce and promote those behaviors."[152]

The *culture* (or climate) of the school is reflected by a number of identifiable characteristics related to both a school's organization and structure (e.g., school site management, parent involvement and support, maximized learning time) and its processes (e.g., collaborative planning and collegial relationships, sense of community, clear goals, and high expectations). The particular "mix" of factors varies from school to school and thus must develop over time from within rather than through external fiat.[153]

A number of scholars have concluded that a key factor in reforming a school and changing its culture is the institutional capacity of the school.[154] School capacity consists of several components, with resources being one of the most important. Several types of resources contribute to school capacity: *material resources*—teachers, textbooks, facilities, etc.; *human resources*, which represents the skills and abilities of teachers, administrators, and staff; and *social resources*, which represent the social relationships or ties among students, parents, teachers, and administrators. One in-depth study of school reform in Chicago found that one particular social resource necessary for school improvement is *relational trust*, which represents the reciprocal social exchanges among all the participants in the schooling enterprise that depend on respect, competence, personal regard for others, and integrity:

> We view the need to develop relational trust as an essential complement both to governance efforts that focus on bringing new incentives to bear on improving practice and to instructional reforms that seek to deepen the technical capacities of school professionals. Absent more supportive social relations among all adults who share responsibility for student development and who remain mutually dependent on each other to achieve success, new policy initiatives are unlikely to produce desired outcomes. Similarly, new technical resources, no matter how sophisticated in design or well supported in implementation, are not likely to be used well, if at all.[155]

Social resources and relational trust contribute to a school's professional community (and culture), which has been shown to impact teachers' *collective* responsibility for student learning, and their instructional practices.[156] Such collective responsibility contributes to a school's internal accountability, in which school staff set clear standards for student performance and monitor student success, and exerts peer pressure to achieve school goals.[157]

Another important component of school capacity is *productivity*, which is "the ability of the school to translate resources into expected outcomes."[158] One common criticism of schools is that they do not use their resources efficiently.[159] Productivity depends, in part, on not just the amount and types of resources and programs (including their standards, curriculum, and assessment), but whether they are aligned with one another and are working together to achieve the same objectives.[160] Productivity also depends on the coherence between current reform efforts and other reforms and policies that may be placing additional or conflicting demands on the school that can impede or undermine the current reform efforts.[161] Additionally, the reform itself may undercut productivity and dilute capacity by the demands it places on the organization, such as the need to adopt new programs and produce quick results in response to accountability demands.[162] The evaluation of the Annenberg challenge grant in Los Angeles, for example, cited the turbulence from changes in state policy as impeding attempts to improve instructional practice in the schools.[163]

If will and capacity are fundamental to successful school reform, one important question is whether both must be present in sufficient amounts before reform strategies can be successfully implemented, or whether the reform itself can sufficiently alter the will and capacity of educators and schools to ensure successful implementation. A study of school reform in Chicago found that indicators of school capacity predicted whether reforms would work, with high-capacity schools showing three times greater impact than low-capacity schools.[164] The lack of capacity in teachers, administrators, schools, and districts was cited in a number of the evaluations as the major reason for the weak implementation and impact of several major reform efforts, as well as the widespread variability among schools and sites. Some evidence also suggests that capacity is generally lower in high schools than in middle or elementary schools.[165]

Although all reform initiatives include a combination of materials, professional development, and technical assistance to build capacity, in many cases the support was unable to raise capacity sufficiently to ensure successful implementation. Many reform strategies also attempt to ensure sufficient will by requiring faculty votes before initiating reforms, although the process for securing buy-in is sometimes coercive and fails to secure genuine willingness to implement the reforms.[166] The study of Chicago school reform found that relationship trust (a component of school capacity) is easier to build in schools that both students and teachers have chosen, thereby ensuring a shared commitment.[167] This literature suggests that it may be necessary to recruit and select teachers with at least some preexisting will and capacity before undertaking school reform. This is one advantage that charter schools typically enjoy over comprehensive school reform—charter schools select their teachers (and may not be required to hire union, district teachers), while comprehensive school reform models are implemented in existing schools and often with existing staffs.

Yet other research suggests that, at least in some instances, "belief or commitment can follow mandated or coerced involvement at both the individual and system level."[168] For example, changing practice and show-ing teachers that effective practices work can change their beliefs about students' ability to learn.[169] Some reform developers point out an impor-tant distinction between the will of district and school leadership versus the will of teachers:

> District leaders remaining on the sidelines, "waiting and seeing," passively undermining grassroots efforts will trump even strong school staff (administrator and teacher) buy-in every time. Top district leaders and those running key central office functions must be on board from the get-go. Teacher buy-in is important but comes *after* leadership buy-in (district and building) and for many staff only comes after implementation and early successes.[170]

In addition, certain organizational features, such as smaller school size and shared decision-making, may facilitate the development of teachers' will and capacity even as they may require new skills and commitment to effectively operate in the restructured organizational arrangements.[171]

The issue of whether, or the extent to which, a certain level of will and capacity must exist before reforms are introduced is difficult to resolve. On the one hand, greater preexisting levels of will and capacity should help— but by no means guarantee—more successful implementation. On the other hand, low levels of will and capacity can be addressed if reforms are properly designed, funded, and matched to the existing needs and capacity of the school, assuming the preexisting needs and capacity of the school can be determined.

The evaluations and existing research literature have identified a num-ber of more specific factors that influence the implementation and impact of school reform strategies, at least in part, through their impact on will and capacity.

THE NATURE OF THE REFORM. Virtually all reforms, no matter their type, are designed to improve the capacity of educators and schools to im-prove student outcomes. Several features of the reform affect successful implementation. One is whether the reform is locally or externally developed.

The research literature suggests that externally developed reform strategies are generally faster and easier to implement in a local site.[172] Another feature of the reform strategy is its specificity—the degree to which it is prescriptive and content-focused versus more process-oriented. Instructional strategies appear to be more successful if they focus on pedagogy rather than curriculum or particular instructional programs.[173] In contrast, comprehensive school reform models that emphasize prescriptive approaches seem to be more successfully implemented than those with more process-oriented approaches.[174] Similarly, specific charter school models such as KIPP and the Harlem Promise Academy appear to have stronger and more consistent impacts than charter schools generally. The need for specificity in reforming schools may depend on existing capacity. One view is that excellent teachers need more autonomy in their choice and application of instructional approaches, while weak or novice teachers benefit from more guidance.[175] Thus, instructional programs that are uniformly prescriptive may be less effective than flexible ones tailored to the teacher's capabilities and the students' needs. A recent evaluation of two supplemental literacy programs for struggling ninth-grade readers appears to bear this out, finding larger effects in the flexible program than the prescriptive one that required teachers to deliver course content in precise and systematic fashion.[176]

A final feature of the reform strategy is the amount and type of support provided in the form of materials, time, professional development, and technical assistance from district staff or outside technical assistance providers. Technical assistance includes developing implementation benchmarks, monitoring the implementation process using these benchmarks, and providing feedback.[177]

SELECTION PROCESS. The selection process is generally considered a critical factor in building will and support to implement reform. Research has shown that teacher buy-in is essential for mounting and sustaining reform efforts in existing schools, with the principal playing a crucial role in promoting teachers' active participation in the selection process.[178] Some comprehensive school reform models, as part of their design, work toward building teachers' and principals' understanding of the reform and, in some cases, help shape the reform to the needs and capacity of the school, a process known as "adaptive implementation."[179] Yet at least one study of the federal Comprehensive School Reform program found that the selection process was less important in ensuring successful implementation than the school-level supports that were provided, reinforcing the idea that will can be altered after successful implementation.[180]

CONTEXT. A number of contextual factors at the school, district, state, and federal levels affect successful implementation. At the school level, studies have found that reforms are easier to adopt in smaller versus larger schools, and in elementary versus secondary schools.[181] Another contextual factor is teacher and administrator stability; it is harder to mount and sustain reform efforts if staff turnover is high, although features of the reform and the process of selection can affect stability by providing support and promoting staff buy-in. There is no consistent evidence on whether student demographics matter—the NAS evaluation did find implementation levels were lower in schools serving significant populations of both poor and minority students.[182] At the district level, studies have found that implementation is more successful in districts that: are more supportive and have more stable leadership that backs the reform efforts; provide more school-level autonomy; have a more coherent program of reform; are not burdened with crises or other distractions; and have trusting relationships among district staff, the school board, and the unions.[183] A 2010 Hechinger report attributed the failure of the Portland, Oregon, school system to improve its graduation rate, despite introducing popular and widely adopted reforms—alternative schools, small academies in large traditional high schools, and targeted extra support for at-risk ninth graders—to its inability to confront "the political, cultural, and bureaucratic forces that typically undermine reform."[184] At the state and federal levels, existing policies, particularly those related to meeting short-term accountability requirements, impact implementation by creating program incoherence and organizational inefficiency at the school level.

Beyond simply identifying factors that promote or impede reform, it is important to identify a *theory of action* to explain the underlying causal process of how reform is supposed to bring about improved student and school performance. A number of prior reform efforts had an explicit theory of action, or at least a stated premise underlying the reform initiative. In some cases, as in the Gates initiative, the theory changed over time in response to initial monitoring of the reform effort. But it is probably safe to say that the conclusion drawn from the Rand evaluation of the NAS applies to virtually all reform initiatives: that the theory of action underlying the reforms "was largely under-developed and underspecified."[185]

Implications

Evaluations of past reform efforts and the existing research literature on implementation provide a number of implications for developing more successful efforts in the future:

1. *Improvement strategies, especially more comprehensive ones, will not be successful until critical aspects of capacity and context are improved.* This was one of the major implications from the NAS evaluation.[186] Most evaluations cited school and district capacity as critical factors in implementation success. The capacity of individuals—teachers and administrators—as well as the institutional capacity of the school itself are key factors to successful implementation. School capacity depends on having sufficient and correct alignment of resources (including sufficient time); it also depends on coherence in its efforts across all the demands placed on schools and their staffs by districts, as well as state and federal policy requirements. Building capacity also depends on having sufficient will or readiness, especially among school and district leadership, to build capacity and initiate reform. Contextual factors in the school (such as student composition and the stability of school personnel) and in the district (such as the harmony between the superintendent, school board, and teachers' union) are much harder to improve.

2. *Districts should be the focal point of high school improvement efforts.* Districts play a critical role in initiating and sustaining school improvement efforts.[187] They also can help create coherence and improve productivity in individual schools engaging in reform efforts by coordinating all the reform efforts within the districts. Moreover, districts that take more control in selecting school improvement strategies tend to provide more support for those efforts.[188] Finally, districts can create new schools, including alternative education schools, so they are in the best position to create a coherent, systemwide effort that involves reforming existing high schools and creating new schools to meet the needs of all students in the districts.

3. Successful improvement efforts depend on selecting not just the most appropriate strategy, but also the most appropriate technical assistance provider. Although some schools and districts can develop local improvement efforts, most require assistance from outside developers and technical assistance providers for materials, information, professional development, implementation monitoring, and guidance.[189] But technical assistance providers vary in their capacity to provide sufficient support to schools and districts. Therefore, it is important that schools and districts select a technical assistance provider that meets their needs and can provide the proper support.[190] In particular, it is important for technical assistance providers to provide consistent, clear, and frequent communication and assistance to districts and schools.[191]

4. Improvement strategies need sufficient time to be fully implemented and to observe meaningful changes in student outcomes. Improving high school performance requires making fundamental changes in the beliefs and practices of school personnel, and ultimately in changing the culture of the school, including the relationships between students and teachers and among school staff.[192] Such changes, especially those concerning instructional practice, take years. Yet accountability systems often require year-to-year improvements in student outcomes, which can thwart long-term investment in building capacity for short-term strategies to raise test scores. In addition, many evaluations tend to focus on the first years of implementation, which may not be sufficient to observe changes in instructional practice that result in improved student outcomes. This implies that evaluations of improvement strategies should be done over long enough periods of time to allow those changes to occur—probably five years or more.

There has been no shortage of efforts to improve dropout and graduation rates in the United States over the past several decades. Efforts range from developing targeted programs for students most at risk for dropping out to large-scale initiatives to improve high school performance. Literally billions of dollars have been spent on these efforts, but there is little to show for it. Why? Two reasons come to mind. First, few targeted programs or high school reform initiatives have proven successful. The most success has been documented by a few specific reform models of targeted programs, comprehensive school reforms, and new charter schools. Second, these proven interventions have yet to be adopted widely where they have the potential to impact large numbers of students. Put differently, the federal and state governments have yet to learn how to scale up successful educational reforms.

What are the prospects for reversing this trend? Are current efforts likely to be more successful than past efforts? Can dropout and graduation rates be improved substantially through widespread school reform efforts alone, or will it require efforts to improve families and communities as well? I address these questions in the concluding chapter.

9

WHAT SHOULD BE DONE TO SOLVE THE DROPOUT CRISIS

Although the term is often overused, the issue of high school dropouts in the United States can rightly be called a crisis. First, the problem is severe, with an estimated 1.3 million students from the class of 2010—about 25 percent—failing to graduate.[1] This is among the highest in developed countries, which include our economic competitors in the world economy. More disturbing, the current high school graduation rate in the United States is no higher than it was more than forty years ago. Second, the problem is costly. Economists estimate that the economic losses from dropouts in a single high school graduating class amount to $335 billion over their lifetimes.[2]

The severity of the crisis is now widely recognized and has commanded the attention of government officials, business leaders, educators, private foundations, national organizations, and advocacy groups. Some of the nation's most influential citizens have publicized the problem before national audiences:

- On February 26, 2005, Bill Gates addressed the nation's governors and declared that "America's high schools are obsolete," noting that only 68 out of every 100 ninth graders graduate.[3]
- On April 11, 2006, Oprah Winfrey dedicated her television show to the nation's dropout crisis.[4]
- On February 24, 2009, before a joint session of Congress, newly elected President Barack Obama declared, "Dropping out of high school is no longer an option."[5]
- On September 27, 2010, NBC News presented a weeklong event examining the state of education in America, including speakers General and Mrs. Colin Powell.[6]

The growing awareness of the dropout crisis has spawned widespread efforts by the public and private sectors to address the problem at the national, state, and local levels. These efforts focus on four major activities:

- Informing the larger public about the nature and severity of the problem and to promote a sense of urgency and broad-based support to address the problem.
- Developing and advocating for specific federal and state policies to address the problem.
- Mobilizing and supporting key stakeholders to take action to address the problem.
- Funding, developing, implementing, evaluating, and scaling up effective dropout prevent programs.

Some of these efforts focus specifically on the dropout crisis itself, while others are directed toward strengthening the public educational system, particularly high schools, in an effort to improve a number of educational outcomes of all students, including dropout and graduation rates. They include not only getting more students to graduate from high school, but also getting all students to graduate from high school sufficiently prepared for college and work.

Although these efforts are extensive and will likely lead to improvements in dropout and graduation rates, they are also likely to fall short of making sizeable improvements, especially for the most disadvantaged students and schools. In this chapter, I first describe recent and ongoing efforts to address America's dropout crisis at the national, state, and local levels. I then explain why these efforts are likely to be insufficient to overcome the problem. Finally, I identify some actions that are likely to lead to more substantial improvements in dropout and graduation rates.

Current Efforts

A wide range of efforts are under way to address the dropout crisis at the national, state, and local levels by private organizations as well as government agencies.

National

A number of private organizations are mobilizing efforts to address the dropout crisis at the national level. One of those is the Alliance for Excellent Education, which was founded in 2001 with a mission "to promote high school transformation to make it possible for every child to graduate prepared for postsecondary learning and success in life."[7] Directed by Bob Wise, the former governor of West Virginia, the alliance "focuses on America's six million most at-risk secondary school students—those in the lowest achievement quartile—who are most likely to leave school without a diploma or to graduate unprepared for a productive future." It produces reports, briefs, and other publications, maintains a website to disseminate this information, and hosts and makes presentations at meetings and conferences across the country "to encourage public awareness and action that support effective secondary school reform." And it works to develop and implement national policies by synthesizing and distributing research and information about promising practices that "enlightens the national debate about education policies and options" and by directly working with and advising key stakeholders.

Another prominent organization addressing the dropout crisis is the America's Promise Alliance, a partnership of more than 300 corporations, nonprofits, faith-based organizations, and advocacy groups dedicated to "improving lives and changing outcomes for children" that includes "ensuring that all young people graduate from high school ready for college, work and life."[8] The organization, founded in 1997 by General Colin Powell and Alma Powell, has focused on the third dropout activity, mobilizing action. In April 2009, it introduced the Dropout Prevention Campaign to promote and fund dropout summits in all fifty states and in fifty-five cities with the largest dropout rates.[9] And on March 1, 2010, it announced the formation of Grad Nation, a ten-year campaign to mobilize the nation to reverse the dropout crisis with a goal of ensuring that 90 percent of America's fourth graders graduate from high school on time, to help fulfill the president's pledge to be the world leader in the proportion of college graduates by 2020.[10]

Other national organizations have also been actively involved in dropout prevention efforts. Civic Enterprises, a public policy firm in Washington, D.C., issued the influential report *Silent Epidemic* in April 2006, which helped focus national attention on the dropout crisis, and teamed with America's Promise Alliance to host the national dropout summit in May 2007.[11] Civic Enterprises works closely with America's Promise Alliance and has continued to issue reports on the crisis and on the progress in addressing it. The National Education Association, the largest teacher professional organization, "supports making high school graduation a national priority" by pledging to invest $10 billion over the next ten years to support dropout prevention efforts, which includes supporting the work of the America's Promise Alliance.[12] The Education Trust, which promotes high academic achievement and narrowed education achievement gaps by issuing reports, participating in policy debates, and working with stakeholders to transform schools and colleges, has issued a series of reports about the dropout crisis at the national, state, and local levels.[13] *Education Week*, the leading education newspaper in the United States, also plays an important role in disseminating information about the dropout crisis, including issuing its annual "Diplomas Count" reports.[14]

The federal government is also actively involved in addressing the dropout crisis, through both legislation and ongoing activities in the U.S. Department of Education (USDOE). Within the USDOE, the National Center for Education Statistics, the federal agency charged with collecting, analyzing, and reporting data related to education, issues the annual *Dropout Rates in the United States*, along with other statistical reports. With input from the National Governors Association, it has adopted a common definition of dropout and graduation rates for federal reporting and accountability purposes. The federal government is also supporting the development of state longitudinal data systems to better track students' progress through school and to generate true cohort graduation rates. And the Institute for Education Sciences supports the What Works Clearinghouse, which reviews and synthesizes research evidence on effective educational interventions, including dropout prevention interventions; it also supports the Doing What Works website, which illustrates research-based practices online.[15]

President Obama has highlighted the dropout crisis as a national priority in his administration, mentioning it in his first address to the joint session of Congress on February 24, 2009, and in subsequent remarks to the Hispanic Chamber of Commerce on March 10, 2009.[16] On March 1, 2010, the president highlighted the steps his administration will take to combat the dropout crisis and to ensure students graduate prepared for college and careers:

- Commit $3.5 billion to fund transformational changes in America's persistently low-performing schools (which produce 50 percent of America's dropouts) and request an additional $900 million in the FY 2010 budget.

- Commit $50 million in the Graduation Promise Fund to invest in innovative dropout recovery and prevention strategies.
- Request $100 million in FY 2011 to fund a new College Pathways Program to increase access to college-level, dual credit, and other accelerated courses in high schools.[17]

These efforts are part of a larger education reform agenda the administration is pursuing under the American Recovery and Reinvestment Act of 2009 (Recovery Act), which Obama signed into law on February 17, 2009, and allocates $105 billion to education to advance four "essential education reforms":

- College- and career-ready standards and high-quality, valid, and reliable assessments for all students.
- Development and use of pre-K through postsecondary and career data systems.
- Increasing teacher effectiveness and ensuring an equitable distribution of qualified teachers.
- Turning around the lowest-performing schools.[18]

The Recovery Act added $3 billion to an existing Title I program, the School Improvement Fund, to target the "persistently lowest-performing schools" in each state with one of four school intervention models:

- *Turnaround model*, which includes, among other actions, replacing the principal and rehiring no more than 50 percent of the school's staff, adopting a new governance structure, and implementing an instructional program that is research-based and vertically aligned from one grade to the next as well as aligned with the state's academic standards.
- *Restart model*, in which the school district converts the school or closes and reopens it under the management of a charter school operator, a charter management organization (CMO), or an education management organization (EMO) selected through a rigorous review process.
- *School closure*, in which the school district closes the school and enrolls the students who attended the school in other, higher-achieving schools in the district.
- *Transformation model*, which addresses four specific areas—teachers and leader effectiveness (including replacing the principal),

instructional and support strategies, extended learning and planning time, and operating flexibility and sustained support.

The Recovery Act also funded two competitive programs: Race to the Top, which provides $4.35 billion to states to "help trail-blaze effective reforms," and Investing in Innovation Fund, which provides $650 million to school districts and schools to expand innovative practices.[19]

These efforts focus not only on dropout prevention, but also on dropout recovery designed to reconnect so-called disconnected youth. Although there are various definitions and estimates of disconnected youth, the term generally refers to the population of young adults sixteen to twenty-four years old who are not working or going to school, and are members of various "vulnerable" populations: high school dropouts, homeless and runaway youth, teen mothers, incarcerated youth, or youth who have aged out of foster care.[20] Estimates of the number of disconnected youth range from 2 million to 5 million, representing up to 20 percent of the total youth population, although a recent longitudinal study found that up to 40 percent of young people are at risk for being disconnected from school or work at some time between the ages of eighteen and twenty-four.[21] A wide variety of government and private programs are designed to reconnect youth to education and training,[22] and while some have shown positive effects, the effects are generally modest or relatively short-lived.[23] New efforts are under way, with the Gates Foundation committing $69 million to double the number of postsecondary degrees earned by low-income students by age twenty-six and the Lumina Foundation for Education establishing a goal of increasing the percentage of Americans with high-quality degrees and credentials to 60 percent by 2025.[24] The federal government has also allocated funds to specifically target disconnected youth, including funds from the 2009 Recovery Act.[25]

Future federal efforts to improve student outcomes will be addressed through upcoming revisions to the 1965 Elementary and Secondary Education Act (ESEA), which was last reauthorized in 2002 as the No Child Left Behind (NCLB) Act. NCLB has been the subject of widespread criticism and study, particularly its accountability provisions, which mandate that all children in America achieve proficiency in reading and math by 2014.[26] In anticipation of its reauthorization, major education stakeholders have issued a number of reports recommending significant changes.[27] The Obama administration released its own blueprint for revising NCLB on March 13, 2010.[28] At this point it is unclear to what extent improving high school graduation rates will be addressed in the reauthorization, although it is likely to be more prominent given all the attention to the issue. In addition, there are a number of bills pending before Congress that focus on improving middle and high schools, and on revising the data and accountability systems for measuring and reporting graduation rates.[29]

State

While states have long been concerned with improving their education systems, the growth of state and federal accountability has lent more urgency to their efforts. States have taken a particularly strong, collective interest in the issue of high school reform in the past few years, both individually and through several national organizations that represent their collective interests.

In 2005, the National Governors Association and Achieve sponsored the National Education Summit on High Schools and issued a report, *An Action Agenda to Improve America's High Schools*, that made five recommendations:

- *Restore value to the high school diploma* by revising academic standards, upgrading curricula and coursework, and developing assessments that align with the expectations of college and the workplace.
- *Redesign the American high school* to provide all students with the higher-level knowledge and skills, educational options, and support they need to succeed.
- *Give high school students the excellent teachers and principals* they need by ensuring teachers and principals have the necessary knowledge and skills and by offering incentives to attract and retain the best and brightest to the neediest schools and subjects.
- *Hold high schools and colleges accountable* for student success by setting meaningful benchmarks, intervening in low-performing schools, and demanding increased accountability of postsecondary institutions.
- *Streamline educational governance* so that the K–12 and postsecondary systems work more closely together.[30]

In January 2009, four state-level organizations—National Governors Association Center for Best Practices, National Conference of State

Legislatures, National Association of State Boards of Education, and Council of Chief State School Officers—issued a joint report, *Accelerating the Agenda: Actions to Improve America's High Schools*, that renews the agenda, documents progress, and discusses the remaining challenges in moving forward.[31]

In the agenda item to redesign high schools, the new report provides more emphasis on "expanding the supply of high-quality schools through new models such as early college high schools and alternative delivery mechanisms such as charter schools and virtual schools; and preventing students from dropping out and reengaging out-of-school youth through youth development programs and alternative high schools,"[32] while acknowledging the need to transform or close existing, low-performing high schools "by seeding innovative practices, evaluating progress, sustaining promising efforts, replicating effective models, and closing persistently failing high schools."[33] The agenda item also restates the need to "identify and support struggling students" and to "reengage out-of-school youth."[34] These recommendations cover several of the general reform strategies discussed earlier: student support programs, alternative programs, comprehensive school reform, and new schools. *What is not specified is the specific nature of these redesigned strategies or how they can be most effectively carried out.*

In October 2009, the National Governors Association Center for Best Practices released a report, *Achieving Graduation for All: A Governor's Guide to Dropout Prevention and Recovery*, which recommends four basic strategies to address the nation's dropout crisis:

1. *Promote high school graduation for all* by: raising the maximum compulsory and allowable school attendance ages; counting graduation rates heavily in state accountability systems; championing higher graduation rates; and assigning responsibility for dropout prevention and recovery.
2. *Target youth at risk of dropping out* by: supporting the development of early warning data systems; targeting investments in promising strategies; and connecting students to existing supports.
3. *Reengage youth who have dropped out of school* by: creating incentives for dropout recovery; employing outreach strategies to reengage out-of-school youth; and establishing school reentry options for juvenile offenders.

4. *Provide rigorous, relevant options for earning a high school diploma* by: creating new effective schools; turning around low-performing schools; and awarding credit for performance, not seat time.[35]

These strategies are very similar to the high school reform strategies the National Governors Association (NGA) released earlier in the year. *Similarly, they provide more information on what should be done than on how to do it.* To provide some guidance on moving forward, in January 2010 the NGA Center selected six states—Colorado, Massachusetts, Minnesota, New Hampshire, Tennessee, and West Virginia—"to develop comprehensive state dropout prevention and recovery policies" based on the recommendations in the report.[36]

Finally, in January 2011 the National Conference of State Legislatures' Task Force on School and Dropout Prevention and Recovery issued its report, *A Path to Graduation for Every Child*, which recommended nine actions that state legislatures can take to address the dropout crisis:

1. Create and sustain urgency to improve high school graduation rates.
2. Insist on high expectations and a rigorous curriculum for all students.
3. Provide options and pathways to engage all students.
4. Put excellent teachers, principals, and other caring adults in schools.
5. Identify and support struggling students.
6. Develop dropout recovery programs to reengage out-of-school youth.
7. Build capacity to transform or replace low graduation-rate high schools.
8. Conduct policy audits, eliminate counterproductive policies and provide incentives for collaboration.
9. Hold schools and districts accountable for improving high school graduation rates.[37]

I have also embarked on an effort to address the dropout crisis in my home state by establishing the California Dropout Research Project in December 2006 at the University of California, Santa Barbara.[38] The project has three goals:

1. To *generate research knowledge* to inform policy makers, educators, and the general public about the nature, causes, consequences, and solutions to the dropout crisis in California.

2. To *develop a meaningful policy agenda* to address the problem.
3. To *disseminate project findings* via publications, the project website, and the media.

Through December 2010, the project has published sixty-six reports, policy briefs, statistical briefs, and dropout profiles for the seventeen largest cities in California. In March 2007, the project established a policy committee composed of state legislators, educators, and researchers that issued a report in February 2008, *Solving California's Dropout Crisis*, recommending a series of actions that the state, local school districts, and schools should undertake to address the crisis.[39] The recommendations are designed to effect change through a combination of *pressure* and *support*: (1) pressure to get educators, policy makers, and the public to stay focused on the problem and to seek solutions, and (2) support for educators and educational institutions to build their capacity to address the problem. The report recommends that the state should:

1. Fix the accountability system to maintain pressure and to allow sufficient time to address the problem.
2. Collect and report more useful data on dropouts and the state's progress in improving graduation rates.
3. Develop high school reform standards and create "lighthouse" districts to implement them in schools with high dropout rates.
4. Undertake middle school reform.
5. Make strategic investments in proven dropout prevention strategies targeting the most disadvantaged students and schools.
6. Reexamine state high school graduation requirements.

The project has achieved some success: more than 50,000 copies of its publications have been downloaded from the website; project publications have received considerable media coverage throughout the state and nationwide; and four bills incorporating recommendations from the report were introduced in the state legislature over the past three years, three of which were signed into law by the governor. However, no legislative or State Department action has been taken on the other recommendations because of the severe budget constraints.

Local

The national and state efforts have spurred many local efforts to address the dropout crisis. America's Promise has supported fifty-five local dropout summits in major cities across the United States and provided materials "to build a sense of urgency around the crisis, secure a commitment to action from leaders in all sectors and most importantly, to result in follow-up action plans to strengthen current efforts and initiate new strategic activity to help more young people graduate from high school ready for college, work and life."[40]

The federal government is in the process of awarding $3.5 billion in School Improvement Grants to turn around the nation's persistently lowest-achieving schools. By the fall of 2010, the U.S. Department of Education had awarded grants to forty-four states and the District of Columbia.[41] In the 2010–11 school year, 730 schools (48 percent of them high schools) began implementing one of the four required intervention models. A review of the initial applications reveals that most schools receiving the funds will adopt the transformation model, which many educators consider to be the least disruptive compared to the other models, which required replacing most of the staff, closing the school, or restarting the school as a charter.[42] The federal government has also awarded $650 million in grants to forty-nine local applicants for the Investing in Innovation Fund, including thirteen grants that target persistently low-performing schools.[43] However, only two of the larger grants target high schools: one targeting sixty middle and high schools in fourteen school districts with a proven whole-school reform model and a student support model,[44] and the other supporting the charter restart model of school transformation in the cities of New Orleans, Memphis, and Nashville.[45]

Finally, a growing number of new, innovative schools are being developed and expanded through national networks and organizations, including:

- *Early college high schools* (200 schools in 24 states) that enable high school students to take community college courses and early college credits and degrees.[46]
- *Big Picture Learning schools* (131 schools in 17 states and Washington, D.C., and 4 other countries) that promote relevant and authentic learning through individualized programs and workplace internships.[47]

There are also efforts to expand "multiple pathways" in high schools that combine rigorous academic and technical coursework with real-world applications and work-based learning.[48]

Are Current Efforts Enough?

Judging by public awareness, private and public activities, and private and public funding, an extraordinary national effort appears to be under way in the United States to address the country's dropout crisis. Yet, these efforts are unlikely to make a sizeable dent in the problem for three reasons:

1. Insufficient targeting of true dropout factories. A popular belief held by many leaders of the dropout effort, including President Barack Obama, is that the dropout crisis is concentrated in so-called dropout factories. The Alliance for Excellent Education has created a database that computes the promoting power of every U.S. high school, because no national dropout data exist for U.S. high schools. The promoting power simply measures the ratio of twelfth graders in a school to ninth-graders three years earlier. Schools with promoting power of 60 percent or less are then identified as "dropout factories" and are said to account for 50 percent of the nation's dropouts.[49] Not only is the promoting power index an inaccurate indicator of dropout rates,[50] it is also misleading because it excludes the large number of alternative schools in the United States that educate a high proportion of at-risk students and account for a high proportion of the dropouts. In California, alternative schools enrolled 8 percent of students in 2005–06 but accounted for 33 percent of the dropouts.[51] Charter schools, a growing number of which serve at-risk students, enrolled another 8 percent of students and accounted for an additional 16 percent of the state's dropouts. More important, dropout factories should be identified not by their dropout rate, but by the actual number of dropouts they produce. *To make a dent in the nation's dropout rate, efforts should focus on **true** dropout factories.*

Yet it does not appear recent efforts are indeed targeting such schools. The federal government's School Improvement Grants are supposed to target each state's persistently lowest-achieving schools. But school performance is judged by a composite measure, with more (or even all) of the weight given to test scores than to graduation rates. Schools could also qualify if their graduation rate was below 60 percent (so-called dropout factories), but because graduation rates can be computed on inflated measures, few schools may qualify. In California, which uses an inflated, federally approved graduation rate, only 5 high schools (out of 2,437 in the state) qualified as persistently lowest-achieving based on graduation rates below 60 percent![52] On November 16, 2010, the federal government released a list of 730 schools (350 high schools) from 44 states that were awarded School Improvement Grants. Comparing the list of schools with dropout figures from California and Texas shows that few high dropout schools received grants. In Texas, none of the 25 schools with the most dropouts (4,798 dropouts total) received any grants.[53] In California, none of the 10 schools that produced the most dropouts (12,188 dropouts total) were even eligible to receive any school improvement funds.[54] For instance, Los Angeles Alternative School, with 1,988 dropouts in 2007–08 and a 50 percent dropout rate, received no funding.

2. *Insufficient funding to develop and implement dropout prevention and recovery strategies.* High school reform efforts alone are unlikely to significantly improve dropout and graduation rates. As the What Works Clearinghouse practice guide, *Dropout Prevention*, documents, students at risk of dropping out need additional supports—mentoring, tutoring, etc.—beyond those typically provided in most school reform efforts, even effective comprehensive school reform models. This can be viewed as another form of differentiated education, where students receive a continuum of support in school depending on their needs and available resources. Thus, government agencies and private organizations should continue to develop, fund, evaluate, and implement specific dropout and recovery prevention strategies and programs, along with comprehensive and systemic school reform strategies. The current funding of $50 million for the High School Graduation Initiative is woefully insufficient.

3. *Lack of attention to costs, sustainability, and scalability.* The federal government has led a national effort to require and support rigorous evaluations of educational interventions. The National Center for Education Research (NCER) supports rigorous research, including efficacy studies to evaluate the effectiveness of programs and practices;[55] the National Center for Education Evaluation and Regional Assistance (NCEE) conducts large-scale evaluations of federally funded educational programs;[56] and the What Works Clearinghouse reviews and synthesizes research evaluations of educational interventions.[57] While this effort is commendable and has helped policy makers and educators learn about the need for rigorous evidence to determine what educational interventions actually work, three areas need further attention.

First, more attention needs to be paid to program costs. As described in the previous chapter, policy makers and practitioners should consider the costs as well as the benefits in determining which interventions to adopt. Interventions that are the most effective or the least costly are not necessarily the most cost-effective. Yet while the federal government is investing considerable resources in determining whether educational interventions are effective, it does not appear to be investing anywhere near comparable resources in measuring costs and determining the cost-effectiveness of interventions. As a result, policy makers and practitioners lack valuable information on where to invest scarce resources that will yield the most impact on improving student outcomes—the most "bang for the buck."[58] Levin and Belfield show that a number of educational interventions, from preschool to high school reform, can improve high school graduation rates, but some are more cost-effective than others. In the current reform agenda, it would be valuable to know the cost-effectiveness of the various high school improvement models that the federal government is funding.

Second, more attention needs to be paid to sustainability. Many educational interventions require additional resources not just to design and implement, but also to sustain. For example, a proven dropout intervention program, Check and Connect, assigns students to a "monitor" who works with and advocates for at-risk students.[59] Often such interventions are supported with external grants. But what happens when the grants run out? How is the program sustained even if found to be successful? Those questions are not typically addressed in intervention studies, but they should be. The government, as well as foundations, should not focus simply on identifying effective or even cost-effective interventions, but also on how cost-effective interventions can be sustained in the current climate of fiscal constraints when the grant funding runs out.

Third, more attention needs to be paid to scalability. One of the great challenges in improving America's education system is not simply to find and sustain cost-effective practices and programs, but to scale up the most cost-effective ones to other schools and districts. Reviews of past large-scale reform efforts in Chapter 8 consistently found widespread variability on the impact of the interventions, supporting an earlier observation that "variability is the rule and uniformity is the exception."[60] This is another area that requires more research. The most recent federal government Investing in Innovation grants included several to scale up some proven interventions, including two to improve the performance of persistently low-achieving schools.[61] And the NCER just funded the National Research and Development Center on Scaling Up Effective Schools, which will identify effective schools and design a process to transfer those practices to other schools.[62] But more needs to be done.

For one thing, it is important to know the barriers, both technical and political, to scaling up successful programs and practices in new locations. For example, if charter schools are successful in part because they select their teachers and are not bound by district union contracts, then the feasibility of scaling up charter schools districtwide would have to confront that issue. It would also be useful to have evaluations identify the effectiveness of key components of interventions and their costs to further broaden our knowledge base about which reforms to scale up.

For another thing, it is also important to consider resource requirements. For example, the average charter school student in New York City spends 8 hours a day and 192 days a year in school.[63] KIPP charter schools, which just received a $50 million federal i3 grant, raise millions of dollars from private foundations and spend an estimated $1,100 to $1,500 more per pupil than regular public schools.[64] If charter schools indeed require higher per student costs, then how scalable are they in the current fiscal climate?

Moving Beyond Current Efforts

Current efforts should lead to some improvement in U.S. dropout and graduation rates. But generating and sustaining significant improvements in dropout and graduation rates will require five additional and more fundamental changes in the U.S. educational system.

Redefining High School Success

As documented in Chapter 2, public officials, parents, and students have always supported broad goals for public education, including a high school education. At the same time, an increasing body of evidence finds that success in college and the labor market, as well as healthy youth development, requires a broad array of both cognitive and noncognitive skills.[65] Yet federal and state accountability systems judge the performance of students and schools on a very narrow range of cognitive skills, particularly reading and math. States and districts are also raising high school graduation requirements by increasing the number and rigor of required academic courses and by adding exit exams. Already twenty-one states have adopted the rigorous, college- and career-ready curriculum, including four years of challenging math, advocated by Achieve and other organizations.[66] As a result, high school is getting harder and success more narrowly defined. The current mantra is "college-ready for all."

Continuing down this path could increase rather than decrease the number of high school dropouts. Moreover, two recent projections find that fewer than two-thirds of job openings in the U.S. economy between 2008 and 2018 will require *any* postsecondary education.[67] These projections reflect a long-standing and continued shift, documented by MIT economist David Autor, of "a pronounced 'polarization' of job opportunities in the U.S., with growth concentrated in relatively high-skill, high wage and in low-skill, low-wage jobs—at the expense of 'middle skill' jobs."[68]

Not only is it important to consider the level of skills that future jobs will require, but also the kinds of skills. Increasingly, a number of economists, including Nobel economist James Heckman, have documented the need for noncognitive or so-called soft skills in the labor market, such as motivation, perseverance, risk aversion, self-esteem, and self-control.[69] Indeed, a 2001 report from the National Association of Manufacturers found the top skill deficiency in both current workers and job applicants was a lack of basic employability skills (attendance, timeliness, work ethic, etc.).[70] The Partnership for 21st Century Skills, a national advocacy organization with a wide range of industry members, argues that—in addition to core academic subject knowledge—students need eleven essential skills and literacies, such as critical thinking, problem solving, communication, and collaboration.[71] In the fall of 2010, the Hewlett Foundation announced a new focus on what it calls "deeper learning" that includes, in addition to mastery of core academic content, critical thinking and problem solving, working collaboratively in groups, communicating clearly and effectively, and learning how to learn.[72]

Finally, high school should prepare adolescents not just for work and careers, but for successful lives as adults. A long-term study by sociologist John Clausen tracked children born in the Great Depression for six decades and found that those whose lives turned out best—they obtained more education, had lower rates of divorce, had more orderly careers, achieved higher occupational status, and experienced fewer life crises, such as unemployment—shared something he labeled "planful competence," a combination of dependability, intellectual involvement, and self-confidence, that was evident in high school: "Predicting to age 70, there's nothing that predicts better than what they were like in high school."[73] This perspective is consistent with Howard Gardner's notion of "multiple intelligences," which include musical, spatial, bodily-kinesthetic intelligences, Daniel Goleman's notion of emotional intelligence, and a growing body of research documenting the benefits of social and emotional learning.[74]

So, instead of defining success solely in terms of mastering a college-preparatory curriculum, we should develop a broader measure of high school success, one that includes vocational and technical education as well as the arts and humanities. A 2011 report from the Harvard Graduate School of Education also questions our current academic, classroom-based approach to reform and instead argues for expanded pathways and work-based learning opportunities to better prepare our young people for a successful adult life.[75] As Stanford education professor Nel Noddings commented in a recent *Education Week* exchange on common standards:

> It is politically incorrect today to suggest that some kids have neither the interest nor aptitude for academic mathematics. Nevertheless, it is true. When I taught high school math (everything from general math to Advanced Placement calculus), I was continually astonished at the range of achievement that appeared in every course. It was wonderful to work with kids who were eager to learn more and more. But it was also gratifying to help less interested students find material connected to their own purposes, and it was humbling to learn something about the impressive range of human talents. There are many intelligent, industrious, morally decent, creative people who dislike academic math and really don't need it.
>
> We do not need to standardize. We need to differentiate—to offer a greater variety of courses—and we should work on the quality of these courses.[76]

Supporting this idea is a growing body of research evidence that career and technical education (CTE) in high school increases attendance rates, improves high school completion rates, and improves earnings and employment prospects of high school graduates regardless of whether they attend college.[77] International comparisons further reveal that countries offering more access to vocational options have higher high school completion rates and higher scores on international tests.[78] Such courses can also provide another way of teaching rigorous academic content. The University of California, for example, is helping teachers design so-called integrated high school CTE courses that meet the university's entry requirements.[79]

The idea of redefining and broadening the definition of high school success is perhaps best exemplified in Big Picture Learning high schools, where learning is tailored to the interests and goals of each student and pursued through a combination of individualized school-based and work-based learning experiences.[80] Such an approach could be used to redefine high school graduation requirements where students must demonstrate mastery of an area that most interests them—whether it is math, physics, cooking, mechanics, sports—while achieving acceptable proficiency in core academic and other areas. Such an approach could better develop the broad array of non-cognitive skills and multiple intelligences needed for adult life rather than forcing every student through the same college-preparatory curriculum.

Changing Accountability Systems to Provide Incentives to Educate All Students

As discussed earlier, there has been a long-standing effort to define an accurate and suitable graduation rate. The NGA led the effort in 2005 by defining a cohort graduation rate based on the number of regular diplomas awarded to students within four years of entering ninth grade.[81] The U.S. Department of Education adopted new graduation rate regulations in 2008 similar to the NGA's that states must begin reporting in the 2010–11 school year.[82] And some pending legislation proposes to create still other graduation rate measures that would include students who earn diplomas beyond the standard four years.[83] Common to all these definitions is that students who transfer from their original high school to another high school would no longer be considered a member of the original school's ninth-grade cohort and thus be excluded in calculating the school's graduation rate. Because schools are accountable for improving the achievement of current students, this provision provides an incentive for schools to encourage transfers of the most challenging students to alternative schools or other comprehensive high schools.

Instead, schools should be provided incentives to successfully educate all the students who enter as ninth graders. One way to do this is to include all students who spend at least one semester of ninth grade in that school's ninth-grade cohort when calculating their graduation rate, regardless of whether the student remains in the school. That way, schools will have a greater incentive to ensure that if students do transfer, they transfer to a school that is likely to improve their chances of graduating. They could also receive more "credit" for successfully graduating a student the longer the student remains in the school. So a school that educated a student for three years would be more accountable for that student than a school that educated a student for only one year. This approach will be adopted in California when recent legislation is implemented that requires the assignment of test scores and other accountability data of students enrolled in alternative education programs back to the school or district of residence.[84] Implementing this recommendation would be facilitated by states' longitudinal student data systems that track students who transfer from one public school to another.

Building Capacity of the Educational System

Evaluations of past reform efforts by the federal government, state governments, and private organizations have consistently concluded that these reform efforts have largely failed because educational institutions lacked sufficient capacity to implement and sustain school reform. Reform efforts have also been hampered by contextual factors such as personnel turnover, political instability, and poor fiscal health. Reform efforts have largely utilized mandates and resources to force schools and staffs to change their practices over the short term rather than building their capacity to improve over the long run.

Unfortunately, current reform efforts largely follow the same formula: increasing standards, mandating reform strategies, and providing more funding to states and schools that adopt these measures. But without a clear and focused effort to improve the capacity at all levels of the educational system—the federal level, the state level, the local district and school level—these efforts will likely fail. For example, one current federal reform strategy—transforming a school by replacing the majority of the staff—is a form of reconstitution that has been tried previously in districts and found to be ineffective because it failed "to address the broad contextual forces that mediate the capacity of schools to fundamentally alter their performance."[85] The importance of building capacity was recognized in the current principles for reforming the No Child Left Behind Act released by the Center for Education Policy;[86] it was also recognized by the California Dropout Research Project Policy Committee as a key strategy for solving the state's dropout crisis.[87] Building capacity should include using state and local data systems for ongoing evaluations of innovative programs and practices together with a mechanism for disseminating and scaling those that are proven effective.

Desegregating Schools

Schools in the United States are highly segregated by race and poverty because communities are segregated and most students still attend neighborhood schools. As a result, black and Hispanic students are much more likely than white and Asian students to attend schools where the majority of other students are poor minorities.[88] Both the racial and socioeconomic composition of schools affect achievement. One recent study found that the average socioeconomic status of the student body had about the same impact on student achievement growth in U.S. high schools as students' individual socioeconomic status.[89] Another study found that two-thirds of all high schools in the United States with more than 90 percent minority enrollment had fewer than six in ten students remain in school from ninth to twelfth grade.[90] In short, it matters with whom one goes to school.

Yet the United States has largely retreated from active pursuit of policies to desegregate its public schools, resulting in a deepening segregation of black and Latino students by race and poverty.[91] While some of the inequalities associated with segregated schools, such as teacher quality and fiscal resources, can be addressed without desegregating schools, segregated schools would still remain "inherently unequal," as the Supreme Court found in the 1954 *Brown v. Board of Education* decision. Continued efforts need to be made to integrate schools to provide equal opportunity for all students.[92]

Strengthening Families and Communities

School-based approaches alone, even with the addition of targeted dropout interventions, are also unlikely to solve the dropout crisis without providing adequate support to families and communities. In particular, even widespread school reform that raised the persistently lowest-achieving schools to even average achievement levels will unlikely raise the graduation rate sufficiently and at best eliminate about one-third of the achievement differences between racial and socioeconomic groups.[93] Therefore, improving graduation rates and closing gaps in graduation will require interventions in two other arenas: families and communities.

Family background remains the most important predictor of success or failure in school. Many students—particularly racial, ethnic, and linguistic minorities—come from families with insufficient fiscal, human, and social resources to guarantee success in school. One in five American children lives in poverty, with the proportion exceeding one in three for black and Hispanic children.[94] Based on an international definition of relative poverty, a 2005 United Nations report found that the United States had the highest rate of child poverty among all twenty-four OECD (Organisation for Economic and Co-operative Development) countries, exceeded only by Mexico.[95] The report further found that variation in government policy—particularly the extent to which the government provides social transfer programs for low-income families—explains most of the variation in poverty rates among countries. A follow-up report examined six dimensions of child well-being—material well-being, health and safety, educational well-being, family and peer relationships, behaviors and risks, and subjective well-being—in twenty-one industrialized nations of the world, and the United States ranked twentieth.[96] Maybe it is not a coincidence that the United States ranks twentieth in the world in high school graduation rates and twentieth in the world in child well-being.[97] If the United States ever hopes to achieve Obama's stated goal of becoming first in the world in college completion rates, then it is imperative that we greatly increase rates of high school graduation and child well-being.

One valuable investment is in early childhood education and preschool. Numerous studies have documented the educational benefits of preschool, including improved graduation rates and reduced crime.[98] Investment in high-quality preschool is also cost-effective.[99] Early education interventions are particularly important in overcoming achievement gaps, which are already sizeable by the time children start school.[100] Research finds that "on average, the later the remediation is given to a disadvantaged child, the less effective it is."[101] Early interventions develop not only cognitive skills but also noncognitive skills that help to foster cognitive skills.

U.S. communities also vary widely in the levels of resources and supports they provide their residents. Black families in particular are more likely to live in communities of concentrated disadvantage than other families, compounding the disadvantages of having high rates of family poverty. Just as it is unlikely the United States can ever attain world dominance in educational attainment without also achieving world dominance in child well-being, it is unlikely that the United States can improve high school graduation rates, especially for African-Americans, without eliminating communities of concentrated disadvantage.

Improving U.S. dropout and graduation rates is likely to be a never-ending goal, akin to improving health care or the environment. Setting specific targets—such as the 90 percent high school completion rate for the year 2000 that U.S. governors set in 1989 or Obama's goal of the United States achieving the highest college completion rate in the world by 2020—are probably less useful in achieving sustained improvements than undertaking a more fundamental commitment to improving the lives of children and strengthening the families, schools, and communities that serve them. Ultimately, it will require a fundamental commitment to improving educational opportunity in the United States and eliminating long-standing and deep inequities in American society, a challenge clearly stated by sociologist James Coleman during America's last large-scale commitment to civil rights, during the 1960s:

> In some part, the difficulties and complexity of any solution derive from the premise that our society is committed to overcoming, not merely inequalities in the distribution of educational *resources* (classroom teachers, libraries, etc.), but inequalities in the opportunity for educational *achievement*. This is a task far more ambitious than has ever been attempted by any society:— not just to offer, in a passive way, equal access to educational resources, but to provide an educational environment that will free a child's potentialities for learning from the inequalities imposed upon him by the accident of birth into one or another home and social environment.[102]

This challenge Coleman identified more than four decades ago remains just as formidable today.

NOTES

INDEX

NOTES

1. Introduction

1. The names of the student and of the school are pseudonyms. This account comes from a dropout-intervention program conducted by the author and a colleague in the school. See Katherine A. Larson and Russell W. Rumberger, "ALAS: Achievement for Latinos through Academic Success," in *Staying in School: A Technical Report of Three Dropout Prevention Projects for Middle School Students with Learning and Emotional Disabilities*, ed. H. Thorton (Minneapolis: University of Minnesota, Institute on Community Integration, 1995).

2. Robert Stillwell, Jennifer Sable, and Chris Plotts, *Public School Graduates and Dropouts from the Common Core Data: School Year 2008–09* (NCES 2011-312) (Washington, DC: National Center for Education Statistics, U.S. Department of Education, 2011), http://nces.ed.gov/Pubsearch/Pubsinfo.Asp?Pubid= 2011312 (accessed May 9, 2011), table 4.

3. "Diplomas Count 2010: Graduation by the Numbers: Putting Data to Work for Student Success," *Education Week*, June 10, 2010, www.edweek.org/Ew/Toc/ 2010/06/10/Index.html (accessed August 28, 2010), 25.

4. Thomas D. Snyder and Sally A. Dillow, *Digest of Education Statistics 2010* (NCES 2011-015) (Washington, DC: National Center for Education Statistics, U.S. Department of Education, 2011), http://nces.ed.gov/Pubsearch/Pubsinfo .Asp?Pubid=2011015 (accessed May 9, 2011), table 9.

5. Stillwell, Sable, and Plotts, *Public School Graduates*, table 4.

6. Snyder and Dillow, *Digest of Education Statistics 2010*, table 37.

7. "Diplomas Count 2010," 24.

8. Special-education students are entitled to receive services for a specified number of years, often until they reach age twenty-one. They may exit school at that time with a regular diploma, an alternative diploma, a certificate of attendance, or no certificate. See Snyder and Dillow, *Digest of Education Statistics 2010*, table 117.

9. Russell W. Rumberger, *Tenth Grade Dropout Rates by Native Language, Race/ Ethnicity, and Socioeconomic Status* (Santa Barbara: University of California

Linguistic Minority Research Institute, 2006), http://lmri.ucsb.edu/Publications (accessed January 17, 2011), figure 1.

10. "Diplomas Count 2010," 25.

11. Elaine Allensworth, *Graduation and Dropout Trends in Chicago: A Look at Cohorts of Students from 1991 through 2004* (Chicago: Consortium on Chicago School Research, 2005), http://ccsr.uchicago.edu/content/publications .php?pub_id=61&list=t (accessed January 17, 2011), table 5.1.

12. James J. Heckman and Paul A. Lafontaine, "The American High School Graduation Rate: Trends and Levels," *Review of Economics and Statistics* 92 (2010): 244–262.

13. "Meeting Summary," 2005 NGA Winter Meeting and Education Summit, Washington, DC, February 26–March 1, www.nga.org/portal/site/nga/menuitem .f3e4d086ac6dda968a278110501010a0/?vgnextoid=cf9f28a5f7ca7110VgnVC M1000001a01010aRCRD (accessed February 15, 2011).

14. "What the Bill and Melinda Gates Foundation Wants You to Know," www.oprah.com/dated/oprahshow/oprahshow_20060411 (accessed February 15, 2011).

15. See www.americaspromise.org/Our-Work/Grad-Nation.aspx.

16. "Remarks by the President at the America's Promise Alliance Education Event, U.S. Chamber of Commerce, Washington, D.C.," March 1, 2010, www .whitehouse.gov/the-press-office/remarks-president-americas-promise-alliance -education-event (accessed August 27, 2010).

17. *National Goals for Education* (Washington, DC: U.S. Department of Education, 1990).

18. *The 1963 Dropout Campaign* (Washington, DC: U.S. Department of Health, Education, and Welfare, 1964).

19. Sherman Dorn, *Creating the Dropout: An Institutional and Social History of School Failure* (Westport, CT: Praeger, 1996).

20. The largest of these was the School Dropout Demonstration Assistance Program (SDDAP), which funded $294 million in targeted and school reform programs from 1989 to 1996. An evaluation of the last and largest phase of the program found that most programs had little impact on reducing dropout rates. See Mark Dynarski and Philip Gleason, *How Can We Help? What We Have Learned from Federal Dropout-Prevention Programs* (Princeton, NJ: Mathematica Policy Research, 1998).

21. *College Enrollment and Work Activity of 2010 High School Graduates* (Washington, DC: U.S. Department of Labor, Bureau of Labor Statistics, 2011), www .bls.gov/schedule/archives/all_nr.htm#HSGEC (accessed May 9, 2011), table 1.

22. *Labor Force Statistics from the Current Population Survey* (Washington, DC: Bureau of Labor Statistics, U.S. Department of Labor, 2010), www.bls.gov/Cps/ Tables.Htm#Nempstat_M (accessed January 17, 2011), table A-16.

23. Susan Aud et al., *The Condition of Education 2010* (NCES 2010-028) (Washington, DC: National Center for Education Statistics, 2010), http://nces.ed.gov/ pubsearch/pubsinfo.asp?pubid=2010028 (accessed January 17, 2011), table A-17-1.

24. Cecilia E. Rouse, "Consequences for the Labor Market," in *The Price We Pay: Economic and Social Consequences of Inadequate Education*, ed. C. R. Belfield and H. M. Levin (Washington, DC: Brookings Institution Press, 2007), 99–141. Rouse estimates that if dropouts who completed high school attended college at rates similar to those of high school graduates, the difference would exceed $550,000.

25. Susan Rotermund, *Education and Economic Consequences for Students Who Drop Out of High School*, Statistical Brief 5 (Santa Barbara: California Dropout Research Project, University of California, 2007), http://cdrp.ucsb .edu/Dropouts/Pubs_Statbriefs.Htm#5 (accessed January 17, 2011), figure 1.

26. Ibid., Figure 2.

27. Clive Belfield and Harry M. Levin, eds., *The Price We Pay: Economic and Social Consequences of Inadequate Education* (Washington, DC: Brookings Institution Press, 2007).

28. Becky Pettit and Bruce Western, "Mass Imprisonment and the Life Course: Race and Class Inequality in U.S. Incarceration," *American Sociological Review* 69 (2004): 151–169.

29. Henry M. Levin and Clive R. Belfield, "Educational Interventions to Raise High School Graduation Rates," in *The Price We Pay: Economic and Social Consequences of Inadequate Education*, ed. C. R. Belfield and H. M. Levin (Washington, DC: Brookings Institution Press, 2007), 177–199, 194.

30. Aud et al., *The Condition of Education 2010*.

31. Rick Fry and Felisa Gonzales, *One-in-Five and Growing Fast: A Profile of Hispanic Public School Students* (Washington, DC: Pew Hispanic Center, 2008), http://pewhispanic.org/Files/Reports/92.Pdf (accessed January 17, 2011), i.

32. Russell W. Rumberger and Sun Ah Lim, *Why Students Drop Out of School: A Review of 25 Years of Research* (Santa Barbara: California Dropout Research Project, University of California, 2008), http://cdrp.ucsb.edu/Dropouts/Pubs_ Reports.Htm#15 (accessed January 17, 2011).

33. Michele D. Kipke, ed., *Risks and Opportunities: Synthesis of Studies on Adolescence*, National Research Council and Institute of Medicine, Forum on Adolescence (Washington, D.C.: National Academic Press, 1999), 11–12.

34. Susan Rotermund, *Why Students Drop Out of High School: Comparisons from Three National Surveys*, Statistical Brief 2 (Santa Barbara: California Dropout Research Project, University of California, 2007), http://cdrp.ucsb.edu/ Dropouts/Pubs_Statbriefs.Htm#2 (accessed January 17, 2011). See also John M. Bridgeland, John J. DiIulio Jr., and Karen Burke Morison, *The Silent*

Epidemic: Perspectives on High School Dropouts (Washington, DC: Civil Enterprises, 2006).

35. Robert Haveman, Barbara Wolfe, and James Spaulding, "Childhood Events and Circumstances Influencing High School Completion, "*Demography* 28 (1991): 133–157; Russell W. Rumberger, "Dropping Out of Middle School: A Multilevel Analysis of Students and Schools," *American Educational Research Journal* 32 (1995): 583–625; Russell W. Rumberger and Katherine A. Larson, "Student Mobility and the Increased Risk of High School Dropout," *American Journal of Education* 107 (1998): 1–35; Christopher B. Swanson and Barbara Schneider, "Students on the Move: Residential and Educational Mobility in America's Schools," *Sociology of Education* 72 (1999): 54–67; Jay D. Teachman, Kathleen Paasch, and Karen Carver, "School Capital and Dropping Out of School." *Journal of Marriage and the Family* 58 (1996): 773–783.

36. Rumberger and Larson, "Student Mobility."

37. Kipke, *Risks and Opportunities*, 12.

38. Richard Jessor, "Successful Adolescent Development among Youth in High-Risk Settings," *American Psychologist* 48 (1993): 117–126.

39. National Research Council Panel on High-Risk Youth, *Losing Generations: Adolescents in High-Risk Settings* (Washington, DC: National Academy Press, 1993).

40. Gary W. Evans, "The Environment of Childhood Poverty," *American Psychologist* 59 (2004): 77–92.

41. See, for example, Henry T. Trueba, George Spindler, and Louise Spindler, eds., *What Do Anthropologists Have to Say about Dropouts?* (New York: Falmer Press, 1989).

42. Russell W. Rumberger and Gregory J. Palardy, "Multilevel Models for School Effectiveness Research," in *Handbook of Quantitative Methodology for the Social Sciences*, ed. D. Kaplan (Thousand Oaks, CA: Sage Publications, 2004), 235–258.

43. See Rumberger and Lim, *Why Students Drop Out of School*. Rumberger and Lim reviewed 203 empirical studies from academic journals published over the 25-year period from 1983 to 2007. The summary in the text is based on that review.

44. Russell W. Rumberger, Rita Ghatak, Gary Poulos, Philip L. Ritter, and Sanford M. Dornbusch, "Family influences on dropout behavior in one California high school." *Sociology of Education* 63 (1990): 283–299; Rumberger, "Dropping Out of Middle School."

45. Michelle Fine, *Framing Dropouts: Notes on the Politics of an Urban Public High School* (Albany: State University of New York Press, 1991); Carolyn Riehl, "Labeling and Letting Go: An Organizational Analysis of How High School

Students Are Discharged as Dropouts," in *Research in Sociology of Education and Socialization*, ed. A. M. Pallas (New York: JAI Press, 1999), 231–268.

46. Rebecca L. Clark, *Neighborhood Effects on Dropping Out of School Among Teenage Boys* (Washington, DC: The Urban Institute); Jonathan Crane, "The Epidemic Theory of Ghettos and Neighborhood Effects on Dropping Out and Teenage Childbearing," *American Journal of Sociology* 96 (1991): 1226–1259.

47. Robert J. Sampson, Jeffrey D. Morenoff, and Thomas Gannon-Rowley, "Assessing 'Neighborhood Effects': Social Processes and New Directions in Research," *Annual Review of Sociology* 28 (2002): 443–478.

48. Tama Leventhal and Jeanne Brooks-Gunn, "The Neighborhoods They Live in: The Effects of Neighborhood Residence on Child and Adolescent Outcomes," *Psychological Bulletin* 126 (2000): 309–337; Maureen T. Hallinan and Richard A. Williams, "Students' Characteristics and the Peer-influence Process," *Sociology of Education* 63 (1990): 122–132; William J. Wilson, *The Truly Disadvantaged: The Inner City, the Underclass, and Public Policy* (Chicago: The University of Chicago Press, 1987).

49. Karl L. Alexander, Doris R. Entwisle, and Nadir S. Kabbini, "The Dropout Process in Life Course Perspective: Early Risk Factors at Home and School," *Teachers College Record* 103 (2001): 760–882; Byron L. Barrington and Bryan Hendricks, "Differentiating Characteristics of High School Graduates, Dropouts, and Nongraduates," *Journal of Educational Research* 82 (1989): 309–319; Robert B. Cairns, Beverley D. Cairns, and Holly J. Necherman, "Early School Dropout: Configurations and Determinants," *Child Development* 60 (1989): 1437–1452; Margaret E. Ensminger and Anita L. Slusacick, "Paths to High School Graduation or Dropout: A Longitudinal Study of a First-Grade Cohort," *Sociology of Education* 65 (1992): 95–113; Helen E. Garnier, Judith A. Stein, and Jennifer K. Jacobs, "The Process of Dropping Out of High School: A 19-Year Perspective," *American Educational Research Journal* 34 (1997): 395–419; Melissa Roderick, *The Path to Dropping Out* (Westport, CT: Auburn House, 1993).

50. See Mark Dynarski et al., *Dropout Prevention: A Practice Guide* (NCEE 2008-4025) (Washington, DC: National Center for Education Evaluation and Regional Assistance, U.S. Department of Education, 2008), http://ies.ed.gov/ncee/wwc (accessed January 17, 2011).

51. Flavio Cunha and James J. Heckman, "Investing in Our Young People" (working paper 16201, National Bureau of Economic Research, Cambridge, MA, 2010), http://papers.nber.org/papers/w16201 (accessed January 17, 2011).

52. Aud et al., *The Condition of Education 2010*, table A-32-1; Chen-Su Chen, *Numbers and Types of Public Elementary and Secondary Schools from the Common Core of Data: School Year 2009–10 - First Look* (Washington, DC: National Center for Education Statistics, U.S. Department of Education,

2011), http://nces.ed.gov/pubsearch/pubsinfo.asp?pubid=2011345 (accessed May 14, 2011), tables 2 and 3.

53. Marshall S. Smith and Jennifer O'Day, "Systemic School Reform," in *The Politics of Curriculum and Testing,* ed. S. H. Fuhrman and B. Malen (Philadelphia: Falmer Press, 1991), 233–267.

54. *WWC Topic Report: Dropout Prevention* (Washington, DC: What Works Clearinghouse, U.S. Department of Education, 2008), http://ies.ed.gov/ncee/wwc/reports/dropout/topic (accessed January 17, 2011).

55. For a review of the research, see John H. Tyler, "Economic Benefits of the GED: Lessons from Recent Research," *Review of Educational Research* 73 (2003): 369–398.

56. For example, the federal accountability established under the No Child Left Behind (NCLB) Act requires states to improve high school graduation rates where only regular diplomas are counted. See "Elementary and Secondary Education: A Uniform Comparable Graduation Rate," www.ed.gov/policy/elsec/reg/proposal/uniform-grad-rate.html (accessed February 15, 2011).

57. Comprehensive School Reform Quality Center, *CSRQ Center Report on Middle and High School Comprehensive School Reform Models* (Washington, DC: American Institutes for Research, 2006); Sarah Hooker and Betsy Brand, *Success at Every Step: How 23 Programs Support Youth on the Path to College and Beyond* (Washington, DC: American Youth Policy Forum, 2009), www.aypf.org/Publications/Index.Htm (accessed August 27, 2010); Tali Klima, Marna Miller, and Corey Nunlist, *What Works? Targeted Truancy and Dropout Programs in Middle and High School* (Olympia: Washington State Institute for Public Policy, 2009), www.wsipp.wa.gov/topic.asp?cat=11&subcat=0&dteslct=0 (accessed January 17, 2011).

58. Levin and Belfield, "Educational Interventions," table 9-6.

59. Anthony P. Carnevale, Nicole Smith, and Jeff Strohl, *Help Wanted: Projections of Jobs and Education Requirements through 2018* (Washington, DC: Center for Education and the Workforce, Georgetown University, 2010), http://cew.georgetown.edu (accessed January 17, 2011), Figure 2.2.

60. For a detailed description of the project, see Larson and Rumberger, "ALAS: Achievement for Latinos through Academic Success."

61. See *Graduation Counts* (Washington, DC: National Governors Association Task Force on State High School Graduation Data, 2005), www.nga.org/Files/Pdf/0507GRAD.pdf (accessed January 17, 2011).

62. For more information, visit the project website, www.cdrp.ucsb.edu (accessed February 15, 2011).

63. Angela Valenzuela, *Subtractive Schooling: U.S.-Mexican Youth and the Politics of Caring* (Albany: State University of New York Press, 1999);

Nilda Flores-González, *School Kids/Street Kids: Identity Development in Latino Students* (New York: Teachers College Press, 2002); Fine, *Framing Dropouts.*

64. Harriett D. Romo and Toni Falbo, *Latino High School Graduation: Defying the Odds* (Austin: University of Texas Press, 1996).

65. Deirdre M. Kelly, *Last Chance High: How Girls and Boys Drop In and Out of Alternative Schools* (New Haven, CT: Yale University Press, 1993).

66. Mark S. Fleisher, *Dead End Kids: Gang Girls and the Boys They Know* (Madison: University of Wisconsin Press, 1998).

67. Kathryn Edin and Maria Kefalas, *Promises I Can Keep: Why Poor Women Put Motherhood before Marriage* (Berkeley: University of California Press, 2005).

68. Mercer L. Sullivan, *"Getting Paid": Youth Crime and Work in the Inner City* (Ithaca, NY: Cornell University Press, 1989).

2. The Varying Requirements and Pathways for Completing High School

1. Stephen Lamb, *Alternative Pathways to High School Graduation: An International Comparison* (Santa Barbara, CA: California Dropout Research Project, 2008), http://cdrp.ucsb.edu/dropouts/pubs_reports.htm#7 (accessed January 17, 2011).

2. Sherman Dorn, *Creating the Dropout: An Institutional and Social History of School Failure* (Westport, CT: Praeger, 1996), 36.

3. Thomas D. Snyder and Sally A. Dillow, *Digest of Education Statistics 2010* (NCES 2011-015) (Washington, DC: National Center for Education Statistics, U.S. Department of Education, 2011), http://nces.ed.gov/Pubsearch/Pubsinfo.Asp?Pubid=2011015 (accessed May 9, 2011), table 50.

4. Dorn, *Creating the Dropout,* 39.

5. Marvin Lazerson and W. Norton Grubb, *American Education and Vocationalism: A Documentary History, 1870–1970* (New York: Teachers College Press, 1974), 2–32.

6. This account is taken from Dorn, *Creating the Dropout,* 44.

7. David B. Tyack, *The One Best System* (Cambridge, MA: Harvard University Press, 1974), 188.

8. Raymond E. Callahan, *Education and the Cult of Efficiency* (Chicago: University of Chicago Press, 1962).

9. As quoted in Tyack, *The One Best System,* 188.

10. Richard Rothstein, Rebecca Jacobsen, and Tamara Wilder, *Grading Education: Getting Accountability Right* (Washington, DC, and New York: Economic Policy Institute and Teachers College Press, 2008), 19.

11. As quoted in Dorn, *Creating the Dropout,* 41.

12. All the material in this paragraph is taken from Dorn, *Creating the Dropout,* 42.

13. Tyack, *The One Best System,* 204.

14. Ibid., 200.
15. As quoted in Dorn, *Creating the Dropout*, 47.
16. Ibid., 49.
17. Rothstein et al., *Grading Education: Getting Accountability Right.*
18. Ibid., 17.
19. Ibid., 27.
20. Ibid., 101.
21. Ibid., 31.
22. As quoted in ibid., 31.
23. Gillian Hampden-Thompson, Siri Warkentein, and Bruce Daniel, *Course Credit Accrual and Dropping Out of High School, Student Characteristics* (NCES 2009-035) (Washington, DC: National Center for Education Statistics, U.S. Department of Education, 2009), http://nces.ed.gov/pubsearch/pubsinfo .asp?pubid=2009035 (accessed May 9, 2011).
24. *State College- and Career-Ready High School Graduation Requirements* (Washington, DC: Achieve, 2010), www.achieve.org/state-college-and-career -ready-high-school-graduation-requirements-comparison-table (accessed January 17, 2011).
25. *Ready or Not: Creating a High School Diploma that Counts* (Washington, DC: America Diploma Project, 2004), www.achieve.org/ReadyorNot (accessed January 17, 2011), 8–9.
26. See Common Core State Standards Initiative, www.corestandards.org (accessed February 15, 2010).
27. See *State College- and Career-Ready High School Graduation Requirements.*
28. See http://notebook.lausd.net/portal/page?_pageid=33,161841&_dad=ptl& _schema=PTL_EP (accessed January 17, 2011).
29. Tony Barboza, "Santa Ana Seeks to Ease High School Graduation Require-ments," *Los Angeles Times*, February 8, 2009, www.latimes.com/news/local/ orange/la-me-graduation8-2009feb08,0,3520667.story (accessed January 17, 2011).
30. The historical figures come from John Robert Warren, Krista N. Jenkins, and Rachel B. Kulick, "High School Exit Examinations and State-Level Comple-tion and GED Rates 1975–2002," *Educational Evaluation and Policy Analysis* 28 (2006): 131–152.
31. The most recent data on types of exams was from 2006, when twenty-two states required exams. See Snyder et al., *Digest of Education Statistics 2008*, table 167.
32. *High School Graduation Requirements Questions and Answers* (Baltimore: Maryland State Department of Education, 2008), www.marylandpublicschools .org/MSDE/Testing/Hsg_Qa (accessed January 17, 2011), 8.
33. Ying Zhang reports that nineteen of the twenty-six states with exit exams in 2009 offered alternative pathways for regular education students to graduate without earning passing scores in all tested subjects, twenty-two states offered

specific alternative pathways for students with disabilities, and only two states offered alternatives for English-language learners; Ying Zhang, *State High School Exit Exams: Trends in Test Programs, Alternative Pathways, and Pass Rates* (Washington, DC: Center on Education Policy, 2009), www.Cep-Dc .Org/Index.Cfm?Fuseaction=Page.Viewpage&Pageid=493&Parentid=481 (accessed January 17, 2011), 2. Martha L. Thurlow et al. found forty-six alternative routes in their study, twenty-three for all students, and twenty-three for students with disabilities; Martha L. Thurlow, Damien C. Cormier, and Miong Vang, "Alternative Routes to Earning a Standard High School Diploma," *Exceptionality* 17 (2009): 135–149.

34. College Now, "High School Graduation: Credit and Regents Requirements," http://collegenow.cuny.edu/nextstop/finish_hs/creditreq (accessed March 4, 2009).

35. Jay P. Heubert and Robert M. Hauser, eds., *High Stakes: Testing for Tracking, Promotion, and Graduation* (Washington, DC: National Research Council, Committee on Appropriate Test Use, National Academies Press, 1999), 166.

36. Ibid., 164, 166.

37. As reported in ibid., 163.

38. See, for example, lawsuits over California's high school exit exam by one public-interest law firm, Public Advocates, www.publicadvocates.org/ourwork/ education/index.html#CAHSEE (accessed January 17, 2011).

39. Heubert et al., *High Stakes*, 214.

40. See www.p12.nysed.gov/osa/sam/secondary/section1.html.

41. *Aligning High School Graduation Requirements with the Real World: A Road Map for States* (Washington, DC: Achieve, 2007), www.achieve.org/Aligning HighSchoolGradRequirements (accessed January 17, 2011), 2.

42. *Ready or Not*, 82.

43. See "Additional Information on Honors Policy for Mathematics Honors Course," www.ucop.edu/a-gGuide/ag/a-g/math_reqs.html (accessed January 17, 2011).

44. GED Testing Service, *2009 GED Testing Program Statistical Report* (Washington, DC: American Council on Education, 2010), www.acenet.edu/Content/ Navigationmenu/Ged/Index.Htm (accessed January 17, 2011).

45. Ibid., 3.

46. For a list of GED credentials awarded by states and their requirements, see ibid., appendix A.

47. GED Testing Service, *2008–09 GED Option Statistical Report* (Washington, DC: American Council on Education, 2009), www.acenet.edu/Content/ Navigationmenu/Ged/Pubs/GEDTS_Pubs.Htm (accessed January 17, 2011).

48. James J. Heckman, John Eric Humphries, and Nicholas S. Mader, "The GED" (working paper 16064, National Bureau of Economic Research, Cambridge, MA, 2010), www.Nber.Org/Papers/W16064 (accessed January 17, 2010), 50.

49. Jeannie Oakes, *Keeping Track: How Schools Structure Inequality*, 2nd ed. (New Haven, CT: Yale University Press, 2005), 41.

50. Ibid., 43–44.

51. Ibid., 45–46.

52. Michael Planty, Robert Bozick, and Steven J. Ingels, *Academic Pathways, Preparation, and Performance: A Descriptive Overview of Transcripts from the High School Graduating Class of 2003–04* (NCES 2007-316) (Washington, DC: National Center for Education Statistics, U.S. Department of Education, 2006), 8.

53. Ibid., tables 3–6.

54. Oakes, *Keeping Track*, 3.

55. Ibid., 76–78.

56. Ibid., 85.

57. Ibid., 98–101.

58. Ibid., 105–112.

59. Ibid., chapter 6.

60. Ibid., 40.

61. Adam Gamoran and Mark Berends, "The Effects of Stratification in Secondary Schools: Synthesis of Survey and Ethnographic Research," *Review of Educational Research* 57 (1987): 415–435; Samuel Roundfield Lucas, *Tracking Inequality: Stratification and Mobility in American High Schools* (New York: Teachers College Press, 1999).

62. Oakes, *Keeping Track*, xi.

63. Tyack, *The One Best System*, 110–111.

64. Ibid., 217.

65. As quoted in ibid., 228–229.

66. U.S. Bureau of the Census, "Percentage of the Population 3 Years Old and Over Enrolled in School, by Age, Sex, Race, and Hispanic Origin: October 1947 to 2007," www.census.gov/population/www/socdemo/school.html (accessed March 6, 2009), table A-2.

67. Gary Orfield and Chungmei Lee, *Historical Reversals, Accelerating Resegregation, and the Need for New Integration Strategies* (Los Angeles: Civil Rights Project/Proyecto Derechos Civiles, UCLA, 2007), table 8.

68. Ibid., 31.

69. Susan Aud, Mary Ann Fox, and Angelina KewalRamani, *Status and Trends in the Education of Racial and Ethnic Groups* (NCES 2010-015) (Washington, DC: National Center for Education Statistics, U.S. Department of Education, 2010), http://nces.ed.gov/pubsearch/pubsinfo.asp?pubid=2010015 (accessed January 17, 2011), figure 4.

70. James S. Coleman et al., *Equality of Educational Opportunity* (Washington, DC: U.S. Government Printing Office, 1966).

71. James S. Coleman, *Equality and Achievement in Education* (Boulder, CO: Westview Press, 1990), 86.

72. Susan E. Mayer, "How Much Does a High School's Racial and Socioeconomic Mix Affect Graduation and Teenage Fertility Rates?" in *The Urban Underclass*, ed. C. Jencks and P. Peterson (Washington, DC : Brookings Institution Press, 1991), 321–341; Charles T. Clotfelter, *After Brown: The Rise and Retreat of School Desegregation* (Princeton, NJ: Princeton University Press, 2004).

73. Michelle Fine, "Why Urban Adolescents Drop Into and Out of Public High School," *Teachers College Record* 87 (1986): 393–409; Angela Valenzuela, *Subtractive Schooling: U.S.-Mexican Youth and the Politics of Caring* (Albany: State University of New York Press, 1999); Nilda Flores-Gonzalez, *School Kids/ Street Kids: Identity Development in Latino Students* (New York: Teachers College Press, 2002).

74. Valenzuela, *Subtractive Schooling*, 5.

75. Tyack, *The One Best System*, 186–189.

76. Deirdre M. Kelly, *Last Chance High: How Girls and Boys Drop In and Out of Alternative Schools* (New Haven, CT: Yale University Press, 1993), 39–40.

77. Ibid., p. 35.

78. Ibid., 215.

79. Ibid., 108.

80. Ibid., 49.

81. Chen-Su Chen, *Numbers and Types of Public Elementary and Secondary Schools from the Common Core of Data: School Year 2009–10—First Look* (NCES 2011-345) (Washington, DC: National Center for Education Statistics, U.S. Department of Education, 2011), http://nces.ed.gov/Pubsearch/Pubsinfo. Asp?Pubid=2011345 (May 14, 2011), B-1.

82. Ibid., Tables 2 and 3.

83. These figures are based on data from the U.S. Department of Education, Common Core of Data, Build a Table website, http://nces.ed.gov/ccd/bat/index .asp (accessed July 21, 2010).

84. Camilla A. Lehr, Eric J. Lanners, and Cheryl M. Lange, *Alternative Schools: Policy and Legislation across the United States* (Minneapolis: University of Minnesota, Institute on Community Integration, 2003), http://ici.umn.edu/ Alternativeschools/Publications/Default.html (accessed January 17, 2011).

85. Susan Rotermund, *Alternative Education Enrollment and Dropouts in California High Schools*, Statistical Brief 6 (Santa Barbara: California Dropout Research Project, University of California, 2007), http://cdrp.ucsb.edu/ Dropouts/Pubs_Statbriefs.Htm#6 (accessed January 17, 2011).

86. Deirdre M. Kelly, "'Choosing' the Alternative: Conflicting Missions and Constrained Choice in a Dropout Prevention Program," in *Debating*

Dropouts. Critical Policy and Research Perspectives on School Leaving, ed. D. Kelly and J. Gaskell (New York: Teachers College Press, 1996), 108.

87. Ibid., 114.

88. Adult Education Annual Report to Congress 2004–05 (Washington, DC: U.S. Department of Education, 2007), www2.ed.gov/about/offices/list/ovae/pi/AdultEd/congressionalreport04-05.pdf (accessed January 17, 2011), 1.

89. From U.S. Department of Education, Office of Vocational and Adult Education National Reporting System, http://wdcrobcolp01.ed.gov/CFAPPS/OVAE/NRS/reports (accessed July 16, 2010). Unfortunately, the data do not distinguish between regular and equivalency diplomas.

90. From U.S. Department of Labor, Job Corps Performance and Planning website, www.jobcorps.gov/AboutJobCorps/performance_planning.aspx (accessed July 16, 2010). The percentage of Job Corps participants who received a regular diploma in 2008, 25 percent, was much higher than the 5 percent reported in an earlier evaluation based on data from the mid-1990s. Peter Z. Schochet, John Burghardt, and Sheena McConnell, "Does Job Corps Work? Impact Findings from the National Job Corps Study," American Economic Review 98 (2008): 1864-1886.

91. Gateway to College National Network, www.gatewaytocollege.org (accessed July 22, 2010).

3. The Nature and Extent of the Dropout Crisis

1. Russell W. Rumberger and Katherine A. Larson, "Toward Explaining Differences in Educational Achievement among Mexican-American Language Minority Students," Sociology of Education 71 (1998): 69–93, table 1.

2. Jacob Alex Klerman and Lynn A. Karoly, "Young Men and the Transition to Stable Employment," Monthly Labor Review 117 (1994): 31–48.

3. Emily Forrest Cataldi, Jennifer Laird, and Angelina KewalRamani, High School Dropout and Completion Rates in the United States: 2007 (NCES 2009-064) (Washington, DC: National Center for Education Statistics, U.S. Department of Education, 2009), http://nces.ed.gov/pubsearch/pubsinfo.asp?pubid=2009064 (accessed January 17, 2011), A-2.

4. Ibid.

5. "Defining and Calculating Dropout and Completion Rates Using the CPS," http://nces.ed.gov/pubs2007/dropout05/DefiningDropoutAndCompletion.asp (accessed January 17, 2011).

6. California Longitudinal Pupil Achievement Data System (CALPADS): CALPADS Data Guide (Sacramento: California Department of Education, 2010), www.cde.ca.gov/ds/sp/cl/systemdocs.asp (accessed April 24, 2011), 139.

7. "A Uniform, Comparable Graduation Rate: How the Final Regulations for Title I Hold Schools, Districts, and States Accountable for Improving Gradua-

tion Rates," www.ed.gov/policy/elsec/reg/proposal/uniform-grad-rate.html (accessed February 15, 2011).

8. *Graduation Counts* (Washington, DC: National Governors Association Task Force on State High School Graduation Data, 2005), www.Nga.Org/Files/Pdf/0507GRAD.pdf (accessed January 17, 2011), 15.

9. *Geographic Mobility: 2008 to 2009* (Washington, DC: U.S. Census Bureau, 2009), www.census.gov/population/www/socdemo/migrate/Cps2009.html (accessed January 17, 2011), detailed table 1.

10. Russell W. Rumberger and Katherine A. Larson, "Student Mobility and the Increased Risk of High School Dropout," *American Journal of Education* 107 (1998): 1–35, table 2.

11. NAEP Data Explorer, http://nces.ed.gov/nationsreportcard/nde/criteria.asp (accessed January 14, 2009).

12. *Many Challenges Arise in Educating Students Who Change Schools Frequently* (GAO-11-40) (Washington, DC: U.S. Government Accountability Office, 2010), www.Gao.Gov/Products/GAO-11-40?Source=Ra (accessed January 17, 2011), table 2. This study did not distinguish between school changes associated with promotion from one school level to another (e.g., elementary to middle) and nonpromotional school changes, so the extent of nonpromotional student mobility is unknown.

13. See Russell W. Rumberger et al., *The Educational Consequences of Mobility for California Students and Schools* (Berkeley: Policy Analysis for California Education, 1999), table 2.1.

14. See "IESP Policy Brief: From One to Eight: A Longitudinal Portrait of the First Grade Class of 1995–1996," http://steinhardt.nyu.edu/scmsAdmin/uploads/001/402/IESPBrief_from%20one%20to%20eight.pdf (accessed February 15, 2011).

15. David Silver, Marisa Saunders, and Estela Zarate, *What Factors Predict High School Graduation in the Los Angeles Unified School District?* (Santa Barbara: California Dropout Research Project, University of California, 2008), http://Cdrp.Ucsb.Edu/Dropouts/Pubs_Reports.Htm#14 (accessed January 17, 2011), table 3.

16. The Data Quality Campaign (DQC), a national effort to support the development of state longitudinal data systems, surveys states every year to identify their progress in implementing what it considers the ten essential elements of a robust longitudinal data system. According to the most recent survey, in 2009–10, all states had implemented at least some of the elements, although some states (such as Idaho) were far from having all the elements in place. See http://dataqualitycampaign.org (accessed February 15, 2011).

17. Data retrieved from Dataquest, http://data1.cde.ca.gov/dataquest (accessed May 8, 2011).

18. Rumberger and Larson, "Student Mobility and the Increased Risk of High School Drop Out," table 3.

19. Silver et al., *What Factors Predict High School Graduation*, table 3.
20. David Hurst, Dana Kelly, and Daniel Princiotta, *Educational Attainment of High School Dropouts 8 Years Later* (NCES 2007-019) (Washington, DC: National Center for Education Statistics, U.S. Department of Education, 2004), http://nces.ed.gov/Pubsearch/Pubsinfo.Asp?Pubid=2005026 (accessed January 17, 2011).
21. Russell W. Rumberger and Susan Rotermund, *What Happened to Dropouts from the High School Class of 2004?* Statistical Brief 10 (Santa Barbara: California Dropout Research Project, University of California, 2008), www.cdrp.ucsb.edu/pubs_stetbriefs.htm (accessed January 17, 2011).
22. See the Civil Rights Project, www.civilrightsproject.ucla.edu, and Achieve, www.achieve.org (accessed February 15, 2010).
23. See "Dropouts Concentrated in 35 Cities, While Federal Data on Dropouts Underestimates Problem," www.gse.harvard.edu/news/features/conf01132001.html (accessed January 19, 2005).
24. Christopher B. Swanson, "The New Math on Graduation Rates," www.urban.org/publications/1000675.html (accessed February 16, 2011).
25. Russell W. Rumberger and Daniel J. Losen, "Other View: Under NCLB, State Tinkers with Dropout Rates," http://education.ucsb.edu/rumberger/papers.htm (accessed February 16, 2011).
26. See Manhattan Institute for Policy Research, www.manhattan-institute.org (accessed February 16, 2011).
27. Jay P. Greene, *High School Graduation Rates in the United States* (New York: Manhattan Institute, 2001).
28. *Telling the Whole Truth (Or Not) about High School Graduation* (Washington, DC: Education Trust, 2003), www2.Edtrust.Org/Edtrust/Product+Catalog/Main.Htm (accessed January 17, 2011).
29. Lawrence Mishel and Joydeep Roy, *Rethinking High School Graduation Rates and Trends* (Washington, DC: Economic Policy Institute, 2006).
30. See Lawrence Mishel, "The Exaggerated Dropout Crisis," *Education Week*, March 7, 2006, www.edweek.org/ew/articles/2006/03/08/26mishel.h25.html?r=323797944 (accessed January 26, 2009); Jay P. Greene, Marcus A. Winters, and Christopher B. Swanson, "Missing the Mark on Graduation Rates," *Education Week*, March 28, 2006, www.edweek.org/ew/articles/2006/03/29/29greene.h25.html?qs=jay+greene (accessed January 26, 2009).
31. Debra Viadero, "Debate over Dropouts Renewed as Scholars Issue Dueling Reports," *Education Week*, April 21, 2006, www.edweek.org/ew/articles/2006/04/26/33grad.h25.html?qs=jay+greene (accessed January 26, 2009).
32. "Diplomas Count: An Essential Guide to Graduation Policies and Rates," *Education Week*, www.edweek.org/ew/articles/2006/06/22/41s_about.h25.html (accessed January 21, 2009).
33. Ibid., 10.

34. See report abstract, National Institute of Statistical Sciences/Education Statistics Services Institute Task Force on Graduation, Completion, and Dropout Indicators, *Final Report* (Washington, DC: National Center for Education Statistics, U.S. Department of Education, 2004), http://nces.ed.gov/pubsearch/pubsinfo.asp?pubid=2005105 (accessed January 20, 2009).

35. Ibid.

36. Jennifer Laird et al., *Dropout Rates in the United States: 2002 and 2003* (NCES 2006-062) (Washington, DC: National Center for Education Statistics, U.S. Department of Education, 2006), http://nces.ed.gov/Pubsearch/Pubsinfo.Asp?Pubid=2006062 (accessed January 17, 2011), tables 12-A and 12-B.

37. Gary Orfield et al., *Losing Our Future: How Minority Youth Are Being Left Behind by the Graduation Rate Crisis* (Cambridge, MA: Civil Rights Project at Harvard University, 2004); *Telling the Whole Truth (Or Not).*

38. *Graduation Counts.*

39. See "A Compact on State High School Graduation Data," www.nga.org/Files/pdf/0507GRADCOMPACT.PDF (accessed January 17, 2011).

40. See "A Uniform, Comparable Graduation Rate," www.ed.gov/policy/elsec/reg/proposal/uniform-grad-rate.html (accessed January 19, 2009).

41. For examples, see Jing Miao and Walt Haney, "High School Graduation Rates: Alternative Methods and Implications," *Education Policy Analysis Archives* 12 (2004): http://Epaa.Asu.Edu/epaa/v12n55 (accessed January 17, 2011); John Robert Warren, "State-Level High School Completion Rates: Concepts, Measures, and Trends," *Education Policy Analysis Archives* 13 (2005), http://Epaa.Asu.Edu/epaa/v13n51 (accessed January 17, 2011).

42. James J. Heckman and Paul A. LaFontaine, "The American High School Graduation Rate: Trends and Levels," *Review of Economics and Statistics* 92 (2010): 244–262. An earlier working paper examines some issues in greater depth than the 2010 paper; James J. Heckman and Paul A. LaFontaine, "The American High School Graduation Rate: Trends and Levels" (working paper 13670, National Bureau of Economic Research, Cambridge, MA, 2007), www.Nber.Org/papers/w13670 (accessed January 17, 2011).

43. Ibid., 253.

44. Robert M. Hauser and Judith Anderson Koenig, eds., *High School Dropout, Graduation, and Completion Rates: Better Data, Better Measures, Better Decisions*, National Research Council and National Academy of Education, Committee for Improved Measurement of High School Dropout and Completion Rates: Expert Guidance on Next Steps for Research and Policy Workshop, Center for Education, Division of Behavioral and Social Sciences and Education (Washington, DC: National Academic Press, 2011). The author was a member of the committee.

45. Thomas D. Snyder and Sally A. Dillow, *Digest of Education Statistics 2010* (NCES 2011-015) (Washington, DC: National Center for Education Statistics, U.S. Department of Education, 2011), http://nces.ed.gov/Pubsearch/Pubsinfo .Asp?Pubid=2011015 (accessed May 9, 2011), table 113.

46. The vast majority of high schools enroll students in grades nine through twelve. See ibid., table 99.

47. See "A Uniform, Comparable Graduation Rate: How the Final Regulations for Title I Hold Schools, Districts, and States Accountable for Improving Gradua- tion Rates," October 2008, www2.ed.gov/policy/elsec/reg/proposal/uniform -grad-rate.html (accessed February 17, 2011).

48. Jeff Archer, "Houston Case Offers Lesson on Dropouts," *Education Week*, September 24, 2003, www.edweek.org/ew/articles/2003/09/24/04houston.h23. html (accessed January 17, 2011).

49. *Census 2000 Basics* (Washington, DC: Census Bureau, U.S. Department of Commerce, 2002), www.census.gov/Dmd/www/Products.html (accessed January 17, 2010), 2. The 2010 Census asked all respondents ten questions (none pertaining to education) and no longer used the "long-form" questions. See http://2010.census.gov/2010census/how/about-the-form.php.

50. See "Current Population Survey (CPS)," www.census.gov/cps (accessed January 22, 2009).

51. See "About the ACS," www.census.gov/acs/www/SBasics (accessed January 22, 2009).

52. See "What Is the CCD?" http://nces.ed.gov/ccd/aboutCCD.asp (accessed January 22, 2009).

53. See "Overview," http://nces.ed.gov/surveys/hsls09 (accessed July 14, 2010).

54. See "Overview: Purpose," http://nces.ed.gov/surveys/els2002 (accessed January 22, 2009).

55. See "National Longitudinal Surveys," www.bls.gov/nls (accessed January 22, 2009).

56. See "NLS97," www.bls.gov/nls/y97summary.htm (accessed January 22, 2009).

57. Heckman and LaFontaine, "The American High School Graduation Rate"; Heckman and LaFontaine, "The American High School Graduation Rate" (working paper 13670).

58. Heckman and LaFontaine, "The American High School Graduation Rate," 249. Heckman and LaFontaine estimate that excluding the prison population biases the overall graduation rate upward by about one percentage point and the male graduation rate by two percentage points.

59. Becky Pettit and Bruce Western, "Mass Imprisonment and the Life Course: Race and Class Inequality in U.S. Incarceration," *American Sociological Review* 69 (2004): 151–169, table 4.

60. See Heckman and LaFontaine, "The American High School Graduation Rate," 249.

61. Cataldi et al., *High School Dropout and Completion Rates in the United States*, table 6.
62. Phillip Kaufman, Martha N. Alt, and Chris D. Chapman, *Dropout Rates in the United States: 2001* (NCES 2005-046) (Washington, DC: National Center for Education Statistics, U.S. Department of Education, 2004), table 4.
63. Heckman and LaFontaine, "The American High School Graduation Rate," 249; Warren, "State-Level High School Completion Rates," 29. Warren also found that including recent immigrants biased the estimated graduation rate downward by about two percentage points nationally, but by three to four percentage points in states with high proportions of immigrants, such as California and Arizona.
64. Bruce D. Spencer et al., *National Education Longitudinal Study of 1988: Base Year Sample Design Report* (NCES 90-463) (Washington, DC: U.S. Department of Education, 1990), 9.
65. See Heckman and LaFontaine, "The American High School Graduation Rate," 22–23 (working paper 13670).
66. Heckman and LaFontaine, "The American High School Graduation Rate," 250.
67. Nicole Scanniello, *Comparison of ACS and ASEC Data on Educational Attainment: 2004* (Washington, DC: U.S. Census Bureau, 2004), www.census.gov/acs/www/Downloads/library/2007/2007_Scanniello_01.pdf (accessed January 31, 2011).
68. A 2006 report on CPS design and methodology states that demographic data on household members are generally reported during the initial personal-visit interview, with subsequent data collected via telephone. See *Design and Methodology: Current Population Survey*, Technical Paper 66 (Washington, DC: U.S. Department of Labor, Bureau of Labor Statistics, 2006), www.bls.gov/Cps/Publications.Htm (accessed January 17, 2011), chapter 7.
69. See GED Testing Service, *2009 GED Testing Program Statistical Report* (Washington, DC: American Council on Education, 2010), appendix A.
70. Heckman and LaFontaine, "The American High School Graduation Rate," 252.
71. Figure taken from Chapter 2, 45
72. See GED Testing Service, *2007 GED Testing Program Statistical Report*, appendix A.
73. The types of rates calculated and reported in the annual report, *Dropout Rates in the United States*, has varied over the twenty years that the report has been issued. See, for example, Kaufman et al., *Dropout Rates in the United States*; Cataldi et al., *High School Dropout and Completion Rates in the United States*.
74. Some studies find that students from private schools are more likely to transfer to public schools instead of drop out. See Valerie E. Lee and David T. Burkam, "Transferring High Schools: An Alternative to Dropping Out?"

American Journal of Education 100 (1992): 420–453; Rumberger and Larson, "Student Mobility and the Increased Risk of High School Drop Out."

75. The U.S. Census Bureau also computes and reports educational attainment, high school completion or higher, for the adult population age twenty-five and over. See, for example, Snyder and Dillow, *Digest of Education Statistics 2010*, table 8.

76. Warren, "State-Level High School Completion Rates," 15–16. As Warren points out, there can still be some bias in using eighth graders as a proxy for first-time ninth graders, although he concludes the bias is relatively minor.

77. Heckman and LaFontaine, "The American High School Graduation Rate," 251.

78. Texas Education Agency, *Grade Level Retention in Texas Public Schools, 2008–09* (Austin: Texas Education Agency, 2010), www.Tea.State.Tx.Us/Index4 .Aspx?Id=4108 (accessed January 17, 2011), tables 3 and 5.

79. Hauser and Koenig, eds., *High School Dropout, Graduation, and Completion Rates*. The NRC Committee for Improved Measurement of High School Dropout and Completion Rates discourages the use of CCD-based cohort graduation rates because of the inherent biases involved.

80. Christopher B. Swanson and Duncan Chaplin, *Counting High School Graduates When Graduates Count: Measuring Graduation Rates under the High Stakes of NCLB* (Washington, DC: Urban Institute, 2003).

81. Miao and Haney, "High School Graduation Rates"; Warren, "State-Level High School Completion Rates." Both show how differences in choice of measure can affect not only the estimated graduation rate but also the relative ranking of states' graduation rates.

82. Anna Habash, *Counting on Graduation: An Agenda for State Leadership* (Washington, DC: Education Trust, 2008). www2.edtrust.org/Edtrust/ Product+Catalog/Main.Htm (accessed January 17, 2011).

83. Nonetheless, both measures are biased, which is why the NRC Committee for Improved Measurement of High School Dropout and Completion Rates discourages the use of CCD-based rates and recommends that they be phased out.

84. Heckman and LaFontaine, "The American High School Graduation Rate," 252; Warren, "State-Level High School Completion Rates," 18. Both found almost identical results in their comparisons, with Heckman and LaFontaine estimating the NELS rate at 79.7 percent and the CCD rate at 76.6 percent, while Warren estimated the NELS rate at 79.6 percent and the CCD rate at 78.4 percent.

85. Heckman and LaFontaine, "The American High School Graduation Rate."

86. See Data Quality Campaign, *10 Essential Elements of a State Longitudinal Data System*, http://dataqualitycampaign.org/build/elements/ (Accessed April 24, 2011).

87. See Data Quality Campaign, *State Analysis by Essential Element*, http:// dataqualitycampaign.org/stateanalysis/elements/8/ (accessed April 24, 2011).

88. See "Statewide Graduation Rates," http://data1.cde.ca.gov/dataquest/Comple-tionRate/CompRate1.asp?cChoice=StGradRate&cYear=2006-07&level=State (accessed February 17, 2011). The state is expected to issue four-year cohort graduation rates in the summer of 2011.

89. 2008 *Comprehensive Annual Report on Texas Public Schools* (Austin: Texas Education Agency, 2008), http://ritter.tea.state.tx.us/research/pdfs/2008_comp _annual.pdf (accessed January 17, 2011), 65.

90. Archer, "Houston Case Offers Lesson on Dropouts."

91. In 2008–09, there were 2,930 providers of adult education. See http://wdcrobcolp01.ed.gov/CFAPPS/OVAE/NRS/reports/index.cfm (accessed July 20, 2010).

92. The California Department of Education instructions to school districts state: "Students under the age of 21 who enroll in adult education programs during the 2007–08 school year are counted as dropouts unless the school system remains responsible for the student." See www.cde.ca.gov/ds/sd/cb/ssidguide08 .asp#gls (accessed July 20, 2010).

93. Robert Balfanz and Nettie Legters, "Locating the Dropout Crisis: Which High Schools Produce the Nation's Dropouts?" in *Dropouts in America*, ed. G. Orfield (Cambridge, MA: Harvard Education Press, 2004), 57–84.

94. As the NRC Committee report notes, this indicator produces demonstrably biased estimates and should be phased out. See Hauser and Koenig, eds., *High School Dropout, Graduation, and Completion Rates*, recommendation 4-3.

95. Ibid.; the figure that dropout factors account for half of the nation's dropouts does not appear in their study, but does appear on a website that documents their work. See www.every1graduates.org/Analytics/LocatingTheDropoutCrisis .html. A more rigorous academic study of a national sample of 247 high schools also found that high dropout rates were concentrated in relatively few schools. See Russell W. Rumberger and Scott L. Thomas, "The Distribution of Dropout and Turnover Rates among Urban and Suburban High Schools," *Sociology of Education* 73 (2000): 39–67.

96. In his remarks at the U.S. Chamber of Commerce on March 1, 2010, President Obama remarked, "Because we know that about 12 percent of America's schools produce 50 percent of America's dropouts . . ." See "Remarks by the President at the America's Promise Alliance Education Event," www.white house.gov/the-press-office/remarks-president-americas-promise-alliance -education-event (accessed July 16, 2010).

97. Thurston Domina, Bonnie Ghosh-Dastidar, and Marta Tienda, "Students Left Behind: Measuring 10th to 12th Grade Student Persistence Rates in Texas High Schools," *Educational Evaluation and Policy Analysis* 32 (2010): 341–343.

98. Chen-Su Chen, *Numbers and Types of Public Elementary and Secondary Schools from the Common Core of Data: School Year 2008–09—First Look*

(NCES 2010-345) (Washington, DC: National Center for Education Statistics, U.S. Department of Education, 2010), http://nces.ed.gov/pubsearch/pubsinfo .asp?pubid=2010345 (accessed January 17, 2011), table 1. Alternative schools and programs are more likely to serve secondary than elementary school students. See Priscilla Ruse Carver and Laurie Lewis, *Alternative Schools and Programs for Public School Students at Risk of Educational Failure: 2007–08* (NCES 2010-026) (Washington, DC: National Center for Education Statistics, U.S. Department of Education, 2010), http://nces.ed.gov/pubsearch/pubsinfo .asp?pubid=2010026 (accessed January 17, 2011), table 5.

99. Susan Rotermund, *Alternative Education Enrollment and Dropouts in California High Schools*, Statistical Brief 6 (Santa Barbara: California Dropout Research Project, University of California, 2007), http://cdrp.ucsb.edu/dropouts/ pubs_statbriefs.htm#6 (accessed January 17, 2011).

100. Jun Tang and Jennifer Sable, *Characteristics of the 100 Largest Public Elementary and Secondary School Districts in the United States: 2006–07* (NCES 2009-342) (Washington, DC: National Center for Education Statistics, U.S. Department of Education, 2009), http://nces.ed.gov/Pubsearch/Pubsinfo.Asp ?Pubid=2009342 (accessed January 17, 2011), table A-12.

101. See, for example, Dan Walters, "Dan Walters: High School Graduation Rate Puts California to Shame," *Sacramento Bee*, June 27, 2010, 3A.

102. Heckman and LaFontaine reached a similar conclusion in their analysis of high school graduation rates in the United States. See Heckman and LaFontaine, "The American High School Graduation Rate."

103. The number of persons passing the GED increased from 227 in 1971 to 448 in 2009. See Snyder and Dillow, *Digest of Education Statistics 2010*, table 114.

104. Thomas L. Friedman, *The World Is Flat: A Brief History of the Twenty-First Century* (New York: Farrar, Straus & Giroux, 2005).

105. Robert D. Atkinson and Scott M. Andes, *The Atlantic Century: Benchmarking EU and U.S. Innovation and Competitiveness* (Washington, DC: Information Technology and Innovation Foundation, 2009), www.itif.org/index .php?id=226 (accessed January 17, 2011). The authors use sixteen indicators to determine a global competitiveness score. The indicators are: higher education attainment in the population ages twenty-five to thirty-four; the number of science and technology researchers per 1,000 employed; corporate investment in research and development (R&D); government investment in R&D; share of the world's scientific and technical publications; venture capital investment; new firms; e-government; broadband telecommunications; corporate investment in information technology; effective marginal corporate tax rates; ease of doing business; trade balance; foreign direct investment inflows; real GDP per working-age adult; and productivity.

106. Stephen Lamb and Eifred Markussen, "School Dropout and Completion: An International Perspective," in *School Dropout and Completion: International Comparative Studies in Theory and Policy*, ed. S. Lamb et al. (New York: Springer, 2011), 1–18. The authors suggest that the OECD figures are inaccurate compared to national data. The OECD, for example, reports that the upper secondary graduation rate for Norway was 100 percent in 2004, whereas national data show a completion rate closer to 70 percent. Lamb (personal communication) also claims that the OECD includes certificates, such as vocational certificates, which do not entitle the holder to enter all forms of postsecondary education.

107. *Education at a Glance 2010* (Paris: Organisation for Economic Co-operation and Development, 2010), www.oecd.org/Edu/Eag2010 (accessed January 17, 2011).

4. The Individual Consequences of Dropping Out

1. Daniel Patrick Moynihan, *The Negro Family: The Case for National Action* (Washington, DC: Office of Policy Planning and Research, U.S. Department of Labor, 1965).

2. Samuel Bowles, Steven N. Durlauf, and Karla Hoff, eds., *Poverty Traps* (Princeton, NJ: Princeton University Press, 2006).

3. Douglas Massey and Nancy Denton, *American Apartheid: Segregation and the Making of the Underclass* (Cambridge, MA: Harvard University Press, 1993); William Julius Wilson, *The Truly Disadvantaged: The Inner City, The Underclass, and Public Policy* (Chicago: University of Chicago Press, 1987); Robert J. Sampson, "Racial Stratification and the Durable Tangle of Neighborhood Inequality," *Annals of the American Academy of Political and Social Science* 621 (2009): 260–280.

4. Sampson, "Racial Stratification and the Durable Tangle of Neighborhood Inequality," 265.

5. "Ten Famous Millionaire High School Dropouts!" www.socyberty.com/People/10-Famous-Millionaire-High-School-Dropouts.56831 (accessed July 23, 2009).

6. John M. Bridgeland, John J. DiIulio Jr., and Karen Burke Morison, *The Silent Epidemic: Perspectives on High School Dropouts* (Washington, DC: Civil Enterprises, 2006), 10.

7. Allison Sherry, "GED's Appeal Gains with Dropouts as Jobs Dwindle," *Denver Post*, March 31, 2009, www.denverpost.com/news/ci_12033273 (accessed August 1, 2009).

8. *Labor Force Statistics from the Current Population Survey* (Washington, DC: Bureau of Labor Statistics, U.S. Department of Labor, 2010), www.bls.gov/Cps/Tables.Htm#Nempstat_M (accessed January 17, 2011), table A-16,

9. Ibid.

10. Mercer L. Sullivan, *"Getting Paid": Youth Crime and Work in the Inner City* (Ithaca, NY: Cornell University Press, 1989), 34.

11. See "NLSY97," www.bls.gov/nls/nlsy97.htm (accessed February 17, 2011).

12. *America's Youth at 23: School Enrollment, Training, and Employment Transitions between Ages 22 and 23* (Washington, DC: Bureau of Labor Statistics, U.S. Department of Labor, 2010), www.bls.gov/nls/nlsy97 (accessed May 14, 2011), table 3.

13. Daniel Kuehn, et al., *Vulnerable Youth and the Transition to Adulthood: Multiple Pathways Connecting School to Work*, ASPE Research Brief (Washington, DC: Urban Institute, 2009), www.urban.org/Url.Cfm?ID=411948 (accessed January 17, 2011).

14. *Labor Force Statistics from the Current Population Survey*, table A-16.

15. Ibid.

16. *Annual Table: Employment Status by Educational Attainment, Sex, Race, and Hispanic Ethnicity* (Washington, DC: Bureau of Labor Statistics, U.S. Department of Labor, 2010), www.bls.gov/Cps/Demographics.Htm#Education (accessed July 28, 2010).

17. Ibid.

18. Julie A. Yates, "The Transition from School to Work: Education and Work Experiences," *Monthly Labor Review* 128 (2005): 21–32.

19. Susan Aud et al., *The Condition of Education 2010* (NCES 2010-028) (Washington, DC: National Center for Education Statistics, U.S Department of Education, 2010), http://nces.ed.gov/pubsearch/pubsinfo.asp?pubid=2010028 (accessed January 17, 2011), table A-17-1.

20. Cecilia E. Rouse, "Consequences for the Labor Market," in *The Price We Pay: Economic and Social Consequences of Inadequate Education*, ed. C. R. Belfield and H. M. Levin (Washington, DC: Brookings Institution Press, 2007), 99–141, table 1.

21. *Characteristics of Minimum Wage Workers: 2009* (Washington, DC: Bureau of Labor Statistics, U.S. Department of Labor, 2010), www.Bls.Gov/Cps/Earnings .Htm#Minwage (accessed January 17, 2011), table 6; *A Profile of the Working Poor, 2009* (Washington, DC: Bureau of Labor Statistics, U.S. Department of Labor, 2010), www.bls.gov/Cps/Earnings.Htm#Workpoor (accessed January 17, 2011), table 3; *A Profile of the Working Poor, 2007.* (Washington, DC: Bureau of Labor Statistics, U.S. Department of Labor, 2009), www.bls.gov/Cps/ Publications.Htm (accessed January 17, 2011).

22. *Income, Poverty, and Health Insurance Coverage in the United States: 2009* (Washington, DC: Census Bureau, U.S. Department of Commerce, 2010), www.census.gov/hhes/www/poverty/data/incpovhlth/2009/index.html (accessed January 17, 2011), table POV29.

23. Tracy A. Loveless and Jan Tin, *Dynamics of Economic Well-Being: Participa-tion in Government Programs, 2001 through 2003: Who Gets Assistance?* (Washington, DC: Census Bureau, U.S. Department of Commerce, 2006), 70–108, www.census.gov/sipp/p70s/p70s.html (accessed January 17, 2011), figures 16 and 18; See also Sandy Baum and Jennifer Ma, *Education Pays 2007: The Benefits of Higher Education for Individuals and Society* (Washing-ton, DC: College Board, 2007), figure 1.12.

24. Aud et al., *The Condition of Education 2010*, table A-17-1.

25. Rouse, "Consequences for the Labor Market."

26. Figures from ibid., table 5.3, based on a discount rate of 3.5 percent and an annual productivity growth rate of 1.5 percent.

27. Baum and Ma, *Education Pays 2007*, figure 1.2.

28. *America's Youth at 19: School Enrollment, Training, and Employment Transi-tions between Ages 18 and 19* (Washington, DC: Bureau of Labor Statistics, U.S. Department of Labor, 2007), www.bls.gov/Nls/Nlsy97.Htm (accessed January 17, 2011), table 2.

29. *America's Youth at 20: School Enrollment, Training, and Employment Transi-tions between Ages 19 and 20* (Washington, DC: Bureau of Labor Statistics, U.S. Department of Labor, 2008), www.bls.gov/Nls/Nlsy97.Htm (accessed January 17, 2011), table 2.

30. *America's Youth at 21: School Enrollment, Training, and Employment Transi-tions between Ages 20 and 21* (Washington, DC: Bureau of Labor Statistics, U.S. Department of Labor, 2009), www.bls.gov/Nls/Nlsy97.Htm (accessed January 17, 2011).

31. Russell W. Rumberger and Susan Rotermund, *What Happened to Dropouts from the High School Class of 2004?* Statistical Brief 10 (Santa Barbara: California Dropout Research Project, University of California, 2008), www.cdrp.ucsb.edu/pubs_statbriefs.htm#10 (accessed January 17, 2011).

32. Susan Rotermund, *Education and Economic Consequences for Students Who Drop Out of High School*, Statistical Brief 5 (Santa Barbara: California Dropout Research Project, University of California, Santa Barbara, 2007), http://cdrp.ucsb.edu/Dropouts/Pubs_Statbriefs.Htm#5 (accessed January 17, 2011).

33. Stephen V. Cameron and James J. Heckman, "The Nonequivalence of High School Equivalents," *Journal of Labor Economics* 11 (1993): 1–47.

34. James J. Heckman, John E. Humphries, and Nicholas S. Mader, "The GED" (working paper 16064, National Bureau of Economic Research, Cambridge, MA, 2010), www.nber.org/papers/w16064 (accessed January 17, 2011); J. H. Tyler, "Economic Benefits of the GED: Lessons from Recent Research," *Review of Educational Research* 73 (2003): 369–398. A 2010 study found that Hispanic full-time, full-year workers with a GED had about the same mean annual

earnings as Hispanic full-time, full-year workers with a high school diploma. See Richard Fry, *Hispanics, High School Dropouts and the GED* (Washington, DC: Pew Hispanic Center, 2010), http://pewresearch.org/pubs/1593/hispanic -black-white-ged-high-school-dropout-rate (accessed July 28, 2010), ii.

35. Heckman et al., "The GED"; James J. Heckman, Jora Stixrud, and Sergio Urzua, "The Effects of Cognitive and Noncognitive Abilities on Labor Market Outcomes and Social Behavior," *Journal of Labor Economics* 24 (2006): 411–482; Flavio Cunha and James J. Heckman "The Economics and Psychology of Inequality and Human Development," *Journal of the European Economic Association* 7 (2009): 320–364.

36. Heckman et al., "The GED"; James J. Heckman and Yona Rubinstein, "The Importance of Noncognitive Skills: Lessons from the GED Testing Program," *American Economic Review* 91 (2001): 145–149.

37. John H. Tyler, Richard J. Murnane, and John B. Willett, "Who Benefits from a GED? Evidence for Females from High School and Beyond." *Economics of Education Review* 22 (2003): 237–247.

38. *America's Youth at 21*, table 2.

39. Ibid.

40. Tom Philpott, "Army Signs More Dropouts," *Military.Com*, November 22, 2006, www.military.com/features/0,15240,119382,00.html (accessed January 17, 2011).

41. Lance Lochner and Enrico Moretti, "The Effect of Education on Crime: Evidence from Prison, Arrests, and Self-Reports," *American Economic Review* 94 (2004): 155–189, table 13.

42. Heather C. West, *Prison Inmates at Midyear 2009—Statistical Tables* (Washington, DC: Bureau of Justice Statistics, U.S. Department of Justice, 2010), http://bjs.ojp.usdoj.gov/index.cfm?ty=pbdetail&iid=2200 (accessed December 30, 1020), tables 15 and 16.

43. Ibid., table 18.

44. David P. Farrington, "Developmental and Life-Course Criminology: Key Theoretical and Empirical Issues—the 2002 Sutherland Award Address," *Criminology* 41 (2003): 221–255.

45. Gary Sweeten, "Who Will Graduate? Disruption of High School Education by Arrest and Court Involvement," *Justice Quarterly* 23 (2006): 462–480.

46. Philip Oreopoulos and Kjell G. Salvanes, "How Large Are Returns to Schooling? Hint: Money Isn't Everything" (working paper 15339, National Bureau of Economic Research, Washington, DC, 2009), www.nber.org/papers/ w15339 (accessed January 17, 2011), figure 4.

47. Andrew Sum et al., *The Consequences of Dropping Out of High School: Joblessness and Jailing for High School Dropouts and the High Costs for Taxpay-*

ers (Boston, MA: Center for Labor Market Studies, Northeastern University, 2009), chart 6.

48. Ibid., chart 8.

49. Bruce Western and Christopher Wildeman, "The Black Family and Mass Incarceration," *Annals of the American Academy of Political and Social Science* 621 (2009): 221–242.

50. Ibid., table 1.

51. David Garland, "Introduction: The Meaning of Mass Imprisonment," in *Mass Imprisonment: Social Causes and Consequences,* ed. D. Garland (Thousand Oaks, CA: Sage, 2001), 1–3.

52. Western and Wildeman, "The Black Family and Mass Incarceration," 227.

53. Richard B. Freeman, "Why Do So Many Young American Men Commit Crimes and What Might We Do about It?" *Journal of Economic Perspectives* 10 (1996): 25–42; Lance Lochner, "Education Policy and Crime" (working paper 15894, National Bureau of Economic Research, Cambridge, MA, 2010), http://papers.nber.org/papers/w15894 (accessed January 17, 2011); Enrico Moretti, "Crime and the Costs of Criminal Justice," in *The Price We Pay: Economic and Social Consequences of Inadequate Education,* ed. C. R. Belfield and H. M. Levin (Washington, DC: Brookings Institution Press, 2007), 142–159.

54. Brian A. Jacob and Lars Lefgren, "Are Idle Hands the Devil's Workshop? Incapacitation, Concentration, and Juvenile Crime," *American Economic Review* 93 (2003): 1560–1577; Jeremy Luallen, "School's Out . . . Forever: A Study of Juvenile Crime, At-Risk Youths and Teacher Strikes," *Journal of Urban Economics* 59 (2006): 75–103.

55. Mark S. Fleisher, *Dead End Kids: Gang Girls and the Boys They Know* (Madison: University of Wisconsin Press, 1998), 213–214.

56. Sullivan, *"Getting Paid,"* 245.

57. The summary in this paragraph is taken from Gary Sweeten, Shawn D. Bushway, and Raymond Paternoster, "Does Dropping Out of School Mean Dropping into Delinquency?" *Criminology* 47 (2009): 47–91.

58. Diane S. Kaplan, Kelly R. Damphouse, and Howard B. Kaplan, "Moderating Effects of Gender on the Relationship between Not Graduating from High School and Psychological Dysfunction in Young Adulthood," *Journal of Educational Psychology* 88 (1996): 760–774; Sweeten et al., "Does Dropping Out of School Mean Dropping into Delinquency?"

59. Robert J. Sampson and John H. Laub, "A Life-Course View of the Development of Crime," *Annals of the American Academy of Political and Social Science* 602 (2005): 16.

60. Ibid., 18.

61. John H. Laub, Daniel S. Nagin, and Robert J. Sampson, "Trajectories of Change in Criminal Offending: Good Marriages and the Desistance Process," *American Sociological Review* 63 (1998): 237.

62. For a summary of research, see Misaki N. Natsuaki, Xiaojia Ge, and Ernst Wenk, "Continuity and Changes in the Developmental Trajectories of Criminal Career: Examining the Roles of Timing of First Arrest and High School Graduation," *Journal of Youth and Adolescence* 37 (2008): 432.

63. See Terrie Moffitt, "Adolescence-Limited and Life-Course-Persistent Antisocial Behavior: A Developmental Taxonomy," *Psychological Review* 100 (1993): 674–701; Sampson and Laub, "A Life-Course View of the Development of Crime."

64. Natsuaki et al., "Continuity and Changes in the Developmental Trajectories," 433.

65. See, for example, Karl L. Alexander, Doris R. Entwisle, and Nadir S. Kabbini, "The Dropout Process in Life Course Perspective: Early Risk Factors at Home and School," *Teachers College Record* 103 (2001): 760–882; Sweeten et al., "Does Dropping Out of School Mean Dropping into Delinquency?"; Barbara S. Mensch and Denise B. Kandel, "Dropping Out of High School and Drug Involvement," *Sociology of Education* 61 (1988): 95–113; Jay D. Teachman et al., "School Capital and Dropping Out of School," *Journal of Marriage and the Family* 58 (1996): 773–783.

66. Natsuaki et al., "Continuity and Changes in the Developmental Trajectories,"

67. Sweeten et al., "Does Dropping Out of School Mean Dropping into Delinquency?"

68. Fleisher, *Dead End Kids*, 216.

69. Lochner and Moretti, "The Effect of Education on Crime," table 11.

70. Ibid.

71. Eric D. Gould, Bruce A. Weinberg, and David B. Mustard, "Crime Rates and Local Labor Market Opportunities in the United States: 1979–1997," *Review of Economics and Statistics* 84 (2002): 45–61; Jeffrey T. Grogger, "Market Wages and Youth Crime," *Journal of Labor Economics* 16 (1998): 756–791; Steven Raphael and Rudolph Winter-Ebmer, "Identifying the Effect of Unemployment on Crime," *Journal of Law & Economics* 44 (2001): 259–283.

72. Kathryn Edin and Maria Kefalas, *Promises I Can Keep: Why Poor Women Put Motherhood before Marriage* (Berkeley: University of California Press, 2005), 168–169.

73. Rebekah L. Coley, Jodi E. Morris, and Daphne Hernandez, "Out-of-School Care and Problem Behavior Trajectories among Low-Income Adolescents:

Individual, Family, and Neighborhood Characteristics as Added Risks," *Child Development* 75 (2004): 948–965.

74. Joyce A. Martin et al., *Births: Final Data for 2008 National Vital Statistical Reports*, vol. 59, no. 7 (Hyattsville, MD: National Center for Health Statistics, U.S. Department of Health and Human Services, 2010), table B. The data for 2008 are final, based on a complete census of birth certificates. Provision data are available for more recent periods.

75. Ibid., tables 3, 7, 8

76. Coley et al., "Out-of-School Care and Problem Behavior Trajectories"; Russell W. Rumberger and Sun Ah Lim, *Why Students Drop Out of School: A Review of 25 Years of Research* (Santa Barbara: California Dropout Research Project, 2008), http://cdrp.ucsb.edu/Dropouts/Pubs_Reports.Htm#15 (accessed January 17, 2011).

77. Kate Perper, Kristen Peterson, and Jennifer Manlove, *Diploma Attainment among Teen Mothers*, Fact Sheet 2010-01 (Washington, DC: Child Trends, 2010), www.childtrends.org/_Files/Child_Trends-2010_01_22_FS_Diploma Attainment.pdf (accessed January 17, 2011), figure 1.

78. See, for example, Jason M. Fletcher and Barbara L. Wolfe, "Education and Labor Market Consequences of Teenage Childbearing: Evidence Using the Timing of Pregnancy Outcomes and Community Fixed Effects," *Journal of Human Resources* 44 (2009): 303–325.

79. Jennifer Manlove, "The Influence of High School Dropout and School Disengagement on the Risk of School-Age Pregnancy," *Journal of Research on Adolescence* 8 (1998): 187–220, table 1.

80. Ibid.; Jennifer E. Glick, Stacey D. Ruf, Michael J. White, and Frances Goldscheider, "Educational Engagement and Early Family Formation: Differences by Ethnicity and Generation," *Social Forces* 84 (2006): 1391–1415.

81. Dawn M. Upchurch and James McCarthy, "The Timing of a First Birth and High School Completion," *American Sociological Review* 55 (1990): 230–231; Manlove, "The Influence of High School Dropout."

82. Dmitry M. Kissin et al., "Is There a Trend of Increased Unwanted Childbearing among Young Women in the United States?" *Journal of Adolescent Health* 43 (2008): 364–371; Cassandra Logan et al., *The Consequences of Unintended Childbearing* (Washington, DC: Child Trends, 2007).

83. Jennifer S. Barber and Patricia L. East, "Home and Parenting Resources Available to Siblings Depending on Their Birth Intention Status," *Child Development* 80 (2009): 921–939.

84. Kissin et al., "Is There a Trend of Increased Unwanted Childbearing," table 1.

85. Ibid., table 2.

86. Stephanie J. Ventura, *Changing Patterns of Nonmarital Childbearing in the United States*, Data Brief 18 (Hyattsville, MD: National Center for Health Statistics, U.S. Department of Health & Human Services, 2009), 2.
87. Ibid., figure 3.
88. Ibid., 3.
89. Ibid., figure 5.
90. Sara McLanahan, "Fragile Families and the Reproduction of Poverty," *Annals of the American Academy of Political and Social Science* 621 (2009): 111–131, table 1. For more information on this study, see the Fall 2010 issue of *The Future of Children*, www.futureofchildren.org/futureofchildren/publications/journals/journal_details/index.xml?journalid=73 (accessed February 17, 2011).
91. Ibid.
92. Ibid.
93. Ibid., table 2.
94. Ibid.
95. Ibid., table 1.
96. Ibid., table 3.
97. Ibid., 120.
98. Ibid., 121.
99. Ibid., 122.
100. Ibid., 122–127.
101. Tama Leventhal and Jeanne Brooks-Gunn, "The Neighborhoods They Live in: The Effects of Neighborhood Residence on Child and Adolescent Outcomes," *Psychological Bulletin* 126 (2000): 309–337; Christopher Jencks and Susan E. Mayer, "The Social Consequences of Growing up in a Poor Neighborhood," in *Inner-City Poverty in the United States*, ed. L. Lynn Jr. and M. G. H. McGeary (Washington, DC: National Academies Press, 1990), 111–186; Anne K. Driscoll et al., "Community Opportunity, Perceptions of Opportunity, and the Odds of an Adolescent Birth," *Youth & Society* 37 (2005): 33–61.
102. James S. Coleman, "Social Capital in the Creation of Human Capital," *American Journal of Sociology* 94 (1988): S95–S120; Erin McNamara Horvat, Elliot B. Weininger, and Annette Lareau, "From Social Ties to Social Capital: Class Differences in the Relations between Schools and Parent Networks," *American Educational Research Journal* 40 (2003): 319–351; Jennie G. Noll et al., "The Cumulative Burden Borne by Offspring Whose Mothers Were Sexually Abused as Children: Descriptive Results from a Multigenerational Study," *Journal of Interpersonal Violence* 24 (2009): 424–449; Robert K. Ream, "Toward Understanding How Social Capital Mediates the Impact of Mobility on Mexican American Achievement," *Social Forces* 84 (2005): 201–224; Robert K. Ream and Gregory J. Palardy, "Reexamining Social Class Differences in

the Availability and the Educational Utility of Parental Social Capital," *American Educational Research Journal* 45 (2008): 238–273; Ricardo D. Stanton-Salazar, "A Social Capital Framework for Understanding the Socialization of Racial Minority Children and Youths," *Harvard Educational Review* 67 (1997): 1–40; Noll et al., "The Cumulative Burden Borne by Offspring."

103. Edin and Kefalas, *Promises I Can Keep*, 170–172.

104. Ibid., 179.

105. Trina L. Hope et al., "The Relationships among Adolescent Pregnancy, Pregnancy Resolution, and Juvenile Delinquency," *Sociological Quarterly* 44 (2003): 555–576.

106. Elizabeth Zachry, "Getting My Education: Teen Mothers' Experiences in School before and after Motherhood," *Teachers College Record* 107 (2005): 2566–2598.

107. Ann M. Beutel, "The Relationship between Adolescent Nonmarital Childbearing and Educational Expectations: A Cohort and Period Comparison," *Sociological Quarterly* 41 (2000): 297–314.

108. William Julius Wilson, *More than Just Race: Being Black and Poor in the Inner City* (New York: W. W. Norton & Company, 2009), 118.

109. Edin and Kefalas, *Promises I Can Keep*, 194.

110. See discussion in Jennifer March Augustine, Timothy Nelson, and Kathryn Edin, "Why Do Poor Men Have Children? Fertility Intentions among Low-Income Unmarried U.S. Fathers," *Annals of the American Academy of Political and Social Science* 624 (2009): 99–117.

111. Wilson, *More than Just Race*, 120.

112. Ibid., 122.

113. Sara McLanahan, "Fragile Families and the Reproduction of Poverty," *Annals of the American Academy of Political and Social Science* 621 (2009): 121.

114. Ibid., 122.

115. Arland Thorton, William G. Axinn, and Jay D. Teachman, "The Influence of School Enrollment and Accumulation on Cohabitation and Marriage in Early Adulthood," *American Sociological Review* 60 (1995): 762–774.

116. John R. Pleis, Jacqueline W. Lucas, and Brian W. Ward, *Summary Health Statistics for U.S. Adults: National Health Interview Survey, 2009*, Vital and Health Statistics Series 10, no. 249 (Washington, DC: National Center for Health Statistics, U.S. Department of Health and Human Services, 2010), www.cdc.gov/Nchs/Nhis/Nhis_Series.Htm#09reports (accessed January 17, 2011), table 21; See also Baum and Ma, *Education Pays 2007*, figure 1.13a.

117. David M. Cutler and Adriana Lleras-Muney, "Education and Health: Evaluating Theories and Evidence" (working paper 12352, National Bureau of Economic Research, Cambridge, MA, 2006), http://papers.nber.org/papers/w12352 (accessed January 17, 2011), 3–4.

118. Oreopoulos and Salvanes, "How Large Are the Returns to Schooling?" figure 4.
119. Arthur J. Reynolds and Catherine E. Ross, "Social Stratification and Health: Education's Benefit beyond Economic Status and Social Origins," *Social Problems* 45 (1998): 221–247.
120. John Mirowsky and Catherine Ross, "Education and Self-Rated Health—Cumulative Advantage and Its Rising Importance," *Research on Aging* 30 (2008): 93–122; David M. Cutler et al., "Explaining the Rise in Educational Gradients in Mortality" (working paper 15678, National Bureau of Economic Research, Cambridge, MA, 2010), http://papers.nber.org/papers/w15678 (accessed January 17, 2011).
121. Jiaquan Xu et al., *Deaths: Final Data for 2007*, National Vital Statistics Reports 58, no. 19 (Washington, DC: Centers for Disease Control and Prevention, 2010), www.cdc.gov/Nchs/Nvss.Htm (accessed July 29, 2010), 22.
122. Mitchell D. Wong et al., "Contribution of Major Diseases to Disparities in Mortality," *New England Journal of Medicine* 347 (2002): 1585–1592.
123. Adriana Lleras-Muney, "The Relationship between Education and Adult Mortality in the United States," *Review of Economic Studies* 721 (2005): 189–221, 215.
124. Catherine E. Ross and Chia-Ling Wu, "The Links between Education and Health," *American Sociological Review* 60 (1995): 719–745; see also Cutler and Lleras-Muney, *Education and Health.*
125. David Dooley, Jonathan Fielding, and Lennart Levi, "Health and Unemployment," *Annual Review of Public Health* 17 (1996): 449–465.
126. John Wirt, Susan Choy, Patrick Rooney, Stephen Provasnik, Anindita Sen, and Richare Tobin, *The Condition of Education, 2004* (NCES 2004—77) (Washington, DC: National Center for Education Statistics, U.S. Department of Education, 2004), http://nces.ed.gov/Pubsearch/Pubsinfo.Asp?Pubid=2004077 (accessed January 17, 2011), table 12-1.
127. Oreopoulos and Salvanes, "How Large Are the Returns to Schooling?" figure 4.
128. Ibid., figure 2.
129. Ibid., figure 3.
130. Ross and Wu, "The Links between Education and Health"; Karen Danna and Ricky W. Griffin, "Health and Well-Being in the Workplace: A Review and Synthesis of the Literature," *Journal of Management* 25 (1999): 357–384; Reynolds and Ross, "Social Stratification and Health."
131. Timothy A. Judge and Charlice Hurst, "How the Rich (and Happy) Get Richer (and Happier): Relationship of Core Self-Evaluations to Trajectories in Attaining Work Success," *Journal of Applied Psychology* 93 (2008): 849–863.
132. Ross and Wu, "The Links between Education and Health," 723.

133. Zuzana Skodova et al., "Socioeconomic Differences in Psychosocial Factors Contributing to Coronary Heart Disease: A Review," *Journal of Clinical Psychology in Medical Settings* 15 (2008): 204–213.

134. Adela Yarcheski et al., "A Meta-Analysis of Predictors of Positive Health Practices," *Journal of Nursing Scholarship* 36 (2004): 102–108.

135. Thomas D. Snyder and Sally A. Dillow, *Digest of Education Statistics 2010* (NCES 2011-015) (Washington, DC: National Center for Education Statistics, U.S. Department of Education, U.S. Government Printing Office, 2011), http://nces.ed.gov/Pubsearch/Pubsinfo.Asp?Pubid=2011015 (accessed January 17, 2011), table 401.

136. Kate E. Fothergill and Margaret E. Ensminger, "Childhood and Adolescent Antecedents of Drug and Alcohol Problems: A Longitudinal Study," *Drug and Alcohol Dependence* 82 (2006): 61–76; Thomas C. Harford, Hsiao-ye Yi, and Michael E. Hilton, "Alcohol Abuse and Dependence in College and Noncollege Samples: A Ten-Year Prospective Follow-Up in a National Survey," *Journal of Studies on Alcohol* 67 (2006): 803–809.

137. Data from "Health Effects of Smoking," www.cdc.gov/tobacco/data_statistics/fact_sheets/health_effects/effects_cig_smoking (accessed July 30, 2010).

138. Data from "Alcohol and Drug Use," www.cdc.gov/HealthyYouth/alcoholdrug (accessed July 30, 2010).

139. Pleis et al., *Summary Health Statistics for U.S. Adults*, table 29.

140. Data from "Physical Activity and Health," www.cdc.gov/physicalactivity/everyone/health (accessed July 30, 2010).

141. *Income, Poverty, and Health Insurance Coverage*, table HI01.

142. Ibid., table 9.

143. Institute of Medicine, *America's Uninsured Crisis: Consequences for Health and Health Care* (Washington, DC: National Academies Press, 2009), 5.

144. Cutler and Lleras-Muney, "Education and Health," 4.

145. Michael Grossman, "Education and Nonmarket Outcomes," in *Handbook of the Economics of Education, Volume 1*, ed. E. A. Hanushek and F. Welch (New York: Elsevier, 2006), 577–633.

146. Aekaterini Galimanis et al., "Lifestyle and Stroke Risk: A Review," *Current Opinion in Neurology* 22 (2009): 60–68.

147. Anna Aizer and Laura Stroud, "Education, Knowledge, and the Evolution of Disparities in Health" (working paper 15840, National Bureau of Economic Research, Cambridge, MA, 2010), http://papers.nber.org/papers/w15840 (accessed January 17, 2011).

148. Gary S. Becker and Casey B. Mulligan, "The Endogenous Determination of Time Preference," *Quarterly Journal of Economics* 112 (1997): 735–736.

149. Oreopoulos and Salvanes, "How Large Are the Returns to Schooling?" 13–14.

150. Gabriel Picone, Frank Sloan, and Donald Taylor Jr., "Effects of Risk and Time Preference and Expected Longevity on Demand for Medical Tests," *Journal of Risk and Uncertainty* 28 (2004): 39–53.

151. Gilbert C. Gee and Devon C. Payne-Sturges, "Environmental Health Disparities: A Framework Integrating Psychosocial and Environmental Concepts," *Environmental Health Perspectives* 112 (2004): 1645–1653; Gary W. Evans and Elise Kantrowitz, "Socioeconomic Status and Health: The Potential Role of Environmental Risk Exposure," *Annual Review of Public Health* 23 (2002): 303–331.

152. Aizer and Strond, "Education, Knowledge, and the Evolution of Disparities." Aizer and Strond found that educated women surrounded by more educated peers were more likely to reduce smoking than those surrounded by less educated peers.

153. Jannet Currie, "Healthy, Wealthy, and Wise: Socioeconomic Status, Poor Health in Childhood, and Human Capital Development," *Journal of Economic Literature* 47 (2009): 87–122; Cutler and Lleras-Muney, *Education and Health.*

154. Cutler and Lleras-Muney, "Education and Health," 11.

155. Ibid., 12–13; Lleras-Muney, "The Relationship between Education and Adult Mortality."

156. As quoted in Richard Rothstein, Rebecca Jacobsen, and Tamara Wilder, *Grading Education: Getting Accountability Right* (Washington, DC, and New York: Economic Policy Institute and Teachers College Press, 2008), 17.

157. *Voting and Registration in the Election of 2008* (Washington, DC: Census Bureau, U.S. Department of Commerce, 2009), www.census.gov/Hhes/www/Socdemo/Voting/Publications/P20/2008/Tables.html (accessed January 17, 2011), table 5.

158. Oreopoulos and Salvanes, "How Large Are the Returns to Schooling?" figure 6.

159. Baum and Ma, *Education Pays 2007*, figures 1.17 and 1.18.

160. Eric M. Uslaner, "Producing and Consuming Trust," *Political Science Quarterly* 115 (2000): 569–590, 569.

161. Ibid.

162. Ibid.; Eric M. Uslaner and Mitchell Brown, "Inequality, Trust, and Civic Engagement," *American Politics Research* 33 (2005): 868–894.

163. John F. Helliwell, "Well-Being, Social Capital, and Public Policy: What's New?" *Economic Journal* 116 (2006): C34–C45.

164. Oreopoulos and Salvanes, "How Large Are the Returns to Schooling?" figure 6.

165. Uslaner and Brown, "Inequality, Trust, and Civic Engagement," 875.

166. Baum and Ma, *Education Pays 2007*, figure 1.20.

167. Thomas Dee, "Are There Civic Returns to Education?" *Journal of Public Economics* 88 (2004): 1697–1720.

168. Ibid. Dee (footnote 4) also suggests that education may have indirect effects on voting because some states prohibit ex-felons from voting. Since dropouts are much more likely to engage in crime and become incarcerated, they would also vote less. Another indirect effect is through the "motor-voter" policies that require a driver's license to vote. Because dropouts are more likely to be poor and to live in urban ghettos without cars, they would also be less likely to vote as a result.

169. Kevin Milligan, Enrico Moretti, and Philip Oreopoulos, "Does Education Improve Citizenship? Evidence from the United States and the United Kingdom," *Journal of Public Economics* 88 (2004): 1669. Although voting rates have generally declined in the United States over time, Milligan estimates that they would have declined even more without the increase in educational attainment over the past three decades (p. 1693).

170. Felicia A. Huppert, Nick Baylis, and Barry Keverne, *The Science of Well-Being* (New York: Oxford University Press. 2005).

171. Richard Desjardins, "Researching the Links between Education and Well-Being," *European Journal of Education* 43 (2008): 23–35.

172. John F. Helliwell and Christopher P. Barrington-Leigh, "Measuring and Understanding Subjective Well-Being" (working paper 15887, National Bureau of Economic Research, Cambridge, MA, 2010), http://papers.nber.org/papers/w15887 (accessed January 17, 2011); Daniel Kahneman and Allan B. Krueger, "Developments in the Measurement of Subjective Well-Being." *Journal of Economic Perspectives* 20 (2006): 3–24.

173. See United Nations website, http://hdr.undp.org/en. Researchers at Columbia University issue an annual modified American human development index, using different indicators of three basic dimensions; see Sarah Burd-Sharps, Kristen Lewis, and Eduardo Borges Martins, *The Measure of America: American Human Development Report 2008–09* (New York: Columbia University Press, 2008).

174. The specific dimensions and indicators vary somewhat among these three reports (Organisation for Economic Co-operation and Development, 2009a; Annie E. Casey Foundation, 2010; Foundation for Child Development, 2010).

175. See "Survey of Income and Program Participation," www.census.gov/sipp (accessed February 18, 2011).

176. *Extended Measures of Well-Being: Living Conditions in the United States, 2005* (Washington, DC: Census Bureau, U.S. Department of Commerce, 2009), www.census.gov/population/www/socdemo/extended-05.html (accessed January 17, 2011), table 9.

177. Oreopoulos and Salvanes, "How Large Are the Returns to Schooling?" 3–4.

178. Sandy Baum, Jennifer Ma, and Kathleen Payea, *Education Pays 2010: The Benefits of Higher Education for Individuals and Society* (Washington, DC:

College Board, 2010), http://trends.collegeboard.org/education_pays (accessed January 17, 2011), figure 1.9a.

179. Desjardins, "Researching the Links between Education and Well-Being."

180. Baum and Ma, *Education Pays 2007*, figure 1.9.

181. Gary S. Becker, "Family Economics and Macro Behaviors," *American Economic Review* 78 (1988): 10.

182. Samuel Bowles and Herbert Gintis, "The Inheritance of Inequality," *Journal of Economic Perspectives* 16 (2002): 21–22.

183. Emily Beller and Michael Hout, "Intergenerational Social Mobility: The United States in Comparative Perspective," *Future of Children* 16 (2006): 19–36; Bhashkar Mazumder, "Fortunate Sons: New Estimates of Intergenerational Mobility in the United States Using Social Security Earnings Data," *Review of Economics and Statistics* 87 (2005): 235–255.

184. Caroline Ratcliffe, Signe-Mary McKernan, *Childhood Poverty Persistence: Facts and Consequences*, Brief 14 (Washington, DC: Urban Institute, 2010), www.urban.org/publications/412126.html (accessed July 30, 2010), table 1.

185. M. Corcoran, "Rags to Rags: Poverty and Mobility in the United States," *Annual Review of Sociology* 21 (1995): 247.

186. *Income, Poverty, and Health Insurance Coverage in the United States: 2009* (Washington, DC: Census Bureau, U.S. Department of Commerce, 2010) www.census.gov/hhes/www/cpstables/032009/pov/new29_100_01.htm (accessed July 30, 2010), table POV29.

187. Lisa A. Keister, *Getting Rich: America's Rich and How They Got that Way* (New York: Cambridge University Press, 2005), table 2.10.

188. Beller and Hout, "Intergenerational Social Mobility."

189. Richard J. Herrnstein and Charles Murray, *The Bell Curve: Intelligence and Class Structure in American Life* (New York: Free Press, 1994).

190. See Corcoran, "Rags to Rags," 251; Wilson, *More than Just Race*, 137. Wilson further argues that the measures of family background that Hernnstein and Murray uses—family education, family income, father's education—are insufficient to capture differences in environmental backgrounds among racial groups.

191. Bruce Sacerdote, "How Large Are the Effects from Changes in Family Environment? A Study of Korean American Adoptees," *Quarterly Journal of Economics* 122 (2007): 139.

192. Eric Turkheimber et al., "Socioeconomic Status Modifies Heritability of IQ in Young Children," *Psychological Science* 14 (2003): 623–628.

193. K. Paige Harden, Eric Turkheimber, and John C. Loehlin, "Genotype by Environment Interaction in Adolescents' Cognitive Aptitude," *Behavior Genetics* 37 (2007): 273–283.

194. Corcoran, "Rags to Rags."

195. Baum and Ma, *Education Pays 2007*, figure 1.16b.
196. Corcoran, "Rags to Rags," 250.
197. W. Steven Barnett and Clive R. Belfield, "Early Childhood Development and Social Mobility," *Future of Children* 16 (2006): 73–98.
198. Cecilia E. Rouse and Lisa Barrow, "U.S. Elementary and Secondary Schools: Equalizing Opportunity or Replicating the Status Quo?" *Future of Children* 16 (2006): 99–123.
199. Sara McLanahan and Christine Percheski, "Family Structure and the Reproduction of Inequalities," *Annual Review of Sociology* 34 (2008): 264.
200. Ibid., 265–267.
201. Ibid., 265–269.
202. McLanahan, "Fragile Families and the Reproduction of Poverty," 127–128.
203. Corcoran, "Rags to Rags," 244.
204. Ibid., 254–256.
205. Wilson, *More than Just Race*, chapter 2.
206. Ibid., 133–134.
207. Ibid., 136.
208. Corcoran, "Rags to Rags," 256–260; Sandra E. Black and Paul J. Devereux, "Recent Developments in Intergenerational Mobility" (working paper 15889, National Bureau of Economic Research, Cambridge, MA, 2010), http://papers.nber.org/papers/w15889 (accessed January 17, 2011); Robert J. Sampson, Jeffrey D. Morenoff, and Thomas Gannon-Rowley, "Assessing 'Neighborhood Effects': Social Processes and New Directions in Research," *Annual Review of Sociology* 28 (2002): 443–478.
209. Robert Haveman and Timothy Smeeding, "The Role of Higher Education in Social Mobility," *Future of Children* 16 (2006): table 3. The ratio of income to needs is the average real value of the family's income while the youths were age two to fifteen, divided by the national poverty line (for a family of that size) and the average wealth (net worth) of the family in 1984, when the youths ranged in age from fifteen to eighteen.
210. Richard Breen and Jan O. Jonsson, "Inequality of Opportunity in Comparative Perspective: Recent Research on Educational Attainment and Social Mobility," *Annual Review of Sociology* 31 (2005): 223–243.
211. Baum and Ma, *Education Pays 2007*, figure 1.16a.
212. Robert J. Sampson, Patrick Sharkey, and Stephen W. Raudenbush, "Durable Effects of Concentrated Disadvantage on Verbal Ability among African-American Children," *Proceedings of the National Academy of Sciences of the United States of America* 105 (2008): 845–852.
213. Samuel Bowles, Herbert Gintis, and Melissa Osborne Groves, "Introduction," in *Unequal Chances: Family Background and Economic Success*, ed. S. Bowles, H. Gintis, and M. Osborne Groves (New York: Russell Sage, 2005), 4; Heckman

et al., "The Effects of Cognitive and Noncognitive Abilities"; Robert H. Haveman and Barbara L. Wolfe, "The Determinants of Children's Attainments: A Review of Methods and Findings," *Journal of Economic Literature* 33 (1995): 1829–1878; George Farkas, "Cognitive Skills and Noncognitive Traits and Behaviors in Stratification Processes," *Annual Review of Sociology* 29 (2003): 541–562.

214. Samuel Bowles, Herbert Gintis, and Melissa Osborne, "The Determinants of Earnings: A Behavioral Approach," *Journal of Economic Literature* 39 (2001): 1149.

215. Currie, "Healthy, Wealthy, and Wise."

216. Barbara Bloom, Robin A. Cohen, and Gulnur Freeman, *Summary Health Statistics for U.S. Children: National Health Interview Survey, 2009*, Vital Health Statistics 10, no. 247 (Washington, DC: National Center for Health Statistics, U.S. Department of Health and Human Services, 2010), table 6.

217. Janet Currie and Enrico Moretti, "Mother's Education and the Intergenerational Transmission of Human Capital: Evidence from College Openings," *Quarterly Journal of Economics* 118 (2003): 1495–1532.

218. Douglas Almond, "Is the 1918 Influenza Pandemic Over? Long-Term Effects of In Utero Influenza Exposure in the Post-1940 US Population," *Journal of Political Economy* 114 (2006): 672–712.

219. Douglas Almond and Bhashkar Mazumder, "The 1918 Influenza Pandemic and Subsequent Health Outcomes: An Analysis of SIPP Data," *American Economic Review* 95 (2005): 258–262.

220. Ronald C. Kessler et al., "Social Consequences of Psychiatric Disorders 1: Educational Attainment," *American Journal of Psychiatry* 152 (1995): 1026–1032.

221. Jane D. McLeod and Karen Kaiser, "Childhood Emotional and Behavioral Problems and Educational Attainment," *American Sociological Review* 69 (2004): 636–658.

222. Reynolds and Ross, "Social Stratification and Health," 240.

223. Fleisher, *Dead End Kids*, 67–68.

224. Ibid., 207.

5. The Social Consequences of Dropping Out

1. Henry M. Levin, *The Costs to the Nation of Inadequate Education* (Washington, DC: U.S. Government Printing Office, 1972).

2. Ibid., ix.

3. See www.tc.columbia.edu/centers/EquityCampaign/index.asp (accessed February 18, 2011).

4. Clive R. Belfield and Harry M. Levin, eds., *The Price We Pay: Economic and Social Consequences of Inadequate Education.* (Washington, DC: Brookings Institution Press, 2007.

5. Stephen J. Carroll and Emre Erkut, *The Benefits to Taxpayers from Increases in Students' Educational Attainment* (Santa Monica, CA: Rand Corporation, 2009).

6. They also use different assumptions about the discount rate used to estimate present values of benefits. Levin and colleagues use a 3.5 percent discount rate, while Carroll and Erkut use a 3 percent discount rate.

7. Clive R. Belfield and Henry M. Levin, "The Education Attainment Gap: Who's Affected, How Much, and Why It Matters," in *The Price We Pay: Economic and Social Consequences of Inadequate Education*, ed. C. R. Belfield and H. M. Levin (Washington, DC: Brookings Institution Press, 2007), 9–10. Levin and colleagues use modest assumptions that college attendance rates for "new" high school graduates would be equivalent to those of high school students in the lowest reading quartile and college completion rates would be equivalent to those of beginning college students in the lowest third of socioeconomic status.

8. For a comparison of estimates with and without the assumption of productivity increases, see Cecilia E. Rouse, "Consequences for the Labor Market," in *The Price We Pay: Economic and Social Consequences of Inadequate Education*, ed. C. R. Belfield and H. M. Levin (Washington, DC: Brookings Institution Press, 2007), 99–141, table 5-3; Rouse and Levin both assume a productivity growth rate of 1.5 percent. See Levin et al., *The Costs and Benefits of an Excellent Education*, 15; Carroll and Erkut assume zero productivity growth. See Carroll and Erkut, *The Benefits to Taxpayers*, 4.

9. The three studies vary in the specific taxes they include in their estimates and in the method used to estimate taxes. See Sandy Baum and Jennifer Ma, *Education Pays 2007: The Benefits of Higher Education for Individuals and Society* (Washington, DC: College Board, 2007); Rouse, "Consequences for the Labor Market"; Andrew Sum et al., *The Consequences of Dropping Out of High School: Joblessness and Jailing for High School Dropouts and the High Costs for Taxpayers* (Boston, MA: Center for Labor Market Studies, Northeastern University, 2009).

10. Rouse, "Consequences for the Labor Market," table 5-3. Figures are based on 3.5 percent discount rate and 1.5 percent annual productivity growth rate.

11. Ibid., 117–118.

12. Henry M. Levin and Clive R. Belfield, "Educational Interventions to Raise High School Graduation Rates," in *The Price We Pay: Economic and Social Consequences of Inadequate Education*, ed. C. R. Belfield and H. M. Levin (Washington, DC: Brookings Institution Press, 2007), 177–199, 194, table 9.5.

13. Carroll and Erkut, *The Benefits to Taxpayers*, table 7.2.

14. Clive R. Belfield and Henry M. Levin, *The Economic Losses from High School Dropouts in California* (Santa Barbara: California Dropout Research Project,

2007), http://cdrp.ucsb.edu/dropouts/pubs_reports.htm#1 (accessed January 17, 2011), tables 7 and 8.

15. Ibid., table 3.

16. See California Dropout Research Project website, www.cdrp.ucsb.edu (accessed February 18, 2011).

17. See "The Economic Benefits of Reducing the Dropout Rate in the Nation's Largest Metropolitan Areas," www.all4ed.org/publication_material/EconMSA (accessed February 18, 2011).

18. It is impossible to compare these figures with those from the Levin and Carroll studies because little details are given on the specific techniques and assumptions used to derive the estimates.

19. See "The Economic Benefits of Reducing the Dropout Rate among Students of Color in the Nation's Largest Metropolitan Areas," www.all4ed.org/publication_material/EconMSAsoc (accessed February 18, 2011).

20. See "Education," www.whitehouse.gov/issues/education (accessed February 18, 2011).

21. *Education at a Glance 2010* (Paris: Organisation for Economic Co-operation and Development, 2010), chart A3.2.

22. Ibid., table A3.2.

23. James J. Heckman and Paul A. LaFontaine, "The American High School Graduation Rate: Trends and Levels," *Review of Economics and Statistics* 92 (2010): 260.

24. Ibid.

25. John Bound, Michael Lovenheim, and Sarah Turner, "Why Have College Completion Rates Declined? An Analysis of Changing Student Preparation and Collegiate Resources" (working paper 15566, National Bureau of Economic Research, Cambridge, MA, 2009), http://papers.nber.org/papers/w15566 (accessed January 17, 2011).

26. *Getting to 2025: Can California Meet the Challenges?* Research Brief Issue 100, ed. E. Hanak and M. Baldassare (San Francisco: Public Policy Institute of California, 2005), www.ppic.org/content/pubs/rb/RB_605MBRB.pdf (accessed January 17, 2011), 1.

27. Lance Lochner and Enrico Moretti, "The Effect of Education on Crime: Evidence from Prison, Arrests, and Self-Reports," *American Economic Review* 94 (2004): table 13.

28. Ibid., 182–183.

29. Details of study can be found in Henry Levin, Clive Belfield, Peter Muennig, and Cecilia Rouse, *The Costs and Benefits of an Excellent Education for All of America's Children: Technical Appendix* (New York: Center for Cost-Benefit Studies of Education Teachers College, Columbia University, 2007), www

.cbcse.org/pages/cost-benefit-research/leeds-natl-benefit-cost.php (accessed January 17, 2011).

30. Ibid., tables 5.4 and 5.5.

31. Ibid., table 5.5.

32. Carroll and Erkut, *The Benefits to Taxpayers from Increases*, table 7.2.

33. Belfield and Levin, *The Economic Losses*, table 13.

34. Ibid., table 17. Total losses equal $21,370 in state and local government crime expenditures plus $79,890 in victim costs times 118,494 dropouts. The figures exclude the estimated $26,840 in education savings from dropouts leaving school early.

35. Clive Belfield and Harry M. Levin, *High School Dropouts and the Economic Losses from Juvenile Crime in California* (Santa Barbara: California Dropout Research Project, 2009), from http://cdrp.ucsb.edu/dropouts/pubs_reports.htm #16 (accessed January 17, 2011).

36. Ibid., table 1.

37. Ibid., table 5.

38. Ibid., table 9.

39. Welfare reform in 1990s reduced benefits. See Pamela J. Loprest and Sheila R. Zedlewski, *The Changing Role of Welfare in the Lives of Low-Income Families with Children* (occasional paper 73, Urban Institute, Washington, DC, 2006), www.urban.org/Publications/311357.html (accessed January 17, 2011).

40. Levin et al., "Educational Interventions to Raise High School Graduation Rates," table 6.1; another study found similar differences. See Baum and Ma, *Education Pays 2007*, figure 1.12.

41. Levin et al., *The Costs and Benefits of an Excellent Education*, table 6.3.

42. Ibid., table 4.1.

43. Ibid.

44. Ibid., table 4.3.

45. Carroll and Erkut, *The Benefits to Taxpayers*, 19.

46. Ibid., table 7.2.

47. Larry M. Bartels, *Unequal Democracy: The Political Economy of the New Gilded Age* (Princeton, NJ: Princeton University Press, 2008).

48. Ibid., 286.

49. Ibid., 284.

50. Levin et al., *The Costs and Benefits of an Excellent Education*, table 7.1.

51. Carroll and Erkut, *The Benefits to Taxpayers*, table 7.2.

52. Sum et al., *The Consequences of Dropping Out*, table 3. Sum et al. considered federal, state, and local taxes together with cash and in-kind transfer costs, and imposed incarceration costs. But they provide no detail for how they estimated

these costs, so it is impossible to determine why their figure is so much higher than the one from Levin et al.

53. Belfield and Levin, *The Economic Losses from High School Dropouts.*
54. Ibid., tables 18 and 19.
55. See California Dropout Research Project website, www.cdrp.ucsb.edu (accessed February 18, 2011).
56. "Remarks by the President at the America's Promise Alliance Education Event," www.whitehouse.gov/the-press-office/remarks-president-americas -promise-alliance-education-event (accessed July 30, 2010).
57. Henry M. Levin and Carolyn Kelley, "Can Education Do It Alone?" *Economics of Education Review* 13 (1994): 97–108.
58. Clark Kerr, "Is Education Really All that Guilty?" *Education Week*, February 21, 1991, www.edweek.org/ew/articles/1991/02/27/10160021.h10.html?qs=Educat ion+Really+All+that+Guilty? (accessed January 17, 2011).

6. Understanding Why Students Drop Out

1. Jerald G. Bachman, Swayzer S. Green, and Ilona D. Wirtanen, *Youth in Transition, Vol. III: Dropping Out: Problem or Symptom?* (Ann Arbor: Institute for Social Research, University of Michigan, 1971, 169.
2. Jeremy D. Finn, "Withdrawing from School," *Review of Educational Research* 59 (1989): 117–142.
3. Margaret E. Ensminger and Anita L. Slusarcick, "Paths to High School Graduation or Dropout: A Longitudinal Study of a First-Grade Cohort," *Sociology of Education* 65 (1992): 95–113.
4. Helen E. Garnier, Judith A. Stein, and Jennifer K. Jacobs, "The Process of Dropping Out of High School: A 19-Year Perspective," *American Educational Research Journal* 34 (1997): 395–419.
5. Karl L. Alexander, Doris R. Entwisle, and Nadir S. Kabbini, "The Dropout Process in Life Course Perspective: Early Risk Factors at Home and School," *Teachers College Record* 103 (2001): 763.
6. Arthur J. Reynolds, Suh-Ruu Ou, and James W. Topitzes, "Paths of Effects of Early Childhood Intervention on Educational Attainment and Delinquency: A Confirmatory Analysis of the Chicago Child-Parent Centers," *Child Development* 75 (2004): 1299–1328.
7. Vincent Tinto, *Leaving College: Rethinking the Causes and Cures for Student Attrition* (Chicago: University of Chicago Press, 1987).
8. Russell W. Rumberger and Katherine A. Larson, "Student Mobility and the Increased Risk of High School Dropout," *American Journal of Education* 107 (1998): 1–35.
9. Gary G. Wehlage et al., *Reducing the Risk: Schools as Communities of Support* (New York: Falmer Press, 1989).

10. Ibid., 117.
11. Ibid., chapter 5.
12. Ibid., 177.
13. Ibid., 179.
14. Richard M. Lerner and Nancy L. Galambos, "Adolescent Development: Challenges and Opportunities for Research, Programs, and Policies," *Annual Review of Psychology* 49 (1998): 413–446. Lerner and Galambos review the literature related to various key risk factors of contemporary adolescence.
15. Sara Battin-Pearson et al., "Predictors of Early High School Dropout: A Test of Five Theories," *Journal of Educational Psychology* 92 (2000): 568–582.
16. Gary Sweeten, "Who Will Graduate? Disruption of High School Education by Arrest and Court Involvement," *Justice Quarterly* 23 (2006): 462–480.
17. Russell W. Rumberger, "High School Dropouts: A Review of Issues and Evidence," *Review of Educational Research* 57 (1987): 111.
18. Deirdre M. Kelly, *Last Chance High: How Girls and Boys Drop In and Out of Alternative Schools* (New Haven, CT: Yale University Press, 1993), 29.
19. Fred M. Newman, Gary G. Wehlage, and Susie D. Lamborn, "The Significance and Sources of Student Engagement," in *Student Engagement and Achievement in American Secondary Schools*, ed. F. M. Newman (New York: Teachers College Press, 1992), 12.
20. Ibid., 13.
21. Ibid., 17.
22. National Research Council, Committee on Increasing High School Students' Engagement and Motivation to Learn, *Engaging Schools: Fostering High School Students' Motivation to Learn* (Washington, DC: National Academies Press, 2004).
23. For a review, see Jacquelynne S. Eccles and Allan Wigfield, "Motivational Beliefs, Values, and Goals," *Annual Review of Psychology* 53 (2002): 109–132.
24. James P. Connell and James G. Wellborn, "Competence, Autonomy, and Relatedness: A Motivational Analysis of Self-Systems Processes," in *Minnesota Symposium on Child Psychology, Volume 23*, ed. M. R. Gunnar and L. A. Stroufe (Hillsdale, NJ: Lawrence Erlbaum, 1991), 43–77.
25. Jennifer A Fredricks, Phyllis C. Blumenfeld, and Alison H. Paris, "School Engagement: Potential of the Concept, State of the Evidence," *Review of Educational Research* 74 (2004): 59–109.
26. James J. Appleton, Sandra L. Christenson, and Michael J. Furlong, "Student Engagement with School: Critical Conceptual and Methodological Issues of the Construct," *Psychology in the Schools* 45 (2008): 369–386.
27. Urie Bronfenbrenner, *The Ecology of Human Development* (Cambridge, MA: Harvard University Press, 1979); See also Lerner and Galambos, "Adolescent

Development"; Laurence Steinberg and Amanda S. Morris, "Adolescent Development," *Annual Review of Psychology* 52 (2001): 83–110.

28. National Research Council, Panel on High-Risk Youth, *Losing Generations: Adolescents in High-Risk Settings* (Washington, DC: National Academies Press, 1993), 1.

29. See, for example, Kathryn Edin and Maria Kefalas, *Promises I Can Keep: Why Poor Women Put Motherhood before Marriage* (Berkeley: University of California Press, 2005); Gary W. Evans, "The Environment of Childhood Poverty," *American Psychologist* 59 (2004): 77–92; Mercer L. Sullivan, *"Getting Paid": Youth Crime and Work in the Inner City* (Ithaca, NY: Cornell University Press, 1989); William Julius Wilson, *The Truly Disadvantaged: The Inner City, the Underclass, and Public Policy* (Chicago: University of Chicago Press, 1987).

30. John M. Bridgeland, John J. DiIulio Jr., and Karen Burke Morison, *The Silent Epidemic: Perspectives on High School Dropouts* (Washington, DC: Civic Enterprises, 2006). The study was conducted in association with Peter D. Hart Research Associates for the Bill & Melinda Gates Foundation.

31. Ibid., 22.

32. Ibid.

33. Ibid., 3.

34. Ibid.

35. Ibid., 4.

36. Ibid., 5.

37. Ibid., 6.

38. Ben Dalton, Elizabeth Glennie, and Steven J. Ingels, *Late High School Dropouts: Characteristics, Experiences, and Changes across Cohorts* (NCES 2009-307) (Washington, DC: National Center for Education Statistics, U.S. Department of Education, 2009), http://nces.ed.gov/Pubsearch/Pubsinfo.Asp ?Pubid=2009307 (accessed January 17, 2011), table 9.

39. The reasons are similar to those reported in an earlier longitudinal study of eighth graders who dropped out between 1988 and 1994. See Jennifer Berktold, Sonya Geis, and Phillip Kaufman, *Subsequent Educational Attainment of High School Dropouts* (NCES 98-085)(Washington, DC: National Center for Education Statistics, U.S. Department of Education, 1998), http://nces.ed.gov/pubsearch/pubsinfo.asp?pubid=98085 (accessed January 17, 2011), table 5.

7. Predictors of Dropping Out

1. Some excellent studies have been conducted. See Michelle Fine, *Framing Dropouts: Notes on the Politics of an Urban Public High School* (Albany: State

University of New York Press, 1991); Nilda Flores-González, *School Kids/Street Kids: Identity Development in Latino Students* (New York: Teachers College Press, 2002); Deirdre M. Kelly, *Last Chance High: How Girls and Boys Drop In and Out of Alternative Schools* (New Haven, CT: Yale University Press, 1993); Harriett D. Romo and Toni Falbo, *Latino High School Graduation: Defying the Odds* (Austin : University of Texas Press, 1996); Angela Valenzuela, *Subtractive Schooling: U.S.-Mexican Youth and the Politics of Caring* (Albany: State University of New York Press, 1999).

2. For a recent review of 203 quantitative studies published from 1983 to 2008, see Russell W. Rumberger and Sun Ah Lim, *Why Students Drop Out of School: A Review of 25 Years of Research* (Santa Barbara: California Dropout Research Project, 2008), http://cdrp.ucsb.edu/Dropouts/Pubs_Reports.Htm#15 (accessed January 17, 2011).

3. See, for example, James S. Coleman and Thomas Hoffer, *Public and Private High Schools: The Impact of Communities* (New York: Basic Books, 1987); Robert K. Ream, "Toward Understanding How Social Capital Mediates the Impact of Mobility on Mexican American Achievement," *Social Forces* 84 (2005): 201–224.

4. Barbara Schneider et al., *Estimating Causal Effects Using Experimental and Observational Designs*, report from the Governing Board of the American Educational Research Association Grants Program (Washington, DC: American Educational Research Association, 2007).

5. Rumberger and Lim, *Why Students Drop Out of School.*

6. Similar factors predict whether students return to school, although few studies have investigated reenrollment behavior. One study found, for example, that students of higher socioeconomic status and higher-achieving students were less likely to drop out and that higher socioeconomic status and higher-achieving dropouts were more likely to return to school. See Hwei-Lin Chuang, "High School Youths' Dropout and Re-enrollment Behavior," *Economics of Education Review* 16 (1997): 171–186.

7. Elaine Allensworth and John Q. Easton, *The On-Track Indicator as a Predictor of High School Graduation* (Chicago: Consortium on Chicago School Research, University of Chicago, 2005), http://ccsr.uchicago.edu/content/publications.php?pub_id=10 (accessed January 17, 2011).

8. Ibid., figures 3 and 6.

9. Ibid., 7.

10. Ibid., figure 5.

11. David Silver, Marisa Saunders, and Estela Zarate, *What Factors Predict High School Graduation in the Los Angeles Unified School District?* (Santa Barbara: California Dropout Research Project, 2008), http://cdrp.ucsb.edu/Dropouts/Pubs_Reports.Htm#14 (accessed January 17, 2011), 14.

12. Ibid., table 3.
13. Marisa Saunders, David Silver, and Estela Zarate, *The Impact of High Schools on Student Achievement within the Los Angeles Unified School District*, LSEAT policy brief (Los Angeles: Institute for Democracy, Education, and Access, 2008), http://idea.gseis.ucla.edu/publications (accessed February 18, 2011), 2.
14. Michal Kurlaender, Sean F. Reardon, and Jacob Jackson, *Middle School Predictors of High School Achievement in Three California School Districts* (Santa Barbara: California Dropout Research Project, 2008), http://cdrp.ucsb.edu/Dropouts/Pubs_Reports.Htm#13 (accessed January 17, 2011), figure 2.
15. Heckman and LaFontaine, "The American High School Graduation Rate," figure 2.
16. *Grade Level Retention in Texas Public Schools, 2008–09* (Austin: Texas Education Agency, 2010), www.tea.state.tx.us/Index4.Aspx?Id=4108 (accessed January 17, 2011), table 3.
17. Ibid., table 5.
18. Silver et al., *What Factors Predict High School Graduation?*
19. The most recent data compiled by the U.S. Department of Education identified ten states that reported using minimum-competency testing in student promotion decisions. See Thomas D. Snyder, Sally A. Dillow, and Charlene M. Hoffman, *Digest of Education Statistics, 2008* (NCES 2008-022) (Washington, DC: National Center for Education Statistics, U.S. Department of Education, 2009), http://nces.ed.gov/Pubsearch/Pubsinfo.Asp?Pubid=2009020 (accessed January 17, 2011).
20. *Grade Level Retention*, 4.
21. Susan Stone and Mimi Engel, "Same Old, Same Old? Students' Experiences of Grade Retention under Chicago's Ending Social Promotion Policy," *American Journal of Education* 113 (2007): 605–634.
22. Jill Walston, Amy Rathbun, and Elvira G. Huasken, *Eighth Grade: First Findings from the Final Round of the Early Childhood Longitudinal Study, Kindergarten Class of 1998–99 (ECLS-K)* (Washington, DC: National Center for Education Statistics, U.S. Department of Education, 2008), http://nces.ed.gov/Pubsearch/Pubsinfo.Asp?Pubid=2008088 (accessed January 17, 2011), 15. This is similar to the 12 percent rate for 2006 that Heckman and LaFontaine estimated by comparing ninth-grade enrollment in public schools with eighth-grade enrollment one year earlier (figure VI).
23. Eric R. Eide and Mark H. Showalter, "The Effect of Grade Retention on Educational and Labor Market Outcomes," *Economics of Education Review* 20 (2001): table 1. Data from Texas also show grade one with the highest retention rate. See *Grade Level Retention*, table 2.

24. A number of studies used NELS:88 data that included a variable indicating whether the student was ever retained between grade one and grade eight, so we put those students in the elementary school category.

25. Shane R. Jimerson, Gabrielle E. Anderson, and Angela D. Whipple, "Winning the Battle and Losing the War: Examining the Relation between Grade Retention and Dropping Out of High School," *Psychology in the Schools* 39 (2002): 441–457. The authors did not identify whether the retention occurred in elementary, middle, or high school.

26. Karl L. Alexander, Doris R. Entwisle, and Nadir S. Kabbini, "The Dropout Process in Life Course Perspective: Early Risk Factors at Home and School," *Teachers College Record* 103 (2001): 760–882; Gary Sweeten, "Who Will Graduate? Disruption of High School Education by Arrest and Court Involvement," *Justice Quarterly* 23 (2006): 462–480.

27. Alexander et al., "The Dropout Process," table 9.

28. An earlier study based on data from the NELS:88 longitudinal study of 1988 eighth graders similarly found that retention in grades 5–8 had a larger negative impact on dropping out in grades 8–10 than retention in grades K–4. See Phillip Kaufman and Denise Bradbury, *Characteristics of At-Risk Students in the NELS:88* (Washington, DC: National Center for Education Statistics, U.S. Department of Education, 1992).

29. Romo and Falbo, *Latino High School Graduation*, 45.

30. Eide and Showalter, "The Effect of Grade Retention," 2001.

31. *School Enrollment—Social and Economic Characteristics of Students: October 2008* (Washington, DC: Census Bureau, U.S. Department of Commerce, 2009), www.census.gov/population/www/socdemo/school/cps2008.html (accessed January 17, 2011), table 2.

32. Jane Arnold Lincove and Gary Painter, "Does the Age that Children Start Kindergarten Matter? Evidence of Long-Term Educational and Social Outcomes," *Educational Evaluation and Policy Analysis* 28 (2006): 153–179.

33. Silver et al., *What Factors Predict High School Graduation?* table 4.

34. For more information about the study, see Catherine Haggerty et al., *National Education Longitudinal Study (NELS:88/94): Methodology Report* (Washington, DC: National Center for Education Statistics, U.S. Department of Education, 1996).

35. Silver et al., *What Factors Predict High School Graduation*, 16.

36. Kurlaender, Reardon, and Jackson, *Middle School Predictors of High School Achievement*, table 4. The study relied on district data, so estimated graduation rates were probably lower than actual graduation rates because some students who left the district could have reenrolled and graduated from other high schools.

37. Ibid., figure 1.

38. Ibid., figure 2.
39. Rumberger and Lim, *Why Students Drop Out of School*, table 2.
40. Donald J. Hernandez, *Double Jeopardy: How Third-Grade Reading Skills and Poverty Influence High School Graduation* (Baltimore, MD: The Annie E. Casey Foundation, 2011), www.aecf.org/~/media/Pubs/Topics/Education/Other/DoubleJeopardyHowThirdGradeReadingSkillsandPovery/Double-JeopardyReport040511FINAL.pdf (accessed May 14, 2011), 3.
41. Ream, "Toward Understanding How Social Capital Mediates"; Russell W. Rumberger, "The Causes and Consequences of Student Mobility," *Journal of Negro Education* 72 (2003): 6–21.
42. Joseph E. Kahne et al., "Small High Schools on a Larger Scale: The Impact of School Conversions in Chicago," *Educational Evaluation and Policy Analysis* 30 (2008): 281–315.
43. Russell W. Rumberger and Katherine A. Larson, "Student Mobility and the Increased Risk of High School Dropout," *American Journal of Education* 107 (1998): 1–35.
44. Christopher B. Swanson and Barbara Schneider, "Students on the Move: Residential and Educational Mobility in America's Schools," *Sociology of Education* 72 (1999): 54–67.
45. Silver et al., *What Factors Predict High School Graduation?* table 3.
46. Ibid.
47. Rumberger and Larson, "Student Mobility and the Increased Risk," table 5.
48. Swanson and Schneider, "Students on the Move," table 2.
49. *Many Challenges Arise in Educating Students Who Change Schools Frequently* (GAO-11-40) (Washington, DC: U.S. Government Accountability Office, 2010), www.gao.gov/new.items/d1140.pdf (accessed January 17, 2011). The study did not account for promotional school changes, such as moving from an elementary to a middle school.
50. Ben Dalton, Elizabeth Glennie, and Steven J. Ingels, *Late High School Dropouts: Characteristics, Experiences, and Changes across Cohorts* (NCES 2009-307) (Washington, DC: National Center for Education Statistics, U.S. Department of Education, 2009), http://nces.ed.gov/Pubsearch/Pubsinfo.Asp?Pubid=2009307 (accessed January 17, 2011), table 3.
51. Several of the studies were based on the NELS:88 data set, which asks the parents to indicate the number of nonpromotional school changes from grades one through eight. These studies are unable to disentangle the effects of mobility during elementary school and mobility during middle school. In our review, we included these predictors in the elementary school category.
52. Ream, "Toward Understanding How Social Capital Mediates"; Robert K. Ream and Russell W. Rumberger, "Student Engagement, Peer Social Capital,

and School Dropout among Mexican American and Non-Latino White Students," *Sociology of Education* 81 (2008): 109–139.

53. Shana Pribesh and Douglas B. Downey, "Why Are Residential and School Moves Associated with Poor School Performance?" *Demography* 36 (1999): 521–534.

54. Russell W. Rumberger et al., *The Educational Consequences of Mobility for California Students and Schools* (Berkeley: Policy Analysis for California Education, 1999).

55. Ibid., 39.

56. Ibid.

57. Ibid., 41.

58. Rumberger and Lim, *Why Students Drop Out of School*, table 2.

59. Romo and Falbo, *Latino High School Graduation*, 102.

60. Melissa Roderick, *The Path to Dropping Out* (Westport, CT: Auburn House, 1993).

61. Kelly, *Last Chance High*, 96.

62. Ibid., 94.

63. Ibid., 102.

64. Margaret W. Cahalan et al., *United States High School Sophomores: A Twenty-Two Year Comparison, 1980–2002* (NCES 2006-327) (Washington, DC: National Center for Education Statistics, U.S. Department of Education, 2006), tables 23 and 24.

65. Walston et al., *Eighth Grade*, table 4.

66. Ralph B. McNeal, "Extracurricular Activities and High School Dropouts," *Sociology of Education* 68 (1995): 62–80; Robert B. Pittman, "Social Factors, Enrollment in Vocational/Technical Courses, and High School Dropout Rates," *Journal of Educational Research* 84 (1991): 288–295; Zenog N. Yin and Justin B. Moore, "Re-Examining the Role of Interscholastic Sport Participation in Education," *Psychological Reports* 94 (2004): 1447–1454.

67. Romo and Falbo, *Latino High School Graduation*, 132–133.

68. Dalton et al., *Late High School Dropouts*, A-22.

69. Ibid., table 7.

70. Isabelle Archambault et al., "Student Engagement and Its Relationship with Early High School Dropout," *Journal of Adolescence* 32 (2009): 651–670; Isabelle Archambault et al., "Adolescent Behavioral, Affective, and Cognitive Engagement in School: Relationship to Dropout," *Journal of School Health* 79 (2009): 408–415; Michel Janosz et al., "School Engagement Trajectories and Their Differential Predictive Relations to Dropout," *Journal of Social Issues* 64 (2008): 21–40; Susan L. Rotermund, "The Role of Psychological Antecedents and Student Engagement in a Process Model of High School Dropout" (PhD

diss., Gevirtz Graduate School of Education, University of California, Santa Barbara, 2010).

71. Alexander et al., "The Dropout Process in Life Course Perspective."

72. Sara Battin-Pearson et al., "Predictors of Early High School Dropout: A Test of Five Theories," *Journal of Educational Psychology* 92 (2000): 568–582; Michael D. Newcomb et al., "Mediational and Deviance Theories of Late High School Failure: Process Roles of Structural Strains, Academic Competence, and General Versus Specific Problem Behaviors," *Journal of Counseling Psychology* 49 (2002): 172–186.

73. Battin-Pearson et al., "Predictors of Early High School Dropout," 572.

74. Newcomb et al., "Mediational and Deviance Theories," 176.

75. Jeremy D. Finn, Reva M. Fish, and Leslie A. Scott, "Educational Sequelae of High School Misbehavior," *Journal of Educational Research* 101 (2008): 259–274. This study did not control for the effects of other variables, such as academic achievement.

76. Mercer L. Sullivan, *"Getting Paid": Youth Crime and Work in the Inner City* (Ithaca, NY: Cornell University Press, 1989), 37.

77. Rumberger and Lim, *Why Students Drop Out of School*, table 2.

78. Suh-Ruu Ou et al., "Alterable Predictors of Educational Attainment, Income, and Crime: Findings from an Inner-City Cohort," *Social Service Review* 81 (2007): 85–128.

79. Sullivan, *"Getting Paid,"* 56.

80. Kelly, *Last Chance High*, table 3.

81. Sweeten, "Who Will Graduate?" 468; for another example, see Lance Hannon, "Poverty, Delinquency, and Educational Attainment: Cumulative Disadvantage or Disadvantage Saturation?" *Sociological Inquiry* 73 (2003): 580.

82. See, for example, Sweeten, "Who Will Graduate?"

83. Lance Hannon, "Poverty, delinquency, and educational attainment: Cumulative disadvantage or disadvantage saturation?" *Sociological Inquiry* 73 (2003): 575–594; Barbara S. Mensch and Denise B. Kandel, "Dropping out of high school and drug involvement," *Sociology of Education* 61 (1988): 95–113; Howard B. Kaplan and Xiaordu Liu, "A Longitudinal Analysis of Mediating Variables in the Drug-Use Dropping-Out Relationship," *Criminology* 32 (1994): 415–439; Suh-Ruu Ou, Joshua P. Mersky, Arthur J. Reynolds, and Kristy M. Kohler, "Alterable predictors of educational attainment, income, and crime: Findings from an inner-city cohort." *Social Service Review* 81 (2007): 85–128.

84. Jön G. Bernburg and Marvin D. Krohn, "Labeling, Life Chances, and Adult Crime: The Direct and Indirect Effects of Official Intervention in Adolescence on Crime in Early Adulthood," *Criminology* 41 (2003): 1287–1318; Hannon, "Poverty, Delinquency, and Educational Attainment"; Sweeten, "Who Will Graduate?"

85. Sweeten, "Who Will Graduate?" 473.

86. Sullivan, *"Getting Paid,"* 202.

87. Ibid., 203, 229.

88. Phyllis Ellickson et al., "Does Early Drug Use Increase the Risk of Dropping Out of High School?" *Journal of Drug Issues* 28 (1998): 357–380; Battin-Pearson et al., "Predictors of Early High School Dropout."

89. Jeremy W. Bray et al., "The Relationship between Marijuana Initiation and Dropping Out of High School," *Health Economics* 9 (2000): 9–18.

90. Rebekah Levine Conley and P. Lindsay Chase-Lansdale, "Adolescent Pregnancy and Parenthood: Recent Evidence and Future Directions," *American Psychologists* 53 (1998): 152–166; Jeff Grogger and Stephen Bronars, "The Socioeconomic Consequences of Teenage Childbearing—Findings from a Natural Experiment," *Family Planning Perspectives* 25 (1993): 156–174.

91. Kate Perper, Kristen Peterson, and Jennifer Manlove, *Diploma Attainment among Teen Mothers*, Fact Sheet 2010-01 (Washington, DC: Child Trends, 2010), www.childtrends.org/Files/Child_Trends-2010_01_22_FS_Diploma Attainment.pdf (accessed January 17, 2011), figure 1.

92. Saul D. Hoffman, E. Michael Foster, and Frank F. Furstenberg, "Reevaluating the Costs of Teenage Childbearing," *Demography* 30 (1993): 1–13; V. Joseph Hotz, Susan Williams McElroy, and Seth G. Sanders, "Teenage Childbearing and Its Life Cycle Consequences—Exploiting a Natural Experiment," *Journal of Human Resources* 40 (2005): 683–715. Hotz et al. discusses the relative merits of the various approaches.

93. Roberto M. Fernandez, Ronnelle Paulsen, and Marsha Hirano-Nakanishi, "Dropping Out among Hispanic Youth," *Social Science Research* 18 (1989): 21–52.

94. Grogger and Bronars, "The Socioeconomic Consequences of Teenage Childbearing"; Renata Forste and Marta Tienda, "Race and Ethnic Variation in the Schooling Consequences of Female Adolescent Sexual-Activity," *Social Science Quarterly* 73 (1992): 12–30.

95. Grogger and Bronars, "The Socioeconomic Consequences of Teenage Childbearing"; Hoffman, Foster, and Furstenberg, "Reevaluating the Costs."

96. V. Joseph Hotz, Charles H. Mullin, and Seth G. Sanders, "Bounding Causal Effects Using Data from a Contaminated Natural Experiment: Analyzing the Effects of Teenage Childbearing," *Review of Economic Studies* 64 (1997): 575–603; Hotz, McElroy, and Sanders, "Teenage Childbearing."

97. Jason M. Fletcher and Barbara L. Wolfe, "Education and Labor Market Consequences of Teenage Childbearing: Evidence Using the Timing of Pregnancy Outcomes and Community Fixed Effects," *Journal of Human Resources* 44 (2009): 303–325; Hoffman et al., "Reevaluating the Costs of Teenage Childbearing."

98. Jacquelynne S. Eccles, "The Development of Children Ages 6 to 14," *Future of Children* 9 (1999): 30–44; Richard M. Lerner and Nancy L. Galambos, "Adolescent Development: Challenges and Opportunities for Research, Programs, and Policies," *Annual Review of Psychology* 49 (1998): 413–46; Allison M. Ryan, "Peer Groups as a Context for the Socialization of Adolescents' Motivation, Engagement, and Achievement in School," *Educational Psychologist* 35 (2000): 101–111.

99. Ream, "Toward Understanding How Social Capital Mediates"; Ricardo D. Stanton-Salazar, "A Social Capital Framework for Understanding the Socialization of Racial Minority Children and Youths." *Harvard Educational Review* 67 (1997): 1–40.

100. Robert B. Cairns, Beverley D. Cairns, and Holly J. Necherman, "Early School Dropout: Configurations and Determinants," *Child Development* 60 (1989): 1437–1452.

101. Russell W. Rumberger, "Dropping Out of Middle School: A Multilevel Analysis of Students and Schools," *American Educational Research Journal* 32 (1995): 583–625; Elizabeth Stearns et al., "Staying Back and Dropping Out: The Relationship between Grade Retention and School Dropout," *Sociology of Education* 80 (2007): 210–240.

102. Jeffrey Fagan and Edward Pabon, "Contributions of Delinquency and Substance Use to School Dropout among Inner-City Youths," *Youth & Society* 21 (1990): 306–354; Pittman, "Social Factors, Enrollment in Vocational/Technical Courses."

103. Battin-Pearson et al., "Predictors of Early High School Dropout"; Cairns et al., "Early School Dropout"; William J. Carbonaro, "A Little Help from My Friend's Parents: Intergenerational Closure and Educational Outcomes," *Sociology of Education* 71 (1998): 295–313; Diane S. Kaplan, Mitchell B. Peck, and Howard B. Kaplan, "Decomposing the Academic Failure-Dropout Relationship: A Longitudinal Analysis," *Journal of Educational Research* 90 (1997): 331–343; Albert Saiz and Elena Zoido, "Listening to What the World Says: Bilingualism and Earnings in the United States," *Review of Economics and Statistics* 87 (2005): 523–538.

104. Caroline Glesmann, Barry Krisberg, and Susan Marchionna, *Youth in Gangs: Who Is at Risk?* (Oakland, CA: National Council on Crime and Delinquency, 2010), figure 1.

105. Rachel Dinkes, Jana Kemp, and Katrina Baum, *Indicators of School Crime and Safety: 2009* (NCES 2010-012/NCJ 228478) (Washington, DC: National Center for Education Statistics, U.S. Department of Education and Bureau of Justice Statistics, U.S. Department of Labor, 2009), http://nces.ed.gov/Pubsearch/Pubsinfo.Asp?Pubid=2010012 (accessed January 17, 2011), table 8.1.

106. James C. Howell and Arlen Egley Jr., "Moving Risk Factors into Developmental Theories of Gang Membership," *Youth Violence and Juvenile Justice* 3 (2005):334–354.

107. Mark S. Fleisher, *Dead End Kids: Gang Girls and the Boys They Know* (Madison: University of Wisconsin Press, 1998), 5.

108. Cahalan et al., *United States High School Sophomores.*

109. John Robert Warren and Emily Forrest Cataldi, "A Historical Perspective on High School Students' Paid Employment and Its Association with High School Dropout," *Sociological Forum* 21 (2006): 113–143.

110. Ellen Greenberger and Laurence Steinberg. *When Teenagers Work: The Psychological and Social Costs of Adolescent Employment* (New York: Basic Books, 1986).

111. Melanie J. Zimmer-Gembeck and Jeylan T. Mortimer, "Adolescent Work, Vocational Development, and Education," *Review of Educational Research* 76 (2006): 537–566.

112. Michael J. Shanahan and Brian P. Flaherty, "Dynamic Patterns of Time Use in Adolescence," *Child Development* 72 (2001): 385–401; John Robert Warren, "Reconsidering the Relationship Between Student Employment and Academic Outcomes: A New Theory and Better Data," *Youth & Society* 33 (2002): 366–393.

113. Jennifer S. Lee and Jeremy Staff, "When Work Matters: The Varying Impact of Work Intensity on High School Dropout," *Sociology of Education* 80 (2007): 158–178; Herbert W. Marsh and Sabina Kleitman, "Consequences of Employment during High School: Character Building, Subversion of Academic Goals, or a Threshold?" *American Educational Research Journal* 42 (2005): 331–369; Zimmer-Gembeck and Mortimer, "Adolescent Work, Vocational Development, and Education."

114. See Ronald D'Amico, "Does Employment during High School Impact Academic Progress?" *Sociology of Education* 57 (1984): 152–164; McNeal, "Extracurricular Activities and High School Dropouts"; Zimmer-Gembeck and Mortimer, "Adolescent Work, Vocational Development, and Education"; Doris R. Entwisle, Karl L. Alexander, and Linda Steffel Olson, "Temporary as Compared to Permanent High School Dropout," *Social Forces* 82 (2004): 1181–1205. D'Amico found that students who worked fewer than twenty hours per week were less likely to drop out, while McNeal found that students who worked fewer than seven hours were less likely to drop out. Zimmer-Gembeck and Mortimer found that students who worked consistently throughout their high school careers were less likely to drop out, which perhaps reflects a long-term commitment and perseverance. Entwisle, Alexander, and Olson found that among a sample of dropouts, those who

were employed prior to dropping out were more likely to complete high school by age twenty-two.

115. D'Amico, "Does Employment during High School Impact Academic Progress?"; Pete Goldschmidt and Jia Wang, "When Can Schools Affect Dropout Behavior? A Longitudinal Multilevel Analysis," *American Educational Research Journal* 36 (1999): 715–738; Kathryn Monahan, Joanna M. Lee, and Laurence Steinberg, "Revisiting the Impact of Part-Time Work on Adolescent Adjustment: Distinguishing Between Selection and Socialization Using Propensity Score Matching," *Child Development* 82 (2011): 96–112; Krista Perreira, Kathleen Mullan Harris, and Dohoon Lee, "Making It in America: High School Completion by Immigrant and Native Youth," *Demography* 43 (2006): 511–536; John Robert Warren and Jennifer C. Lee, "The Impact of Adolescent Employment on High School Dropout: Differences by Individual and Labor-Market Characteristics," *Social Science Research* 32 (2003): 98–128; Warren and Cataldi, "A Historical Perspective on High School Students' Paid Employment."

116. D'Amico, "Does Employment during High School Impact Academic Progress?"; Ralph B. McNeal, "Are Students Being Pulled Out of High School? The Effect of Adolescent Employment on Dropping Out," *Sociology of Education* 70 (1997): 206–220; Perreira et al., "Making It in America"; Warren and Cataldi, "A Historical Perspective on High School Students' Paid Employment."

117. Lee and Staff, "When Work Matters."

118. Eccles, "The Development of Children Ages 6 to 14," 37.

119. Jacquelynne S. Eccles and Allan Wigfield, "Motivational Beliefs, Values, and Goals," *Annual Review of Psychology* 53 (2002): 109–132. Eccles and Wigfield provide an in-depth discussion of student beliefs, values, and attitudes.

120. Alexander et al., "The Dropout Process in Life Course Perspective."

121. Ibid., 810–812.

122. Ibid., table 9.

123. Ibid., 796.

124. Eccles and Wigfield, "Motivational Beliefs, Values, and Goals."

125. Sullivan, "*Getting Paid*," 54.

126. Dalton et al., *Late High School Dropouts*, table 5.

127. Ibid.

128. National Research Council, Committee on Increasing High School Students' Engagement and Motivation to Learn, *Engaging Schools: Fostering High School Students' Motivation to Learn* (Washington, DC: National Academies Press, 2004).

129. Mimi Bong and Einar M. Skaalvik, "Academic Self-Concept and Self-Efficacy: How Different Are They Really?" *Educational Psychology Review* 15 (2003): 1–40.

130. Ibid.
131. Romo and Falbo, *Latino High School Graduation*, 52–53.
132. Alexander et al., "The Dropout Process in Life Course Perspective"; Ruth B. Ekstrom et al., "Who Drops Out of High School and Why? Findings from a National Study," *Teachers College Record* 87 (1986): 356–373; Russell W. Rumberger, "Dropping Out of High School: The Influence of Race, Sex, and Family Background," *American Educational Research Journal* 20 (1983): 199–220.
133. Dalton et al., *Late High School Dropouts*, table 9.
134. Ibid.
135. Rumberger, "Dropping Out of Middle School."
136. Kyle Crowder and Scott J. South, "Neighborhood Distress and School Dropout: The Variable Significance of Community Context," *Social Science Research* 32 (2003): 659–698.
137. Daniel T. Lichter, Gretchen T. Cornwell, and David J. Eggebeen, "Harvesting Human-Capital—Family-Structure and Education among Rural Youth," *Rural Sociology* 58 (1993): 53–75.
138. Jessica W. Davis and Kurt J. Bauman, *School Enrollment in the United States: 2006* (Washington, DC: Census Bureau, U.S. Department of Commerce, 2008), www.census.gov/prod/2008pubs/p20=559.pdf (accessed January 17, 2011), figure 6.
139. Susan Aud, Mary Ann Fox, and Angelina KewalRamani, *Status and Trends in the Education of Racial and Ethnic Groups* (NCES 2010-015) (Washington, DC: National Center for Education Statistics, U.S. Department of Education, 2010), http://nces.ed.gov/pubsearch/pubsinfo.asp?pubid=2010015 (accessed January 17, 2011), table 18.1b.
140. Michael J. White and Gayle Kaufman, "Language Use, Social Capital, and School Completion among Immigrants and Native-Born Ethnic Groups," *Social Science Quarterly* 78 (1997): 385–398.
141. Rumberger, "Dropping Out of Middle School."
142. Anne K. Driscoll, "Risk of High School Dropout among Immigrant and Native Hispanic Youth," *International Migration Review* 33 (1999): 857–875; Perreira et al., "Making It in America"; Rumberger, "Dropping Out of Middle School"; Roger A. Wojtkiewicz and Katherine M. Donato, "Hispanic Educational Attainment: The Effects of Family Background and Nativity," *Social Forces* 74 (1995): 559–574.
143. William Velez, "High School Attrition among Hispanic and Non-Hispanic White Youths," *Sociology of Education* 62 (1989): 119–133.
144. Wojtkiewicz and Donato, "Hispanic Educational Attainment."
145. Barbara A. Zsembik and Daniel Llanes, "Generational Differences in Educational Attainment among Mexican Americans," *Social Science Quarterly* 77 (1996): 363–374.

146. Amy Lutz, "Barriers to High-School Completion among Immigrant and Later-Generation Latinos in the USA—Language, Ethnicity and Socioeconomic Status," *Ethnicities* 7 (2007): 323–342.

147. Grace Kao and Marta Tienda, "Optimism and Achievement: The Educational Performance of Immigrant Youth," *Social Science Quarterly* 76 (1995): 1–19.

148. Perreira et al., "Making It in America."

149. Valenzuela, *Subtractive Schooling*, 5.

150. Margaret A. Gibson, "Complicating the Immigrant/Involuntary Minority Typology," *Anthropology & Education Quarterly* 28 (1997): 431–454.

151. Pátricia Gandara and Russell W. Rumberger, "Defining an Adequate Education for English Learners," *Journal of Education Finance and Policy* 3 (2008): 130–148; Pátricia Gandara and Russell W. Rumberger, "Immigration, Language, and Education: How Does Language Policy Structure Opportunity?" *Teachers College Record* 111 (2009): 750–782, www.tcrecord.org/Content.Asp ?Contentid=15343 (accessed January 17, 2011).

152. Bryan W. Griffin and Mark H. Heidorn, "An Examination of the Relationship between Minimum Competency Test Performance and Dropping Out of High School," *Educational Evaluation and Policy Analysis* 18 (1996): 243–252; Perreira et al., "Making It in America"; Zsembik and Llanes, "Generational Differences in Educational Attainment." Zsembik and Llanes found significant benefits from English language proficiency, while Driscoll did not.

153. Lutz, "Barriers to High-School Completion."

154. Amy L. Reschly and Sandra Christenson, "Prediction of Dropout among Students with Mild Disabilities—A Case for the Inclusion of Student Engagement Variables," *Remedial and Special Education* 27 (2006): 276–292.

155. Brian Powell and Lala Carr Steelman, "The Educational Benefits of Being Spaced Out—Sibship Density and Educational Progress," *American Sociological Review* 58(3) (1993): 367–381.

156. M. Christopher Roebuck, Michael T. French, and Michael L. Dennis, "Adolescent Marijuana Use and School Attendance," *Economics of Education Review* 23 (2004): 133–141.

157. Joshua Breslau, *Does Poor Health Contribute to Dropping Out of High School?* (Santa Barbara: California Dropout Research Project, University of California, 2010), http://cdrp.ucsb.edu/dropouts/pubs_reports.htm (accessed January 17, 2010).

158. Jane D. McLeod and Karen Kaiser, "Childhood Emotional and Behavioral Problems and Educational Attainment," *American Sociological Review* 69 (2004): 636–658.

159. Stephanie S. Daniel et al., "Suicidality, School Dropout, and Reading Problems among Adolescents," *Journal of Learning Disabilities* 39 (2006):

507–514; Farah Farahati, David E. Marcotte, and Virginia Wilcox-Gok, "The Effects of Parents' Psychiatric Disorders on Children's High School Dropout," *Economics of Education Review* 22 (2003): 167–178; John Hagan and Holly Foster, "Youth Violence and the End of Adolescence," *American Sociological Review* 66, no. 6 (2001): 874–899; Chadwick L. Menning, "Nonresident Fathering and School Failure," *Journal of Family Issues* 27 (2006): 1356–1382; Scott J. South, Dana L. Haynie, and Sunita Bose, "Student Mobility and School Dropout," *Social Science Research* 36 (2007): 68–94.

160. James P. Connell et al., "Hanging in There: Behavioral, Psychological, and Contextual Factors Affecting Whether African-American Adolescents Stay in High School," *Journal of Adolescent Research* 10 (1995): 41–63; Robert G. Croninger and Valerie E. Lee, "Social Capital and Dropping Out of High School: Benefits to At-Risk Students of Teachers' Support and Guidance," *Teachers College Record* 103 (2001): 548–581; Valerie E. Lee and David T. Burkam, "Transferring High Schools: An Alternative to Dropping Out?" *American Journal of Education* 100 (1992): 420–453.

161. Michael R. Benz, Lauren Lindstrom, and Paul Yovanoff, "Improving Graduation and Employment Outcomes of Students with Disabilities: Predictive Factors and Student Perspectives," *Exceptional Children* 66 (2000): 509–529; Alberto F. Cabrera and Steven M. La Nasa, "on the Path to College: Three Critical Tasks Facing America's Disadvantaged," *Research in Higher Education* 42 (2001): 119–149.

162. Croninger and Lee, "Social Capital and Dropping Out of High School."

163. Robert Balfanz, Liza Herzog, and Douglas J. MacIver, "Preventing Student Disengagement and Keeping Students on the Graduation Path in Urban Middle-Grades Schools: Early Identification and Effective Interventions," *Educational Psychologist* 42 (2007): 223–235.

164. Rumberger and Lim, *Why Students Drop Out of School*, table 2.

165. Michel Janosz et al., "Predicting Different Types of School Dropouts: A Typological Approach with Two Longitudinal Cohorts," *Journal of Educational Psychology* 92 (2000): 171–190.

166. Rex B. Kline, *Principles and Practice of Structural Equation Modeling*, 3rd ed. (New York: Guilford Publications, 2010).

167. See, for example, Battin-Pearson et al., "Predictors of Early High School Dropout"; Margaret E. Ensminger and Anita L. Slusarcick, "Paths to High School Graduation or Dropout: A Longitudinal Study of a First-Grade Cohort," *Sociology of Education* 65 (1992): 95–113; Helen E. Garnier, Judith A. Stein, and Jennifer K. Jacobs, "The Process of Dropping Out of High School: A 19-Year Perspective," *American Educational Research Journal* 34 (1997): 395–419; Arthur J. Reynolds, Suh-Ruu Ou, and James W. Topitzes, "Paths of

Effects of Early Childhood Intervention on Educational Attainment and Delinquency: A Confirmatory Analysis of the Chicago Child-Parent Centers," *Child Development* 75 (2004): 1299–1328; Archambault et al., "Student Engagement and Its Relationship."

168. James S. Coleman et al., *Equality of Educational Opportunity* (Washington, DC: U.S. Government Printing office, 1966); Christopher Jencks, Marshall Smith, Henry Acland, Mary J. Bane, David Cohen, Herbert Gintis, Barbara Heyns, and Stephan M. Michelson, *Inequality: A reassessment of the effects of family and schooling in America* (New York: Basic Books, 1972).

169. Coleman et al., *Equality of Educational Opportunity*; Eva M. Pomerantz, Elizabeth A. Moorman, and Scott D. Litwack, "The How, Whom, and Why of Parents' Involvement in Children's Academic Lives: More Is Not Always Better," *Review of Educational Research* 77 (2007): 373–410.

170. Thomas D. Snyder and Sally A. Dillow, *Digest of Education Statistics 2010* (NCES 2011-015) (Washington, DC: U.S. National Center for Education Statistics, U.S. Department of Education, 2011), http://nces.ed.gov/Pubsearch/Pubsinfo.Asp?Pubid=2011015 (accessed May 14, 2011), table 24. These figures differ somewhat from those reported by another NCES report, which shows that 67 percent of families in 2007 were married-couple families (Aud et al., *Status and Trends in the Education of Racial and Ethnic Groups*, table 3).

171. Sara McLanahan, "Fragile Families and the Reproduction of Poverty," *Annals of the American Academy of Political and Social Science* 621 (2009): 111–131.

172. Romo and Falbo, *Latino High School Graduation*, 80–82.

173. Ibid., 80.

174. Snyder and Dillow, *Digest of Education Statistics 2010*, Table 27.

175. Nan Marie Astone and Sara S. McLanahan, "Family Structure, Parental Practices and High School Completion," *American Sociological Review* 56 (1991): 309–320; McLanahan, "Fragile Families and the Reproduction of Poverty."

176. Krista M. Perreira, Kathleen. M. Harris, and Dohoon Lee, "Making it in America: High school completion by immigrant and native youth," *Demography* 43 (2006): 511–536; Russell W. Rumberger, "Dropping out of middle school: A multilevel analysis of students and schools," *American Educational Research Journal* 32 (1995): 583–625; Rumberger and Lim, *Why Students Drop Out of School*, table 3.

177. Judith A. Seltzer, "Consequences of Marital Dissolution for Children," *Annual Review of Sociology* 20 (1994): 235–266.

178. Steven Garasky, "The Effects of Family-Structure on Educational-Attainment—Do the Effects Vary by the Age of the Child?" *American Journal of Economics and Sociology* 54 (1995): 89–105.

179. Suett-Ling Pong and Don-Beom Ju, "The Effects of Change in Family Structure and Income on Dropping Out of Middle and High School," *Journal of Family Issues* 21 (2000): 147–169.

180. Karl L. Alexander, Doris R. Entwisle, and Carrie S. Horsey, "From First Grade Forward: Early Foundations of High School Dropout," *Sociology of Education* 70 (1997): 87–107; Alexander et al., "The Dropout Process in Life Course Perspective"; Garnier et al., "The Process of Dropping Out"; Robert Haveman, Barbara Wolfe, and James Spaulding, "Childhood Events and Circumstances Influencing High School Completion," *Demography* 28 (1991): 133–157.

181. Cara Bohon, Jason Garber, and Judy L. Horowitz, "Predicting School Dropout and Adolescent Sexual Behavior in Offspring of Depressed and Nondepressed Mothers," *Journal of the American Academy of Child and Adolescent Psychiatry* 46 (2007): 15–24; Margaret E. Ensminger et al., "Maternal Psychological Distress: Adult Sons' and Daughters' Mental Health and Educational Attainment," *Journal of the American Academy of Child and Adolescent Psychiatry* 42 (2003): 1108–1115.

182. *Geographic Mobility: 2008 to 2009* (Washington, DC: Census Bureau, U.S. department of Commerce, 2009), www.census.gov/population/www/socdemo/migrate/cps2009.html (accessed January 17, 2011), table 9.

183. Christine Humke and Charles Schaeffer, "Relocation: A Review of the Effects of Residential-Mobility on Children and Adolescents," *Psychology* 32 (1995): 16–24.

184. Dana L. Haynie, Scott J. South, and Sunita Bose, "The Company You Keep: Adolescent Mobility and Peer Behavior," *Sociological Inquiry* 76 (2006): 397–426; Ream, "Toward Understanding How Social Capital Mediates"; Ream and Rumberger, "Student Engagement, Peer Social Capital, and School Dropout."

185. Rumberger and Lim, *Why Students Drop Out of School*, table 3.

186. Arthur J. Reynolds, Chin-Chih Chen, and Janette E. Herbers, *School Mobility and Educational Success: A Research Synthesis and Evidence on Prevention*, paper prepared for the Workshop on the Impact of Mobility and Change on the Lives of Young Children, Schools, and Neighborhoods, June 29–30 (Washington, DC: National Academies Press, 2009), www.bocyf.org/Children _Who_Move_Workshop_Presentations.html (accessed January 6, 2011).

187. Ensminger et al., "Maternal Psychological Distress."

188. D. Wayne Osgood, E. Michael Foster, and Mark E. Courtney, "Vulnerable Populations and the Transition to Adulthood," *Future of Children* 20 (2010): 209–229.

189. Paul A. Toro, Amy Dworsky, and Patrick J. Fowler, "Homeless Youth in the United States: Recent Research Findings and Intervention Approaches," paper developed for the National Symposium on Homelessness Research held on

March 1–2, 2007, http://aspe.hhs.gov/hsp/homelessness/symposium07/toro (accessed June 22, 2011). Regarding the difficulty in disentangling the effects of poverty from those of homelessness, see John C. Buckner, "Understanding the Impact of Homelessness on Children: Challenges and Future Research Directions," *American Behavioral Scientist* 51 (2008): 721–736.

190. Martha Burt et al., *Helping America's Homeless: Emergency Shelter or Affordable Housing?* (Washington, DC: Urban Institute Press, 2001), table 5.6.

191. Osgood et al., "Vulnerable Populations and the Transition to Adulthood."

192. This is the index used in NELS:88, one of the most common sources of data in the studies identified in our review. See Steven J. Ingels, Leslie A. Scott, Judith T. Lindmark, Martin R. Frankel, and Sharon L. Myers, *National Education Longitudinal Study of 1988, First Follow-up: Student Component Data File User's Manual* (NCES 92-030) (Washington, DC: National Center for Education Statistics, U.S. Department of Education, 1992).

193. Dalton et al., *Late High School Dropouts*, table 1.

194. Rumberger and Lim, *Why Students Drop Out of School*, table 3.

195. Caroline Ratcliffe and Signe-Mary McKernan, *Childhood Poverty Persistence: Facts and Consequences*, Brief 14 (Washington, DC: Urban Institute, 2010), www.urban.org/Url.Cfm?ID=412126 (accessed July 30, 2010), table 1.

196. Croninger and Lee, "Social Capital and Dropping Out of High School."

197. James S. Coleman, "Social Capital in the Creation of Human Capital," *American Journal of Sociology* 94 (1988): S95–S120.

198. Xitao Fan and Michael Chen, "Parental Involvement and Students' Academic Achievement: A Meta-Analysis," *Educational Psychology Review* 13 (2001): 1–22; William H. Jeynes, "The Relationship between Parental Involvement and Urban Secondary School Student Academic Achievement—A Meta-Analysis," *Urban Education* 42 (2007): 82–110; Pomerantz et al., "The How, Whom, and Why of Parents' Involvement"; Christopher Spera, "A Review of the Relationship among Parenting Practices, Parenting Styles, and Adolescent School Achievement," *Educational Psychological Review* 17 (2005): 120–146. Spera discusses the distinction between parenting practices and parenting styles.

199. Astone and McLanahan, "Family Structure, Parental Practices and High School Completion."

200. Carbonaro, "A Little Help from My Friend's Parents"; Susan Stone, "Correlates of Change in Student Reported Parent Involvement in Schooling: A New Look at the National Education Longitudinal Study of 1988," *American Journal of Orthopsychiatry* 76 (2006): 518–530. Using the same data set as Carbonaro, Stone examined the effects of the changes in three composite measures of parental involvement—home communication about school, monitoring, and direct parent interaction with the school—between grades eight and ten, and

found that only one—a decrease in home communication—increased the odds of dropping out by a very modest 5 percent.

201. Brian A. Jacob, "Getting Tough? The Impact of High School Graduation Exams," *Educational Evaluation and Policy Analysis* 23 (2001): 99–121; Russell W. Rumberger and Scott L. Thomas, "The Distribution of Dropout and Turnover Rates among Urban and Suburban High Schools," *Sociology of Education* 73 (2000): 39–67; Jay D. Teachman et al., "School Capital and Dropping Out of School," *Journal of Marriage and the Family* 58 (1996): 773–783; Jay D. Teachman, Kathleen Paasch, and Karen Carver, "Social Capital and the Generation of Human Capital," *Social Forces* 75 (1997): 1343–1359.

202. Gary Orfield, *Reviving the Goal of an Integrated Society: A 21st Century Challenge* (Los Angeles: Civil Rights Project/Proyecto Dereshos Civiles at UCLA, 2009), http://civilrightsproject.ucla.edu/research/k-12-education/integration-and-diversity (accessed January 17, 2011).

203. Valerie E. Lee, "Using Hierarchical Linear Modeling to Study Social Contexts: The Case of School Effects," *Educational Psychologist* 35 (2000): 125–141; Stephen W. Raudenbush and J. Douglas Willms, "The Estimation of School Effects," *Journal of Educational and Behavioral Statistics* 20 (1995): 307–335; Russell W. Rumberger and Gregory J. Palardy, "Multilevel Models for School Effectiveness Research," in *Handbook of Quantitative Methodology for the Social Sciences*, ed. D. Kaplan (Thousand Oaks, CA: Sage Publications, 2004), 235–258.

204. Rumberger and Palardy, "Multilevel Models for School Effectiveness Research." Multilevel models allow researchers to partition the variability in student outcomes to various levels of the educational system—students, classrooms, schools, districts, and states. Most studies find that about 75 percent of the variability is at the student level, with the remaining variability attributable to other levels. For example, Mingliang Li estimated that 23 percent of the variability in dropout was at the school level and 5 percent at the state level, with the remaining 72 percent at the student level. See Mingliang Li, "Bayesian Proportional Hazard Analysis of the Timing of High School Dropout Decisions," *Econometric Reviews* 26 (2007): 529–556.

205. Steffi Pohl et al., "Unbiased Causal Inference from an Observational Study: Results of a Within-Study Comparison," *Educational Evaluation and Policy Analysis* 31 (2009): 463–479; Schneider et al., *Estimating Causal Effects*.

206. Eric A. Hanushek, "The Economics of Schooling: Production and Efficiency in Public Schools," *Journal of Economic Literature* 24 (1986): 1141–1177.

207. Adam Gamoran, "Social Factors in Education," in *Encyclopedia of Educational Research*, ed. M. C. Alkin, (New York: Macmillan, 1992), 1222–1229.

208. James S. Coleman, *Equality and Achievement in Education* (Boulder, CO: Westview Press, 1990), 119.

209. For example, one recent study found that the social class background of the student body had an almost as large—and sometimes larger—effect on student learning in high school as students' own social class background. See Russell W. Rumberger and Gregory J. Palardy, "Does Segregation Still Matter? The Impact of Student Composition on Academic Achievement in High School," *Teachers College Record* 107 (2005): 1999–2045. A recent reanalysis of Coleman's data found that the racial/ethnic and social class composition was almost twice as important than a student's own race, ethnicity, and social class in explaining educational outcomes. See Geoffrey Borman and Maritza Dowling, "Schools and Inequality: A Multilevel Analysis of Coleman's Equality of Opportunity Data," *Teachers College Record* 112 (2010): 1201–1246. An international study found that in the United States the effects of school socioeconomic status (SES) on student achievement (not achievement growth) were about twice as large as the effects of individual SES. See *Knowledge and Skills for Life: First Results from the OECD Programme for International Student Assessment (PISA) 2000* (Paris: Organisation for Economic Co-Operation and Development, 2001), 199.

210. Charles T. Clotfelter et al., "High Poverty Schools and the Distribution of Teachers and Principals," *North Carolina Law Review* 85 (2007): 1345–1379; Eric A. Hanushek, John F. Kain, and Steven G. Rivkin, "Why Public Schools Lose Teachers," *Journal of Human Resources* 39 (2004): 326–354; Deborah Reed, *Educational Resources and Outcomes in California, by Race and Ethnicity* (San Francisco: Public Policy Institute of California, 2005).

211. Richard D. Kahlenberg, *All Together Now: Creating Middle-Class Schools through Public School Choice* (Washington, DC: Brookings Institution Press, 2001); Christopher Jencks and Susan E. Mayer, "The Social Consequences of Growing up in a Poor Neighborhood," in *Inner-City Poverty in the United States*, ed. L. Lynn Jr. and M. G. H. McGeary (Washington, DC: National Academies Press, 1990), 111–186; Ryan, "Peer Groups as a Context."

212. Anthony S. Bryk and Yeow Ming Thum, "The Effects of High School Organization on Dropping Out: An Exploratory Investigation," *American Educational Research Journal* 26 (1989): 353–383; Ralph B. McNeal, "High School Dropouts: A Closer Examination of School Effects," *Social Science Quarterly* 78 (1997): 209–222; William Sander, "Chicago Public Schools and Student Achievement," *Urban Education* 36, no. 1 (2001): 27–38; Rumberger, "Dropping Out of Middle School"; Rumberger and Thomas, "The Distribution of Dropout and Turnover Rates"; Russell W. Rumberger and Gregory J. Palardy, "Test Scores, Dropout Rates, and Transfer Rates as Alternative Indicators of High School Performance," *American Educational Research Journal* 41 (2005): 3–42; Argun Saatcioglu, "Disentangling School-

and Student-Level Effects of Desegregation and Resegregation on the Dropout Problem in Urban High Schools: Evidence from the Cleveland Municipal School District, 1977–1998," *Teachers College Record* 112 (2010): 1391–1442.

213. William N. Evans, Wallace E. Oates, and Robert M. Schwab, "Measuring peer group effects: A study of teenage behavior," *The Journal of Political Economy* 100 (1992): 966–991; Steven G. Rivkin, "Tiebout sorting, aggregation and the estimation of peer group effects," *Economics of Education Review* 20 (2001): 201–209.

214. One study found that three measures of school social composition—mean SES, the proportion of students whose families had moved between grades ten and twelve, and the proportion of students from nontraditional families—were no longer significant predictors of dropping out after controlling for a number of structural, resource, and school practice variables that had direct effects on dropout rates. See Rumberger and Palardy, "Test Scores, Dropout Rates, and Transfer Rates," table 2. Another study found that mean SES had no direct effects on dropout rates after controlling for a number of other school characteristics, including school size, academic climate, and teacher relations. See Valerie E. Lee and David T. Burkam, "Dropping Out of High School: The Role of School Organization and Structure," *American Educational Research Journal* 40 (2003): 353–393.

215. Flores-González, *School Kids/Street Kids*; Valenzuela, *Subtractive Schooling*.

216. John Wirt, Susan Choy, Stephen Provasnik, Patrick Rooney, Anindita Sen, and Richard Tobin, *The Condition of Education 2003* (NCES 2003—67) (Washington, DC: National Center for Education Statistics, U.S. Department of Education, 2003), indicator 30.

217. David I. Levine and Gary Painter, "The Nels Curve: Replicating the Bell Curve Analyses with the National Education Longitudinal Study," *Industrial Relations* 38, no. 3 (1999): 364–406; Herbert W. Marsh, "Employment during High School: Character Building or a Subversion of Academic Goals?" *Sociology of Education* 64 (1991): 172–189; Rumberger and Larson, "Student Mobility and the Increased Risk"; William Sander and Anthony C. Krautmann, "Catholic Schools, Dropout Rates and Educational Attainment," *Economic Inquiry* 33 (1995): 217–233.

218. Ronald H. Heck and Rochelle Mahoe, "Student Transition to High School and Persistence: Highlighting the Influences of Social Divisions and School Contingencies," *American Journal of Education* 112 (2006): 418–446; Rumberger and Thomas, "The Distribution of Dropout and Turnover Rates."

219. Pong and Ju, "The Effects of Change in Family Structure and Income"; Rumberger, "Dropping Out of Middle School"; Rumberger and Larson,

"Student Mobility and the Increased Risk"; Swanson and Schneider, "Students on the Move."

220. Lee and Burkam, "Dropping Out of High School"; Marsh, "Employment during High School"; Rumberger and Palardy, "Test Scores, Dropout Rates, and Transfer Rates."

221. Maureen A. Pirog and Christopher Magee, "High School Completion: The Influence of Schools, Families, and Adolescent Parenting," *Social Science Quarterly* 78 (1997): 710–724; Rumberger and Thomas, "The Distribution of Dropout and Turnover Rates."

222. Bryk and Thum, "The Effects of High School Organization"; Jeffrey T. Grogger, "Local Violence and Educational Attainment," *Journal of Human Resources* 32 (1997): 659–682; McNeal, "High School Dropouts"; Rumberger, "Dropping Out of Middle School"; Sander, "Chicago Public Schools and Student Achievement"; Richard A. Van Dorn, Gary L. Bowen, and Judith R. Blau, "The Impact of Community Diversity and Consolidated Inequality on Dropping Out of High School," *Family Relations* 55 (2006): 105–118.

223. Lee and Burkam, "The Impact of Adolescent Employment on High School Dropout."

224. Robert B. Pittman and Perri Haughwout, "Influence of High School Size on Dropout Rate," *Educational Evaluation and Policy Analysis* 9 (1987): 337–343.

225. Rumberger and Palardy, "Test Scores, Dropout Rates, and Transfer Rates."

226. Anthony S. Bryk, Valerie E. Lee, and Peter B. Holland, *Catholic Schools and the Common Good* (Cambridge, MA: Harvard University Press, 1993); James Samuel Coleman, Thomas Hoffer, and Sally Kilgore, *High School Achievement: Public, Catholic, and Private Schools Compared* (New York: Basic Books, 1982); James S. Coleman and Thomas Hoffer, *Public and private high schools: The impact of communities* (New York: Basic Books, 1987).

227. William N. Evans and Robert M. Schwab, "Finishing High School and Starting College: Do Catholic Schools Make a Difference?" *Quarterly Journal of Economics* 110 (1995): 941–974; Rumberger and Larson, "Student Mobility and the Increased Risk"; Rumberger and Thomas, "The Distribution of Dropout and Turnover Rates"; Rumberger and Palardy, "Test Scores, Dropout Rates, and Transfer Rates"; Sander and Krautmann, "Catholic Schools, Dropout Rates and Educational Attainment"; William Sander, "Catholic High Schools and Rural Academic Achievement," *American Journal of Agricultural Economics* 79 (1997): 1–12; Teachman et al., "Social Capital and the Generation of Human Capital."

228. Coleman and Hoffer, *Public and private high*; Coleman, Hoffer, and Kilgore, *High school achievement*; Bryk, Lee, and Holland, *Catholic Schools*.

229. Lee and Burkam, "Dropping Out of High School"; Rumberger and Thomas, "The Distribution of Dropout and Turnover Rates."

230. Eric A. Hanushek, "The Impact of Differential Expenditures on School Performance," *Educational Researcher* 18 (1989): 45–62; Eric A. Hanushek, "Assessing the Effects of School Resources on Student Performance: An Update," *Educational Evaluation and Policy Analysis* 19 (1997): 141–164; Eric A. Hanushek and Dale W. Jorgenson, eds., *Improving America's Schools: The Role of Incentives* (Washington, DC: National Academies Press, 1996); Larry V. Hedges, Richard D. Laine, and Rob Greenwald, "Does Money Matter? A Meta-Analysis of Studies of the Effects of Differential School Inputs on Student Outcomes," *Educational Researcher* 23, no. 3 (1994): 5–14; Robe Greenwald, Larry V. Hedges, and Richard D. Laine, "The Effect of School Resources on Student Achievement," *Review of Educational Research* 66 (1996): 361–396; Eric A. Hanushek, "Money Might Matter Somewhere: A Response to Hedges, Laine, and Greenwald," *Educational Researcher* 23, no. 4 (1994): 5–8.

231. Spyros Konstantopoulos, "Effects of Teachers on Minority and Disadvantaged Students' Achievement in the Early Grades," *Elementary School Journal* 110 (2009): 92–113; Barbara Nye, Spyros Konstantopoulos, and Larry V. Hedges, "How Large Are Teacher Effects?" *Educational Evaluation and Policy Analysis* 26 (2004): 237–257; Gregory J. Palardy and Russell W. Rumberger, "Teacher Effectiveness in First Grade: The Importance of Background Qualifications, Attitudes, and Instructional Practices for Student Learning," *Educational Evaluation and Policy Analysis* 30 (2008): 111–140; Steven G. Rivkin, Eric A. Hanushek, and John F. Kain, "Teachers, Schools, and Academic Achievement," *Econometrica* 73 (2005): 417–458; Andrew J. Wayne and Peter Youngs, "Teacher Characteristics and Student Achievement Gains: A Review," *Review of Educational Research* 73 (2003): 89–122; Corey Koedel, "Teacher Quality and Dropout Outcomes in a Large, Urban School District," *Journal of Urban Economics* 64 (2008): 560–572.

232. See Vincent J. Roscigno and Martha L. Crowley, "Rurality, Institutional Disadvantage, and Achievement/Attainment," *Rural Sociology* 66 (2001): 268–293; Maureen A. Pirog and Christopher Magee, "High School Completion: The Influence of Schools, Families, and Adolescent Parenting," *Social Science Quarterly* 78 (1997): 710–724; Rumberger and Palardy, "Test Scores, Dropout Rates, and Transfer Rates"; Rumberger and Thomas, "The Distribution of Dropout and Turnover Rates"; McNeal, "High School Dropouts"; Li, "Bayesian Proportional Hazard Analysis"; Pirog and Magee, "High School Completion." Roscigno and Crowley found that higher per pupil spending increased graduation rates, particularly for students attending rural schools. Of six analyses (in two studies), Pirog and Magee and Rumberger and Palardy found that higher mean teacher salaries were associated with lower dropout or

higher graduation rates. Rumberger and Thomas and McNeal found that a higher student-teacher ratio was associated with higher dropout rates. Li, McNeal, Pirog and McNeal, Pirog and Magee, and Rumberger and Thomas found no significant relationship between teacher quality, as measured by the percentage of teachers with advanced degrees, and dropout or graduation rates.

233. Koedel, "Teacher Quality and Dropout Outcomes."
234. Li, "Bayesian Proportional Hazard Analysis"; Susanna Loeb and Marianne E. Page, "Examining the Link between Teacher Wages and Student Outcomes: The Importance of Alternative Labor Market Opportunities and Non-Pecuniary Variation," *Review of Economics and Statistics* 82 (2000): 393–408; John Robert Warren, Krista N. Jenkins, and Rachel B. Kulick, "High School Exit Examinations and State-Level Completion and GED Rates 1975–2002," *Educational Evaluation and Policy Analysis* 28 (2006): 131–152.
235. Loeb and Page, "Examining the Link between Teacher Wages."
236. Jacqueline Ancess, *Beating the Odds: High Schools as Communities of Commitment* (New York: Teachers College Press, 2003); Anthony S. Bryk and Barbara Schneider, *Trust in Schools: A Core Resource for Improvement* (New York: Russell Sage, 2002); Richard F. Elmore, *School Reform from the Inside Out* (Cambridge, MA: Harvard Education Press, 2004); Wayne K. Hoy, C. John Tarter, and Anita Woolfolk Hoy, "Academic Optimism of Schools: A Force for Student Achievement," *American Educational Research Journal* 43 (2006): 425–446.
237. Christine Bowditch, "Getting Rid of Troublemakers: High School Disciplinary Procedures and the Production of Dropouts," *Social Problems* 40 (1993): 493–509; Fine, *Framing Dropouts*.
238. Carolyn Riehl, "Labeling and Letting Go: An Organizational Analysis of How High School Students Are Discharged as Dropouts," in *Research in Sociology of Education and Socialization*, ed. A. M. Pallas (New York: JAI Press, 1999), 231.
239. Flores-González, *School Kids/Street Kids*, 58.
240. Kelly, *Last Chance High*, 24.
241. Romo and Falbo, *Latino High School Graduation*, 34.
242. Valenzuela, *Subtractive Schooling*, 5.
243. Fine, *Framing Dropouts*, chapter 3.
244. Ibid., 69.
245. Frank C. Worrell and Robert L. Hale, "The Relationship of Hope in the Future and Perceived School Climate to School Completion," *School Psychology Quarterly* 16 (2001): 370–388.
246. Rumberger and Thomas, "The Distribution of Dropout and Turnover Rates."

247. Bryk and Thum, "The Effects of High School Organization on Dropping Out"; Lee and Burkam, "Dropping Out of High School"; Rumberger and Palardy, "Test Scores, Dropout Rates, and Transfer Rates."

248. Bryk and Thum, "The Effects of High School Organization on Dropping Out"; Pittman, "Social Factors, Enrollment in Vocational/Technical Courses"; Rumberger, "Dropping Out of Middle School"; Rumberger and Palardy, "Does Segregation Still Matter?"

249. Croninger and Lee, "Social Capital and Dropping Out of High School"; Rumberger and Palardy, "Does Segregation Still Matter?"

250. Tama Leventhal and Jeanne Brooks-Gunn, "The Neighborhoods They Live in: The Effects of Neighborhood Residence on Child and Adolescent Outcomes," *Psychological Bulletin* 126 (2000): 309–337.

251. Robert J. Sampson, "Racial Stratification and the Durable Tangle of Neighborhood Inequality," *Annals of the American Academy of Political and Social Science* 621 (2009): 260–280.

252. Sullivan, "*Getting Paid*," 231.

253. Kathryn Edin and Maria Kefalas, *Promises I Can Keep: Why Poor Women Put Motherhood before Marriage* (Berkeley: University of California Press, 2005).

254. Flores-González, *School Kids/Street Kids*, 60.

255. Jeanne Brooks-Gunn, Greg J. Duncan, Pamela Kato Klebanov, and Naomi Sealand, "Do Neighborhoods Influence Child and Adolescent Development?" *American Journal of Sociology* 99 (1993): 353–395; Jonathan Crane, "The Epidemic Theory of Ghettos and Neighborhood Effects on Dropping Out and Teenage Childbearing," *American Journal of Sociology* 96 (1991): 1226–1259; Margaret E. Ensminger, Rebecca P. Lamkin, and Nora Jacobson, "School Leaving: A Longitudinal Perspective Including Neighborhood Effects," *Child Development* 67 (1996): 2400–2416; McNeal, "Are Students Being Pulled Out of High School?"; E. Michael Foster and Sara McLanahan, "An Illustration of the Use of Instrumental Variables: Do Neighborhood Conditions Affect a Young Person's Chance of Finishing High School?" *Psychological Methods* 1 (1996): 249–260.

256. Brooks-Gunn et al., "Do Neighborhoods Influence Child and Adolescent Development?"; Ensminger et al., "School Leaving."

257. Derek A. Neal, "The Effects of Catholic Secondary Schooling on Educational Achievement," *Journal of Labor Economics* 15 (1997): 98–123.

258. Foster and McLanahan, "An Illustration of the Use of Instrumental Variables."

259. Fagan and Pabon, "Contributions of Delinquency and Substance"; Grogger, "Local Violence and Educational Attainment."

260. Rumberger and Lim, *Why Students Drop Out of School*, table 3.

261. Loeb and Page, "Examining the Link between Teacher Wages"; Warren et al., "High School Exit Examinations."

262. Laurence Steinberg, Sanford M. Dornbusch, and B. Bradford Brown, "Ethnic Differences in Adolescent Achievement," *American Psychologist* 47 (1992): 723–729; John U. Ogbu, "The Individual in Collective Adaptation: A Framework for Focusing on Academic Underperformance and Dropping Out among Involuntary Minorities," in *Dropouts from School: Issues, Dilemmas, and Solutions*, ed. L. Weis, E. Farrar and H. G. Petrie (Albany: State University of New York Press, 1989), 181–204.

263. National Research Council, Panel on High-Risk Youth, *Losing Generations: Adolescents in High-Risk Settings* (Washington, DC: National Academies Press, 1993).

264. Pátricia Gandara and Frances Contreras, *The Latino Education Crisis: The Consequences of Failed Social Policies* (Cambridge, MA: Harvard University Press, 2009).

265. Fernandez et al., "Dropping Out among Hispanic Youth"; Rumberger, "Dropping Out of High School"; Velez, "High School Attrition."

266. Susan E. Mayer, "How Much Does a High School's Racial and Socioeconomic Mix Affect Graduation and Teenage Fertility Rates?" in *The Urban Underclass*, eds. C. Jencks and P. Peterson (Washington, DC: Brookings Institution Press, 1991), 321–341.

267. Ogbu, "The Individual in Collective Adaptation"; John U. Ogbu, "Understanding Cultural Diversity and Learning," *Educational Researcher* 21 (1992): 5–14.

268. Ogbu, "Understanding Cultural Diversity and Learning," 9–10.

269. James W. Ainsworth-Darnell and Douglas B. Downey, "Assessing the Oppositional Culture Explanation for Racial/Ethnic Differences in School Performance," *American Sociological Review* 63 (1998): 536–553; Philip J. Cook and Jens Ludwig, "Weighing the Burden of 'Acting White': Are There Race Differences in Attitudes toward School?" *Journal of Policy Analysis and Management* 16 (1997): 256–278; George Farkas, Robert P. Grobe, Daniel Sheehan, and Yuan Shuan, "Cultural Resources and School Success: Gender, Ethnicity, and Poverty Groups within an Urban District," *American Sociological Review* 55 (1990): 127–142; Maria Eugenia Matute-Bianchi, "Ethnic Identities and Patterns of School Success and Failure among Mexican-Descent and Japanese-American Students in a California High School: An Ethnographic Analysis," *American Journal of Education* 95 (1986): 233–255; Gibson, "Complicating the Immigrant/Involuntary Minority Typology."

270. Steinberg, Dornbusch, and Brown, "Ethnic Differences in Adolescent Achievement." Scholars have also found cultural differences in achievement motivation. See Kao and Tienda, "Optimism and Achievement."

271. Will J. Jordan, Julia Lara, and James M. McPartland, "Exploring the causes of early school dropout among race-ethnic and gender groups," *Youth & Society* 28 (1996): 62–94.; Rumberger, "Dropping Out of Middle School"; Ream and Rumberger, "Student Engagement, Peer Social Capital, and School Dropout."

272. Claude M. Steele, "The Threat in the Air: How Stereotypes Shape Intellectual Identify and Performance," *American Psychologist* 52 (1997): 613–629.

273. William Julius Wilson, *More than Just Race: Being Black and Poor in the Inner City* (New York: W. W. Norton & Company, 2009), 133.

274. Valenzuela, *Subtractive Schooling*, 4.

8. *Learning from Past Efforts to Solve the Dropout Crisis*

1. *The 1963 Dropout Campaign* (Washington, DC: U.S. Department of Health, Education, and Welfare, 1964).

2. National Commission on Excellence in Education, *A Nation at Risk* (Washington, DC: U.S. Department of Education, 1983).

3. *National Goals for Education* (Washington, DC: U.S. Department of Education, 1990).

4. Russell W. Rumberger, "Can NCLB Improve High School Graduation Rates?" in *Holding NCLB Accountable: Achieving Accountability, Equity, and School Reform*, ed. G. L. Sunderman (Thousand Oaks, CA: Corwin Press, 2008), 209–222.

5. The largest of these was the School Dropout Demonstration Assistance Program, which funded $294 million in targeted and school reform programs from 1989 to 1996. For an evaluation of the last and largest phase of the program that found that most programs had little impact on reducing dropout rates, see Mark Dynarski and Philip Gleason, *How Can We Help? What We Have Learned from Federal Dropout-Prevention Programs* (Princeton, NJ: Mathematica Policy Research, 1998).

6. *2009 Annual Letter from Bill Gates* (Seattle: Bill & Melinda Gates Foundation, 2009), www.gatesfoundation.org/Annual-Letter/Pages/2009-Bill-Gates-Annual-Letter.Aspx (accessed January 17, 2011), 11.

7. Deirdre M. Kelly, *Last Chance High: How Girls and Boys Drop In and Out of Alternative Schools* (New Haven, CT: Yale University Press, 1993).

8. Chen-Su Chen, *Numbers and Types of Public Elementary and Secondary Schools from the Common Core of Data: School Year 2009-10 - First Look* (Washington, DC: National Center for Education Statistics, U.S. Department of Education, 2011), nces.ed.gov/pubsearch/pubsinfo.asp?pubid=2011345 (Accessed May 14, 2011), table 1.

9. Susan Rotermund, *Alternative Education Enrollment and Dropouts in California High Schools*, Statistical Brief 6 (Santa Barbara: California Dropout

Research Project, University of California, 2007), http://cdrp.ucsb.edu/
Dropouts/Pubs_Statbriefs.Htm#6 (accessed January 17, 2011).

10. Dynarski and Gleason, *How Can We Help?*

11. For example, a recent study found that having friends who drop out or who do not value education can increase the risk of dropping out. See Robert K. Ream and Russell W. Rumberger, "Student Engagement, Peer Social Capital, and School Dropout among Mexican American and Non-Latino White Students," *Sociology of Education* 81 (2008): 109–139.

12. *Comprehensive School Reform (CSR) Program Guidance* (Washington, DC: U.S. Department of Education, 2002), www.ed.gov/Programs/Compreform/ Legislation.html (accessed January 17, 2011).

13. Ibid.

14. Geoffrey D. Borman et al., "Comprehensive School Reform and Achievement: A Meta-Analysis," *Review of Educational Research* 73 (2003): 125–230.

15. Julian R. Betts and Paul T. Hill, eds., *Taking Measure of Charter Schools: Better Assessments, Better Policymaking, Better Schools* (Lanham, MD: Rowman & Littlefield, 2010); Martin Carnoy et al., *The Charter School Dust-Up: Examining the Evidence on Enrollment and Achievement* (Washington, DC, and New York: Economic Policy Institute and Teachers College Press, 2005); Chester E. Finn Jr., Bruno V. Manno, and Gregg Vanourek, *Charter Schools in Action: Renewing Public Education* (Princeton, NJ: Princeton University Press, 2000); Jeffrey R. Henig, *Spin Cycle: How Research Is Used in Policy Debate: The Case of Charter Schools* (New York: Russell Sage Foundation, 2008); Ron Zimmer et al., *Charter Schools in Eight States: Effects on Achievement, Attainment, Integration, and Competition* (Santa Monica, CA: Rand Corporation, 2009).

16. Susan Aud et al., *The Condition of Education 2010* (NCES 2010-028) (Washington, DC: National Center for Education Statistics, U.S. Department of Education, 2010), http://nces.ed.gov/pubsearch/pubsinfo.asp?pubid= 2010028 (accessed January 17, 2011), table A-32-1. Chen, *Numbers and Types of Public Elementary and Secondary Schools from the Common Core of Data*, tables 2 and 3.

17. According to data from the National Alliance of Public Charter Schools, 22 percent of charter schools in 2009–10 were high schools, 9 percent were middle/high schools, and 11 percent were elementary/middle/high schools, www.publiccharters.org/dashboard/schools/page/conf/year/2010 (accessed August 19, 2010).

18. "Public Charter School Dashboard," www.publiccharters.org/dashboard/ schools/page/conv/year/2010 (accessed August 19, 2010).

19. These partnerships can be initiated by individual schools or by district offices. For a case study of the latter, see Mavis Sanders, "Collaborating for Change: How an Urban School District and a Community-Based Organization

Support and Sustain School, Family, and Community Partnerships," *Teachers College Record* 111 (2009): 1693–1712.

20. National Research Council, Panel on High-Risk Youth, *Losing Generations: Adolescents in High-Risk Settings* (Washington, DC: National Academies Press, 1993), 193.

21. The average size of high schools in the United States was 876 students in 2006–07, compared to an average size of 593 students for middle schools and 446 for elementary schools. See Hoffman, *Numbers and Types of Public Elementary and Secondary Schools*, table 5.

22. Tom Corcoran and Megan Silander, "Instruction in High Schools: The Evidence and the Challenge," *Future of Children* 19 (2009): 157–183.

23. Thomas D. Snyder and Sally A. Dillow, *Digest of Education Statistics, 2010* (NCES 2011-015) (Washington, DC: National Center for Education Statistics, U.S. Department of Education, 2011), http://nces.ed.gov/Pubsearch/Pubsinfo.Asp?Pubid=2011015 (accessed May 14, 2011), table 75.

24. In 2008, more than 21 percent of children ages five through seventeen spoke a language other than English at home, more than twice the percentage of 1979. See Aud, *The Condition of Education 2010, Figure 5-1*.

25. Tom Loveless, *The 2009 Brown Center Report on American Education: How Well Are American Students Learning?* (Washington, DC: Brown Center on Education Policy, Brookings Institution, 2009), www.brookings.edu/Reports/2010/0317_Education_Loveless.Aspx (accessed August 19, 2010), 28. Loveless found little change in achievement for two groups of schools in California that converted from traditional public schools to charter schools. Scott A. Imberman, *Achievement and Behavior in Charter Schools: Drawing a More Complete Picture* (occasional paper 142, National Center for the Study of Privatization in Education, Teachers College, Columbia University, New York, 2007). Imberman found that startup charter schools in an anonymous large urban school district improved student behavior and attendance, but conversion charters did not.

26. Marshall S. Smith and Jennifer O'Day, "Systemic School Reform," in *The Politics of Curriculum and Testing*, ed. S. H. Fuhrman and B. Malen (Philadelphia: Falmer Press, 1991), 233–267.

27. John M. Bridgeland, John J. DiIulio Jr., and Ryan Streeter, *Raising the Compulsory School Attendance Age: The Case for Reform* (Washington, DC: Civic Enterprises, 2008).

28. Melinda Mechur Karp and Katherine L. Hughes, "Supporting College Transitions through Collaborative Programming: A Conceptual Model for Guiding Policy," *Teachers College Record* 110 (2008): 838–866; Carl Krueger, *Dual Enrollment: Policy Issues Confronting State Policymakers*, policy brief (Denver: Education Commission of the States, 2006); Brian P. Gill et al.,

Rhetoric versus Reality: What We Know and What We Need to Know about Vouchers and Charter Schools (Santa Monica, CA: Rand Corporation, 2001); Clive Belfield and Harry M. Levin, "Vouchers and Public Policy: When Ideology Trumps Evidence," *American Journal of Education* 111 (2005): 548–567; John Robert Warren, *Graduation Rates for Choice and Public School Students in Milwaukee, 2003–2008* (Milwaukee: School Choice Wisconsin, 2010), www.schoolchoicewi.org/Library/Research.Cfm (accessed August 21, 2010).

29. Richard J. Shavelson and Lisa Towne, eds., *Scientific Research in Education*, National Research Council Committee on Scientific Principles for Education Research (Washington, DC: National Academies Press, 2002).

30. Robert E. Slavin, "What Works? Issues in Synthesizing Educational Program Evaluations," *Educational Researcher* 37 (2008): 5–14.

31. Ibid., 5.

32. Barbara Schneider et al., *Estimating Causal Effects Using Experimental and Observations Designs*, report from the Governing Board of the American Educational Research Association Grants Program (Washington, DC: American Educational Research Association, 2007).

33. Shavelson and Towne, eds., *Scientific Research in Education*.

34. Jeremy D. Finn and Charles M. Achilles, "Tennessee's Class Size Study: Findings, Implications, Misconceptions," *Educational Evaluation and Policy Analysis* 21 (1999): 97–110.

35. Thomas D. Cook, "Randomized Experiments in Educational Policy Research: A Critical Examination of the Reasons the Educational Evaluation Community Has Offered for Not Doing Them," *Educational Evaluation and Policy Analysis* 24 (2002): 175–199.

36. S. W. Raudenbush, A. Martinez, and J. Spybrook, "Strategies for Improving Precision in Group-Randomized Experiments," *Educational Evaluation and Policy Analysis* 29 (2007): 5–29.

37. Schneider et al., *Estimating Causal Effects*.

38. Zimmer et al., *Charter Schools in Eight States*, 21–26.

39. See, for example, the articles in the January/February 2008 issue of *Educational Researcher*.

40. For an earlier review that identified only six dropout prevention programs that meet their standards of evidence, see Robert E. Slavin and Olatokunbo S. Fashola, *Show Me the Evidence!: Proven and Promising Programs for America's Schools* (New York: Corwin, 1998). See also Cathy Hammond et al., *Dropout Risk Factors and Exemplary Programs: A Technical Report* (Clemson, SC: National Dropout Prevention Center/Network, Clemson University and Communities in Schools, 2007). A more recent review identified twenty-five significant risk factors for school dropout and fifty "exemplary" programs that

addressed one or more of those risk factors. Thus, not all these programs demonstrated that they directly improved dropout and graduation rates.

41. This center operated from 2003 to 2006. See "Comprehensive School Reform Quality Center," www.csrq.org (accessed February 22, 2011).

42. Comprehensive School Reform Quality Center, *CSRQ Center Report on Middle and High School Comprehensive School Reform Models* (Washington, DC: American Institutes for Research, 2006).

43. WWC *Topic Report: Dropout Prevention* (Washington, DC: What Works Clearinghouse, U.S. Department of Education, 2008), http://ies.ed.gov/ncee/wwc/reports/dropout/topic (accessed January 17, 2011).

44. Sarah Hooker and Betsy Brand, *Success at Every Step: How 23 Programs Support Youth on the Path to College and Beyond* (Washington, DC: American Youth Policy Forum, 2009), www.aypf.org/publications/index.htm (accessed January 17, 2011).

45. See "Washington State Institute for Public Policy," www.wsipp.wa.gov (accessed February 22, 2011).

46. Tali Klima, Marna Miller, Corey Nunlist, *What Works? Targeted Truancy and Dropout Programs in Middle and High School* (Olympia: Washington State Institute for Public Policy, 2009), www.Wsipp.Wa.Gov/Topic.Asp?Cat=11&Subcat=0&Dteslct=0 (accessed January 17, 2011).

47. Larry V. Hedges, "What Are Effect Sizes and Why Do We Need Them?" *Child Development Perspectives* 2 (2008): 167–171.

48. Jacob Cohen, *Statistical Power Analysis for the Behavioral Sciences*, 2nd ed. (Hillsdale, NJ: Erlbaum, 1988), 25–26. See also Carolyn J. Hill et al., "Empirical Benchmarks for Interpreting Effect Sizes in Research," *Child Development Perspectives* 2 (2008): 172–177. Instead of a universal benchmark, Hill et al. argue that different benchmarks be used depending on the nature of the intervention, its target population, and the outcome measure(s) being used.

49. Klima et al., *What Works*, appendix C.

50. U.S. Department of Education, Institute of Education Sciences, What Works Clearinghouse, *WWC Topic Report: Dropout Prevention 2008*, http://ies.ed.gov/Ncee/Wwc/Reports/Topic.Aspx?Tid=06 (accessed January 17, 2011), figure 1.

51. Ibid., figures 1 and 3.

52. National Research Council, Committee on Increasing High School Students' Engagement and Motivation to Learn, *Engaging Schools: Fostering High School Students' Motivation to Learn* (Washington, DC: National Academies Press, 2004), 94–95.

53. Eric M. Camburn, "Embedded Teacher Learning Opportunities as a Site for Reflective Practice: An Exploratory Study," *American Journal of Education* 116 (2010): 463–489; Judith Warren Little, "Inside Teacher Community: Representations of Classroom Practice," *Teachers College Record* 105 (2003): 913–945;

K. S. Louis and H. M. Marks, "Does Professional Community Affect the Classroom? Teachers' Work and Student Experiences in Restructuring Schools," *American Journal of Education* 106 (1998): 532–575; Milbrey W. McLaughlin and Joan E. Talbert, *Professional Communities and the Work of High School Teaching* (Chicago: University of Chicago Press, 2001); Etienne Wenger, *Communities of Practice: Learning, Meaning, and Identity* (New York: Cambridge University Press, 1998); Ronald Gallimore et al., "Moving the Learning of Teaching Closer to Practice: Teacher Education Implications of School-Based Inquiry Teams," *Elementary School Journal* 109 (2009): 537–553.

54. James P. Connell et al., *Going Small and Getting Smarter: Small Learning Communities as Platforms for Effective Professional Development* (Washington, DC: U.S. Department of Education, 2006), www.csos.jhu.edu/pubs/edweek/ SLC%20IssPap%20Book.pdf (accessed January 17, 2011); Elena Silva, *Teachers at Work: Improving Teacher Quality through School Redesign* (Washington, DC: Education Sector, 2009).

55. John Dewey, *The School and Society* (Chicago: University of Chicago Press, 1899).

56. Jeannie Oakes and Marisa Saunders, eds., *Beyond Tracking: Multiple Pathways to College, Career, and Civic Participation* (Cambridge, MA: Harvard Education Press, 2008).

57. Jeffrey L. Pressman and Aaron Wildavsky, *Implementation: How Great Expectations in Washington Are Dashed in Oakland; Or, Why It's Amazing that Federal Programs Work at All, This Being a Saga of the Economic Development Administration as Told by Two Sympathetic Observers Who Seek to Build Morals on a Foundation of Ruined Hopes* (Berkeley: University of California Press, 1973).

58. For a review of these studies, see Laura Desimone, "How Can Comprehensive School Reform Models Be Successfully Implemented?" *Review of Educational Research* 72 (2002): 433–479.

59. See What Works Clearinghouse "Practice Guides," http://ies.ed.gov/ncee/wwc/ publications/practiceguides (accessed February 23, 2011).

60. Mark Dynarski et al., *Dropout Prevention: A Practice Guide* (NCEE 2008-4025) (Washington, DC: National Center for Education Evaluation and Regional Assistance, U.S. Department of Education, 2008), http://Ies.Ed.Gov/ Ncee/Wwc (accessed January 17, 2011), 6; Members of the expert panel were Mark Dynarski (Mathematica Policy Research), Brian Cobb (Colorado State University), Linda Clarke (City of Houston), Jeremy Finn (State University of New York, Buffalo), Russell Rumberger (University of California, Santa Barbara), and Jay Smink (National Dropout Prevention Center, Clemson University).

61. National Research Council, Committee on Increasing High School Students' Engagement and Motivation to Learn, *Engaging Schools*, 103.

62. Similar strategies were identified in a 2007 conference of leaders from twenty-two midsize urban districts. See Janet Quint, Saskia Levy Thompson, and Margaret Bald, *Relationships, Rigor, and Readiness* (New York: MDRC, 2008), www.mdrc.org/publications/498/preface.html (accessed January 17, 2011).

63. W. Steven Barnett and Clive R. Belfield, "Early Childhood Development and Social Mobility," *Future of Children* 16 (2006): 73–98; Kevin M. Gorey, "Early Childhood Education: A Meta-Analytic Affirmation of the Short- and Long-Term Benefits of Educational Opportunity," *School Psychology Quarterly* 16 (2001): 9–30; Gregory Camilli et al., "Meta-Analysis of the Effects of Early Education Interventions on Cognitive and Social Development," *Teachers College Record* 112 (2010): 579–620.

64. Barnett and Belfield, "Early Childhood Development and Social Mobility," 84.

65. Gorey, "Early Childhood Education," table 3.

66. Arthur J. Reynolds, Suh-Ruu Ou, and James W. Topitzes, "Paths of Effects of Early Childhood Intervention on Educational Attainment and Delinquency: A Confirmatory Analysis of the Chicago Child-Parent Centers," *Child Development* 75 (2004): 1299–1328, table 3.

67. Suh-Ruu Ou, "Pathways of Long-Term Effects of an Early Intervention Program on Educational Attainment: Findings from the Chicago Longitudinal Study," *Journal of Applied Developmental Psychology* 26 (2005): 578–611; Reynolds et al. "Paths of Effects of Early Childhood Intervention."

68. Phyllis Levenstein et al., "At-Risk Toddlers: An Exploratory Study of High School Outcomes in the Replication of the Mother-Child Home Program," *Journal of Applied Developmental Psychology* 19 (1998): 267–285.

69. Jeremy D. Finn et al., "The Enduring Effects of Small Classes," *Teachers College Record* 103 (2001): 146.

70. Jeremy D. Finn, Susan B. Gerber, and Jayne Boyd-Zaharias, "Small Classes in the Early Grades, Academic Achievement, and Graduating from High School," *Journal of Educational Psychology* 97 (2005): 214–223.

71. Other systemic reforms have been shown to impact high school dropout and graduation rates. A recent study found that welfare reform instituted in the 1990s, which promoted work rather than education, significantly increased the probability of young women's staying in high school by about 16 percent. See Dhaval M. Dave, Nancy E. Reichman, and Hope Corman, "Effects of Welfare Reform on Educational Acquisition of Young Adult Women" (working paper 14466, National Bureau of Economic Research, Cambridge, MA, 2008), http://papers.nber.org/papers/w14466 (accessed January 17, 2011), 37.

72. Bridgeland et al., *Raising the Compulsory School Attendance Age*.
73. Dean R. Lillard and Philip P. DeCicca, "Higher Standards, More Dropouts? Evidence within and across Time," *Economics of Education Review* 20 (2001): 459–473; Mingliang Li, "Bayesian Proportional Hazard Analysis of the Timing of High School Dropout Decisions," *Econometric Reviews* 26 (2007): 529–556; John Robert Warren, Krista N. Jenkins, and Rachel B. Kulick, "High School Exit Examinations and State-Level Completion and GED Rates 1975–2002," *Educational Evaluation and Policy Analysis* 28 (2006): 131–152.
74. Snyder and Dillow, *Digest of Education Statistics 2010*, table 176.
75. Lillard and DeCicca, "Higher Standards, More Dropouts?"; Warren et al., "High School Exit Examinations."
76. Elaine Allensworth, Takako Nomi, Nicholas Montgomery, and Valerie E. Lee, "College Preparatory Curriculum for All: Academic Consequences of Requiring Algebra and English I for Ninth Graders in Chicago," *Educational Evaluation and Policy Analysis* 31 (2009): 367–391; Nicholas Montgomery, Elaine Allensworth, and Macarena Correa, *Passing through Science: The Effects of Raising Graduation Requirements in Science on Course-Taking and Academic Achievement in Chicago* (Chicago: Consortium on Chicago School Research, University of Chicago, 2010), http://ccsr.uchicago.edu/content/ publications.php?pub_id=138 (accessed January 17, 2011); Christopher Mazzeo, *College Prep for All? What We've Learned from Chicago's Efforts* (Chicago: Consortium on Chicago School Research, University of Chicago, 2010), http://ccsr.uchicago.edu/content/publications.php?pub_id=149 (accessed August 26, 2010).
77. Lillard and DeCicca, "Higher Standards, More Dropouts?"; Warren et al., "High School Exit Examinations."
78. Chandra Muller, "The Minimum Competency Exam Requirement, Teachers' and Students' Expectations and Academic Performance," *Social Psychology of Education* 2 (1998): 199–216; John Robert Warren and Jennifer C. Lee, "The Impact of Adolescent Employment on High School Dropout: Differences by Individual and Labor-Market Characteristics," *Social Science Research* 32 (2003): 98–128; John Robert Warren and Melanie R. Edwards, "High School Exit Examinations and High School Completion: Evidence from the Early 1990s," *Educational Evaluation and Policy Analysis* 27 (2005): 53–74.
79. Bryan W. Griffin and Mark H. Heidorn, "An Examination of the Relationship between Minimum Competency Test Performance and Dropping Out of High School," *Educational Evaluation and Policy Analysis* 18 (1996): 243–252; Brian A. Jacob, "Getting Tough? The Impact of High School Graduation Exams," *Educational Evaluation and Policy Analysis* 23 (2001): 99–121.

80. Sean F. Reardon et al., *Effects of California High School Exit Exam on Student Persistence, Achievement, and Graduation* (Stanford, CA: Institute for Research on Education Policy and Practice, Stanford University, 2009), www.stanford.edu/group/irepp/cgi-bin/joomla/index.php (accessed January 17, 2011); Sean F. Reardon et al., "Effects of Failing a High School Exit Exam on Course Taking, Achievement, Persistence, and Graduation," *Educational Evaluation and Policy Analysis* 32 (2010): 498–520; Warren et al., "High School Exit Examinations."

81. Belfield and Levin, "Vouchers and Public Policy"; Clive Belfield and Harry M. Levin, "The Effects of Competition between Schools on Educational Outcomes: A Review for the United States," *Review of Educational Research* 72 (2002): 279–341; Henig, *Spin Cycle*; Christopher Lubienski, Peter Weitzel, and Sarah Theule Lubienski, "Is There a 'Consensus' on School Choice and Achievement? Advocacy Research and the Emerging Political Economy of Knowledge Production," *Educational Policy* 23 (2009): 161–193; Patrick J. McEwan, "The Potential Impact of Large-Scale Voucher Programs," *Review of Educational Research* 70 (2000): 103–149.

82. See Middle College National Consortium website, http://mcnc.us (accessed February 23, 2011).

83. One exception is a recent study that found that startup (but not conversion) charter schools in an anonymous urban school district were effective in improving student behavior and attendance but had no statistical impact on test scores. See Imberman, *Achievement and Behavior in Charter Schools*, 26.

84. Julian R. Betts and Y. Emily Tang, *Value-Added and Experimental Studies of the Effect of Charter Schools on Student Achievement* (Seattle: University of Washington, Bothell, Center on Reinventing Public Education, National Charter School Research Project, 2008), www.crpe.org/cs/crpe/view/csr_pubs/253 (accessed August 19, 2010), 3.

85. Ibid., 10.

86. Ibid., tables 3 and 4.

87. Ibid., 26.

88. Zimmer, *Charter Schools in Eight States*, xii–xv.

89. *Multiple Choice: Charter School Performance in 16 States* (Stanford, CA: Center for Research on Education Outcomes, Stanford University, 2009), http://credo.stanford.edu (accessed August 20, 2010), 3–6.

90. Philip Gleason et al., *The Evaluation of Charter School Impacts: Final Report* (NCEE 2010-4029) (Washington, DC: National Center for Education Evaluation and Regional Assistance, Institute of Education Sciences, U.S. Department of Education, 2010), http://ies.ed.gov/Ncee/Pubs/20104029/Index.Asp (accessed August 20, 2010), xvii.

91. See KIPP website, www.kipp.org (accessed February 23, 2011).

92. Joshua D. Angrist et al., "Who Benefits from KIPP?" (working paper 15740, National Bureau of Economic Research, Cambridge, MA, 2010), www.nber.org/ papers/w15740 (accessed January 17, 2011); Katrina R. Woodworth et al., *San Francisco Bay Area KIPP Schools: A Study of Early Implementation and Achievement, Final Report* (Menlo Park, CA: SRI International, 2008), http:// policyweb.sri.com/cep/publications/SRI_ReportBayAreaKIPPSchools_Final.pdf (accessed January 17, 2011); Christina Clark Tuttle et al., *Student Characteristics and Achievement in 22 KIPP Middle Schools* (Washington, DC: Mathematica Policy Research, 2010), www.Mathematica-Mpr.Com/Newsroom/Releases/ 2010/KIPP_6_10.Asp (accessed January 17, 2011), xi.

93. Tuttle et al., *Student Characteristics and Achievement*, xv.

94. The largest effects were found for Harlem Children's Zone's Promise (middle school) Academy and the Boston charter middle schools. See Will Dobbie and Roland G. Fryer Jr., "Are High Quality Schools Enough to Close the Achievement Gap? Evidence from a Social Experiment in Harlem" (working paper 15473, National Bureau of Economic Research, Cambridge, MA, 2009), www .nber.org/papers/w15473 (accessed August 21, 2010); Atila Abdulkadiroglu et al., "Accountability and Flexibility in Public Schools: Evidence from Boston's Charters and Pilots" (working paper 15549, National Bureau of Economic Research, Cambridge, MA, 2009), www.nber.org/papers/w15549 (accessed August 21, 2010).

95. Kevin Booker et al., *Achievement and Attainment in Chicago Charter Schools* (Santa Monica, CA: Rand Corporation, 2009), www.rand.org/pubs/technical _reports/TR585-1/ (accessed August 21, 2010), x.

96. Douglas Lee Lauren, "To Choose or Not to Choose: High School Choice and Graduation in Chicago," *Educational Evaluation and Policy Analysis* 31 (2009): 195.

97. Ibid., 196.

98. Caroline M. Hoxby, Sonali Murarka, and Jenny Kang, *How New York City's Charter Schools Affect Achievement* (Cambridge, MA: New York City Charter Schools Evaluation Project, 2009), www.nber.org/~schools/charterschoolseval (accessed August 21, 2010), tables IVf and IVh. But the effect on graduating was significant at the 0.15 level, which is far from the standard in social science research of 0.05. See Sean F. Reardon, *Review of "How New York City's Charter Schools Affect Achievement"* (Boulder, CO, and Tempe, AZ: Education and the Public Interest Center and Education Policy Research Unit, 2009), http:// epicpolicy.org/Thinktank/Review-How-New-York-City-Charter (accessed August 21, 2010), 12.

99. Lisa Barrow and Cecilia E. Rouse, "School Vouchers: Recent Findings and Unanswered Questions," *Federal Reserve Bank of Chicago Economic Perspectives* 32 (2008): 12.

100. Warren, *Graduation Rates for Choice and Public School,* table 1.
101. Ibid., 7.
102. Henry M. Levin, "Cost-Effectiveness and Educational Policy," *Educational Evaluation and Policy Analysis* 10 (1988): 51–69; Henry M. Levin and Patrick J. McEwan, *Cost-Effectiveness Analysis,* 2nd ed. (Thousand Oaks, CA: Sage, 2000).
103. Henry M. Levin and Clive R. Belfield, "Educational Interventions to Raise High School Graduation Rates," in *The Price We Pay: Economic and Social Consequences of Inadequate Education,* eds. C. R. Belfield and H. M. Levin (Washington, DC: Brookings Institution Press, 2007), 177–199.
104. A 2011 study based on data collected up to age 26, from participants of the Chicago Child Parent Centers, found that the preschool program provided a total social benefit (including increased earnings of more than ten dollars for each dollar invested, while the school-age program generated a benefit of four dollars per dollar invested). See Arthur J. Reynolds, Judy A. Temple, Barry A. B. White, Suh-Ruu Ou, and Dylan L. Robertson, "Age 26 Cost-Benefit Analysis of the Child-Parent Center Early Education Program," *Child Development* 82 (2011): 379–404.
105. Much of material for this section first appeared in Russell W. Rumberger, *What the Federal Government Can Do to Improve High School Performance* (Washington, DC: Center on Education Policy, 2009), www.cep-dc.org/Index .Cfm?Fuseaction=Page.Viewpage&Pageid=536&Parentid=481 (accessed January 17, 2011).
106. Dynarski and Gleason, *How Can We Help?*; Mark Dynarski, "Interpreting the Evidence from Recent Federal Evaluations of Dropout-Prevention Programs: The State of Scientific Evidence," in *Dropouts in America: Confronting the Graduation Rate Crisis,* ed. Gary Orfield (Cambridge, MA: Harvard Education Press, 2004), 255–267.
107. Dynarski and Gleason, *How Can We Help?* 4.
108. Ibid., 14.
109. *Evaluation of the Comprehensive School Reform Program Implementation and Outcomes: Third-Year Report* (Washington, DC: Office of Planning, Evaluation, and Policy Development, Policy and Program Studies Service, U.S. Department of Education, 2008), www.ed.gov/about/offices/list/opepd/ppss/ reports.html (accessed January 17, 2011), xiii.
110. Daniel K. Aladjem et al., *Models Matter—The Final Report of the National Longitudinal Evaluation of Comprehensive School Reform* (Washington, DC: American Institutes for Research, 2006); Milbrey W. McLaughlin, "The Rand Change Agent Study Revisited: Macro Perspectives and Micro Realities," *Educational Researcher* 19 (1990): 11–16.
111. Aladjem et al., *Models Matter,* 51

112. See, for example, the Colorado Children's Campaign, www.coloradokids.org; the Ohio High School Transformation Initiative, www.kwfdn.org; and the Texas High School Project, www.thsp.org (accessed February 23, 2011).

113. Jenifer Harr et al., *Evaluation Study of California's High Priority Schools Grant Program: Final Report* (Palo Alto, CA: American Institutes for Research, 2007).

114. Ibid., 3.

115. Ibid., 4.

116. Mark Berends, Susan J. Bodilly, Sheila Nataraj Kirby, *Facing the Challenges of Whole-School Reform: New American Schools after a Decade* (Santa Monica, CA: Rand Corporation, 2002), xv.

117. Ibid.

118. Ibid., 147.

119. Ibid., xxxii; Desimone, "How Can Comprehensive School Reform Models Be Successfully Implemented?"; McLaughlin, "The Rand Change Agent Study Revisited."

120. Berends et al., *Facing the Challenges of Whole-School Reform*, xxxvi.

121. Ibid., 149.

122. William H. Gates, "Speech: 2005 Education Summit on High Schools," *International Journal of Instructional Technology and Distance Learning* 2 (2005), www.itdl.org/Journal/May_05/Article01.Htm (accessed January 17, 2011).

123. *2009 Annual Letter from Bill Gates*, 11.

124. Aimee Evan et al., *Evaluation of the Bill and Melinda Gates Foundation's High School Grants Initiative: 2001–2005 Final Report* (Washington, DC, and Menlo Park, CA: American Institutes for Research and SRI International, 2006), www.gatesfoundation.org/learning/Documents/Year4EvaluationAIRSRI .pdf (accessed January 17, 2011).

125. Ibid., 3.

126. Ibid., 27–28.

127. Ibid., 26.

128. Ibid., 38.

129. Ibid., 61.

130. Ibid., 67.

131. Ibid., 77.

132. Ibid., 78–79.

133. *2009 Annual Letter from Bill Gates*, 11–12.

134. Julie A. White and Gary Wehlage, "Community Collaboration: If It Is Such a Good Idea, Why Is It So Hard to Do?" *Educational Evaluation and Policy Analysis* 17 (1995): 24.

135. Gary Wehlage, Gregory Smith, and Pauline Lipman, "Restructuring Urban Schools: The New Futures Experience," *American Educational Research Journal* 29 (1992): 51–93; White and Wehlage, "Community Collaboration."

136. Wehlage et al., "Restructuring Urban Schools," 73.

137. Eileen Foley, *Approaches of Foundation–Funded Intermediary Organizations to Structuring and Supporting Small High Schools in New York City* (Washington, DC: Policy Studies Associates, 2010), www.policystudies.com/studies/?id=1 (accessed January 17, 2011), 1.

138. Ibid., 13.

139. Eileen M. Foley, Allan Klinge, and Elizabeth R. Reisner, *Evaluation of New Century High Schools: Profile of an Initiative to Create and Sustain Small, Successful High Schools* (New York: Policy Studies Associates, 2008), www.policystudies.com/studies/?id=3 (accessed January 17, 2011).

140. See U.S. Department of Education, What Works Clearinghouse, *WWC Topic Report.*

141. Academy for Educational Development, Center for School and Community Services, *Small High Schools at Work: A Case Study of Six Gates-Funded Schools in New York City* (Washington, DC: Academy for Educational Development, 2010); Foley, *Approaches to Bill & Melinda Gates Foundation–Funded Intermediary Organizations.*

142. Howard S. Bloom, Saskia Thompson, and Rebecca Unterman, *Transforming the High School Experience: How New York City's New Small Schools Are Boosting Student Achievement and Graduation Rates* (New York: MDRC, 2010), www.mdrc.org/project_29_96.html (accessed August 23, 2010), iii.

143. Richard F. Elmore and Milbrey W. McLaughlin, *Steady Work: Policy, Practice, and the Reform of American Education* (Santa Monica, CA: RAND Corporation, 1988); Milbrey W. McLaughlin, "Learning from Experience: Lessons from Policy Implementation," *Educational Evaluation and Policy Analysis* 9 (1987): 171–178.

144. Elmore and McLaughlin, *Steady Work*, 3.

145. Aladjem et al., *Models Matter.*

146. Elmore and McLaughlin, *Steady Work*, 34–35.

147. McLaughlin, "Learning from Experience"; McLaughlin, "The Rand Change Agent Study Revisited."

148. Elmore and McLaughlin, *Steady Work*, 42–44.

149. Ibid., 45–47.

150. Karen Seashore Louis, Karen Febey, and Roger Schroeder, "State-Mandated Accountability in High Schools: Teachers' Interpretations of a New Era," *Educational Evaluation and Policy Analysis* 27 (2005): 177–204; James P. Spillane, Brian J. Reiser, and Todd Reimer, "Policy Implementation and

Cognition: Reframing and Refocusing Implementation Research,." *Review of Educational Research* 72 (2002): 387–431.

151. Elmore and McLaughlin, *Steady Work*, 45–47.

152. Richard F. Elmore, *School Reform from the Inside Out* (Cambridge, MA: Harvard Education Press, 2004), 38.

153. National Research Council, Committee on Increasing High School Students' Engagement and Motivation to Learn, *Engaging Schools*; Stewart C. Purkey and Marshall S. Smith, "Effective Schools: A Review," *Elementary School Journal* 83 (1983): 426–452; Seymour Bernard Sarason, *Revisiting the Culture of the School and the Problem of Change* (New York: Teachers College Press, 1996).

154. Betty Malen and Jennifer King Rice, "A Framework for Assessing the Impact of Education Reforms on School Capacity: Insights from Studies of High-Stakes Accountability Initiatives," *Educational Policy* 18 (2004): 631–660; Fred M. Newmann, M. Bruce King, and Mark Rigdon, "Accountability and School Performance: Implications from Restructuring Schools," *Harvard Educational Review* 67 (1997): 41–74; Fred M. Newmann, M. Bruce King, and Peter Youngs, "Professional Development that Addresses School Capacity: Lessons from Urban Elementary Schools," *American Journal of Education* 108 (2000): 259–299; Melissa Roderick, John Q. Easton, and Penny Bender Sebring, *The Consortium on Chicago School Research: A New Model for the Role of Research in Supporting Urban School Reform* (Chicago: University of Chicago Urban Education Institute, Consortium on Chicago School Research, 2009), http://ccsr.uchicago.edu/Content/Publications.Php?Pub_Id=131 (accessed January 17, 2011).

155. Anthony S. Bryk and Barbara Schneider, *Trust in Schools: A Core Resource for Improvement* (New York: Russell Sage, 2002), 144.

156. Valerie E. Lee and Julia B. Smith, *Restructuring High Schools for Equity and Excellence* (New York: Teachers College Press, 2001); Little, "Inside Teacher Community"; McLaughlin and Talbert, *Professional Communities*; Karen Seashore Louis, Helen M. Marks, and Sharon D. Kruse, "Teachers' Professional Community in Restructuring Schools," *American Educational Research Journal* 33 (1996): 757–798; Louis and Marks, "Does Professional Community Affect the Classroom?"

157. Elmore, *School Reform from the Inside Out*, chapter 4; Newmann et al., "Accountability and School Performance."

158. Malen and Rice, "A Framework for Assessing the Impact," 635.

159. As economist Eric Hanushek states, "The fundamental problem is not a lack of resources but poor application of available resources." See Eric A. Hanushek and Dale W. Jorgenson, eds., *Improving America's Schools: The Role of Incentives* (Washington, DC: National Academies Press, 1996), 30.

160. W. Norton Grubb, *The Money Myth: School Resources, Outcomes, and Equity* (New York: Russell Sage, 2009); Newmann et al., "Professional Development that Addresses School Capacity."

161. Fred M. Newmann et al., "Instructional Program Coherence: What It Is and Why It Should Guide School Improvement Policy," *Educational Evaluation and Policy Analysis* 23 (2001): 297–321.

162. Malen and Rice, "A Framework for Assessing the Impact." Malen and Rice refer to these organizational responses as "organizational freneticism and fragmentation."

163. Joan L. Herman and Eva L. Baker, *The Los Angeles Annenberg Metropolitan Project: Evaluation Findings* (Los Angeles: National Center for Research on Evaluation, Standards, and Student Testing, 2003), www.cse.ucla.edu/Products/Summary.Asp?Report=591 (accessed January 17, 2011).

164. Roderick et al., *The Consortium on Chicago School Research*, 17.

165. Newmann et al., "Accountability and School Performance."

166. Aladjem et al., *Models Matter*; Amands Datnow, "Power and Politics in the Adoption of School Reform Models," *Educational Evaluation and Policy Analysis* 22 (2000): 357–374.

167. Bryk and Schneider, *Trust in Schools*, 142.

168. McLaughlin, "The Rand Change Agent Study Revisited," 13.

169. Thomas R. Guskey, "Attitude and Perceptual Change in Teachers," *International Journal of Educational Research* 13 (1989): 439–453.

170. James P. Connell et al., *Getting Ready, Willing and Able: Critical Steps toward Successful Implementation of Small Learning Communities in Large High Schools* (Washington, DC: U.S. Department of Education, 2006), www.irre.org/publications/getting-ready-willing-and-able-critical-steps (accessed January 17, 2011), 6.

171. Fred M. Newmann, "Beyond Common Sense in Educational Restructuring," *Educational Researcher* 22 (1993): 4–13, 22; Jacqueline Ancess, "The Reciprocal Influence of Teacher Learning, Teaching Practice, School Restructuring, and Student Learning Outcomes," *Teachers College Record* 102 (2000): 590–619.

172. Desimone, "How Can Comprehensive School Reform Models Be Successfully Implemented?"; Thomas K. Glennan Jr. et al., *Expanding the Reach of Education Reforms: Perspectives from Leaders in the Scale-Up of Educational Interventions* (Santa Monica, CA: Rand Corporation, 2004).

173. Robert E. Slavin et al., "Effective Reading Programs for Middle and High Schools: A Best-Evidence Synthesis," *Reading Research Quarterly* 43 (2008): 290–322; Robert E. Savin, Cynthia Lake, Cynthia Groff, "Effective Programs in Middle and High School Mathematics: A Best-Evidence Synthesis," *Review of Educational Research* 79 (2009) 839–911.

174. Desimone, "How Can Comprehensive School Reform Models Be Successfully Implemented?"; Brian Rowan et al., *School Improvement by Design: Lessons from a Study of Comprehensive School Reform Programs* (Philadelphia: Consortium for Policy Research in Education, 2009).

175. Andrew C. Porter, "External Standards and Good Teaching: The Pros and Cons of Telling Teachers What to Do," *Educational Evaluation and Policy Analysis* 11 (1989): 343–356.

176. William Corrin et al., *The Enhanced Reading Opportunities Study: Findings from the Second Year of Implementation* (NCEE 2009-4036) (Washington, DC: National Center for Education Evaluation and Regional Assistance, U.S. Department of Education, 2009).

177. Desimone, "How Can Comprehensive School Reform Models Be Successfully Implemented?"; Berends et al., *Facing the Challenges of Whole-School Reform.*

178. Ibid.; Glennan Jr. et al., *Expanding the Reach of Education Reforms.*

179. McLaughlin, "The Rand Change Agent Study Revisited," 14.

180. Aladjem et al., *Models Matter.*

181. Berends et al., *Facing the Challenges of Whole-School Reform*; Bryk and Schneider, *Trust in Schools*; Desimone, "How Can Comprehensive School Reform Models Be Successfully Implemented?"

182. Berends et al., *Facing the Challenges of Whole-School Reform.*

183. Ibid; Aladjem et al., *Models Matter*; Desimone, "How Can Comprehensive School Reform Models Be Successfully Implemented?"

184. Betsy Hammond, *Portland: All the Advantage, Nothing to Show for It* (New York: Hechinger Report, Teachers College, Columbia University, July 6, 2010), http://hechingerreport.org/content/portland-all-the-advantages-nothing-to-show-for-it_3322 (accessed August 27, 2010).

185. Berends et al., *Facing the Challenges of Whole-School Reform*, 147.

186. Ibid.

187. Cynthia E. Coburn and Joan E. Talbert, "Conceptions of Evidence Use in School Districts: Mapping the Terrain," *American Journal of Education* 112 (2006): 469–495; James P. Spillane, "School Districts Matter: Local Educational Authorities and State Instructional Policy," *Educational Policy* 10 (1996): 63–87; Jonathan A. Supovitz, *The Case for District-Based Reform: Leading, Building, and Sustaining School Improvement* (Cambridge, MA: Harvard Education Press, 2006).

188. Aladjem et al., *Models Matter.*

189. Glennan Jr. et al., *Expanding the Reach.*

190. Ibid.; Supovitz, *The Case for District-Based Reform.*

191. Berends et al., *Facing the Challenges of Whole-School Reform*, 149.

192. Bryk and Schneider, *Trust in Schools*; Sarason, *Revisiting the Culture of the School*; Purkey and Smith, "Effective Schools."

9. What Should Be Done to Solve the Dropout Crisis

1. *Diplomas Count 2010: Graduation by the Numbers* (Bethesda, MD: Editorial Projects in Education Research Center, 2010), 33.
2. *The High Cost of High School Dropouts: What the Nation Pays for Inadequate High Schools* (Washington, DC: Alliance for Excellent Education, 2009), www.all4ed.org/publication_material/EconImpact (accessed January 17, 2011).
3. William H. Gates, "Speech: 2005 Education Summit on High Schools," *International Journal of Instructional Technology and Distance Learning* 2 (2005), www.itdl.org/Journal/May_05/Article01.Htm (accessed January 17, 2011).
4. See "What Bill and Melinda Gates Want You to Know," www.oprah.com/showinfo/What-Bill-and-Melinda-Gates-Want-You-to-Know (accessed February 23, 2011).
5. "Remarks of President Barack Obama—As Prepared for Delivery Address to Joint Session of Congress Tuesday, February 24th, 2009," www.whitehouse.gov/the_press_office/Remarks-of-President-Barack-Obama-Address-to-Joint-Session-of-Congress (accessed August 21, 2010).
6. See "Education Nation," www.educationnation.com (accessed February 23, 2011).
7. See "About the Alliance," www.all4ed.org/about_the_alliance (accessed February 23, 2011).
8. See "America's Promise: About the Alliance," www.americaspromise.org/About-the-Alliance.aspx (accessed February 23, 2011).
9. See "America's Promise: Dropout Prevention," www.americaspromise.org/Our-Work/Dropout-Prevention.aspx (accessed February 23, 2011).
10. See "Grad Nation," www.americaspromise.org/Our-Work/Grad-Nation.aspx (accessed February 23, 2011).
11. John M. Bridgeland, John J. DiIulio Jr., and Karen Burke Morison, *The Silent Epidemic: Perspectives on High School Dropouts* (Washington, DC: Civic Enterprises, 2006).
12. See "Make High School Graduation a National Priority," www.nea.org/home/19351.htm (accessed February 23, 2011).
13. See "About the Education Trust," www.edtrust.org/dc/about (accessed February 23, 2011).
14. "Diplomas Count 2010: Graduation by the Numbers: Putting Data to Work for Student Success," *Education Week*, June 10, 2010, www.edweek.org/Ew/Toc/2010/06/10/Index.html (accessed August 28, 2010).
15. See "Do What Works," http://dww.ed.gov/topic/?T_ID=24 (accessed February 23, 2011).

16. "Remarks of President Barack Obama—As Prepared for Delivery Address to Joint Session of Congress Tuesday, February 24th, 2009"; "Remarks by the President to the Hispanic Chamber of Commerce on a Complete and Competitive American Education," www.whitehouse.gov/the_press_office/ Remarks-of-the-President-to-the-United-States-Hispanic-Chamber-of-Commerce (accessed August 21, 2010).

17. Information retrieved from "President Obama Announces Steps to Reduce Dropout Rate and Prepare Students for College and Careers," www.white house.gov/the-press-office/president-obama-announces-steps-reduce-dropout -rate-and-prepare-students-college-an (accessed August 24, 2010).

18. See "State Fiscal Stabilization Fund March 7, 2009," www2.ed.gov/policy/gen/ leg/recovery/factsheet/stabilization-fund.html (accessed February 23, 2011).

19. The winners of these two competitions were announced in March and August 2010. Information retrieved from "Race to the Top Fund," www2.ed .gov/programs/racetothetop/index.html, and "Investing in Innovation Fund," www2.ed.gov/programs/innovation/index.html (accessed August 24, 2010).

20. Adrienne Fernandes and Thomas Gabe, *Disconnected Youth: A Look at 16- to 24-Year Olds Who Are Not Working or in School* (Washington, DC: Congressional Research Service, 2009), www.fas.org/sgp/crs/misc (accessed August 25, 2010); *Disconnected Youth: Federal Action Could Address Some of the Challenges Faced by Local Programs that Reconnect Youth to Education and Employment* (Washington, DC: U.S. Government Accountability Office, 2008), www.gao.gov/Products/GAO-08-313 (accessed August 25, 2010); Jacob Rosch, Dana Brinson, and Bryan Hassel, *Youth at High Risk of Disconnection: A Data Update of Michael Wald and Tia Martinez's Connected by 25: Improving the Life Chances of the Country's Most Vulnerable 14–24 Year Olds* (Washington, DC: Annie E. Casey Foundation, 2008) www.aecf.org/KnowledgeCenter/Publications.aspx?pubguid=%7B61CC54FE-28E6-443A-8421 -25CBD8D6B90D%7D (accessed August 25, 2010).

21. Fernandes and Gabe, *Disconnected Youth*, 11; Daniel Kuehn et al., *Vulnerable Youth and the Transition to Adulthood: Multiple Pathways Connecting School to Work* (ASPE research brief) (Washington, DC: Urban Institute, 2009), www .urban.org/Url.Cfm?ID=411948 (accessed January 17, 2011), 2.

22. Dan Bloom, "Programs and Policies to Assist High School Dropouts in the Transition to Adulthood," *Future of Children* 20 (2010): 89–108; Dan Bloom, Saskia Levy Thomason, and Rob Ivry, *Building a Learning Agenda around Disconnected Youth* (New York: MDRC, 2010), www.mdrc.org/publications/ 545/abstract.html (accessed August 25, 2010); *Disconnected Youth*, U.S. Government Accountability Office; Peter Leone and Lois Weinberg. *Addressing*

the Needs of Children and Youth in the Juvenile Justice and Child Welfare Systems (Washington, DC: Center for Juvenile Justice Reform, Georgetown Public Policy Institute, Georgetown University, 2010); D. Wayne Osgood, E. Michael Foster, and Mark E. Courtney, "Vulnerable Populations and the Transition to Adulthood," *Future of Children* 20 (2010): 209–229; Carolyn J. Heinrich and Harry J. Holzer, "Improving Education and Employment for Disadvantaged Young Men: Proven and Promising Strategies," *Annals of the American Academy of Political and Social Science* (forthcoming).

23. Bloom et al., *Building a Learning Agenda,* 11.

24. Information retrieved from "New Initiative to Double the Number of Low-Income Students in the U.S. Who Earn a Postsecondary Degree by Age 26," www.gatesfoundation.org/press-releases/Pages/low-income-postsecondary-degree-081209.aspx, and from "Lumina's Big Goal," www.luminafoundation.org/goal_2025 (accessed August 25, 2010).

25. Fernandes and Gabe, *Disconnected Youth,* 8–10.

26. David K. Cohen and Susan L. Moffitt, *The Ordeal of Equality: Did Federal Regulation Fix the Schools?* (Cambridge, MA: Harvard University Press, 2009); Richard F. Elmore, "Conclusion: The Problem of Stakes in Performance-Based Accountability Systems," in *Redesigning Accountability Systems for Education,* ed. S. H. Furhman and R. F. Elmore (New York: Teachers College Press, 2004), 274–296; Gail L. Sunderman, ed., *Holding NCLB Accountable: Achieving Accountability, Equity, & School Reform* (Thousand Oaks, CA: Corwin Press, 2008); Russell W. Rumberger, "Can NCLB Improve High School Graduation Rates?" in *Holding NCLB Accountable: Achieving Accountability, Equity, and School Reform,* ed. G. L. Sunderman (Thousand Oaks, CA: Corwin Press, 2008), 209–222; Diane Ravitch, *The Death and Life of the Great American School System* (New York: Basic Books, 2010).

27. One was issued by the independent, bipartisan Commission on No Child Left Behind. See its *Beyond NCLB: Fulfilling the Promise to Our Nation's Children* (Aspen, CO: Aspen Institute, 2007), www.aspeninstitute.org/policy-work/no-child-left-behind/reports (accessed January 17, 2011). Another was issued by the Center on Education Policy (CEP), a national, independent advocate for public education presided over by Jack Jennings, former staff director for the U.S. House of Representatives Committee on Education and Labor. See *Better Federal Policies Leading to Better Schools* (Washington, DC: Center on Education Policy, 2010), www.cep-dc.org (accessed January 17, 2011), 508.

28. A *Blueprint for Reform: The Reauthorization of the Elementary and Secondary Education Act* (Washington, DC: U.S. Department of Education, Office of Planning, Evaluation, and Policy Development, Policy and Program Studies

Service, 2010), www2.ed.gov/policy/elsec/leg/blueprint/index.html (accessed August 25, 2010).

29. See "Key Legislation," compiled by the Alliance for Excellent Education, www.all4ed.org/federal_policy/KeyLegislation (accessed February 22, 2011).

30. *An Action Agenda for Improving America's High Schools* (Washington, DC: National Governors Association and Achieve, 2005), 5.

31. *Accelerating the Agenda: Actions to Improve America's High Schools* (Washington, DC: National Governors Association Center for Best Practices, National Conference of State Legislatures, National Association of State Boards of Education, and Council of Chief State School Officers, 2009).

32. Ibid., 2.

33. Ibid., 13.

34. Ibid., 14–17.

35. Daniel Princiotta and Ryan Reyna, *Achieving Graduation for All: A Governor's Guide to Dropout Prevention and Recovery* (Washington, DC: NGA Center for Best Practices, 2009), www.nga.org/portal/site/nga/menuitem.9123e83a1f6786440ddcbeeb501010a0/?vgnextoid=da8b386aa6c74210VgnVCM1000005e00100aRCRD (accessed January 17, 2011).

36. See press release, www.nga.org/portal/site/nga/menuitem.6c9a8a9ebc6ae07eee28aca9501010a0/?vgnextoid=8d2b864e5b4f5210VgnVCM1000005e00100aRCRD&vgnextchannel=759b8f2005361010VgnVCM1000001a01010aRCRD (accessed January 4, 2010).

37. Sunny Deyé, *A Path to Graduation for Every Child: State Legislative Roles and Responsibilities* (Washington, DC: National Conference of State Legislatures, 2011).

38. See California Dropout Research Project, http://cdrp.ucsb.edu (accessed February 23, 2011).

39. See "CDRP Policy Committee Report," http://cdrp.ucsb.edu/dropouts/pubs_policyreport.htm (accessed February 23, 2011).

40. As of December 2010, forty-nine state summits and fifty-five city summits had been held. See www.americaspromise.org/Our-Work/Dropout-Prevention/Summits.aspx (accessed January 8, 2011).

41. See "School Improvement Grants," www.ed.gov/category/program/school-improvement-grants (accessed August 25, 2010).

42. See "Transformation: Most Popular School Improvement Model," http://blogs.edweek.org/edweek/state_edwatch/2010/07/transformation_the_fourth_of_the.html (accessed August 25, 2010).

43. See "Investing in Innovation Fund," www2.ed.gov/programs/innovation/index.html (accessed August 25, 2010).

44. See "Validating the Talent Development–Diplomas Now Secondary School Turnaround Model," http://data.ed.gov/grants/investing-in-innovation/applicant/15275 (accessed August 25, 2010).

45. See "Scaling the New Orleans Charter Restart Model," http://data.ed.gov/grants/investing-in-innovation/applicant/15201 (accessed August 25, 2010).

46. "See Welcome to Early College High School," www.earlycolleges.org (accessed August 27, 2010).

47. Information retrieved from Big Picture Learning, www.bigpicture.org (accessed August 27, 2010).

48. See, for example, the work of the Linked Learning Alliance www.connect edcalifornia.org/alliance (accessed August 27, 2010). There is also a bill before Congress, the Linked Learning Pathways Affording College and Career Success Act, which would expand pathways. See "Key Legislation," www.all4ed.org/federal_policy/KeyLegislation (accessed August 27, 2010).

49. According to the Everyone Graduates Center website, "Approximately 15% of the nation's high schools produce more than half of its dropouts and close to 75% of its minority dropouts." Information retrieved from http://every1gradu ates.org/analytics/item/64-locating-the-dropout-crisis.html (May 7, 2011). A study by Balfanz and Legters shows that 2,007 high schools (excluding alternative high schools and schools with fewer than 300 students) out of 11,129 (18 percent) had promoting power of 60 percent or less. See Robert Balfanz and Nettie Legters, "Locating the Dropout Crisis: Which High Schools Produce the Nation's Dropouts?" in *Dropouts in America*, ed. G. Orfield (Cambridge, MA: Harvard Education Press, 2004), 61.

50. See Robert M. Hauser and Judith Anderson Koenig, eds., *High School Dropout, Graduation, and Completion Rates: Better Data, Better Measures, Better Decisions*, National Research Council and National Academy of Education, Committee for Improved Measurement of High School Dropout and Completion Rates: Expert Guidance on Next Steps for Research and Policy Workshop, Center for Education, Division of Behavioral and Social Sciences and Education (Washington, DC: National Academies Press, 2011).

51. Susan Rotermund, *Alternative Education Enrollment and Dropouts in California High Schools*, Statistical Brief 6 (Santa Barbara: California Dropout Research Project, University of California, 2007), http://cdrp.ucsb.edu/Dropouts/Pubs_Statbriefs.Htm#6 (accessed January 17, 2011).

52. Information retrieved from "Graduation Rate Only Schools," www.cde.ca.gov/ta/ac/pl/graduationrate.asp (accessed August 25, 2010).

53. The list of SIG schools was retrieved from the U.S. Department of Education School Improvement Fund website, www2.ed.gov/programs/sif/index.html (accessed January 16, 2010; Texas dropout data for 2008–09 by school was retrieved from the Texas Education Agency website, http://ritter.tea.state.tx.us/acctres/drop_annual/0809/level.html (accessed January 16, 2011).

54. Information on the high schools was retrieved from "Regular and Cumulative Enrollment and Dropout Rates for California Schools, 2007–08," www.cdrp .ucsb.edu/dropouts/sb13table.php (accessed August 25, 2010). Information on the SIG funding was retrieved from www3.cde.ca.gov/scripts/texis.exe/ webinator/search?pr=default&query=state%20board%20SIG&submit=GO (accessed August 25, 2010).

55. See "Welcome to NCER," http://ies.ed.gov/ncer (accessed February 23, 2011).

56. See "Welcome to NCEE," http://ies.ed.gov/ncee (accessed February 23, 2011).

57. See "Welcome to WWC," http://ies.ed.gov/ncee/wwc (accessed February 23, 2011).

58. Douglas N. Harris, "Toward Policy-Relevant Benchmarks for Interpreting Effect Sizes: Combining Effects with Costs," *Educational Evaluation and Policy Analysis* 31 (2009): 3–29.

59. Information retrieved from "Intervention: Check and Connect," http://ies.ed .gov/ncee/wwc/reports/dropout/check_conn (accessed August 26, 2010).

60. Richard F. Elmore and Milbrey W. McLaughlin, *Steady Work: Policy, Practice, and the Reform of American Education* (Santa Monica: Rand Corporation, 1988), 34–35.

61. Information retrieved from "Investing in Innovation Fund," www2.ed.gov/ programs/innovation/index.html (accessed August 26, 2010).

62. Information retrieved from "NCER Announces New FY 2010 Research Grants," http://ies.ed.gov/ncer/projects/10awards3.asp (accessed August 26, 2010).

63. Caroline M. Hoxby, Sonali Murarka, and Jenny Kang, *How New York City's Charter Schools Affect Achievement* (Cambridge, MA: New York City Charter Schools Evaluation Project, 2009), www.nber.org/~schools/charterschoolseval (accessed August 21, 2010), 1–9.

64. Richard D. Kahlenberg, *Turnaround schools that work: Moving beyond separate but equal* (Washington, DC: Brookings Institution Press, 2010), 15. Another study found that in the 2007–08 academic year KIPP schools received an average of $6,500 more per pupil than local district schools. See Gary Miron, Jessica L. Urschel, and Nicholas Saxton, *What Makes KIPP Work? A Study of Student Characteristics, Attrition, and School Finance* (New York: National Center for the Study of Privatization in Education, Teachers College, Columbia University, 2011) www.ncspe.org/list-papers.php (accessed May 15, 2011).

65. Laura Lippman et al., *A Developmental Perspective on College and Workplace Readiness* (Washington, DC: Child Trends, 2008), www.childtrends.org/Files// Child_Trends-2009_10_14_SP_DevelopmentPer.pdf (accessed January 17, 2011); Tony Wagner, *The Global Achievement Gap: Why Even Our Best Schools Don't Teach the New Survival Skills Our Children Need—and What We Can Do about*

It (New York: Basic Books, 2008); Lynn Olson, "What Does 'Ready' Mean?" *Education Week*, June 12, 2007, www.edweek.org/Ew/Articles/2007/06/12/40overview.h26.html (accessed January 17, 2011).

66. *State College- and Career-Ready High School Graduation Requirements* (Washington, DC: Achieve, 2010), www.achieve.org/state-college-and-career-ready-high-school-graduation-requirements-comparison-table (accessed January 17, 2011).

67. Carnevale, Smith, and Stohl project that 63 percent of future job openings will require at least some college education. See Anthony P. Carnevale, Nicole Smith, and Jeff Strohl, *Help Wanted: Projections of Jobs and Education Requirements through 2018* (Washington, DC: Center for Education and the Workforce, Georgetown University, 2010), http://cew.georgetown.edu (accessed August 26, 2010), figure 2.1. However, Lacey and Wright from the U.S. Bureau of Labor Statistics project that more than one-third of all job openings (such as retail salespeople and waiters and waitresses) will require one month or less of on-the-job experience or instruction to be fully qualified in the occupation. See T. Alan Lacey and Benjamin Wright, "Occupational Employment Projections to 2018," *Monthly Labor Review* 132 (2009): table 3, 89.

68. David Autor, *The Polarization of Job Opportunities in the U.S. Labor Market* (Washington, DC: Center for American Progress and the Hamilton Project, Brookings Institution, 2010), www.americanprogress.org/issues/2010/04/job_polarization_report.html (accessed August 26, 2010), 2.

69. James J. Heckman, Jora Stixrud, and Sergio Urzua, "The Effects of Cognitive and Noncognitive Abilities on Labor Market Outcomes and Social Behavior," *Journal of Labor Economics* 24 (2006): 411–482; Flavio Cunha and James J. Heckman, "Investing in Our Young People" (working paper 16201, National Bureau of Economic Research, Cambridge, MA 2010), http://papers.nber.org/papers/w16201 (accessed January 17, 2011).

70. National Association of Manufacturers, Anderson, and the Manufacturing Institute's Center for Workforce Success, *The Skills Gap 2001* (Washington, DC: National Association of Manufacturers, 2001), 2. For more discussion of the future skill demands of work, see Paul E. Barton, *High School Reform and Work: Facing Labor Market Realities* (Princeton, NJ: Policy Evaluation and Research Center, Educational Testing Service, 2006), www.ets.org/research/policy_research_reports/pic-hswork (accessed January 17, 2011).

71. Information retrieved from "Overview: Framework for 21st Century Learning," www.p21.org/index.php?option=com_content&task=view&id=254&Itemid=119 (accessed January 16, 2011).

72. Information retrieved from "The Quest for 'Deeper Learning' by Barbara Chow," www.hewlett.org/newsroom/quest-deeper-learning (accessed January 16, 2011).

73. John A. Clausen, *American Lives: Looking Back at the Children of the Great Depression* (Berkeley: University of California Press, 1993). Quote is from M. Locke, "Tracking the Lives of a Whole Generation," *Santa Barbara News Press*, September 12, 1993, A4.

74. Howard E. Gardner, *Frames of Mind: The Theory of Multiple Intelligences* (New York: Basic Books, 1983); Howard E. Gardner, *Intelligence Reframed: Multiple Intelligences for the 21st Century* (New York: Basic Books, 1999); Daniel Goleman, *Emotional Intelligence* (New York: Bantam, 1996); Joseph A. Durlak, Roger P. Weissberg, Allison B. Dymnicki, Rebecca D. Taylor, and Kriston B. Schellinger, "The Impact of Enhancing Students' Social and Emotional Learning: A Meta-Analysis of School-Based Universal Interventions," *Child Development* 82 (2011): 405–434.

75. William C. Symonds, Robert B. Schwartz, and Ronald Ferguson, *Pathways to Prosperity: Meeting the Challenge of Preparing Young Americans for the 21st Century* (Cambridge, MA: Graduate School of Education, Harvard University, 2011) www.agi.harvard.edu (Accessed May 15, 2011).

76. Nel Noddings, "Differentiate, Don't Standardize," *Education Week: Quality Counts 2010* 29, no. 17 (2010): 29–31, www.edweek.org/ew/articles/2010/01/14/17noddings-comm.h29.html (accessed January 17, 2011), 29.

77. John H. Bishop and Ferran Mane, "The Impacts of Career-Technical Education on High School Labor Market Success," *Economics of Education Review* 23 (2004): 381–402.

78. UNICEF, *Child Poverty in Rich Countries, 2005*, Innocenti Report Card 6 (Florence, Italy: UNICEF Innocenti Research Centre, 2005).

79. The university sponsors Curriculum Integration Institutes that bring academic and career-technical school teachers together to design CTE courses that meet the university's academic course requirements. See "The University of California Curriculum Integration (UCCI) Institute," www.ucop.edu/ucci/welcome.html (accessed February 23, 2011).

80. Information retrieved from "Big Picture Learning," www.bigpicture.org (accessed August 28, 2010).

81. *Graduation Counts* (Washington, DC: National Governors Association Task Force on State High School Graduation Data, 2005), www.nga.org/Files/Pdf/0507GRAD.pdf (accessed January 17, 2011).

82. See "A Uniform, Comparable Graduation Rate," www2.ed.gov/policy/elsec/reg/proposal/uniform-grad-rate.html (accessed February 23, 2011).

83. For example, the Every Student Counts Act would create a new "cumulative" graduation rate that would include students who graduate more than four years after entering ninth grade. See "Every Student Counts Act (111th)," http://all4ed.org/federal_policy/legislative_updates/ESCA (accessed February 24, 2011).

84. See SB 291, www.leginfo.ca.gov/pub/07-08/bill/sen/sb_0201-0250/sb_219_bill _20071014_chaptered.html (accessed February 24, 2011).

85. Betty Malen et al., "Reconstituting Schools: 'Testing' the 'Theory of Action,'" *Educational Evaluation and Policy Analysis* 24 (2002): 127. See also Jennifer King Rice and Betty Malen, "The Human Costs of Education Reform: The Case of School Reconstitution," *Educational Administration Quarterly* 39 (2003): 635–666.

86. *Better Federal Policies Leading to Better Schools*, 8.

87. Russell W. Rumberger, *Solving California's Dropout Crisis*, report of the California Dropout Research Project Policy Committee (Santa Barbara: California Dropout Research Project, University of California, 2008), http://cdrp.ucsb.edu/Dropouts/Pubs_Policyreport.Htm (accessed January 17, 2011).

88. Gary Orfield, *Reviving the Goal of an Integrated Society: A 21st Century Challenge* (Los Angeles: Civil Rights Project/Proyecto Dereshos Civilies at UCLA, 2009), http://civilrightsproject.ucla.edu/research/k-12-education/integration-and-diversity (accessed January 17, 2011).

89. Russell W. Rumberger and Gregory J. Palardy, "Does Segregation Still Matter? The Impact of Student Composition on Academic Achievement in High School," *Teachers College Record* 107 (2005): 1999–2045.

90. Balfanz and Legters, "Locating the Dropout Crisis," figure 2.

91. Orfield, *Reviving the Goal of an Integrated Society*.

92. Kahlenberg, *All Together Now*; Richard D. Kahlenberg, *Turnaround Schools that Work: Moving beyond Separate but Equal* (New York: Century Foundation, 2010).

93. Raising the national graduation rate would take near-universal adoption of proven school-based interventions. Research by Konstantopoulos and Hedges shows that moving a school from the 10th to the 50th percentile on NAEP achievement scores, which would be quite a challenge, would eliminate only about one-third of the achievement gap between racial and socioeconomic groups. See Spyros Konstantopoulos and Larry V. Hedges, "How Large an Effect Can We Expect from School Reforms?" *Teachers College Record* 110 (2008): 1611–1638.

94. *Income, Poverty, and Health Insurance Coverage in the United States: 2009* (Washington, DC: Census Bureau, U.S. Department of Commerce, 2010), www.census.gov/Hhes/www/Poverty/Data/Incpovhlth/2009/Index.html (accessed January 17, 2011), table B-2.

95. UNICEF, *Child Poverty in Rich Countries*, 2005, figure 1.

96. UNICEF, *Child Poverty in Perspective: An Overview of Child Well-Being In Rich Countries*, Innocenti Report Card 7 (Florence, Italy: UNICEF Innocenti Research Centre, 2007), 2.

97. *Education at a Glance 2010* (Paris: Organisation for Economic Co-operation and Development, 2010), 42.

98. W. Steven Barnett and Clive R. Belfield, "Early Childhood Development and Social Mobility," *Future of Children* 16 (2006): 73–98; Kevin M. Gorey, "Early Childhood Education: A Meta-Analytic Affirmation of the Short- and Long-Term Benefits of Educational Opportunity," *School Psychology Quarterly* 16 (2001): 9–30.

99. James J. Heckman et al., "The Rate of Return to the HighScope Perry Preschool Program," *Journal of Public Economics* 94 (2010): 114–128; Henry M. Levin and Clive R. Belfield, "Educational Interventions to Raise High School Graduation Rates," in *The Price We Pay: Economic and Social Consequences of Inadequate Education*, ed. C. R. Belfield and H. M. Levin (Washington, DC: Brookings Institution Press, 2007), 177–199; Arthur J. Reynolds, Judy A. Temple, Barry A. B. White, Suh-Ruu Ou, and Dylan L. Robertson, "Age 26 cost-benefit analysis of the Child-Parent Center Early Education Program," *Child Development* 82 (2011): 379–404.

100. Carolyn J. Hill et al., "Empirical Benchmarks for Interpreting Effect Sizes in Research," *Child Development Perspectives* 2 (2008): 172–177.

101. Cunha and Heckman, *Investing in Our Young People*, 4.

102. James S. Coleman, "Toward Open Schools," *Public Interest* 9 (1967): 20–21.

INDEX

Absenteeism, 7, 50, 169, 177, 205, 208, 213
Absolute mechanism, 120
Academic integration, 148, 149
Academic mediation theory, 150
Accelerating the Agenda: Actions to Improve America's High Schools, 262
Accountability, 6, 27–28, 272–273
Acevedo, Millie, 102
Achieve, 55–56, 261
Achievement, academic, 41, 154–155, 160–169, 226
Achievement tests, 27–28
Achieving Graduation for All: A Governor's Guide to Dropout Prevention and Recovery, 262–263
ACS (American Community Survey), 61, 63, 64–65
An Action Agenda to Improve America's High Schools, 261
"Adaptive implementation," 250–251
Adolescent development, contextual factors and, 8 (figure)
Adult advocates, 222, 225–226
Adult education, 45, 65, 77–78, 297n92
Age: compulsory schooling age, 13, 30–31 (table), 230; crime and, 98–99; as predictor of dropping out, 164
Alcohol use, 114, 175
Alexander, Karl, 147
Algebra, passing, as dropout predictor, 161
Allensworth, Elaine, 161
Alliance for Excellent Education, 133, 256–257, 266
Alternative credentials, 2, 4, 35–36
Alternative education, 43, 77–78
Alternative models of dropping out, 145–151

Alternative pathways, 13, 33, 36–46, 214, 220, 231, 285n1, 286n33
Alternative schools, 12, 42–45, 209. *See also* Charter schools
American Community Survey (ACS), 61, 63, 64–65
American Diploma Project, 29–32, 35
American Recovery and Reinvestment Act (2009), 259–260
American Youth Policy Forum, 219, 227–228
America's Promise Alliance, 3, 257–258, 264–265
Appleton, James, 153
Aristotle, 139
Armed forces, 95
Assessment, 228, 248, 259, 262; alternative, 33; academic, 34, 222; self-, 180
Attendance, 1, 10, 21, 48, 52, 151, 169–170, 197, 217, 225, 270; compulsory, 24–25, 199, 262; rates, 199, 241, 244, 271
Attitude: behavior and, 154; educational performance and, 155–156; as predictor of dropping out, 178–181
Authoritative parenting style, 9
Autor, David, 270
Averaged Freshman Graduation Rate, 68, 72, 73, 80

Balfanz, Bob, 78, 79
Baltimore Beginning School Study, 147, 163–164, 179
Barrow, Lisa, 233
Bartels, Larry, 138–139
Battin-Pearson, Sara, 150
Becker, Gary, 115–116, 121

Behavior: criminal, 5, 86; problem, 6; as dropout predictor, 7, 169–178; developmental behavioral science, 8; in "frustration-self-esteem" model, 146; attitude and, 154; educational performance and, 155; improving classroom, 226

Behavioral engagement, 153, 186

Belfield, Clive, 131–133, 135–137, 234, 268

Beller, Emily, 122

Betts, Julian, 231

Big Picture Learning schools, 265, 272

Bill & Melinda Gates Foundation, 207, 240–242, 244

Births, unintended, 104. See also Teen parenthood

Blumenfeld, Phyllis, 152–153

Bonding, social, 149

Bowles, Samuel, 126

Bridgeland, John, 156–157

Bronfenbrenner, Urie, 153

Brown, B. Bradford, 204

Burke Morison, Karen, 156–157

Bush, George H. W., 3

Bush, George W., 207

California: graduation rates in, 17, 80; alternative schools in, 44; student mobility in, 54; Data Quality Campaign and, 77; economic losses from dropouts in, 133, 139–140; crime costs in, 135–136; High Priority Schools Grant Program in, 237–238; dropouts and adult education in, 297n92

California Continuation Education Association (CCEA), 43

California Dropout Research Project (CDRP), 17–18, 133, 263–264

Cameron, Stephen, 94

Capacity, will and, 246–249, 252, 273–274

The Cardinal Principles of Secondary Education, 23–24

Career and technical education (CTE), 32, 223, 227, 271–272

Carroll, Stephen, 131, 133, 135, 137–138, 139

Catholic schools, 195–196

Causes of dropping out, 15, 143–145, 156–158. See also Predictors of dropping out

Center on Educational Policy (CEP), 235, 363n27

Charter schools: overview of, 12, 212; in California, 44; debate over, 195; disadvantages of, 213–214; research findings on, 231–232; by school type, 346n17; start-up versus conversion, 347n25, 353n83

Chicago, 2, 18, 23, 87, 109, 110, 124, 126, 146, 161, 166, 198, 200, 230–232, 234, 247, 248

Chicago Longitudinal Study, 147, 229

Childbearing, 101–110, 175–176, 204–205

Choice: student, 38, 44, 248; school, 212, 231–233, 241–242, 244; teacher, 248, 250

Christenson, Sandra, 153

Cigarette smoking, 113–114, 310n152

Civic engagement, 117–119, 138–139, 311n168–169

Civic Enterprises, 257

Civil Rights Act (1964), 40

Civil Rights Project, 55–56

Class size, in elementary school, 13, 216, 229

Clausen, John, 270–271

Cognitive engagement, 153, 186

Cognitive skills, 126, 269–270

Cohabitation, 110

Cohort graduation rate, 59, 68–70, 71 (table), 73–76

Coleman, James, 41, 194, 276

Coleman report, 41

Collaborative relationships, 12, 212–213, 242–243, 245

College enrollments, 134, 315n7

Commission on National Aid to Vocational Education, 22

Committee for Improved Measurement of High School Dropout and Completion Rates, 58, 296nn79, 83

Committee of Ten, 23

Common Core of Data (CCD), 61–62, 65, 68–70, 80, 296nn79, 83

Community: as dropout factor, 10–11, 153–154, 199–201; teen pregnancy and, 107–108; civic engagement and, 117–119; well-being and, 120; poverty and, 124–125; strengthening, 274–275

Competence, planful, 270–271

Completion, high school. *See* High school completion

Comprehensive approaches, to dropout prevention, 12, 210–214

Comprehensive school reform (CSR) model, 12, 13, 210–211, 236–237, 245

Comprehensive School Reform Quality Center, 217, 220

Compulsory schooling age, 13, 30–31 (table), 230

Conant, James Bryant, 25

Concentrated disadvantage, 10, 86–87, 124, 200, 206, 275–276

Conceptual framework of dropout process, 154–156

Concern, over dropout crisis, 4–6

Connell, James, 152

Consequences of dropping out: overview of, 4–6; introduction to, 86–88; labor market outcomes and, 88–95; crime and, 95–101; family formation and, 101–110; health and, 110–116; civic engagement and, 117–119; well-being and, 119–120. *See also* Social consequences of dropping out

Context: for dropouts, 8–11, 153–154; of reform implementation, 251–252

Continuation high schools, 42–43, 44–45, 209

Contreras, Frances, 201

Control: mental health and, 112–113; locus of, 180, 181

Corcoran, Mary, 122–123

Costs, of prevention programs, 233–234, 235 (table), 267–268

Council of Chief State School Officers (CCSSO), 32

Course-taking and requirements, 28–32, 171–172; California, 29, 32; University of California, 32, 35

Crime/criminal behavior, 5, 86, 95–101, 134–136, 173–174

Criminology theories, 98–101

Cross-sectional data, 60–61

Cubberly, Ellwood, 23

Culture: of poverty, 124, 125; youth outcomes and, 202, 204–205; of schools, 246–247, 253

Cumulative mechanism, 120

Cumulative Promotion Index (CPI), 72, 73, 80

Current Population Survey (CPS), 61, 63, 64–65

"Curricular incoherence," 169

Curriculum: differentiated, 21–25, 267; standardization of, 32; tracking and, 36–39; "curricular incoherence," 169

Currie, Janet, 126

Data Quality Campaign, 76–77, 291n16

Death rates, 111

Debra P. v. Turlington (1981), 34

Decennial Census, 61, 63, 64

Dee, Thomas, 118–119

Delinquency, 173–174. *See also* Deviance

Demographic characteristics, as dropout predictor, 181–184

Developmental behavioral science, 8

Deviance, 150–151, 172–176

Deviant affiliation theory, 150

Differentiated curriculum, 21–25, 267

Differentiated schooling, 41, 42–45, 267

DiIulio, John, 156–157

Diploma requirements, 28–35

Disabilities, students with, 2, 63–64, 184, 279n8

Disadvantage, concentrated, 10, 86–87, 124, 200, 206, 275–276

Disconnected youth, 91, 260

Districts, as focal point of improvement efforts, 252

Dorn, Sherman, 4, 21, 25

Dornbusch, Sanford, 204

Driver's licenses, 311n168

Dropout factories, 41, 80, 266, 297nn95–96, 365n49

Dropout Prevention practice guide, 224–225

Dropout rates: overview of, 1–3; measuring, 14, 66–73; debate over, 55–58; defining, 59–60; data for, 60–66, 73–78; by demographic, 78, 79 (table); differences among schools, districts, and states and, 78–80; trends in, 81–84; international comparisons for, 84–85, 134, 298–299nn105–106; race and, 201–205; alternative approaches to improving, 208–215

Dropout recovery programs, 209

Index

Dropouts/dropping out: defining, 47–48, 50, 51; identifying, 49–55

Drug use, 113–114, 175

Du Bois, W. E. B., 40

Early college high schools, 265

Early intervention, 228–229, 275

Earnings: of dropouts, 4, 86, 92, 93; economic well-being and, 119; intergenerational mobility and, 120–129; family income, 191, 313n209

Easton, John, 161

Economic inequality, 138–139

Economic Policy Institute, 56–57

Economy: dropouts' effect on, 4–5, 14–15, 132–134, 139–140; health and, 111–112; economic well-being, 119; intergenerational mobility and, 120–129

Edin, Kathryn, 18, 107–109, 200

Education: postsecondary, 4–5; parental, 9, 191; vocational, 22, 42, 223, 271–272; Jefferson on public, 25–26, 117; goals of public, 26–27; alternative, 43, 77–78; crime and, 96–100; health and, 110–116; well-being and, 120; intergenerational mobility and, 120–129; Obama on, 140–141; for future jobs, 367n67

Educational attainment, data on, 64–66

Educational engagement, 149–153, 155, 169–171, 186, 222–223, 227–228

Educational performance, 41, 154–155, 160–169, 226

Educational Policies Commission, 24–25

Education for All American Youth, 25

Education Longitudinal Study (2002), 62

The Education Trust, 56, 258

Education Week, 1, 2, 56, 57, 72, 73, 80, 258, 271

Effect size, 220

Eighth-grade graduation rate, 71–72

Eisenhower, Dwight, 26

Elementary school: class size in, 13, 216, 229; retention in, 162–163; grades in, as dropout predictor, 166; student mobility and, 167

Eliot, Charles, 23

Emotional engagement, 153

Employment: of dropouts, 4, 86, 88–95; and enrollment for 2009–10 high school dropouts and completers, 89 (table); health and, 111–112; as dropout predictor, 177–178, 201, 329n114; skills for future, 270; education for future, 367n67

Engagement: impediments to, 149–150; role of, in dropout process, 151–153, 155; as dropout predictor, 169–171, 222–223; behavioral and cognitive, 186; improving, 227–228

English-language learners, 63–64, 184, 347n24

Enrollment: identifying dropouts through, 49–50; reenrollment, 54–55, 321n6; rates for, 81; dropout rates and, 82 (table); and employment for 2009–10 high school dropouts and completers, 89 (table)

Ensminger, Margaret, 146–147

Entwisle, Doris, 147

Environment: as dropout factor, 8–11; health and, 116; well-being and, 120; poverty and, 122–125

Equivalency tests. *See* General Education Development (GED) test

Erkut, Emre, 131, 133, 135, 137–138, 139

Evaluation research, 215–216

Event, dropping out as, 47–48, 51–52

Event rates, 59, 66–68

Every Student Counts Act, 368n83

Exercise, 114

Exit exams, 33–34, 165, 230

Expectations, 179–180

Externalities, 120, 139–140

Extracurricular activities, 170–171

Failed courses, 160–162, 205

Falbo, Toni, 18, 163, 169, 171, 180, 188, 192–193, 198

Family: as dropout factor, 9, 153–154, 188–193, 205; consequences of dropping out and, 101–110; intergenerational mobility and, 120–129; strengthening, 274–275

Family income, 191, 313n209

Family socialization theory, 150

Female-headed households, 123

Fine, Michelle, 18, 41, 198–199

Finn, Jeremy, 146, 150, 152

Fleisher, Mark, 18, 100–101, 128, 177
Flores-González, Nilda, 18, 41, 198, 200
Foster care, 190
Fragile Families and Child Wellbeing Study, 105–106, 110, 124
Fredericks, Jennifer, 152–153
Freemont Hustlers, 97–98, 177
Fresno Unified School District, 161, 165
Friedman, Thomas, 84
"Frustration-self-esteem" model, 146, 150
Funding, for prevention programs, 267

Gándara, Patricia, 201
Gangs, 176–177
Garnier, Helen, 147
Gates, Bill, 3, 240. *See also* Bill & Melinda Gates Foundation
Gates High School Grants Initiative, 240–242
Gateway to College, 45
Ge, Xiaojia, 100
GED. *See* General Education Development (GED) test
Gender differences, 170, 181–182
General deviance theory, 150
General Education Development (GED) test, 4, 13, 35–36, 83, 94
Gintis, Herbert, 126
Globalization, 84–85
Goals, for students, 179–180
Goodlad, John, 36–37
Government assistance programs, 92
Grades, 165–166
Graduate/population ratio, 68
Graduation: requirements for, 14, 28–36, 230; defined, 51. *See also* High school completion
Graduation rates: in United States, 1–3; improving, 3–4, 369n93; concern for, 4–6; measuring, 14, 66–73; debate over, 55–58; defining, 59–60, 272–273; data for, 60–66, 73–78; of class of 2000, 69 (table); alternative, by state, 74–75 (table); by demographic, 78; differences among schools, districts, and states and, 78–80; trends in, 81–84; enrollment rates and, 82 (table); international comparisons for, 84–85, 134, 298–299nn105–106; alternative approaches to improving, 208–215

Grants, 265, 266–267
Greene, Jay, 56, 72
Grubb, Norton, 22
Guidance counselors, 25

Happiness, 119–120
Health: dropping out's effect on, 5, 86, 110–116, 137–138; intergenerational mobility and, 126–128; as dropout predictor, 184–185
Health care/health insurance, 114–115, 137
Heckman, James, 3, 58, 62–63, 65, 76, 94, 134, 270
Heredity, 122
Herrnstein, Richard, 122
High-risk settings, 8–11
High school(s): history and goals of, 21–28; high school reform, 210–211, 213–214; redefining success of, 269–272; size of, 347n21
High school completion: introduction to, 20; goals of high school and, 21–28; requirements for, 28–36; alternative pathways to, 36–46, 93–94, 214, 286n33; defining, 50–51; types of, certificates awarded, 66 (table); trends in, 81–82; graduation rates and, 83 (table); Obama on, 140–141; special-education students and, 279n8. *See also* Graduation
High School Graduation Initiative, 235–236
High School Longitudinal Study (2009), 62
Homelessness, 190
Hout, Michael, 122

Identification: of dropouts, 49–55; in "participation-identification" model, 146
IES practice guide, 224–228, 267
Immigration status, 63, 182–184, 204
Incarceration, 5, 63, 95–98, 311n168
Institute for Education Sciences, 258
Integration, social and academic, 148, 149
Intelligence tests, 24, 39
"Intent-to-treat" technique, 216
Intergenerational mobility, 120–129
International graduation rates, 84–85, 134, 298–299nn105–106

Index

Intervention strategies: designing effective, 11–13; of author, 16–18; early, 228–229, 275; systemic interventions, 229–233; costs and benefits of, 233–234, 235 (table), 267–268; under Recovery Act, 259–260. *See also* Prevention programs
Investing in Innovation Fund, 260
Involuntary minorities, 202
Involuntary withdrawal, 10, 197–198

Jacobs, Jennifer, 147
Jacobsen, Rebecca, 25–27
Jefferson, Thomas, 25–26, 117
Job Corps, 45, 65, 77–78
Juvenile crime, 136
Juvenile delinquency, 150–151, 173–174
Juvenile justice systems, 190

Kabbini, Nader, 147
Kefalas, Maria, 18, 107–109, 200
Kelly, Deirdre, 18, 42–43, 44, 151, 170, 173, 182, 198
Kennedy, John F., 4, 207
Kerr, Clark, 141–142
Knowledge Is Power Program (KIPP), 232, 269

Labor market. *See* Employment
LaFontaine, Paul, 62–63, 65, 76
Lamborn, Susie, 151–152
Larson, Katherine, 149
Laub, John, 99
Lazerson, Marvin, 22
Legters, Nettie, 78, 79
Levin, Henry, 130–133, 135–137, 139, 141, 234, 268
Life-course models, 146–147
Lifestyle, health and, 113–116
Linguistic minorities, 63–64, 184, 347n24
Local efforts, 264–265
Locus of control, 180, 181
Longitudinal data, 60–61, 73–78, 291n16
Los Angeles, 16, 49, 133, 140, 267; Unified School District, 1, 32, 53, 54, 80, 161, 162, 164, 165, 167, 248
Losen, Daniel J., 56
Lynd, Helen, 22
Lynd, Robert, 22

Marriage, childbearing and, 104–110
McLanahan, Sara, 123
MDRC studies, 221–223
Medicaid, 137
Medicare, 137
Membership, school, 149, 152
Mental health, 112–113, 128, 185, 189
Middle school: passing, as dropout predictor, 161; retention in, 162–163; achievement in, as dropout predictor, 165; student mobility and, 167
"Middletown" high school case study, 22–23
Migration. *See* Student mobility
Military service, 95
Milwaukee Parental Choice Program, 233
Minorities: dropout crisis and, 5; segregation and, 39–41, 274; prison populations and, 63, 95–96; retention and, 70; dropout rates and, 78; concentrated disadvantage and, 86–87; labor market prospects and, 90, 92; teen birthrates among, 103–104; nonmarital birth rates and, 104; ninth-grade retention rates and, 162; voluntary and involuntary, 202. *See also* Race
Misbehavior. *See* Deviance
Mobility: student, 7, 52–54, 70, 148–149, 166–169; longitudinal data and, 77; intergenerational, 120–129; residential, 189–190
Models of dropping out, 145–151
Morbidity/mortality, 111, 115
Morison, Karen Burke, 156–157
Motivation, 151–152
Moynihan, Daniel Patrick, 86, 124
Muennig, Peter, 135, 136–137
"Multiple pathways," 223
Murray, Charles, 122

National Academy of Education, 28, 58
National Assessment of Educational Progress (NAEP), 27–28, 53
National Center for Education Evaluation and Regional Assistance (NCEE), 267
National Center for Education Research (NCER), 267, 269
National Center for Education Statistics (NCES), 56, 57, 62, 72, 73, 80, 258

National Center for Health Statistics, 110
National Conference of State Legislatures'
     Task Force on School and Dropout
     Prevention and Recovery, 263
National Education Association (NEA), 23,
     257–258
National Education Goals, 3
National Education Longitudinal Study
     (1988), 62, 323nn24,28, 324n51
National efforts, 256–261
National Governors Association Center for
     Best Practices (NGA Center), 32, 58, 76–77,
     261–263
National Guard ChalleNGe program,
     77–78
National Health Interview Survey, 110–111,
     112, 127
National Longitudinal Survey of Youth (1997),
     62, 90–91, 94
National Research Council, 6, 8, 33, 34, 58,
     154, 201; Engaging Schools report, 152, 153,
     186, 222–223, 227
National Survey on Drug Use and Health,
     113–114
Natsuaki, Misaki, 100
Neighborhood: as dropout factor, 10–11,
     199–201; poverty and, 124–125. See also
     Community
New American Schools (NAS) program,
     238–240
New Century High Schools Initiative,
     243–244
New Futures Initiative, 242–243
Newman, Fred, 151–152
New York City's Small School Initiative,
     243–244
Ninth grade: graduation rate, 71–72; passing, as
     dropout predictor, 161; retention and, 162;
     over-age students in, 164
No Child Left Behind Act (2002), 73, 207, 215,
     260–261, 284n56
Noddings, Nel, 271
Noncognitive skills, 94, 126, 270–271
Nonmarital childbearing, 104–105
NRC Committee for Improved Measurement
     of High School Dropout and Completion
     Rates, 58, 296nn79,83

Oakes, Jeannie, 36–39
Obama, Barack, 3, 80, 133–134, 140–141,
     258–260, 297n96
Ogbu, John, 202
Orfield, Gary, 40
Osborne, Melissa, 126
Ou, Suh-Ruu, 147
Over-age students, 164

Parental education, 9, 191
Parental involvement, 191–193, 336n200
Parental resources, 124
Parenthood, teen, 101–110, 175–176, 204–205
Paris, Alison, 152–153
"Participation-identification" model, 146
Past efforts for dropout prevention, 207–208,
     234–235, 244–254
A Path to Graduation for Every Child, 263
Peers, 10–11, 176–177
Percheski, Christine, 123
Personal control, 112–113
Personalized learning environments, 221–222,
     226–227
Planful competence, 270–271
Political participation, 117, 118–119, 138–139,
     311n168–169
Population coverage, 62–64
Poverty, 86–87, 92, 121–125, 127–128, 191,
     202, 275
Powerlessness, 112–113
Practice guides, 224–228
Predictors of dropping out: overview of, 6–11;
     consequences of dropping out and, 87;
     introduction to, 159–160; individual, 160;
     educational performance as, 160–169;
     behavior as, 169–178; attitude as, 178–181;
     background as, 181–185; combining,
     185–187; institutional, 187; family structure
     as, 188–190; schools and, 188–193; family
     resources and, 190–191; family practices as,
     191–193, 336n200; community as, 199–201;
     race and, 201–205; conclusions on, 205–206;
     identifying at-risk students with, 225;
     socioeconomic status as, 321n6; employ-
     ment and, 329n114. See also Causes of
     dropping out
Pregnancy, teen, 101–110, 175–176, 204–205

Preschool, 228–229, 275, 355n104

Prevention programs: past efforts and, 3–4, 207–208; of author, 16–18; alternative, 208–215; effectiveness of, 215–234; evidence on, 218 (table); costs and benefits of, 233–234, 235 (table), 267–268; lessons learned from, 234–235, 244–254; High School Graduation Initiative, 235–236; Comprehensive School Reform (CSR), 236–237; High Priority Schools Grant Program, 237–238; New American Schools (NAS) program, 238–240; Gates High School Grants Initiative, 240–242; New Futures Initiative, 242–243; New York City's Small School Initiative, 243–244; funding for, 267. *See also* Intervention strategies

Principals, 246, 250–251

Prison population, 5, 63, 95–96, 311n168

Private schools, 195–196, 231

Problem behaviors, 5, 146, 172–176

Process, dropping out as, 48, 145–156

Productivity, of schools, 247–248

Project STAR (Student-Teacher Achievement Ratio), 229

Promoting power, 78–80, 266

Promotion, social, 6

Psychological resources, 112–113, 128

Public school event dropout rate, 66

Public schools, 195–196, 231

Public Schools Accountability Act (PSAA), 238

Race: segregation and, 39–42, 274; labor market prospects and, 90, 92; prison populations and, 95–96; teen birthrates and, 103–104; nonmarital birth rates and, 104; poverty and, 121; dropouts' effect on economy by, 132–133; ninth-grade retention rates and, 162; and differences in dropout rates, 201–205; characteristics of children and students by, 203 (table). *See also* Minorities

Race to the Top, 260

Randomized control trials, 215–216

Raudenbush, Stephen, 126

Reconstituting existing high schools, 211, 273

Recovery Act (2009), 259–260

Recovery programs, 209

"Redshirting," 164

Reenrollment, 54–55, 321n6

Reform: for existing high schools, 210–211, 213–214; systemic, 214–215; effectiveness of, 245

Relational trust, 247, 248

Relative mechanism, in education and well-being relationship, 120

Residential mobility, 7, 52–53, 189–190

Restart model, 259

Retention, 7, 70, 162–164

Reynolds, Arthur, 147

Risk factors, 185–186. *See also* Predictors of dropping out

Romo, Harriet, 18, 163, 169, 171, 180, 188, 192–193, 198

Rothstein, Richard, 25–27

Rouse, Cecilia, 93, 132, 135, 136–137, 233

Rumberger, Russell W., 56

Sampson, Robert, 99, 124, 126

San Francisco Unified School District, 32

Santa Ana school district, 32

Scalability, 268–269

School Dropout Demonstration Assistance Program, 235–236, 280n20, 345n5

School Dropout Prevention Program, 235–236

School Improvement Fund, 259–260

School Improvement Grants, 265, 266–267

School misbehavior, 173

School mobility, 7, 52–53, 148–149, 166–169

Schools: as dropout factor, 9–10, 153–154, 193–199; in comprehensive approach to intervention, 12; alternative, 42–45; enrollment in, 49–50, 54–55, 89 (table); membership in, 149, 152; reforming, 210–211; reconstituting, 211, 273; creating, 211–212; choosing, 231–233; will and capacity of, 246–247, 252, 273–274; resources of, 247–248; closing, 259; innovative, 265; composition of, 338n209, 339n214; size of, 347n21

Scientific research, evaluating, 217–221

Segregation, 39–42, 274

Self-concept, 180

Self-esteem, 146, 180

Self-perception, 180–181

Senate Select Committee on High School
Graduation, 18
"Sensemaking," 246
Sharkey, Patrick, 126
The Silent Epidemic (Bridgeland et al.),
156–157
Single-family households, 123
Skills: noncognitive, 94, 126, 270–271;
cognitive, 126, 269–270; social skills, 226
Slusarcick, Anita, 146–147
Small School Initiative, 243–244
Smith-Hughes Vocational Education Act
(1917), 22, 42
Smoking, 113–114, 310n152
Social bonding, 149
Social capital, 113, 191–192, 197, 200
Social composition, 194
Social consequences of dropping out:
introduction to, 130–132; economy and,
132–134, 139–140; crime and, 134–136;
welfare and, 136–137; health and, 137–138;
civic engagement and, 138–139; conclusions
on, 140–142
Social control theory, 98
Social integration, 148, 149
Social promotion, 6
Social resources, 247
Social skills, 226
Social support. *See* Social capital
Socioeconomic status: as dropout factor, 9;
segregation and, 40; as family resource
measure, 190–191; reenrollment and, 321n6;
effects of, 338n209, 339n214
Solutions to dropout crisis: overview of, 15–16;
introduction to, 255–256; current efforts,
256–269; suggestions for, 269–276;
conclusions on, 276
Sorting, 37–39
Special-education students, 279n8
Specificity, in reform strategy, 250
Sports, 170–171
State efforts, 261–264
Status, dropping out as, 47, 48
Status rates, 59, 66, 68
Steele, Claude, 204
Stein, Judith, 147
Steinberg, Darrell, 18

Steinberg, Laurence, 204
Stereotype threat, 204
Strain theory, 98
Structural equation modeling, 186
Structural models of dropping out, 186–187
Structural strains theory, 150
Student background, as predictor of dropping
out, 181–185
Student composition, 194
Student engagement, 151–153, 155, 169–171,
222–223, 227
Student mobility, 7, 52–54, 70, 77, 166–169
Student success, 143–144, 146, 150
Success: student, 143–144, 146, 150; redefining
high school, 269–272
Sullivan, Mercer, 19, 98, 113, 173, 174, 179, 200
"Summer Dropout Campaign," 4, 207
Supplemental programs, 208–209, 210
Sustainability, 268
Swanson, Christopher B., 56, 57
Systemic approaches, to dropout prevention,
12, 13, 214–215, 229–233
Systemic reform, 214–215, 351n71

TANF (Temporary Assistance for Needy
Families), 136
Tang, Emily, 231
Targeted approaches, to dropout prevention,
208–210
Tax revenue, lost, 132–133
Teachers: quality and salaries, 196–197,
341n232; will and capacity of, 246, 248–249;
collective responsibility of, 247; support of,
250–251
Technical assistance, 250, 253
Teen parenthood, 101–110, 175–176, 204–205
Telecommunications, 84
Temporary Assistance for Needy Families
(TANF), 136
Testing: General Education Development
(GED) test, 13, 35–36; achievement tests,
27–28; exit exams, 33–34, 165, 230;
segregation and, 39–40; test scores, 165–166
Texas, longitudinal data and, 77
Theory of action, 239, 251–252
Tinto, Vincent, 147–149, 150
Topitzes, James, 147

Tracking, 36–39, 198
Transformation model, 259–260
Truancy, 50. *See also* Attendance
Trust, 117–118, 247, 248
Turnaround model, 259
Turning points, 99, 108
Tyack, David, 23, 24, 39
Tyler, Ralph, 27
Typologies, 186

Unintended births, 104
U.S. Census, 2, 51, 61, 62–63, 119, 164, 296n75
U.S. Department of Education, 12, 16, 56, 80, 217, 237, 258, 265, 272
Uslaner, Eric, 117–118

Valenzuela, Angela, 18, 41–42, 183–184, 198, 204
Vocational education, 22, 42, 223, 271–272
Vocational Education Act (1963), 42
Voluntary minorities, 202
Voluntary withdrawal, 197–198

Voting, 118, 311n168–169
Vouchers, publicly funded, 231, 233

Warren, Rob, 72–73
Washington State Institute for Public Policy, 219–221
Wehlage, Gary, 149–150, 151–152
Welfare, 124, 136–137, 351n71
Well-being, 16, 111, 118, 119–120, 122, 126, 127, 168, 275
Wellborn, James, 152
Wenk, Ernst, 100
What Works Clearinghouse (WWC), 12–13, 217–219, 220, 224, 258
Wilder, Tamara, 25–27
Will and capacity, 246–249
Wilson, William Julius, 109, 124–125, 204
Winters, Marcus, 72
Withdrawal, voluntary and involuntary, 10, 197–198
Work-based learning, 22, 42, 223, 271–272

Zachry, Elizabeth, 108